Time Signatures

After the Empire:
The Francophone World and
Postcolonial France

Series Editor

Valérie Orlando, Illinois Wesleyan University

Advisory Board

Robert Bernasconi, Memphis University; Alec Hargreaves, Florida State University; Chima Korieh, Rowan University; Françoise Lionnet, UCLA; Obioma Nnaemeka, Indiana University; Kamal Salhi, University of Leeds; Tracy D. Sharpley-Whiting, Vanderbilt University; Nwachukwu Frank Ukadike, Tulane University

See *www.lexingtonbooks.com/series* for the series description and
a complete list of published titles.

Recent and Forthcoming Titles

Time Signatures

Contextualizing Contemporary
Francophone Autobiographical Writing
from the Maghreb

Alison Rice

LEXINGTON BOOKS

A Division of
ROWMAN & LITTLEFIELD PUBLISHERS, INC.
Lanham • Boulder • New York • Toronto • Oxford

LEXINGTON BOOKS

A division of Rowman & Littlefield Publishers, Inc.
A wholly owned subsidiary of The Rowman & Littlefield Publishing Group, Inc.
4501 Forbes Boulevard, Suite 200
Lanham, MD 20706

PO Box 317
Oxford
OX2 9RU, UK

British Library Cataloguing in Publication Information Available

Library of Congress Cataloging-in-Publication Data

Rice, Alison, 1973–
    Time signatures : contextualizing contemporary Francophone autobiographical
writing from the Maghreb / Alison Rice.
      p. cm. — (After the empire)
    Includes bibliographical references and index.
    ISBN 0-7391-1289-9 (cloth : alk. paper) — ISBN 0-7391-1290-2 (pbk. : alk. paper)
    ISBN 978-0-7391-1289-2   ISBN 978-0-7391-1290-8
    1. North African literature (French)—History and criticism. 2. Autobiography in
literature. 3. Self in literature. I. Title. II. Series.
PQ3988.5.N6R488 2006
840.9'492—dc22   2005032204

Printed in the United States of America

♾™ The paper used in this publication meets the minimum requirements of
American National Standard for Information Sciences—Permanence of Paper for
Printed Library Materials, ANSI/NISO Z39.48-1992.

To my mother, for her unfailing love, faith, and drive. To my brother, for his music, and for his humor (even when it's at my expense). But mostly, to my father, for the things that cannot be said, for passion, yearning, and commitment.

I dedicate these pages to you, the immediate, the nuclear, the closest. As we say in French, you are my heart.

Contents

Part III: Abdelkébir Khatibi

~

Acknowledgments

One of the distinctive advantages of working on contemporary writing is the opportunity to know and interact with the author who signs the *œuvre*, and in this case the proper name, along with the signature, take on a particular resonance. I have had the good fortune to become acquainted with the three individuals whose writing inspired this work, and I want to express my profound gratitude to Hélène Cixous, Assia Djebar, and Abdelkébir Khatibi. Their words and friendship are at the heart of this study, composed in their honor with affection and dedication. Jacques Derrida, to whom my debt is beyond expression, was a very real presence in Paris in 2003 as I wrote the pages that follow. Now that I have revised them after his passing, I realize to what extent this book bears witness to the many gifts his work has contributed to the present.

I would like to make special mention of the members of my doctoral committee at the University of California, Los Angeles (UCLA). Emily Apter has moved me with her cleverness and widespread interests; my exchanges with her have unfailingly been enlightening and inspiring. Andrea Loselle has consistently provided solid advice and careful critical readings of my work over the years. Dominic Thomas has had an inestimable impact on my scholarly trajectory; I deeply appreciate his perspectives and his personality. Samuel Weber has given generously, particularly in Paris, where his Program in Critical Theory opened countless new horizons for me. Finally, I cannot find superlatives laudatory enough to praise Françoise Lionnet, the scholar and the person to whom I owe so very much, whose mentorship has made an indelible mark on my life. Françoise is the living embodiment of two concepts I hold dear, hospitality and generosity.

I am also thankful for exchanges with a variety of scholars both in the United States and in France. Mireille Calle-Gruber deserves recognition for her ongoing guidance and support since our very first meeting, as well as for her pedagogical example and contagious enthusiasm. I have also especially enjoyed discussing with and learning from Christiane Chaulet-Achour, Charles Bonn, and Martine Mathieu-Job. I am appreciative of the intellectual proximity and warmth I have found in Hédi Abdel-Jaouad, Anne Donadey, Hafid Gafaïti, Alec Hargreaves, Michel Laronde, Mireille Rosello, Keith Walker, and Jack Yeagar. I would like to acknowledge Mary Jean Green as well, for she has been a wonderful interlocutor and provided valuable feedback on my work.

My new colleagues at the University of Notre Dame have been very supportive of this publication, and I wish to thank them all here, especially Patricio Boyer, Ted Cachey, JoAnn Della Neva, Julia Douthwaite, Louis MacKenzie, Christian Moevs, Catherine Perry, Alain Toumayan, and Ivy Wilson. Shannon Carter and Robin Hoeppner of Notre Dame have facilitated many of the technical aspects of this work with good humor, as have Serena Krombach and Katie Funk at Lexington Books. I am particularly grateful to Valérie Orlando for her longstanding camaraderie and trust.

I am grateful to the editors of *Pacific Coast Philology* and the *CELAAN Review* for their kind permission to reprint portions of previously published articles. Michèle Katz, whose lithographs have accompanied writings by Jacques Derrida in book form, generously provided the artwork for the cover of this publication.

I would be remiss if I did not thank my parents for raising me in a musical environment. While I couldn't have known it at the time, the piano, trumpet, and voice lessons they offered me have assumed great importance in my life. This very book gives evidence to the ways in which early exposure to the marvels of music has left a lasting impression. But my greatest thanks go to Olivier Morel, for his constancy, his depth, and his musings.

〜

Francophony? Legitimacy, Authenticity, and Integrity in French Literature

A modest reason faced with the extreme cruelty of History. What the musician was improvising was so intense and so full of youth that I heard myself say: The "miracle" is this art of improvisation that transforms melancholy into nostalgia, servitude into freedom, freedom into rhythm [. . .] a gift from this century to the memory of men, to their heritage.

—Abdelkébir Khatibi, *Un été à Stockholm* (1990)[1]

A piece of music does not exist outside its interpretation. It must be said that we interpret—but that's obvious—and then hold out the musical sheets to others and tell them: it's your turn to play.

—Philippe Lejeune, "La rédaction finale" (2003)

This book adopts a new approach to Francophone autobiographical writings, reading the texts of Assia Djebar, Hélène Cixous, and Abdelkébir Khatibi in terms of *music*. Their works contain musical elements in rhythm and style, as *enchanting* compositions that draw readers in. They also are musical in theme, as the writers either directly address or allude to music as a topic both in fictional and theoretical texts (and in texts that arguably combine these two elements and blur the distinction between them). The autobiographical corpuses under study do not contain clear presentations of facts, nor do they present linear, chronological developments in a single story; instead, this contemporary writing "plays" (with) musical fragments and communicates the self in "song," so to speak. The resulting textual transpositions do not contain a single resounding refrain, but instead are decidedly "polyphonic," mixing the "*je*" with other voices that interweave in the text at varying *intervals*, both in the musical and the temporal sense. While there is a certain degree of continuity from one text to another (and even from one motif to the next within the same text), there is also *development*: adaptations from one text to another reveal change over time; they reveal that times *can change*, and that they *change us*. The "signatures" of the writers in this study are ever evolving, and their creation is ongoing, just as the lives they parallel. These signatures make their mark in a number of different areas, as revealed by the emphases of the chapters in this study. The self (and *identity*, problematic as that notion is) is a composite construction related to name, religion, history (familial, communal, and "national"), birthplace, itinerary, sexuality, language, and—particularly in the case of the Francophone writer from the Maghreb—translation.

I begin in this Introduction with the concept of "Francophonie" because of the primary place of language throughout this project. Articulations of the self in writing take place for these writers in "La Langue de l'Autre," to quote the title of one of Khatibi's recent publications. I examine here, in different thematic settings, what it means to write in the other's language, working under the assumption that language is not a neutral medium. The French tongue carries a particular worldview, especially when it is associated with colonialism and the "universal" values of what was known as the "*mission civilisatrice*." The focus in this study is on works emerging from the North African region comprising three countries collectively referred to as the Maghreb: Morocco, Algeria, and Tunisia. This geographic space is at once proximate to France, in terms of kilometers, and distant from it, in terms of mindset. This place of birth, childhood, and adolescence is a pervasive presence that profoundly influences the works of these writers.

I am concerned with the *details* that punctuate the autobiographical texts of Cixous, Djebar, and Khatibi. While some of these elements may seem to be "minor" or inconsequential, I argue that even the subtlest accents, even the slightest stress marks, contain crucial fragments of the self.[2] I contend that anecdotes are a powerful way of relating the past and present, as they tell of the idiosyncratic in succinct, memorable manner, similar to a catchy melody. In the close readings of these chapters, I draw from a chorus of texts to cull material that has been overlooked in previous examinations of these writers and their work. My primary preoccupation is to study the texts, but I do not limit my examination to the written publication. I look inside *and* outside these works for context, concentrating on the "vibrations" between *author* and *œuvre*, between *corps* and *corpus*, as I trace the literary history of

an important contemporary phenomenon in French writing. It is not anecdotal that Francophone literature is presently transforming "French literature" and ultimately rendering obsolete this distinction ("French" versus
"Francophone").

In this introduction, I reconsider the term "Francophonie" and indicate a
need to revalorize it in inclusive ways *before* embracing it as appropriate to
describe the works of Cixous, Djebar, and Khatibi. Then, I indicate why this
unprecedented grouping of writers from the Maghreb is pertinent; I argue
that this threesome makes up a *trio*, that their voices interact in concordant
ways, due in many respects to a common inspiration found in a fourth voice,
that of Jacques Derrida. Then, I return to the importance of music, not to repeat the brief comments I have already made, but to develop the ideas contained within the title and to hint that the term "authentic cadence" is at
once appropriate *and* insufficient to describe what takes place in the works
under study. An "authentic cadence" in music means moving from the dominant to the tonic chord and usually implies a sense of harmonic completion.
Such movement is characteristic of the works by Cixous, Djebar, and Khatibi, as they change key and time signature within the same piece and from
one work to another. But these texts do not convey a sense of "completion,"
since they are always evolving, and pointing to the future. One of the common characteristics of these prolific autobiographical composers is the continuing melody of their work. These contemporary writers have not yet
placed the final note on paper; their creativity never ceases to flow and writing the self is a continual source of life, in time. In like manner, this introduction gestures toward the chapters to come, with an indication of the major strains to be played out in their lines.

Of Nominal Insufficiencies: "Francophonie"

The term "Francophonie" is complex and multifaceted, and that is one of the
reasons why it remains a subject of debate and heated discussion, whether
among politicians, writers, or professors, in France, Africa, the United States,
or elsewhere.[3] While its etymological origins appear uncomplicated, the
word has come to mean much more than its components, and it therefore defies easy description. According to Jean-Marc Moura's revisiting of the history of the term, it dates back to 1880, the same year the somewhat simpler
"Francophone" came into being, thanks to a publication titled *France, Algérie et colonies* by a geographer named Onésime Reclus.[4] This second term is
less contentious when it comes to deciphering its significance; most agree
that it designates people (or places) proficient in the French language. It is

important to note, however, that from its inception, the word "Franco-phone," whether used as a noun or an adjective, was not meant to describe French speakers *from France*. Instead, this term applied from the outset to those hailing from other regions of the world: "It thus signifies 'one who speaks French' and designates inhabitants of the French language who are from national or regional entities where French is not the only tongue" (Moura 1). Of course, this comment immediately calls into question the sta-tus of French as the *only tongue* of France, and the author later brings to light the fact that the Hexagon is hardly a monolingual space: "monolingualism is above all a myth, even in France, where French coexists with other regional tongues like Catalan or Breton" (Moura 73).[5]

Even if France itself is not characterized by linguistic uniformity, it is nonetheless considered the "metropolis" for those growing up in its colonies, and the experience of the writers featured in this work reveals that the lan-guage in which they write is seldom dissociated from the country whence it originated. Writing in French inevitably entails a connection to France, and the fact that they spent their early years outside the borders of this nation leaves these writers, in a pun, "tongue-tied," linked to a language and a country that they cannot call their "own." This is in certain respects a boon to a writer, as Jacques Derrida puts it, "I like words too much because I don't have a language of my own" ("Circonfession" 91). Hélène Cixous, born in Algeria seven years after Derrida, pinpoints in like manner the benefits of maintaining a "certain" distance from (one's) language: "If you do not pos-sess a language, you can be possessed by it: let the tongue remain foreign to you. Love it like your fellow creature" ("Coming to Writing" 23). Hélène Cixous, Assia Djebar, and Abdelkébir Khatibi, the three writers at the fore-front of this study, are all, in important ways, "Francophone" writers, and yet I would argue that this term is insufficient to describe their work, if we con-sider it in an exclusionary sense. While it is certainly correct that all three of these writers spent their formative years outside the Hexagon, and while none of them claims French as a "mother tongue," I would like to shift the focus to *their writing* rather than their origins. It is in their writing that these origins come out, in all of their subtlety and complexity, and it is because of the long, lasting, and unfinished textual exploration of self-definitions and belongings that the application of the label "Francophone" is insufficient to cover the multiple factors contributing to their identities and identifica-tions. I contend that both a "return to roots" and an opening up of the term "Francophonie" in *inclusive* ways are pressing and necessary steps to under-standing, and contextualizing, their contemporary autobiographical writing in French.

To understand why this revalorizing of "Francophonie" is necessary, it is essential to underscore the division inherent in the term beginning with its first use. In the online version of the journal *Prétexte*, an interview with Tunisian-born Abdelwahab Meddeb gives the writer an opportunity to reflect on the geographical parameters contained within the word: "The very term 'francophonie' holds within it the somber separation between the Hexagon and the rest of the world." As Meddeb's comment shows, "separation" continues to characterize the word over one hundred years after its first appearance. This assertion is echoed in the words of Moroccan writer Tahar Ben Jelloun who, like Meddeb, has become a "spokesperson" for his native land in his current country of residence, France. Despite his membership in the *Haut Conseil de la francophonie*, Ben Jelloun stumbles in an interview when asked to provide a description of the term. He has recourse to its etymology, indicating that it *should* designate all those who speak French, but then lamenting the fact that the term is never employed in reference to "*écrivains français*."[6] Ben Jelloun made this statement in 1995, on the occasion of the twenty-fifth anniversary of "Francophonie,"[7] and, unfortunately, his words still ring true in many circles. While some scholars, university departments, and even bookstores have begun to consider all French-language literature under the same rubric, placing works by French speakers from France alongside those composed in French by writers of another native tongue and/or country, this move has not yet been adopted in widespread fashion. The result is a split of French-language written works into two categories that do justice to neither: "French" and "Francophone" literatures turn out in many points of view to indicate a hierarchical division, with the latter constituting the "lesser" of the two designations.

In anticipation of the first printing of a new review of Francophone poetry called *Agotem* (published by éditions Obsidiane under the direction of François Boddaert), two prominent contributors granted an interview to Patrick Kéchichian of *Le Monde* in March 2003. Monchoachi, of Antillean origin, had this to say about the label "Francophone": "Speaking of Francophone poetry or Francophone literature never carries positive resonance, but instead gives off the feeling of subjection, of a necessarily devalued subgroup, of a literature of the second zone." The words "second zone" recall Meddeb's comments on France as "center" and other zones as "second,"[8] a division that he undermines by highlighting the presence of the "margins" at the very center of France (and, by extension, I would add "French Culture"): "What remains excluded is at the very heart of the Hexagon [. . .] the notion of a center is dispersed to the margins and every single margin constitutes a center." The creators of *Agotem* take into account the important presence of marginal voices, aiming to make them heard—and seen—in a country where they are often overlooked, according to Monchoachi: "France itself worries very little about the existence of diversity within its own borders." The first issue (June 2003) of this journal—containing poems from a number of foreign authors whose native tongue is not French—boasts a collectively signed introduction that addresses the term "Francophonie" and its problems:

> The goal of *Agotem* [. . .] is certainly not to profit from this strange thing that francophonie has become today, because it is uncertain. And if we clearly advertise our disinterest for what seems to us to be empty excess or a cenotaph, it's because the very concept of francophonie must be redefined in light of a changed world: that of after-colonialism [*l'après-colonialisme*], in the rational sense of the term.

The call to redefine "Francophonie" in light of the term's acquired "uncertain" character is reminiscent of another text in its focus on colonialism and a "changed" contemporary world marked by "globalization."

In their introduction to *Post-Colonial Cultures in France*, Alec Hargreaves and Mark McKinney present a clear, straightforward explanation of a term that itself can be characterized as neither; the editors explain the geographical and political dimensions of "Francophonie" and indicate its connection to *time*, locating it as a "post-colonial" phenomenon.[9] While they admit that "Both terms are profoundly ambiguous" (3), Hargreaves and McKinney indicate a slight preference for "post-colonial" as a "more politically correct concept" (4). They find this word's overly political nature preferable to "Francophonie," a word that obscures its political weight under the guise of a "purely cultural field of reference" (4).[10] But adopting the classification "post-colonial" is not the ideal solution to this problem of naming either, for the term runs the risk of "ensnaring" individuals from formerly colonized areas "by defining cultural projects in terms of a common reference to an earlier period of colonial domination" (4). This is the trap I aim to avoid by examining the specificity of writers *in their own contexts, in their own texts*, taking into account the common experience of "colonial domination,"[11] but devoting *time* to the *individual* expression of the past in view of the present, and giving *space* to the evolving, idiosyncratic development of the self in writing.[12]

The criticisms leveled by the founders of *Agotem* at the word "Francophonie" are harsh, but generally well founded, for they are based on historical fact and present practice. In the words of Nimrod, a poet from Chad: "Francophonie is not simply another exoticism [*un exotisme de plus*] with respect to French; it is no longer anything more than a reserved domain where neocolonial states continue to confiscate the French word."[13] It is interesting that this new publication should address the deficiencies and insufficiencies of "Francophonie" in its current currency, so to speak, in order to reappropriate the language of poetic composition and revalorize the word that describes it. The journal's goal is to provide a place of *distinction* for poetry from "outside France" by removing the *distinction* between it and poetry from "inside," pointing out the ludicrous nature of this division when much of what bears the label "Francophone" is actually composed within the Hexagon. Nimrod doesn't mince words, heading right to the center of the problem in order to reorient the question: "The question is therefore not to distinguish poetry written in Africa from that written in France, but rather to welcome the first at the heart of the hexagonal economy." Bound up with the term "economy" are a number of assumptions about the value, merit, and appeal of "Francophone" literary compositions, and these assumptions are crucial to a reconsideration of "Francophonie" as a term that holds much promise that remains as yet unfulfilled.

Selling "Francophonie"

I have given a new orthography to the term "Francophonie" in the title of this Introduction, transforming the "*phonie*," referring to "speech sound" in French, into "phony," an English word meaning "not real or genuine; fake; false or deceiving." What is interesting about this alteration of the word in English is that it plays on—and defies—the usual addition of "phony" in the "formation of abstract nouns corresponding to nouns ending in 'phone'" (*Random House* 980). The fact that the word "Francophonie" retains its French form in English-speaking academic circles is undoubtedly in part due to this unfavorable overlap in translation, given the pejorative connotations of "phony." I spell "Francophony" this way in my title because of the double-sided questions of legitimacy, and of authenticity, that I perceive in the very concept of "Francophonie," in particular in its use as a literary designation.

Writers from outside France need to "prove themselves" in two very different, but paradoxically complementary arenas. First, they must demonstrate exceptional writing ability, characterized not only by perfect "mastery" of literary French, but also by a creative signature style that sets their compositions apart from the rest. Second, writers from beyond the hexagonal borders must be representative of their native land; their publications are expected to accurately depict their thorough knowledge of and earlier experiences in a different culture—and, often, different language—than the one connected to the French idiom of writing. It is generally understood that "Francophone" writers insert the "foreign" into their texts, and many readers from France (and elsewhere) approach these works with that in mind. If the poet Nimrod argues that "Francophonie" is not just "*un exotisme de plus*," it is because this "exotic" presupposition often accompanies the "Francophone"-labeled text.

The label "Francophone" is not entirely negative, of course. The explosive popularity of literary and cultural studies that bear this name in the United States and the United Kingdom gives evidence of an increasing attraction to works in French that do not fall into the strict, canonical definitions of what constitutes "French literature." The magnetism these publications hold for an American public, for instance, contributes to Ben Jelloun's wholehearted embrace of the "luck" of his situation as a Moroccan-born writer of literature in French:

> I would even say that, as a Moroccan, I'm lucky. The fact is that writing in French when France is not one's native country is a plus. I am translated in the United States, and that's no small feat. I suspect that I am translated much more because I am from Africa, because to the American mind, [. . .] French literature stops at Robbe-Grillet, if it goes that far.[14]

In this interview, Ben Jelloun profits from an opportunity to take a jab at the sacrosanct institution of "French literature" by insisting that it is thanks to the publication of texts known as "Francophone" that literature in French continues to be read and appreciated abroad.[15] But what Ben Jelloun does not mention is that he currently benefits from a trend that is not long-standing. Indeed, this attention to "Francophone" literature has not characterized the United States for long, at least not in the academic milieu; it is a positive development of relatively recent memory, according to Algerian-born Réda Bensmaïa.

In an article published in *Rue Descartes*, the journal of the Collège International de Philosophie, Bensmaïa literally "crosses out" the term "Francophonie," placing two intersecting lines through it in a visual gesture in harmony with his title: "La Langue de l'étranger ou la Francophonie barrée" (65).[16] This visible "X" of course does not prohibit the reader from seeing the word that has been crossed out with these lines; it is instead another layer, an additional tier that creates the effect of a palimpsest, allowing the reader to trace the term underneath despite its partial effacement. From the very first paragraph, it is clear that much is at stake in Bensmaïa's article, but that the primary point is to uproot (and reconsider) the problematic notion of "Francophonie" from its position as separate from and inferior to "French literature." The troublesome status of "Francophone" literature is the "question" that guides his reflections: "the status of literature called 'francophone' and its (uncanny) relationship [*d'inquiétante étrangeté*] to French literature" (65). The crossing out of the word "Francophonie" throughout his text makes perceptible Bensmaïa's retrospective accusations directed at American scholars, himself included: "literature, hypostasized as 'francophone' or 'postcolonial literature,' had become the object in each of us of a veritable *scotomization process* combined with a *primordial interdict*" (70). Bensmaïa creatively employs the French term "*scotomisation*" to evoke a "blind spot" in academic tunnel visions of the past. This diminished sight in the field of "French literary" vision temporarily rendered the immense variety of works in French illegible, if not invisible, by placing them without distinction into what Bensmaïa calls "la catégorie fourre-tout 'francophonie'" (73). The practice of stuffing all publications into this "other" category did a disservice not only to writers and their texts, but also to scholars and students who failed to perceive the "hybrid, multiple, diverse character of this new 'site' or 'place' that Francophonie has become!" (73). The exclamation point that closes this last citation is one of five such punctuation marks in the final paragraph, lauding in enthusiastic, exuberant textual signs the positive potential for "Francophonie" when it is informed by such fields as deconstruction and postcolonial studies. It is thanks to these two currents of thought, in Bensmaïa's experience, that "Francophonie" at long last became a "place" of serious, respected scholarship in the 1980s in the United States.[17]

The "primordial interdict" which Bensmaïa italicizes in the quotation above is a prohibition that exists on the level of language: "this 'interdict' comes from afar and proceeds directly from a (colonial) 'educational' system and a 'law' *in* and *of* the French language that have not left any place for differences that work *both* the 'idioms' *and* the literatures that proceeded from them" (71). For those who know Derrida's work, it will come as no surprise that Bensmaïa quotes at length from *Le Monolinguisme de l'autre*.[18] In this text, as in others, Derrida elegantly interweaves details from his personal history in Algeria with the political and educational circumstances that in many ways shaped his outlook on life in lasting ways. As the title of his reflections indicates, language was crucial to the philosopher's childhood and adolescent experience, and his tormented relation to French is shown in its connection to the colonial environment. This relation did not improve with time. In a foreword to a work published by Galilée in 2003, *Chaque fois unique, la fin du monde*, Derrida ostensibly places the personal possessive pronoun in quotation marks when he refers to this work's appearance in French, two years after an English version went to print at the University of Chicago Press: "I never would have dared to undertake such a collection in France, in 'my' country and 'my' language" (9). This language is not his, these words tell us, and yet they tell us this *in* this language, in a nuanced twist that has become the hallmark of Derrida's writing. Here, a text originally published in translation has returned to its "original" form, and the occasion gives Derrida the chance to again establish a distance from "his" only tongue: "The survivor position that such a collection seems to exhibit will remain for me in 'my' language, even though this language still remains completely other for me, unbearable. Indecent, even obscene" (10). Derrida's bind was that his language of writing had always been French, yet this language was inextricably intertwined with a troubled history. This is also the dilemma of Cixous, Djebar, and Khatibi.[19] While they are all proficient in various other tongues, their language of writing has primarily been French. It is the language of their œuvre and their renown. It is a tongue to which they owe much, and yet their relation to it is fraught with complexity, if not anxiety.

From her earliest publications, Cixous has put on paper her fears about "legitimately" taking up the pen and voicing herself through writing. While many of these reflections are situated within the context of gender expectations and prohibitions, the following passage from "La Venue à l'écriture" reveals that the transgression of sexual boundaries was not the only challenge she faced upon becoming an author:

> You want—to Write? In what language? Property, rights, had always policed me: I learned to speak French in a garden from which I was on the verge of expulsion for being a Jew. I was of the race of Paradise-losers. Write French? With what right? Show us your credentials! What's the password? Cross yourself! Put out your hands, let's see those paws! What kind of nose is that? ("Coming" 13)

Cixous's overwhelming concern is with justifying the appropriating gesture not simply of writing, but writing *in French*. Born outside of metropolitan France without a single ancestor of "French" origin,[20] she "comes to writing" in a language that, like Derrida, she can hardly call her own. Their unique status as "*Juifs d'Algérie*" largely spared them—at least until recently—the need to define themselves according to the "Francophone" or "French" literary divide. Cixous and Derrida—despite unusual surnames that immediately distinguish them from those with "typical" French appellations—were not relegated to the domain of "Francophone" studies. But, they were not exactly "French" either, and the cutting-edge nature of much of their work forestalled any possible quick adoption of the "French" label.[21]

If Cixous does not fit neatly into either the category of "French" or that of "Francophone" literature, she is certainly not the only one to hold ambiguous status. Leïla Sebbar is a writer born to an Algerian father and a French mother in Algeria; she writes in French because it is her only language. In *Lettres parisiennes*, Sebbar explains the complexity of her identity as a person and a writer, and indicates that this complexity sometimes leads her readers to react with hostility. Instead of being attacked for problems of style or coherence, her work is occasionally criticized for its author's indefinable status: "I am not a Maghrebian writer of French expression. . . . I am not a pure French woman. . . . My mother tongue is not Arabic. [. . .] When I say that I don't speak Arabic, people are scandalized" (133). When Sebbar admits to her Arabic-speaking readers that she doesn't know their language, they are scandalized for one specific reason: this lack of competence diminishes her status as (a) "representative" of Algerians in her writing, whether her characters continue to reside in Algeria, have immigrated to France, or have been born in France to Algerian parents. These readers assume that since she is neither "integrated" nor "assimilated" into the "Arab" or "Muslim" culture she represents in writing renders her literary project inadequate, even suspect.[22]

This criticism seems to confuse two separate criteria that both figure in my title: legitimacy and authenticity. While *legitimacy* has to do with the law, with what is legal or lawful, proper, in accordance with rules and principles, and by extension is valid or logical, *authenticity* focuses on what is genuine or real, depending on an origin supported by unquestionable evidence, on that which is worthy of acceptance or belief because it is utterly reliable or trustworthy. In her own defense, Sebbar says that she never makes a claim for authenticity in her work; she doesn't aim to tell *her own* story in her writing, and the situations she evokes in her books are not part of a personal identity quest: "the subjects of my books are not my identity" (134).[23] Sebbar's publications may not therefore be called "authentic," since they explore and create situations that are dependent on Sebbar's imagination, unrelated to her own past or present. But her texts nonetheless benefit from a certain degree of "legitimacy" conferred precisely because of Sebbar's familial and experiential ties to Algeria. Even if she is unable to speak Arabic, and even if she is in some ways a foreigner to the Algeria she portrays in works like *La fille au balcon*, Sebbar has a surname and a history that give her clout in the publishing world. These two factors (the name of the father and the place of her birth) are enough—to put it in stark terms—to *sell books*, a point that brings us back to the question of economy with respect to the "Francophone" text.

A 1996 novel titled *Lila dit ça* published under the indecipherable pseudonym "Chimo" caused quite a stir in France, where critics found it doubtful that such a well-written autobiographical text could be the product of a young person born to immigrant parents in the suburbs of Paris. The book was extremely popular, selling tens of thousands of copies in the original

French version and quickly attracting the attention of foreign markets as well, but the author's true name was never revealed. The resulting controversy centered on the identity of the author, instead of focusing on the value of the book as an anonymous literary creation, and this obsessive concern reveals that much of what is officially recognized as possessing literary worth is dependent on identity (and) politics, as well as on presentation and packaging. Michel Laronde uses the polemical case of this pseudonymous novel to examine the paratextual apparatus and its crucial importance to a publication's success.[24] Linking the "paratexte" to "la politique éditoriale" (8), Laronde points toward *the name* as the crucial element around which the other aspects of launching a book revolve. When the name is clearly a pseudonym and no face can be put to it, critics find themselves in a real dilemma in reacting to the work in question:

> For here, a whole line of reading could be based on the fundamental unknown that destabilizes the media world and feeds controversy: the author is anonymous. And the author's pseudonym, so well fabricated that one can hardly pigeonhole it as belonging to a precise ethnic origin (apart from a certainty that it is not a stereotypically French name), renders completely non-functional the criteria of rank and value that seemed so well established based on the author's origin. (7)

The "missing" identity behind the book puts its readers in a quandary; unable to judge its "authenticity," they are at a loss when it comes to classifying it and determining its value.

The title of the present study, *Time Signatures*, hints at the importance of names herein. The first chapter is devoted to reflections on names and their implications both inside and outside the written text: as the signature of a particular publication; as the heading for an entire œuvre; or as the appellation for the person behind the work, the writer. "NameStakes" examines the importance of the proper name in a broad setting, looking with special interest at the case of Hélène Cixous and placing her textual comments on the name (in personal and theoretical terms) in dialogue with those by Abdelkébir Khatibi and Assia Djebar. Specific examples found in their work reveal that self-naming is often dependent on the names others assign us. In Cixous's fiction, for instance, her name is most often pronounced by others, and her image is thus a reflection of their invocation; as a heading for her work, her name is not uniform or predictable, but open to reiterations that never say exactly the same thing in the same way. This does not preclude the invention of a "signature" style that distinguishes her œuvre from others in decisive ways. If her name—like that of Khatibi or Djebar—is known, it is largely because it is special, distinctive, in a word: inimitable. Recognizing her name is synonymous with recognizing her writing, including the themes and rhythms that set it apart.

Reception and Recognition

One obvious sign of commercial success in the publishing world is widespread availability of the text in bookstores and libraries. In simple economic terms, a work that is in high demand translates into monetary profit for the writer, as well as for all those associated with the book's printing and distribution. What is striking in the case of works by the three writers in my study is that a number of their texts are hard to locate, at best, and out of print, at worst. For instance, Djebar's 1987 novel *Ombre sultane* cannot be found in any bookstores in France, a surprising fact that seems all the more curious when we consider that it was the recipient of a literary prize in Frankfurt, the Prix Liberatur, and is widely used in university classrooms of the United States in English translation. Many of Cixous's early publications are hard to track down as well, including those that have brought her such fame abroad, like *La Jeune née* and "La Venue à l'écriture." The same holds true, to a much greater degree, for texts written by Khatibi. While it is encouraging that an increasing number of Djebar's works originally published by Albin Michel are now coming out in small, accessible, paperback form, ideal for wide distribution,[25] it is disheartening that a similar version of Khatibi's *La Mémoire tatouée* ("collection 10/18") has long been out of print. It makes little sense that this brilliant autobiographical novel, discovered by literary critic Maurice Nadeau in 1971 and then published by Denoël the same year, should now be practically impossible to find, even in specialized bookstores and libraries.

The difficulty of getting hold of Khatibi's texts in the original version may have something to do with his publishing history. He has published far and wide, his name has been associated with Gallimard, Flammarion, Fata Morgana, Denoël, Actes Sud, L'Harmattan, Hazan, Aubier, and others, and while he has published more than one text with some of these *maisons d'édition*, he has found no steady "home." His most recent novel, *Pèlerinage d'un artiste amoureux*, was published by yet another entity, Éditions du Rocher. The fact that he has little continuity in his publishing experience may contribute to the inaccessibility of his work; Khatibi's texts seem to hit the bookstands and fade away. In contrast, Djebar has published a steady stream of texts with Albin Michel, beginning with *Loin de Médine* in 1991 and continuing up to *La Disparition de la langue française* in 2003. Although this has not been her sole publisher (she has also published several recent works with Actes Sud), it has provided her with a regular place to present her work, and it has "revived" some of her older publications, most importantly *L'Amour, la fantasia*, which reappeared in print in 1995, ten years after its initial appearance, thanks to Lattès.[26] Cixous has proved the most faithful to her publishers, producing no fewer than 26 texts for Éditions des femmes (the final one, titled *Osnabrück*, went to print in 1999), and then moving on to Éditions Galilée, where she is sole author of or contributor to fourteen publications to date, including *L'Amour meme: dans la boîte aux lettres*, appearing in September 2005.

The prestige of these writers is undoubtedly related to not only the number and quality of their publications, but to the reputation of the publishing houses to which they have attached themselves. It is also, without question, related to *translation*. There can be little doubt about the role translation has played in establishing Djebar's international renown, as evidenced in the attribution of four respected literary prizes *awarded outside France* for her œuvre: the Prix Maurice-Maeterlinck in Brussels in 1995, the International Literary Neustadt Prize in the United States in 1996, the International Prize of Palmi in Italy in 1998, and the Peace Prize of the German Book Trade in Frankfurt in 2000. Djebar has been honored with other awards for writing, and for filmmaking, but only two of these have come from France.[27] Khatibi has also been largely overlooked in France, I would argue, and also owes much to translation, or to one translation in particular: Richard Howard's English version of *Amour bilingue*, translated as *Love in Two Languages*. American scholars have found this text inspiring, and it is largely due to its appearance that other works by Khatibi, especially the collection of essays titled *Maghreb pluriel*, have caught the attention of critics abroad. This text has not yet been rendered in English, curiously enough. In a special issue of *Yale French Studies* edited by Françoise Lionnet and Ronnie Scharfman, a passage from a much longer text in French appears in translation, and the appearance of "A Colonial Labyrinth," as it is titled, should be applauded. But it is remarkable how much remains untranslated from Khatibi's rich and varied œuvre.

It is also remarkable how much remains untranslated from Cixous's rich and varied œuvre, I would argue, but the sheer prolixity of her prolific publications—and, of course, the difficult nature of translating such densely resonant "poetic" prose—may explain the number of lacunae in her translated corpus.[28] It is the "time lag" in transferring her "French" compositions to English that has in part created a large division between her different reading publics. If Cixous is known as a feminist theorist in the United States, she is renowned as a playwright and professor in France, even if she did receive the Prix Médicis for her first full-length work of fiction, *Dedans*, in 1969. Following that eventful début, much of Cixous's writing has gone un-noticed in the country where she has invested herself,[29] personally and pro-fessionally, since the 1960s, an oversight that, more and more, has been rec-tified in recent years. The three-day conference devoted to her œuvre at the Biblothèque nationale de France in May 2003 was a significant step in "con-secrating" the writer and her work; this occasion coincided with Cixous's gift of her manuscripts to the archives of this great national literary institution, placing her on an elite list of great writers in French from the twentieth (and now, twenty-first) century. This recognition of Cixous as a writer decidedly does not carry the label "Francophone" and, to my knowledge, she has never identified herself as a "Francophone writer," even if she may have much in common with others who do. *Defining herself* is something that Cixous is con-stantly doing; it is an act that takes place repeatedly throughout her œuvre, contributing to an inexhaustible autobiographical project that continually questions the assumptions of such terms as "Francophone," challenging them with personal details that defy all normative labels.

Self-Definitions: The Hesitations of "Francophone" Writers

Assia Djebar published a series of essays in 1999 with a subtitle that illus-trates her hesitancy to fully embrace the term "Francophone" as descriptive of her work: *Ces voix qui m'assiègent . . . en marge de ma francophonie*. As in-dicated, the concept of "Francophonie" pervades the text, beginning with an "Introduction: Un parcours francophone 1957–1997" (9-22) and continuing on to "Écriture francophone au féminin" (59–94), reflecting on the inquisi-tive "Francophonie?" along the way (23–58). A paper originally delivered at a colloquium at the University of Leeds on "Francophone Voices" is perhaps most revelatory of the mixed emotions the writer harbors with respect to this terminology. When she confronts her personal history, she deems it neces-sary to concede the point, calling herself by the term in its adjectival form: "I am, without a doubt, a woman of French education, due to my training in the French language during the time of colonized Algeria. If I add immedi-ately to French education that I am also of Algerian—or Arab-Berber, or even Muslim sensibility, [. . .] then I am indeed a 'Francophone woman' in my intellectual and critical activity" (*Ces voix* 26). If she reluctantly adopts the term "Francophone" to describe a *certain* part of her life "If I am, it is in my public activity, as a university professor," Djebar nonetheless aims to push this "ambiguous notion" in new directions: "to break out of the geo-graphical limits of the French language in order to analyze, discuss, and put into question this ambiguous notion of *francophonie*: a notion that is not always literary, or even cultural, and that, in numerous African countries, is still connected to politics" (26–27). She expresses a desire to test the borders, rather than fit within them, in her work: "in this linguistic territory called 'francophonie,' I place myself at the borders" (27).[30]

Djebar's grappling with the term "Francophone" in these textual reflections goes hand in hand with a similar struggle with her status as a "woman writer." Both designations contain "concessions" of a sort, setting Djebar apart and marking her œuvre in its double specificity as a work composed by a *woman* originating from *outside France*. While such specifications are useful marketing techniques to seduce certain types of readers—and to attract precise sorts of literary awards—they are in some senses derogatory as they *differentiate* the writer from the "norm," establishing different criteria of excellence and setting up different sets of expectations. When Djebar poses the question, "Am I not just a writer, period?" (27), she is highlighting the suspicious nature of hastily "contextualizing" writers, I would say, by providing multiple labels that serve inattentive readers for the sake of a "quick study." Like the blurb on the back of the book, the brief biographical notice that accompanies the written work negatively simplifies the complex nature of its subject. Just as texts deserve careful readings, so the writers who have penned them merit *either* a simple byline *or* a developed exposé, *not* the cursory, elliptical list of labels that serve to classify works and writers that are, by nature, unclassifiable.[31] When Djebar gives a talk titled "Écrivain/Écrivaine" on writing as an Arab woman, she finds herself quoting Maurice Blanchot before she catches herself, in time to bring her thoughts back to the subject at hand: "But I digress: Blanchot is not a woman and is not Arab like me. He's only a writer" (*Ces voix* 63).[32] To be only a writer seems a refreshing option to the burden of bearing "representative" tags.[33]

There is an undeniable responsibility weighing on those who choose to represent certain cultures, and especially people(s), in writing. There is a desire to "be true" to those outside the text, to faithfully represent them within. This is the "weight" Djebar refers to when she addresses the complex challenge of "translating" the voices of Algerian women into the French text in *L'Amour, la fantasia*: "Torch-words which light up my women-companions, my accomplices; these words divide me from them once and for all. And weigh me down as I leave my native land" (*Fantasia* 142). Not only does the act of writing in French separate Djebar from her Algerian companions, it removes her from her homeland as well. What is ironic is that this distance is *necessary* to her writing project, even if it puts into question some of the accuracy, or the "legitimacy" of her depictions of contemporary Algeria and its inhabi-

tants. Of course, the writer has returned to the land of her birth on various occasions following her initial departure, but the crux of her writing depends on
the perspective that distance provides: "I have been writing far from Algeria
for seventeen years now. I find that in order to write, I must come in complete
freedom and ease, with the happiness of space" (Rieck). If Algeria continually
returns in Djebar's writing, as in her recent *La Disparition de la langue française*,
nostalgia and imagination are underscored in her portrayal of this native land,
as she indicates in her doctoral thesis: "As always, living in Paris for ten years,
it is in present-day Algeria that my mind is engaged, that my dreams mixed
with nostalgia return, ferment, and sharpen" ("Le roman" 193). The past,
transposed into French, is not necessarily interpreted "realistically," but it is
portrayed "authentically," *in the light of the present*, in accordance with Edward
Said's analysis: "Authenticity is also about justifying the present . . . in relation to the past. [. . .] It's really misleading to think that authenticity is about
the past. It's about the present and how the present sees and constructs the
past and what past it wants" (*Parallels* 126). Said's understanding of the way
the present views and constructs the past is particularly pertinent to Djebar's
work, I will show in the second and third chapters, devoted to the writer. Her
texts reveal the *montage*—including the *selection* and the *selectivity* of the
past—in treating of history and religion in writing.

It is significant that Said comments on authenticity in a work titled *Parallels and Paradoxes: Explorations in Music and Society*. By focusing on French-
language texts in *musical terms* throughout this book, I intend hereby to propose an alternative to the stale debate between "French" and "Francophone,"
to revalorize the term "*Francophonie*" in its sonorous etymology,[34] and to point
to the ever-changing, moving possibilities it carries for literature. As Khatibi
argues, "the francophone world is métissage, or mixture, with diverse bilin-
gualisms and multilingualisms" (*La Langue* 66). This linguistic mixing, in its
polyphonic diversity, applies to the Francophone world in its entirety, including France, and therefore should not be considered solely in relation to "other"
regions marked by the French tongue. If we consider "Francophonie" in a
larger, inclusive sense, we find that it lends itself well to musical conceptions
and expressions, both thematically and stylistically. Musical terms—often deriving from Italian and transcending linguistic borders intact—abound in contemporary Francophone works by the writers in my study. Transposing life and
its substance into textual compositions, these writers demonstrate the qualities
of true musicians: they possess trained ears and voices. Like composers of musical pieces, they prove attentive and open to external *and internal* rhythms
and transitions, whether harmonic or dissonant, and convincingly transcribe
them on paper, marking their time.

Writing Autobiographically, Authentically

This study brings together three contemporary writers in French: Assia Dje-bar; Hélène Cixous; Abdelkébir Khatibi. Born in 1936, 1937, and 1938, re-spectively, these intellectuals are not only close *in time*, but *in space* as well, since all three were born and grew up in North Africa. While the political situations in their native lands were not identical (the shorter-lived protec-torate in Morocco was less violent than the long presence of the French in Algeria, which began in 1830 with the conquest of this territory and culmi-nated in the Algerian War of 1954–1962), they were nonetheless quite sim-ilar, and the domination that characterizes the two countries' rather recent histories left recognizable traces on those who witnessed and "underwent" this period.

The fact that the three North African countries of Algeria, Morocco, and Tunisia are often referred to collectively as "the Maghreb" reveals the shared characteristics of these lands marked by geographical proximity. This denomination points not only to this common location, but also to a comparable historical and linguistic situation that unites these discrete na-tional entities. Writers from this area have long exhibited solidarity with those from other Maghrebian countries, as evidenced by Kateb Yacine's writings in the 1960s and current exchanges between Jacques Derrida and Abdelkébir Khatibi, whose ongoing (inter)textual dialogue focusing on "Franco-Maghrebian" identity and language(s) is explored in the second part of the seventh chapter.[35]

The deep-seated "problems of *identity*" that Derrida speaks to in *Le Mono-linguisme de l'autre* are addressed in the context of a "Francophone" confer-ence held at Louisiana State University in Baton Rouge (10). Not only is the place of enunciation important here, since particular areas (and particular university departments) of the United States have been especially active in promoting "Francophone" studies, but the *occasion* takes on special signifi-cance as well, as a *gathering* of members of the Francophone "community," in a large sense, including French citizens from France, French-speakers from other countries from Switzerland to Canada to Central Africa, and Maghre-bians who have never held French citizenship (29–30). Derrida describes each of these three categories in order to show that he fits none of them, due to the strange combination of circumstances that made him at once Maghre-bian (not a citizenship) and French (a citizenship), by birth. This unique classification, though unparalleled at the 1992 conference on "problems of *francophonie* outside France," is nonetheless shared by Cixous, whose per-sonal and professional itineraries have much in common with Derrida's. Like

Derrida, Cixous has not long been associated with the country of her birth, and for that reason Cixous may be the unexpected writer in this unprecedented grouping. It is clear that she does not call herself "Maghrebian," that she *could not* "name" herself thus in the same sense as the other two writers in this study. But her presence is essential, indeed *central* to this study, precisely because of the uniqueness of what she calls her "Algériance."[36] The fifth chapter, "*Prelude to a Fugue*, Out of North Africa," concentrates on the importance of Cixous's "Algerian accidence" to her writing career.

While this book does not contain a chapter specifically devoted to him, the presence of Derrida is felt throughout. He is a crucial interlocutor with each of these writers in very real ways. The influence of Derrida's writings is obvious in the many (explicit and implicit) citations of and references to his work in the writings of his friends and colleagues Cixous and Khatibi. In "Settling the Musical Score: Orality, Rhythm, and Repetition in Writing Wrongs," a section called "Dancing with Derrida" provides some insight into the long-standing, highly subtle textual exchanges in Cixous's and Derrida's publications, revealing an easily overlooked mutual influence between Cixous and Derrida that is present from very early on in their writing careers. Djebar does not quote or refer to Derrida directly, but her methods of thinking and writing often find themselves in tandem with his, in part because the two writers are influenced by many of the same readings,[37] and in part because their paths have crossed in various settings, such as in their active participation in the *Parlement International des Écrivains* as founding members in 1994.[38]

Placing the textual voices of Cixous, Djebar, and Khatibi in choral dialogue here, in this publication, is not meant to establish an equivalency among their very different œuvres. While a certain number of fruitful comparisons can be drawn, there are just as many contrasts, and the thrust of my argument is to place these variations, stemming from differences (sexual, religious, historical, familial, ethnic, and linguistic), alongside each other, in order to better see—*and hear*—the divergences in note and tone. The point is not therefore to seek inexorably to establish connections justifying this choice, although many could be given, including the prominent presence of Khatibi at two large colloquia in Paris in 2003, the first titled "Hélène Cixous: Genèses Généalogies Genres" held at the Bibliothèque nationale de France in May, and the second in November at the Maison des écrivains, devoted to "Assia Djebar: nomade entre les murs, Pour une poétique transfrontalière." The aim is, rather, to look at the way similar backgrounds and movements (from the Magheb to Paris, for starters)[39] yield diverging, yet complementary literary works.

Cixous, Djebar, and Khatibi all make, in varying ways, considerable strides in autobiographical writing. While not one has composed a text labeled "autobiography," each has produced a series of "autobiographical" texts that treat of the personal in profound ways. Unconcerned with adhering to models that determine generic classifications, these inventive writers have found within the "foreign" French tongue a space to write the self, in flux, in motion, in change, in a word: authentically. My understanding of this word is influenced by Milan Kundera's comments in *Les Testaments trahis*; his close reading of Leo Tolstoy's *War and Peace* demonstrates that individuals are continually changing, throughout their lives: "Tolstoy thus offers us another conception of man: he is an itinerary; a winding road; a journey whose successive phases not only vary but often represent a total negation of the preceding phases" (213). Given this condition of perpetual change, it is difficult for the reader to judge a literary character, not only according to moral standards, but also according to expectations of authenticity: "It is impossible to say which Bolkonsky is more true to himself" (214). As a critic, Kundera posits an understanding of the self as unstable, as changeable, and therefore, often, as contradictory, and he points to the ever-present potential for self-transformation as it is conveyed in the Russian writer's work: "In Tolstoy, man is the more himself, the more an individual, when he has the strength, the imagination, the intelligence to transform himself" (221).

The possibility for self-transformation is a crucial part of Khatibi's view not only of life, but also of *life writing*. He contends that autobiography is filled with possibility, with *becoming*: "Autobiography, in its different forms, is a gesture or a calligraphy more than a literary genre. It is the possibility of being received as a guest in the language of the other. This release from the self prefigures a memory of becoming" (*La Langue* 29). Writing in the "language of the other," Khatibi maintains, gives him room *to become* (in and through writing), and the outcome is uncertain: "We are rather on the horizon of a promise, of a productive possibility, a game with chance and the unknown" (41). Djebar exhibits a similar attitude toward writing the self as an adventure that can lead in any number of directions: "if it seems that language is, as we often say, 'a means of communication,' it is especially for me as a writer, 'a means of transformation,' insofar as I experience writing as an adventure" (*Ces voix* 42). This view of writing as a place for transformation overthrows assumptions that writing the self means remaining "authentically" true to a lived past, and it places an emphasis on the changing nature of individuals, who are always in movement, inside and outside the text, *transforming* themselves in relation to time. This is the most critical element of Kundera's reading of Tolstoy, when he notes that characters "are different in each phase of their lives" (213). When he implicitly makes a connection between the question of identity and the question of time, highlighting the possibility of evolving over time, Kundera intimates what is at work in the ongoing autobiographical publications of the three writers in my study.

Time Signatures

Time Signatures focuses on the ways in which contemporary writing in French by Cixous, Djebar, and Khatibi pushes the limits of this "foreign" language by creating innovative texts in various genres (poetry, short stories, novels, and theoretical essays). These texts defy traditional categorical classification and problematize preconceived notions of "autobiographical" works. My focus on *language* and *translation* in these authors' written output is not limited to a linguistic analysis of the bilingual or multilingual aspects of their creative production. I understand language and translation in a larger metaphorical sense that includes an examination of music, silence, madness, gender and sexuality, history, tradition, and religion as they are communicated in the text.

The title *Time Signatures* provides an important point of entry into my study of these autobiographical texts. First, *time* is crucial to the work of these contemporary authors who are writing in the aftermath of a specific historical moment they all experienced: the end of French colonization in their native lands. The portrayals of their personal histories during this pivotal period take place within the contexts of larger familial and national histories. Second, the concept of *signatures* is key to my study of the role of proper names in these works and of the "moment" of signing a work that contributes to the authenticity of any literary publication. Then, taken together, *time signatures* is a metaphorical term that refers directly to a piece of music, highlighting the rhythm and the speed of phrasing, and providing a key to reading (or playing) the written work. A musical note in any given composition carries only a relative value that depends on the notes around it in respect to the time signature (provided by the composer); a note's length and its emphasis change according to context. The time signature thus furnishes a guide to reading the individual work by giving specific meaning to signs that acquire this significance *within* the work rather than outside it.

This conception of *time signatures* is particularly applicable to the "musical" compositions of poetical writers like Cixous, Djebar, and Khatibi, who play with words and their meanings, inserting plurality and multiplicity into their texts in polyphonic autobiographical works. Worn words take on new resonance in the autobiographical works by these creative writers who infuse old terms with renewed emotion, who mix familiar expressions with unfamiliar turns of phrase, and the novelty of their literary creations must be properly contextualized in multiple ways: the relations within a singular work; the relations between various writings belonging to the same œuvre; the relations between this oeuvre and other literary texts; the relations between this œuvre and the surrounding historical, political, and geographical climates.

The choice of this title from musical terminology ties together the various threads of this study. For instance, in this introduction, I have explored the way these writers from outside the hexagonal borders of contemporary France effectively establish "legitimacy" and "authenticity" in writing. Their credibility in literary circles is not dependent solely on "telling the truth" by relating discrete elements of veracity in the text. It relies also and more importantly on "hitting the right note," on finding an appropriate voice to communicate a *broader truth* in the literary work. The three writers in my study do not consistently claim to be relating strict facts in their writing, even if they are often exact in their detailing of events; they are more concerned with the contours of the text and its articulations of personal lived experience. They tend to focus not on the major strains of history, but rather on the off beat, on the unaccented notes in the stories of peoples and lands, revealing the private aspects of life that are so frequently missing from official accounts. In this writing, the distinction between truth and fiction becomes obsolete. It is not a question of distinguishing between what "really happened" and how that happening is altered or doctored in its written form. To the contrary, these writings reveal that there is undeniable truth *in* fiction, that autobiographical writing can *make truth* ("*faire la vérité*," as Jacques Derrida describes it in "Circonfession"), and that aspects of writing the self that may seem to be contradictory in nature do not detract from the autobiographical work. Contradictions may in fact *contribute* to a writer's authenticity.

In French, the notion of singing off key is communicated through the expression "*chanter faux*," and this provocative reference to what is "false" (as opposed to what is "*juste*" or "correct") in the musical world is translatable into literary terms. In contrast to music, "approximation" can be effective in literature, and my study seeks to explore the ways Maghrebian writers use supposition and imagination to (re)construct and (re)present events, emotions, and people. While it is often true that words, like musical notes, must be exact or they will not sound right, writings can often bring out resonance *through* dissonance, and communicate the larger meaning of the text, the greater harmony of the autobiographical enterprise as these writers understand it.

Translation occupies a central place in these writers' works since none of them claims the language of writing as their "mother tongue." Hélène Cixous, Assia Djebar, and Abdelkébir Khatibi all explore the plurality of languages that influenced their childhood in multilingual, multiethnic Algeria and Morocco. They find ways to communicate their "mothers' tongues"— whether Berber or German—in the French text in myriad ways, including the direct insertion of untranslated words in italics into the work, the French translations of unusual expressions without explanation or elaboration, the juxtaposition of foreign terms and French equivalents, circumlocutions that explain the concept in the original tongue, footnotes that provide definitions of unfamiliar terms, and syntactic disruptions and variations that infuse the French text with the rhythms of the native language.

An apt term to describe the processes at work in this sort of writing is "transposition," a word that figures in the title of the sixth chapter, "French Transcriptions, French Transpositions: Transportation, *Transnation*, and Transliteration." In music, to "transpose" a piece means to rewrite it, or to play it in a key or pitch other than the one in which it was originally written or in which it is usually performed. By extension, to "transpose" means to take a story or incident out of its usual setting or time and relocate it in another. This is precisely the sort of "translation" that Maghrebian writers of various origins must engage in when composing in French. Their experiences in their native countries must be transposed into another linguistic and cultural context in order to be legible. And the works that result from this transposition are often on the border of the "readable," pushing the limits of textual composition by incorporating new, inventive elements. It is important to note that the verb "to transpose" can also refer to the action of making two things change place; for instance, a transposition on the page can constitute a reversal of the normal order of two letters in a word. The wordplay present in the autobiographical writings in my study is a deliberate action that disrupts ordinary rules of grammar and orthography. Djebar, Cixous, and Khatibi are quick to show the similarities among words and to demonstrate the slippages in language (a single language, French) and among languages (the multiple idioms of the written text).

The languages that find expression in these works are not limited to specific tongues. Significant place is given to songs, for instance, to the words that are sung or chanted in various settings and that carry multiple meanings. The insertion of such lyrics is meant to highlight the way words enter us, the way they form us, sometimes without our conscious awareness. Particularly in childhood and adolescence, in the early formative years of existence, *refrains* become a part of our internal soundtrack before we have an understanding of their import. Music is the focus of the fourth chapter, "Settling the Musical Score: Orality, Rhythm, and Repetition in Writing Wrongs." The writers in my study carefully portray the language of childhood in the text, giving way to the rhythmic, melodic strains that are not always strictly "meaningful" and that thereby evade logical reflection. Orality comes through in specific passages in complex ways; not only is it communicated through the use of distinctly "spoken" terms, direct address of the reader, and repetition, but it is also evoked in the *vocal* rhythms of the writing. Special attention is given to voices in all of these writers' works, and the narrator's inimitable voice finds itself intermingling with voices belonging to others in these polyphonic texts. The inclusion of other voices that have their own stories to tell underscores the fact that the stories of others *make us up*, that they contribute to our *makeup* in crucial ways. The multiple voices in the text do not emerge from a vacuum; their source in real, bodily beings is highlighted in the space devoted to *breath*. The recurrence of the word *"souffle"* in these corpuses reveals that it is not only *what* is said that counts, but also *how* it is said, including pauses and inflections.

Another idiom of crucial importance to these writings is the language of love. These writers from the Maghreb seek to express affection in a foreign tongue, and they reveal that the language of the heart is always already "foreign," that words employed to tell of the deepest desires and the most complex emotions will not come "naturally" and certainly never "logically" to the human subject. It is in representing relations of fondness and tenderness between embodied men and women that the complexities of language are most salient in these literary compositions. The frequently poetic but sometimes faltering amorous expressions found in these texts not only point to advantages but also to larger flaws of language. In fact, the often "illogical" expressions of sentiment in such works as *Amour bilingue* by Khatibi are illustrative of the "madness" of language in general. This text contains expressions of the ineffable experiences of sexuality and sensuality, taking into account the changing nature of desire and pleasure.

For many women writers of Islamic tradition, words of love are simply unpronounceable. In Assia Djebar's *L'Amour, la fantasia*, the narrator describes the aphasia that haunts her when it comes to confessions of affections in French. This censure in her writings is reminiscent of the taboo nature of written avowal of love in the form of exchanged letters during her childhood; as the narrative reveals, a paternal interdict definitively terminated such correspondence. Djebar calls attention to absence, indeed to *silence*, in her writing, and thereby gives the reader a valuable lesson on another aspect of language in Maghrebian autobiographical texts. Contrary to the commonly held belief that silences are empty, it is clear in these writings that the silences are pregnant with meaning. Just as rests are part of the musical score and must be counted as carefully as the notes, so the pauses in the written text must be observed, respected, and *read*. Deciphering the silences in their myriad forms (spaces, ellipses, margins, omissions) is an integral part of reading.

If aphasia characterizes her state in romantic settings, the same cannot be said with respect to religion. Djebar evokes the Islamic faith of her upbringing in outspoken, critical terms that demonstrate the sharp divergence between Islam as it has evolved over time and the worthy precepts that marked its early years. In *"Religio*: Re-thinking and Re-linking Cultural and Religious Tradition," Djebar engages in a close reading of the early texts of this heritage and demonstrates where interpretations have gone wrong. It is noteworthy that she vindicates the rights of women in her work *based on* Islam, not fighting against that Tradition but hoping instead to re-read and transform it from *within*.

As I have already mentioned, "NameStakes: Putting the Proper Name into Textual Play" treats of the proper name. In this first chapter, I examine the specificity of the Maghrebian-born writer in French, and I consider on a number of levels the consequences of writing with a name that is "foreign" to the idiom of composition. It becomes clear that Cixous's sensitivity and careful attention to the names of others stems from her observations of the noisome results of bad naming in the colonial environment of her early years. Her seemingly contradictory impulses with respect to names, wishing at once to preserve them from disrespectful use *and* free them from their charge, is due to the qualifying term, *proper*. Cixous does not claim sole ownership of her literary production, proclaiming instead that her books belong to everyone, to all those who are sung in her texts.

The *time* of my title also makes reference to the *temporality* of the writing and reading of the text.[40] Silences help to shape this temporal dimension of the text, providing a certain rhythm to the reading by spacing the words on the printed page and structuring the reader's experience. The length of sentences and paragraphs, as well as the number of pauses in the form of commas, semicolons, and periods also play an important role in establishing temporality. Explicit references to speed (*la vitesse*) and slowness (*la lenteur*) also serve to influence the reader who is in touch with the writer's pace thanks to these metatextual clues that indicate the appropriate *time signatures*. Silence emerges as an important concept in several chapters, but plays a particularly strong role in the seventh chapter, "Silence and Schizophrenia: Subtle Slips of the Tongue."

My emphasis on the plural in the title is crucial, for not only does it evoke the multiple modes of writing these authors employ, but it sheds light on their time-varied writing even *within* a single text. It is important to know that time signatures can change within a piece; nothing in a composition is set, stable, or fixed. Reading music requires keeping an open eye to see changes in key, mode, and *time*; rhythms and values can change dramatically and suddenly in any work. The autobiographical works by the three writers in my study prove this musical rule to be the case in their compositions. None of their texts can be characterized as "chronological." Instead, they all proceed in a nonlinear fashion that doesn't move toward an "ending" in the sense that implies a plot that "progresses" toward a satisfying conclusion, ultimately tying together all the loose ends so that every element of the text "makes sense." Their fragmentary texts focus on specific moments, often related in the form of anecdotes, as revealed in the third chapter, "*Histoires à Contretemps*: Syncopated Histories: Writing on the Offbeat." These revealing episodes, these chosen instances of intense description, are an important part of these writings that make a mark in time, that mark their writers' time, chronicling and calculating this *before* and *after* of colonization. This time of intense change, of tremendous violence and tumultuous activity to which they bore witness in their native countries is transposed in(to) the written production of these Francophone subjects.

It is because of their birth in the French-occupied territories of the Maghreb that Hélène Cixous, Assia Djebar, and Abdelkébir Khatibi are so keenly aware of questions of language—and particularly the French language—in their writing. In their theoretical reflections, they carefully focus on how language translates experience, and in their novels they enact the "double" translation that takes place when experience is rendered in *another* language, when it is transposed into another key. These three contemporaries hail from a particular region at a particular time; Morocco and, to an even greater extent, Algeria were historical hotbeds during these writers' childhoods, and all three were lastingly affected by their early environment. As Hélène Cixous notes, you cannot decide where you're from, and the chapter "*Prelude to a Fugue*, Out of North Africa: Uprooting and Rerouting in Autobiographical Fiction" explores what the place of origin means in her experience. This chapter shows that the geography of your environment can play an undeniable role in *deciding* you, in determining how you see the world and how you react to it. In the case of the writers in my study, the reactions have yielded innovative literary works of distinction. And to describe these works, I once again have recourse to a musical term: *play*.

There is tremendous "play" at work in autobiographical writings by Maghrebian writers. Just as the musician "plays" a piece of music, readers must seek to "play" the literary text. They must approach the work with great respect for the composer's indications and intentions, but they must also provide their own interpretations, their individual reactions to the work. Since there is arguably a great deal of "play" in these writings, approaches and explanations will be multiple and varied. There is not one single "correct" version of the text, but a number of valid understandings of the meaning inherent in the work. For autobiographical writers, the text is a place to "play out" the many factors of their experience in a complex transcription that defies easy interpretation. This "self writing" is composite and complicated in its sincere effort to give place to the multiple influences that traverse the writing subject.

In conclusion, I would like to propose that my new spelling of "Francophony" could be pronounced Francophony, in accord with the word "cacophony." Contemporary writers from the Maghreb are not always concerned with creating harmony, either in theme or form. In fact, recent writing has been increasingly marked by dissonance, by innovation that departs from established spellings, syntax, and treatment of the past, the personal, and the political. While "cacophony" often carries negative connotations, writing that may initially impress readers as discordant and arrhythmic can strike unique chords if we approach the text in new ways, learning to "read by ear," the only appropriate manner to come to Cixous's writing, in Khatibi's analysis. In order to appreciate the multicultural, multilingual autobiographical text in French, we must understand that music may not be the "universal language" after all, but that heretofore unseen combinations of notes and unheard-of contrasting tones have much to offer "French letters."

Notes

1. Unless otherwise indicated in parenthetical notations and in the bibliography, all translations are mine.

2. Music is cited as a part of "minor literature" as Deleuze and Guattari describe it: "These are the true minor authors. An escape for language, for music, for writing. [. . .] To make use of the polylingualism of one's own language, to make minor or intensive use of it, to oppose the oppressed quality of this language to its oppressive quality, to find points of nonculture or overdevelopment, linguistic Third World zones by which a language can escape, an animal enters into things, an assemblage comes into play" (26–27).

3. There is an unfortunate lack of uniformity in texts that refer to "Francophonie," some placing it within quotation marks, others in italics; some capitalizing the word and others not. I have chosen to capitalize it here to highlight its transformation into English, a tongue in which languages are capitalized, and to place it in quotation

marks. While "Francophone" has made it into English dictionaries, "Francophonie" has not (yet).

4. To read chapter 6 ("La Langue française en Europe, dans le monde") of Reclus's book online, in which these words first appear in print, go to http://languefrancaise .free.fr/promotion/francophonie _texte_reclus.htm. Although "Francophonie" dates back to 1880, the term was rarely used before 1962, when an issue of *Esprit* dedicated to the question of "Français langue vivante" presented an eloquent definition by Senegalese writer and politician Léopold Sédar Senghor: "Francophonie is this integral Humanism that weaves its way around the earth, this symbiosis of 'dominant energies' from all continents and all races that is awakened by their complementary warmth." Moura draws the conclusion that this remarkable statement served to distance the term from its original geographic and linguistic notions and to attach it to "Frenchness [*francité*], designating, beyond language, the spirit of French civilization, of French Culture" (2).

5. Not only is French not the sole language spoken in France, it is of course not a "pure" construct, unaffected by other idioms. Khatibi eloquently recalls the history of the tongue, pointing to its implications for writers of the French language, "French" and "Francophone" alike: "The language for which I was 'historically destined,' French, is an altered form of Latin, a sort of alliance between a Latin lexicon and a local idiomatic syntax. Therein lies its initial identity principle—only schematically explained here—with respect to which we are inscribed, French and francophone, with our languages, our idioms, our cultures, far before colonization and the French Empire" (*La Langue* 37).

6. Ben Jelloun admits that he has no personal definition of "francophonie," and points to the problematic nature of the appellation: "It's very bothersome because for me, the word 'francophone' refers to all those who use the French language. And in the High Council, for instance, the majority of us are foreigners. There are two or three French writers, but it is not customary to use the term 'francophone' to refer to French writers. It sounds strange, and they would possibly take it badly. So, it's a curious phenomenon. I am not very comfortable with the notion."

7. For more on the *Haut Conseil de la Francophonie*, see http://www.francophonie .org. This web site sheds some light on the storied past of "Francophonie," and cites 1970 as the date when the first intergovernmental organism on Francophonie was founded, under the name *Agence de coopération culturelle et technique* (ACCT).

8. Meddeb identifies France as "center" in the political context of "Francophonie": "What we call francophonie covers a constant politics [. . .] of perpetuation of a thought and production emanating from a center and destined to be diffused in zones that are secondary, if not dependent." In Meddeb's analysis, this split between a "center" and "secondary zones" results in a false separation between interrelated literatures of the same language. (*Prétexte*)

9. Hargreaves and McKinney argue that, due to the large number of minorities originating in ex-colonies who have now settled in France, the geographical dimension of the term *francophonie* no longer holds sway: "French-speaking to a very

large extent, yet culturally distinct in other ways and still marked by exclusionary memories of the colonial period, these minorities defy the political logic of fran-cophonie by being residents and in many cases citizens of France while appearing to many among the majority population to belong elsewhere" (4). In a beautiful analysis of "Francophonie," Abdelkébir Khatibi elucidates the historical compo-nent of the term, maintaining that it at once is *and* isn't a "colonial" product and highlighting the anonymous, harmful, "political" aspect of its application: "what we call in such an inconsiderate manner 'la francophonie' or 'francographie' dates and does not date back to the colonial period. That's why the literature whose name we bear—no matter what our origin, citizenship, or nationality—has been forced through its exercise and through poetic work in particular to constitute a territory that belongs to no one, but that is taken over by politics as if it were private prop-erty, to the extent that in certain public sessions, you get the strange feeling that the 'Francophones' are a community of hostages. But of whom and of what?" (*La Langue* 37).

10. Ben Jelloun laments the political aspect of "Francophonie," particularly in its present dimensions. When asked about its role in the world, he asserts first that it is an error to focus solely on the imparting of French culture in other lands and argues that there should be more of an exchange at work, rather than a unilateral relation-ship of instruction. Then he militates in favor of ridding "Francophonie" of its polit-ical mantle: "détacher la francophonie de toute politique." These words echo the lamentations in a 1988 interview of Kateb Yacine who sees through the positive ap-pearance of "Francophonie" to its tarnished political core: "What one calls 'fran-cophonie' is a neocolonial machine that only perpetuates our alienation. I have al-ways denounced it, no matter what my detractors say. I recently said so to François Mitterand himself: the francophonie of a Bokassa who takes himself for Napoleon or a Houphouët-Boigny who receives Le Pen hurts Africa as much as it does France" (Chergui 47).

11. I use the terms "colonial" loosely, to refer to French domination in a general sense. As Hargreaves and McKinney note, none of the areas of North Africa occu-pied by the French was officially called a "colony": "In French and/or international law, none of these territories was formally classified as a colony. Officially regarded as an integral part of French territory, Algeria was subject to the French Interior Min-istry instead of the Colonial Ministry. Morocco and Tunisia were officially 'protec-torates,' nominally retaining internal autonomy while enjoying the external 'protec-tion' of the French Foreign Ministry" (23).

12. "Contextualizing" the works of writers from the Maghreb means placing them in geographical and chronological context with respect to external events, but it also means delving into their truths, closely reading their contents for the specific con-text of each text, and its place within the writer's corpus taken as a whole.

13. Nimrod hopes to disrupt the "central" location of France to the French lan-guage, affirming that "it is time to consider French an African language." http://www.lemonde.fr/web/imprimer_article/0,1-0@2-3260,36-334055,0.html.

14. In support of this statement on the American preference for works penned by non-native French writers, Ben Jelloun recounts an anecdote he overheard while visiting his agent in New York. According to his story, the translation into English of the recently published *Onitsha*, by Jean-Marie Le Clézio, was at stake. The book was sure to be a hit, according to the two interlocutors, because of its emphasis on Africa, but it was a shame the writer was not an "African" himself; in the words of the agent: "if he had been black, that would have been outstanding, we would have had a best-seller."

15. Meddeb makes a similar statement when he touts the creative energies that come from "Francophone" compositions: "It's enough to open one's eyes and admit that the creative energy in the French language is redeploying itself by returning to their place works already produced by the word of 'exotes' (Ségalen)." The term "exotes," taken from Victor Ségalen's *Essai sur l'exotisme: Une Esthétique du divers*, is used to highlight the "exotic," the "other" status that breathes new life into writing in French.

16. A different version of this text is available in English translation. It was published in a volume of *Yale French Studies* titled "French and Francophone: The Challenge of Expanding Horizons."

17. While Bensmaïa indicates that these areas of study also pulsed through France during this period (or shortly thereafter), I would argue that they still have not received the same positive attention in the Hexagon. The number of French institutions that promote courses in "postcolonial" or "Francophone" studies pales in comparison to the U.S., and while classes in deconstruction—and even classes devoted entirely to the writings of Derrida—abound in American schools, I have yet to learn of a single course on this subject in France.

18. This text figures prominently in this study, not only for what it reveals about language and translation in the specific context of the French-speaking subject from Algeria, but also for its attention to the particular difficulties of "identity" and "identification" in such a context.

19. The colonial context, and its critical influence of their approach to the French language, pervades the work of all three writers, beginning with Djebar. In *L'Amour, la fantasia*, the first-person narrative voice treats of the history of French in Algeria in stark, dark terms: "This language was imported in the murky, obscure past, spoils taken from the enemy. [. . .] This language was formerly used to entomb my people" (*Fantasia* 215). Cixous portrays the colonial educational environment of her own childhood in Algeria as inappropriate, even laughable: "Me too. The routine 'our ancestors, the Gauls' was pulled on me. [. . .] What is my name? I want to change life. Who is this 'I'? Where is my place? I am looking. I search everywhere. I read. I ask. I begin to speak. Which language is mine? French? German? Arabic?" ("Sorties" 70). Khatibi addresses the "*clarté*" of the French language with respect to national identity and disrupts both notions when he insists, in personal terms, on colonial history: "They used to say, and they still do, that the clarity of the French language is a national virtue. Illegible is he or she who stirs up the identity principle of the nation. But I was colonized by this nation" (*La Langue* 30).

20. It is important to note that Algeria was officially considered part of France (even if its inhabitants had to obtain passports to travel to the *métropole*), and that Cixous terms the educational environment of her teenage years "Algériefrançaise" in *Les Rêveries de la femme sauvage* (142). Growing up in a "France" that wasn't (France), posed a challenge to an entire generation of writers from Algeria.

21. Here it is important to note a long-standing tendency among the French to "claim" as their own, without hesitation, successful scribblers from beyond French borders, from Jean-Jacques Rousseau to Amélie Nothomb.

22. I have not picked the terms "integrated" and "assimilated" randomly; they are employed by Hélène Cixous in an interview during which she evokes Algeria as her own place of origin, and indicates that it was there that she learned the ways these "political" expressions actually worked to exclude those they supposedly sought to include: "Coming from Algeria, [. . .] I have always been extremely sensitive to what is called in French space, in idiomatic language, integration and assimilation. Regarding the French political scene, I have always told myself that those were heavy, dangerous, not necessarily beneficial words. I felt it when I was young in Algeria, in the politics of exclusion that were called 'integration'; it is true that exclusion has often been called integration" ("La voix étrangère" 111).

23. The writer of autobiographical works who does not establish an equivalency between the person outside the text and the narrator and character within could respond in a similar manner. I would argue that such a statement appears to be a cop-out, for the writer can always say that she is writing a work of fiction and therefore deny all responsibility for its contents. Writing is, however, always an act of responsibility, and inevitably participates in the processes of meaning-making that are dependent on a striving for truth, in a broad sense that transcends the truth/fiction divide.

24. Laronde points to what I would say has sometimes been the unfortunate plight of the "Francophone" text by highlighting the fact that works are esteemed not for their aesthetic value but instead are considered solely for their sociological worth: "socioethnic and sociolinguistic criteria according to which we still classify novels, as para-literature (or 'minor' literature) for their content and as sociolect for the writing, hinting more or less that the works lack aesthetic value" (5).

25. *Loin de Médine*, *Le Blanc de l'Algérie*, and *L'Amour, la fantasia* are now available in "Livre de poche," as are *Les Nuits de Strasbourg* and *Oran, langue morte* in the Babel collection.

26. If we consider that *Ombre sultane* was also published by Lattès, and is presently unavailable, the contrasting availability of *L'Amour, la fantasia* sheds light on the crucial role Albin Michel has played in Djebar's publishing history.

27. Djebar recently received La Médaille Vermeil pour la Francophonie, awarded by the Académie Française in 1999, and was named Commandeur des Arts et des Lettres in France in 2001. In June 2005, another honor of a different aura was bestowed upon her: election to the illustrious Académie Française.

28. My focus here is on translations into English, due to lack of space. Translations into other tongues have also had an important influence on the writing careers of the

three writers in this study. Cixous's work has been published in a number of tongues and a unique collection of reflections on translating her writing into languages as diverse as Japanese and Romanian has recently been published under the title *Joyful Babel*. It is worth noting that Djebar's very first publication, *La Soif*, was translated into Dutch in 1958, three years before it was published in an English version. Jan Versteeg has rendered four of Djebar's more recent publications—from *Ombre sultane* to *Les Nuits de Strasbourg*—in Dutch as well. Other important languages of translation for Djebar's corpus include German, Italian, and Swedish.

29. As Derrida observes, "There is, indeed, an undeniable celebrity, an aura, and a worldwide admiration of Hélène Cixous. But, strangely, they are accompanied by a deep misunderstanding, especially in this country" (Samoyault).

30. Khatibi echoes this desire when he praises the freedom he enjoys when writing in French: "Apparently, I have more freedom than writers of French origin. [. . .] That is why I like paradoxical writers who live a limit-experience of language. I am a border-dweller, a climber, a 'professional foreigner.' It so happens that I invent words" (*La Langue* 80).

31. I am arguing here *for* a comprehension of the subtlety and complexity of both the writer and the work—and thus *against* the prescriptive application of "*étiquettes*" such as "woman" and "Francophone." The inadequacy of such labels parallels the insufficiency of generic classification, as supported by Jacques Derrida's analysis of a "*récit*" by Maurice Blanchot in "The Law of Genre": "Every text *participates* in one or several genres, there is no genreless text, there is always a genre and genres, yet such participation never amounts to belonging" (230).

32. This particular writer is the embodiment of the concise biographical notice! "Maurice Blanchot, novelist and critic, was born in 1907. His life is entirely devoted to literature and its silence" are the only sentences that grace his books.

33. The work of Edward Said is useful to understanding the importance of the particular as related to, but separate from, the universal. In a section titled "Discrepant Experiences" from *Culture and Imperialism*, Said makes clear that "although there is an irreducible subjective core to human experience, this experience is also historical and secular, it is accessible to analysis and interpretation, and—centrally important—it is not exhausted by totalizing theories, not marked and limited by doctrinal or national lines, not confined once and for all to analytical constructs" (31). Said trumpets what he calls a "contrapuntal perspective," an idea I will develop in relation to Assia Djebar's work in Chapter 2, that is explained as follows by Said: "we must be able to think through and interpret together experiences that are discrepant, each with its particular agenda and pace of development" (32). Said's emphasis on "pace" echoes my own concern with rhythm and cadence, and temporality, in the written text. His evocation of history and social setting as crucial to experience resonates with the stress I place on contextualizing works and writers in this study.

34. Djebar gathered reels of audio and visual recordings of women's voices in Algeria during the 1970s. In a number of textual reflections on this period of her life,

the writer reveals the importance of these "sounds" in her writing project. Even though her language of writing is French, her own vision of "Francophonie" is informed by these voices from other tongues: "Thus my francophonie—at the close of these ten years of searching, of researching often in the dark, of polyphonic attempts—cannot be situated any longer except in the enlarging of this field. My francophonie, taken charge of in this fashion, can only wander through mutations and movings [mouvances]" (Ces voix 40). The crucial importance of movement to Djebar's—and to Khatibi's—writing is the topic of the seventh chapter, in which "translation" is taken in the French sense to mean physical displacement and serves as a stimulus for the creative productivity of these writers.

35. Kateb Yacine testifies to the unity among Maghrebian peoples and their histories in Le Poète comme un boxeur: "If we speak of the Maghreb, it's the same thing: Algeria is fully a part of the Maghreb. If we write the history of the Maghreb, if we show what the Moroccan monarchy, the struggle of the Sahraouis, the struggle of Abdelkader or Abdelkrim, [. . .] if we connect that to current events, we don't leave Algeria, for all of that concerns the Algerians" (89). Assia Djebar often expresses (a desire for) Maghrebian unity, as in these words pronounced by a character in Les Nuits de Strasbourg: "We chatted for a long time into the night: of the Maghreb that we wanted to be a single country" (62).

36. It is not an accident that Djebar and Khatibi both cite Cixous's works on occasion. The contributions Cixous has made to contemporary thought in her writings, from the catch-phrase "coming to writing" to her unique style, make her an unavoidable source from which Djebar and Khatibi draw inspiration: "All of this brings me to define my writing, or at least its beginning, its perception ('coming to writing,' Hélène Cixous would say), in a position 'outside languages' ['hors-les-langues'] (Ces voix 26); "I began to read Hélène Cixous's OR this summer, a text that is related to the topic on 'this' French. What a box of treasures! I am moved by this voice that finds its way in a magical night. Spatial, geometric writing, an ascending geometry in free fall" (La Langue 27).

37. Djebar quotes in a number of texts Maurice Blanchot, Paul Celan, Friedrich Hölderlin, and, with the greatest frequency, Saint Augustine, all of whom figure prominently in Derrida's œuvre.

38. In the first publication of the review AUTODAFE in the spring of 2001, the following explanation of the organization's history is given on the final page: "The International Parliament of Writers was born following a call that went out in July 1993 by three hundred writers from around the world, in reaction to the increasing numbers of assassinated writers in Algeria" (271). Derrida (who served for a time as vice president of the IWP), Cixous (also a founding member), and Djebar contributed to this initial issue of the review.

39. Paris figures in the discussion of movement that permeates chapters 6 and 7, on Cixous and on Khatibi and Djebar; it is the city in which Cixous has taken up residence, and in which Djebar also has a home. While Khatibi currently lives in his native country, he asserts that the French capital not only was crucial to his intellectual

formation during the six years he spent there between 1958 and 1964, but also that it remains an unavoidable part of his life: "Paris is my 'supernative' town. My itinerary had to pass through this city; it continues to pass through it and will in the future" (*La Langue* 74).

40. For an insightful treatment of music and temporality, see Bernard Stiegler's *Aimer, s'aimer, nous aimer: Du 11 septembre au 21 avril*, especially pages 38–40.

CHAPTER ONE

~

NameStakes: Putting the
Proper Name into Textual Play

Because of fear, I reinforced love. I alerted all the strengths of life: I
armed love with soul and words, to stop death from winning. To love: to
keep alive: to name.

—Hélène Cixous, "La Venue à l'écriture" (1977)

It seems to go without saying that names are anything but inconsequential,
but it is easy to forget that their importance is not dependent solely on
"meaning." The underlying emphasis throughout this initial chapter is on
the "sound" of the name, on the significance of appellations as they resonate
in (and around) the text. Proper names, like words in general, carry meaning
that is not only rational, but *musical* as well. Just as the way words *sound* influences the way we perceive them, so—to an even greater extent—names
are not only significant in relation to their points of reference. While the history of a name is important, especially if we consider "namesakes" as contributing to the way we see those who bear specific names, it is not the sole
aspect that determines the way names come across. Names also gather meaning thanks to their reverberations. The sound of a name contributes to its
meaning, and the combination of these two elements plays a crucial role in
forming individual identity and shaping personal expression. In this chapter
it will become clear that the act of naming takes on significant dimensions
in writing, especially when it is autobiographical. Putting the proper name
into textual play is an act that requires forethought and awareness on the part

of the writer, who is conscious of the high stakes involved in naming self and others in the text.

Leading In: Names from the Maghreb

In her correspondence with Nancy Huston published under the title *Lettres parisiennes*, Algerian-born writer Leïla Sebbar tells of her personal experience with her name:

> A Moroccan student ordered me to change my name one morning in Lyon. He felt betrayed [*trompé*] because with my name he expected an Arab woman who spoke Arabic, thus legitimate for representing Arabs. In their view, I am suspicious from the outset, more than for the French. The French don't understand why I kept the name of my father if I write in my mother tongue, French, and inscribe myself in French literature as a French writer. To satisfy both camps, I should have an anonymous, neutral, universalizing pen name, and I would be identifiable as a writer fulfilling a writer's function, with a writer's name [*nom d'écrivain*]. (133–34)

I open with this quotation because Sebbar's comments reveal some of the crucial dilemmas with which Francophone writers from the Maghreb inevitably struggle. Their "nom d'écrivain" carries significance for multiple reasons. As the Moroccan student's reaction to Sebbar reveals, names create *expectations*. Publishing fiction under the family name she inherited from her Algerian father, Sebbar gives the impression that she speaks Arabic fluently and is therefore qualified to depict Arabs in her written work, in the student's reasoning. The fact that she may not be proficient in this tongue leads him to doubt her ability to accurately portray Algerian culture.[1] Prior to meeting her in person, he conferred a degree of legitimacy to her work simply because of the name she bore. Upon learning of her linguistic limitations, however, the student felt tricked, almost betrayed, by someone whom he held responsible for the important task of representing the region from which her name originates.

If North African readers respond in this way to Sebbar's name, readers from across the Mediterranean are not much more welcoming. According to Sebbar's account, the French also fail to understand her name. They cannot fathom why she would keep her *father's* name if she has chosen to write in her *mother* tongue and thereby establish herself as a "French" writer of "French" literature.[2] She concludes that an "anonymous," "neutral," "universalizing" *nom de plume* would satisfy both sides of this debate, but I think Sebbar has misunderstood the complaint. Both parties (the Moroccan student and the French reading public) appear to privilege language over origin; they judge the choice to write in French, the adoption of the French language as that of written composition, as the crucial step in determining the writer's name. In spite of this strong opinion shared by her reading public, this writer situated on the border between two cultures and languages has decided not to find a new name that would make her "identifiable as a writer fulfilling a writer's function." She thus declines to yield to the demands of her readers, but that's not all the retention of her name entails. When Sebbar publishes in her family name, she refuses to make an artificial distinction between her personal and professional lives. She acknowledges the genealogical heritage to which her writing is indebted, and embraces her origins on the cover of her work.

The Moroccan student who approaches Sebbar makes clear with his reproach that names are not innocent. They carry baggage—cultural, social, familial—that extends far beyond the personal identities of those who bear them; they implicate larger groups of people and tap into the roots of each individual. For this reason, names create immediate suppositions. Their presence on the cover of books is part of a larger "paratextual" apparatus that shapes the way the public perceives the book. The title of the work, the image on the cover, the blurb on the back, even the shape and style of the book, all combine with the name to provide an initial impression, a "packaging" that is meant to attract people to the work. Grouped with these other factors, the proper name of the "author" sends a message to the reader and often shapes his or her opinion of the work before the written text is even approached. The combination of the proper name, the title, and the publishing house responsible for printing the work and circulating it, sends a complicated message that supposedly communicates the contents of the work in question. The public "comes to reading" with certain presuppositions and (mis)understandings due therefore to the marketing techniques that surround the book, and also due to the name printed thereon. The name is the single greatest referent, because it indicates the source of the writing. Readers want to know from whose pen the book emerged. This quest for origin (and legitimacy) occupies the Moroccan student's mind. The name was his guarantee of authenticity prior to meeting Sebbar; the *person* behind the book, with her linguistic limitations, put into question all of his certainty about the quality of the *work*.

The student's criticism, while misguided, highlights another important prerogative of the writer: the ability to *choose* a name or to *change* a name.[3] Sebbar's proposed solution—finding an appropriately "neutral" writer's name that would appease all her readers—may work in principle, but I don't think it is possible in practice. An "anonymous" name is indeed an oxymoron. A "universalizing" name could not exist. Nor would it be desirable. Names are essential, particularly for writers, because they are distinguishing features. They differentiate and singularize both one writer from another and one written work from the next. They are also perhaps one of the greatest onuses writers must suffer, due to the undeniable difficulty of assigning names to books, to characters, and to oneself.

This chapter is an in-depth study of the proper name in the written work of Francophone writers from North Africa, with an emphasis on the unique case of Hélène Cixous and the inclusion of references to Assia Djebar and Abdelkébir Khatibi. Like Leïla Sebbar, these writers come from *outside* France; like Sebbar, they write *in* French. Like Sebbar's, their names reveal their "foreignness" to the French language and land. And, like hers, their various reflections show they are aware of the importance of names, not just as headings under which they publish their works and thereby seek a place in *literary* history, but also as bonds that tie them to (or alienate them from) *social* and *communal* history. It is because of the significance of names and naming that these writers pay such close attention to the insertion of names and the action of naming in the text. While they recognize the gravity of these acts, however, Cixous, Djebar, and Khatibi, refuse to take them *too* seriously. Their creative and innovative written production *plays* with the name. They are always careful to respect names, but they also know that their writing benefits when names are *at play.*[4]

This "name game" is something Cixous engages in frequently; the rules vary according to context, but consideration of the name seems to fit into every text in some way or another. Whether she is ruminating on her own name; discussing pseudonyms or nicknames; giving, choosing, or changing names, she is constantly *name-dropping*. This expression usually implies an intention to impress, and such an interpretation is sometimes valid. That is, this author puts illustrious proper names into the text: names of famous historical characters, names of biblical personages, names of influential thinkers past and present, names of friends and acquaintances, and *her own* name. But, on occasion, she can be found taking part in name-dropping of a different kind, the literal "dropping" of names. When she *refrains* from mentioning names, these omissions are significant. *Both* placing the name in the text *and* not putting it in constitute meaningful acts. Evasion can be just as striking as inclusion, sometimes more so. This is where her work resonates with that of Khatibi, who is adept at knowing when to include his name in the text and when to leave this appellation unmentioned. This move, while highly political, is also, arguably, literary. The strains of the text work themselves out differently depending on the uses and misuses of callings, and the wordsmiths behind the finished product are aware of the subtleties of their production. Indeed, these Francophone writers are fully conscious of the high stakes involved when they put the(ir) proper name into textual play.

What's in a Name? Singular Cases

Before looking carefully at the "stories" of the names of writers in my study, it will be useful to reflect on the process of naming and the "role" of names in a general way. The act of "giving names" is not something we should take for granted, for it is a process embedded in social, historical, familial, and *linguistic* tradition. In *Excitable Speech: A Politics of the Performative*, Judith Butler addresses the "linguistic performativity" involved in naming. Butler begins a section on "The Injurious Action of Names" by reflecting on the necessary, often implicit, conditions of naming:

> First, a name is offered, given, imposed by someone or by some set of someones, and it is attributed to someone else. It requires an intersubjective context, but also *a mode of address*, for the name emerges as the *addressing of a coinage to another, and in that address, a rendering of that coinage proper*. The scene of naming appears then first as a unilateral action: there are those who address their speech to others, who borrow, amalgamate, and coin a name, deriving it from available linguistic convention, and establish that derivation as *proper* in the act of naming. (29) (Emphasis in original.)

Butler's comments on names in this quotation are important for two reasons. First, they highlight the *arbitrary* nature of the name: the one who *is named* has no say in the matter, since the "scene of naming" appears as a "unilateral action" in which "someone else" either "offers," "gives," or "imposes" the name on its receiver. The first instance of naming usually occurs at the time of birth. For official, legal reasons as well as cultural custom, names are normally assigned to newly born children shortly after they enter the world (or sometimes before, as Butler allows). Butler's reflection underscores the important fact that the name chosen in these instances is derived "from available *linguistic* convention" (my emphasis) and therefore adheres to certain rules of sound and spelling. If we assume that a newborn is "offered" a name in this fashion, the linguistic makeup of his or her name will adhere to the standards of his or her community. The name will clearly reflect the language environment in(to) which the child is born. This is noticeably the case for writers who come from outside of France yet choose to compose their written works in French. Their names bespeak their foreign origin and reveal their "non-native" status as "French" writers.

Highlighting the "foreign" aspect of the names "Cixous" and "Khatibi" may seem like an obvious, even gratuitous gesture, but the fact that these appellations are not widespread in France is more than merely "anecdotal." It is hardly an accident that scholars around the world are perpetually stumped when confronted with the surname "Cixous." Even professors and critics familiar with her work *and with her* vary in their oral versions of the writer's last name, sometimes pronouncing the "s" and sometimes not, and often switching back and forth between sentences. Typographical errors prove easy to produce, even at publishing houses as conscientious as Galilée, as evidenced by the misspelling of "Cixoux" on the cover of the text she coauthored with Jacques Derrida: *Voiles*. Khatibi is subjected to similar "woundings" of the proper name, the frequency of which undoubtedly inspired his printed reflections on the matter in a number of texts, notably *La Blessure du nom propre*. His first name often appears without the customary accent, and his last name—particularly the first syllable—is witness to all kinds of different elocutions. The uncertainty that accompanies the spelling and pronunciation of these writers is significant: they are not easily pinned down, seemingly as slippery and unusual as the sounds and signs that designate them. Hélène Cixous and Abdelkébir Khatibi are singular, unique, unparalleled. Their names alone are enough to stimulate discussion and bring out differences (of opinion, accent, etc.).

Foreign names on the shelves of bookstores in France may reap the benefit of their uncommon appearance; readers may find themselves attracted to novels by authors who evidently come from elsewhere. In these instances, the name successfully fulfills its theoretical role of distinguishing individuals from others in a collectivity; the name assures *singularity* by differentiating one person from another: "What is called by the generic common noun 'proper name' must function, it too, in a system of differences: this or that proper name rather than another designates this or that individual rather than another" (*Jacques Derrida* 105). This "system of differences" threatens to disintegrate in the case of a number of writers with "foreign" names who compose their work in French. While it can be a boon to a writer to have an unusual name that stands out from the crowd, it can also be a risk. French readers may easily forget a name they find difficult to spell or pronounce; they may lapse into a national assignation, referring to a specific writer as "the Moroccan" or "the Algerian" and thereby lumping him or her into a group rather than retaining his or her singularity. The individuality of writers from elsewhere composing in French is important, for each writer has followed a specific trajectory to French land and tongue, and for many of these writers that trajectory is itself inscribed in the name, as we will see. Whether their names are memorable or not to the French reading public, these appellations are dependent on that public for recognition, and the work of Judith Butler reminds us that the "linguistic" constitution of *every* person is fragile, since an individual depends on others to be called into being.

Butler identifies an essential paradox at the heart of naming when she treats of its power: "The jarring, even terrible, power of naming appears to recall this initial power of the name to inaugurate and sustain linguistic existence, to confer singularity in location and time" (29–30). She touches in this sentence on the intensely pejorative potential for naming, but she also underscores its twofold ability to "inaugurate existence" and "confer singularity." The paradox hinges on the concept of singularity, of course, since names are closely tied to circumstances: "Whether the name is shared by others, the name, as a convention, has a generality and a historicity that is in no sense radically singular, even though it is understood to exercise the power of conferring singularity" (29). When their names are removed from the geographical and historical context and recontextualized in the French text, it is my contention that "Hélène Cixous" and "Abdelkébir Khatibi" obtain a newfound singularity that depends not so much on the uniqueness of their moment of birth, but rather on their trajectories. Both of these writers traced their own routes to French land and tongue, paths that were determined in large part by the date and time of their birth and the presence of the French in their native lands, but paths that were also chosen, and the specificity of these trajectories merits attention. It is because they have forged ahead and signed numerous texts that their names have become recognizable. But these names are not entirely of their own making, unlike the pseudonym of fellow Maghrebian-born Assia Djebar. The names they bear that ultimately work to set them apart and distinguish their *œuvre* may, paradoxically, be inextricably tied to a society and a culture that mark them not as *individuals*, but as members of a larger *group*, whether familial, social, national, or transnational.

Name Binding

"Making a name" as a foreign-born author writing in French immediately brings to mind the social and legal aspects of the name. In important ways, the name is *binding*: it is a necessary prerequisite for contracts between two parties.[5] Butler's comments on the "linguistic bearing" that constitutes the subject and makes possible the act of addressing an individual by name also call attention to "vulnerability" (30). The vulnerability of all named subjects is magnified in the case of the immigrant. Neither Cixous, who currently lives in Paris, nor Khatibi, whose present residence is in his native Morocco—but who has spent (and continues to spend) considerable time in the French capital—chooses to call France "home." Their status as "foreigner" in the land referred to as the *"métropole"* in their places of origin makes them particularly sensitive to the case of others who are not "native" to this country. For many underprivileged newcomers to France, it proves to be a hostile environment. It is no accident that Cixous has brought attention to the plight of the *sans-papiers*.[6] At the University of Paris 8 where she founded the *Centre de Recherches en Études Féminines* in the mid-1970s and where she continues to teach and direct doctoral degrees, a remarkable number of Maghrebian students are constantly threatened with expulsion. The fact that these students' right to remain in Paris is regularly challenged has undoubtedly contributed to Cixous's attention to and actions on behalf of those who implore her to take up their cause, *in her name.*

Living and speaking in a non-native country, immigrants are especially fragile and dependent upon the reception of their names. Derrida's prolonged interest in the proper name as a linguistic and textual phenomenon meets with practical concerns for immigrants in *De l'hospitalité*, a text co-authored with Anne Dufourmantelle, based on two meetings from his annual seminar (in January 1996). In this work, Derrida distinguishes between the "foreigner" and the "absolute other" by insisting that the former is equipped with a name. This name carries with it social and legal responsibilities:

> [F]rom the outset, the right to hospitality commits a household, a line of descent, a family, a familial or ethnic group receiving a familial or ethnic group. Precisely because it is inscribed in a right, a custom, an *ethos* and a *Sittlichkeit*, this objective morality [. . .] presupposes the social and familial status of the contracting parties, that it is possible for them to be called by their names, to have names, to be subjects in law, to be questioned and liable, to have crimes imputed to them, to be held responsible, to be equipped with nameable identities, and proper names. A proper name is never purely individual. (23–24)

It is significant that Derrida mentions the "household" and "a line of descent" with respect to the name. Names contain within them "histories," specific stories of ancestors and an ethnic or familial *past*. They also harbor a *present*: affinities with and connections to living people related through blood or land or similar experience. Welcoming foreigners to France means accepting them *with their names, in their names*, providing them legal protection and accountability under these recognized appellations that establish their identity. Because of the ties to (past) land and people, as well as to the (adopted) society, it is in the case of the immigrant that we can see most clearly the "communal" aspects of the proper name. In the instance of writers from elsewhere, like Cixous and Khatibi, it can be said with even greater conviction that "a proper name is never purely individual." The name may seek to designate one unique person, but it almost inevitably carries within it multiple filiations and affiliations.

In his reflections on hospitality, Derrida comes to an impasse regarding the question of the name. His queries into whether it is more hospitable to ask foreigners their names or to accept them wholeheartedly without engaging in such "interrogations" reveal an essential dilemma revolving around names. Asking someone's name generally indicates an interest in a person and a desire to know who he or she is, and therefore is a respectful, even flattering, gesture. However, asking someone's name can also be interpreted as an indecent inquiry into the person's identity, a threatening action that seeks not to know who the person is but rather to pigeonhole the other, to stereotype him or her according to relations and origins. Whether hospitality is better extended to an anonymous person or someone known by name then becomes *the* question, in Derrida's view: "The question of hospitality is thus also the question of the question: but by the same token the question of the subject and the name as hypothesis of descent" (29). If one were to leave the preoccupation with "descent" behind and focus on the "welcome" of the present hospitable gesture, then it would seem that asking the foreigner's name would be superfluous:

> Shouldn't we also submit to a sort of holding back of the temptation to ask the other who he is, what her name is, where he comes from, etc.? Shouldn't we abstain from asking another these questions, which herald so many required conditions, and thus limits, to a hospitality thereby constrained and thereby confined into a law and a duty? (135)

Derrida's comments on hospitality can be effectively applied to the "hospitality" found in the written text. The presence of proper names in the text can be viewed as a sign of acceptance, welcome, and generous treatment, but I contend that the absence of proper names is not *necessarily* the opposite. As in the case of hospitable kindness given to another in one's home, deliberately omitting the proper name from the text can also be a sign of generosity and respect. Free from the confinement of law and duty, proper names may be absent from the text in significant ways. Characters without names are not denied voice in autobiographical fiction. To the contrary, they may communicate very effectively, if Derrida's words on linguistic hospitality ring true: "Keeping silence is already a modality of possible speaking" (135).

My emphasis on the importance of leaving names out of the text must not be misunderstood. I do not mean to ignore the tremendous injustice this sort of "anonymity" often promotes, nor the punishing gesture it metes out. In light of many historical atrocities, it would be impossible to celebrate only the qualities of "missing" names. Acts of injustice have been carried out in the not-so-distant past—and continue to occur in the present—against nameless individuals identified only as members of a certain ethnic group or as possessing a particular racial background. One of the most prominent examples of such group categorization and accompanying individual effacement is found in written accounts of the horrors of the death camp in Auschwitz. In *Paroles suffoquées*, Sarah Kofman draws from texts by Maurice Blanchot and Robert Antelme to demonstrate the loss of identity and the assault on the individual exemplified by the absence of the name and the conversion to a number in "counting" episodes. There could be no distinguishing among the individuals in the crowd, according to these written accounts. Kofman calls attention to the repetition of the "anonymous and indefinite word 'one'" in Antelme's text, "which rings the knell of singularity, neutralizing it and underscoring, through its repetition, the panic felt by the deportee, the loss of the 'I' and the proper name" (47). This stripping of the proper name is undeniably a dehumanizing act of the worst sort; it cannot be condoned for any reason.

As a corrective to the horrors of "un-naming" individuals in this way, Cixous seeks in a very personal way to *restore names* to history. *Hélène Cixous, Photos de racines* is a text that devotes time and place to the exploration of genealogical roots through photographs and an extensive family tree: those who were lost in the horrors of the Holocaust have found their rightful position, for their names and dates figure—as accurately as possible—in print. Fictional works like *Benjamin à Montaigne: Il ne faut pas le dire* demonstrate a tendency in Cixous's writing to move more and more openly toward a quest for names from the past, particularly those that have not been celebrated in the family's history. The Benjamin of the book's title is a forgotten relative whose fate was linked to banishment: the German-born great uncle was sent off to the United States because of reprehensible behavior. What happened to him after his departure remains a mystery, and his very existence has almost slipped from family memory. It is a photograph that serves as the trace of his life for the narrator, who is left to speculate on the details of his character and life path. This wanderer, excluded from his family and expelled from his country, occupies not only the imagination of the narrator, but he captures her heart as well. This text, like many others in Cixous's vast corpus, is attentive to the unfortunate destiny of many whose fate has taken unfortunate turns, and who have no space where they can call themselves "at home," no place where they feel they "belong." Devoting reflection to Benjamin, giving him a privileged role in this book, is one way of restoring lost names for the record, of reinscribing them for memory.

Although naming her characters is a crucial aspect of much of her work, I have nonetheless been insisting that Cixous does not *always* include proper names. When names are not included in her written work, the intention is never to strip individuals of their humanity; nameless characters are not transformed into representatives of any targeted group of people, as we will see. Instead, names are silenced out of respect, in accordance with the Derridian conception of unlimited hospitality that extends generosity and warmth to foreigners regardless of descent, irrespective of familial and social history.

In *Amour bilingue*, Khatibi addresses the question of the foreigner. In autobiographical passages, the narrator explains his own fear, which parallels that of other foreigners, the fear of "fading away" because he is "unnameable": "I was therefore unstable, capable of vibrating, accused of irresponsibility. I believed myself to be the foreigner who must inevitably suffer from his foreignness; and at the same time, fade away as such, appearing only as a useless trace, a scrap, a leftover of the unnameable" (28). The foreigner as "unnameable" appears at first glance to be a negative designation, and the fear seems valid. If a foreigner cannot be called by name, then he or she risks "fading" into anonymity and may not be taken notice of at all. But, as an exploration of Khatibi's text reveals, to be "unnameable" is actually a position of strength, for it opens the door to a multitude of possibilities and eludes any rigid categorization. The narrator later boasts of *unnaming* himself and the pleasure that such a linguistic action provokes: "Whereas, I name myself in two languages in unnaming myself; I unname myself in telling my story. Speaking in this no-name sense, the body experiences pleasure in outbursts of rage, in breakup" (79).[7] Ridding oneself of names is a potentially liberating activity, one that is embodied in the figure of the orphan, lauded in a number of Khatibi's works.

Despite the enjoyment of freeing oneself from names, writers know that names are important in the written text, that their presence or absence matters. As a writer with an unusual family history on both sides of the proverbial tree, Cixous is especially sensitive to her own names and how she came upon them. A quote refering to the work of Jacques Derrida above demonstrated how the proper name works within a "system of differences" to distinguish one person from another. This ability to differentiate among people occasionally loses some of its efficacy when it comes to names from other places, originating in other languages, and when these names bear a close resemblance to one another. In the case of Cixous, however, her surname is one of a kind. When running a search under this author, one is unlikely to come across many works from other pens. Cixous is aware of the idiosyncratic, "foreign," even "exotic" qualities of her inherited name and she reflects on them in various forms in different texts.

Balancing *Hélène* with *Cixous*

Hélène Cixous provides ample commentary on her name in theoretical works like "La Venue à l'écriture" and "My Algeriance." It is interesting to juxtapose these two texts, since they date from very different periods and were intended for quite diverse readerships ("La Venue" was published in a series titled *Féminin futur* by Christian Bourgois in 1976 and "Mon Algériance" first appeared in *Les Inrockuptibles* in 1997); despite the time lapse between them, they reveal a similar attitude toward her difficult, rare name. According to the "younger" text, the writer's early struggle with her name was representative of a larger struggle with her identity. Hélène Cixous found her first and last names to be in conflict, a clash that ultimately proved to be a source of literary stimulation. Her "coming to writing" is due, in her analysis, specifically to her unusual last name:

> I could have been called Hélène; I would have been beautiful and unique, the only one. But I was Cixous. As an enraged mouse. I was so far from Hélène, a name which had actually been innocently transmitted to me from a German great-grandmother. With Cixous, imbeciles (some of them will doubtless recognize themselves) make 'sous.' And other low-level capital. With such a name, how could one not have been concerned with letters? Not have sharp ears? Not have understood that a body is always a substance for inscription? ("Coming" 26)

The two sides of her family are contained in the proper name: her first name is transmitted from her maternal great-grandmother, and her last name comes from her father.[8] This balance, this double heritage, is communicated already through her name, and recalled in texts like *Osnabrück*, where her "belonging" to both her mother's and her father's genealogical line is highlighted.

The final question posed in the above quotation, "Ne pas avoir compris qu'un corps est toujours substance à inscription?" ("La Venue" 36), is important because it calls attention to the body. Coming to terms with her name parallels an acceptance of her body, both of which she acquired at birth, neither of which were of her choosing; they were imposed on her from the outset. It is perhaps partly for this reason that, in her view, the two are tightly interconnected: "Thanks to this name, I knew very early that there was a carnal bond between name and body" ("Coming" 26). But when it came to publishing her first text, Cixous was not obligated to sign her father's name. She easily could have chosen to publish under a different name. As a writer, she had freedom to determine her own appellation; she could have told others what to call her, how to address her and her *oeuvre*. Jacques Derrida remembers the dilemma Cixous faced when she was on the verge of becoming "an author":

> As for her name, her family name or patronym, her name as an author, very quickly after our first meeting thirty-five years ago we spoke of it, even debated it. [. . .] Upon our first meeting, she had hardly published anything yet, and nothing under this name: H.C., Hélène Cixous. [. . .] She did not yet know under what family name to publish" ("H. C. pour la vie" 29)

Cixous's own recollection confirms Derrida's comments.[9] She did indeed vacillate when it came to choosing a name, and she nearly sacrificed the original surname in favor of "easier" names from her mother's side of the family, the German side:[10]

> I almost sacrificed it: when my first book was going to come out, I was advised to use a less apotropaic one. I considered Jonas, the maiden name of Omi, my maternal grandmother. The names of my German Jewish family: Klein, Meyer, Ehrenstein, Jonas or Feuchtwanger. Easy names. I caught myself just in time: my name, my nose too big too aquiline, my prominences. My excessive traits. At the last minute I renounced renouncing my marks. Accept destiny. What I kept away from, in keeping my name and my nose, was the temptation of disavowal. ("My Algeriance" 157–58)

The coupling of the "name" and the "nose" in this passage indicates that the name is as real and binding as a physical trait. It cannot simply be discarded or ignored, any more than a body part can be done away with. Cixous explains that her mother encouraged her to change her facial appearance through plastic surgery; Cixous's refusal to give in to the pressure to conform to standards of physical normalcy or "beauty" finds its echo in her decision to retain her father's name.[11] She remains true to her origins and doesn't alter what is "naturally" hers. The mystery of this name propels her to a quest for meaning, and a desire for roots, that has inspired prolific literary production.[12]

It is true that anyone may have difficulty accepting a name and "adopting" it for the purpose of writing. Cixous's struggles with her name are in part due to the oft-recognized fact that she is a woman, and that taking up the pen and asserting oneself through writing is not an effortless activity for those who are socially and legally defined by belonging: "She is defined by her connections [appartenances], wife of, as she was daughter of, from hand to hand, from bed to niche, from niche to household, woman as the complement-of-a-name has much to do to cut free" ("Coming" 40).

But being a "woman" is not the only obstacle to writing, in Cixous's case. As a Jewish child growing up in a very specific environment, in a particular moment in history, in a place she later termed "Algériefrançaise" (Les Rêveries 132), Cixous had difficulty asserting her right to write. Cixous alludes in "La Venue à l'écriture" to an episode she revisits much later, in a special issue on "Translating Algeria" for parallax: "In Le monolinguisme de l'autre, J. Derrida has described this maneuver, unique in history, of the French State subjugated to Hitler, which made us, we who were 'French' but Jewish, in October 1940 and for two years, we who were born 'French', into passport-less, law-less, shelter-less, identity-less, school-less, profession-less people" ("Letter to Zohra Drif" 189).[13] When Cixous refers to her name and her nose as her "excessive traits" in "Mon Algériance," she is expressing much more than an adolescent crisis: the signature and the body are called into question on a legal level in her native land. Having watched her father remove his name from the door of his medical practice when she was just a toddler, Cixous is not overreacting when she takes on the voices of her inquisitors who demand to see everything from her credentials to her "paws" in "La Venue de l'écriture." The personal question, "In whose name would I write?" (25), takes on new light given her experiences.

In her early essay on writing, "La Venue à l'écriture," Cixous refers to herself prior to publishing as a "skinny, anonymous mouse" with an admittedly problematic relationship to her name:

My tumults were at the very most concentrated under a name, and not just any name! Cixous—itself a tumultuous, indocile name. That, a 'name'? This bizarre, barbarous word, so poorly borne by the French tongue, this was 'my' 'name.' An impossible name. A name to put outside at night. A name which no one ever knew how to spell and which was me. It is still me. A bad name,

I thought when they turned it against me, flaying me by flaying it, one of those foreign, unswallowable, unclassifiable words. I was no one. ("Coming" 35)

Today Cixous is anything but anonymous; she has established herself as a prominent literary critic, novelist, poet, and playwright around the world. Her work is translated into numerous languages and her contributions to feminist theory are recognized in universities in many countries. But in her recent return to the question of her name in "My Algeriance," she takes up many of the same derogatory words and terms to describe her patronymic: "A non-French name. A bizarre, and unknown name. Without origin" (158). She indicates that people still have not *learned* her name: "Still today the way it is treated flayed mispronounced spat out the reactions, the projections, the deformations. An impossible name [. . .] unpronounceable and unspellable: even dictated it is inaudible and inadmissible" (158). I read this echo of the earlier text with a smile, for the success of Cixous as a writer renders less serious the stumblings over her name.[14] In fact, the unfamiliar nature of this appellation may have worked in her favor; it is undeniable that it is representative of her person, and her work: "*inclassable*" is the first adjective that comes to mind when one seeks to categorize this writer whose texts fall under the indefinable name she received at birth, a name she adopted upon her re-birth as a woman writer in France over thirty-five years ago.

Marking Singularity

Abdelkébir Khatibi, unlike Cixous, was never in doubt as to the meaning of his name. The day of his birth determined how he would be called; his name was dictated by the destiny of this date. In the autobiographical novel *La Mémoire tatouée*, Khatibi dedicates the opening passage to his name:

> Born the day of Aïd el Kébir, my name suggests a millenary rite and it happens that, on occasion, I imagine the gesture of Abraham slitting his son's throat. I can do nothing about it, even if I'm not obsessed with the song of killing, there is the nominal tearing at the root. From the maternal arch to my own will, time remains fascinated by childhood, even if writing, in giving me to the world, begins again the shock of my inertia, at the fold of an obscure doubling. I can do nothing about it, I have an easy soul to eternity. (17)

Khatibi's first name is therefore due to a date. He entered the world on the anniversary of an ancient "gesture" revered by his religious tradition: Abraham's willingness to sacrifice his son Isaac. It is important to note that this intended act was never carried out. Abraham did not cut his son's throat, according to written record. God intervened, the son's life was spared, and the sacrifice did not actually take place. But this redemption does not figure in this account of his birth. The image he sees is that of a father harming his son. In his view, he was *sacrificed* at birth.

La Mémoire tatouée was originally published in 1971. In a preface to a later edition ("collection 10/18"), Khatibi reiterates the importance of his birth date. This later version (the *"présentation"* was penned in October of 1978) puts forth a slightly different angle of interpretation of this crucial event, beginning his story with a phrase reminiscent of the invocation to storytelling from *Les Mille et Une Nuits*:

> Tell me a beautiful story or I'll kill you: I was born, I am purported to have been born under the sign of the expiatory sacrifice. We'll say it again, the day of my birth (1938) is the very day of Aïd el Kébir, the festival commemorating Abraham's sacrifice: whence my first name Abdelkébir, servant of the Great, slave of God. The Patriarch has doubly signed my childhood, through the name and circumcision. I was sacrificed in coming into the world, and my head was, in a certain way, offered to God. Have I ever recovered it, beyond any metaphysical destiny? (10)

The reader encounters two descriptions of the name within the space of seven pages in this new version. The repetition highlights the importance of the name and its connection with the date of birth. But the accounts are not entirely identical, of course. Repetition presents itself as similar, yet varied, and this variation opens itself up to interpretation. In this introductory passage, Khatibi mentions his name in greater detail, giving the reader some equivalent expressions in French. These juxtaposed expressions inform us that this appellation means "serf," "servant," "slave" to God. In a sense, then, his life is not *his own*; the significance of his name, recalling an earlier scene of sacrifice, is that of sacrifice itself.[15] His head is therefore not his; it has been separated symbolically from his body through the assignation of this particular name. And his body bears trace of this decapitation: circumcision. Name and body are tightly connected; the Patriarch has "signed" them both.

Khatibi's "signs" can be placed in temporary contrast to Cixous's name and nose, characteristics that accompanied her birth. Cixous's first and last names, as we have seen, derive from her family roots and therefore seem to have "natural," "inherent" qualities to them. Her nose can also be considered a genetic inheritance. But Khatibi's first name seems to have been left to chance; if he had been born a day later, he would have borne an entirely different forename. And Khatibi's circumcision, there can be no doubt, was externally imposed. The cut foreskin is the result of entering a community adhering to the Islamic faith; it is certainly not a trait with which he came into the world.[16] Obviously, this distinction between Khatibi and Cixous is somewhat arbitrary and fails to take into account crucial similarities: *neither* chose the names endured during childhood; neither selected the critical physical features suffered. These are things over which they initially had no control.

There is another difference between the name and the body *chez* Khatibi and Cixous that is arguably of greater importance in their personal formations, and that is *singularity*. Khatibi's first name marks him as part of a community; Muslim men are named according to the ninety-nine attributes of Allah.[17] His surname is also unmistakably of Arab origin, even if it is subject to misspellings and mispronunciations in translation. His full name immediately indicates—even to outsiders—that he is part of a larger cluster of people, a member of a group from an established tradition of beliefs. Circumcision also serves as a sign of belonging to that same community; Khatibi joins all the other male members of this society in this significant ritual act. Cixous's situation is markedly different. Her distinctive nose, in contrast, sets her apart from others because of its size and shape. While it could be considered a typical trait of her "race," the fact that she is not a member of a Jewish community transforms her nose into a feature that *singularizes* its bearer. Located in the middle of her face, it is visible for all to see, proclaiming her individuality, her uniqueness. She chooses not to have her nose adjusted. Such an operation would render her like others; she embraces her individuality by opting to remain as she is. Her surname is equally unusual and noticeable. It may be unrecognizable at first, as evidenced by the fact that people struggle with its spelling and stumble over its pronunciation; but once she has established this name, she has a monopoly on it. She could have been confused with other *Kleins* had she chosen to publish under her mother's maiden name. But no one questions which *Cixous* has written the latest French novel. Her name is her trademark; it *is* she, unchanged since birth.

If Khatibi's first name has not undergone transformation since his childhood, the same cannot be said for his last name. In an essay on language and writing, *La Langue de l'Autre*, Khatibi explains that his surname has not remained steady over the years: "I was born with my first name that refers to one of the 99 attributes of Allah, a god who had said everything, according to my entourage. My first name has remained stable until today, whereas I had to change my last name on 14 February 1956. My older brother chose a last name according to the code of the civil state several days before the official end of the Protectorate. Was that my 'decolonization,' between a predestined first name and a substituted surname?" (39). His name was changed without his voice; he had no say in the matter. The date is noted as precisely as his birth date: it has imposed itself in just as arbitrary a manner. At least there was *some choice* involved in this momentous act, but Abdelkébir Khatibi himself played no role in that process. He owes his current last name to his brother, who acted according to the civil code just prior to the end of the French Protectorate in Morocco.[18] So, while Cixous had the option to hold onto her original surname, Khatibi saw his change in an instant; his original last name disappeared right out from under his nose.[19]

Signing Otherwise

At the age of twelve, Khatibi published his first poems under a pseudonym. This early memory spurs him to ask some provocative questions about the role of pseudonymous writing as a stimulus for creative work:

> I wrote my first poems at the age of twelve. In Arabic, then in French, under the unavoidable influence of Baudelaire. I sent them to radio stations and magazines under pseudonyms. Does the use of a pseudonym destine one for writing, and under what conditions? [. . .] What is a pseudonymous signature? [. . .] Why accentuate illegibility from self to self, why veil in this way the social transparency of one's identity? (*La Langue* 40)

Following this early experience with writing undercover, Khatibi began to publish in his "real" name. Emphasizing his name becomes a very important theme in his autobiographical work; though he only inserts his name into the autobiographical text in the two notable examples from *La Mémoire tatouée* cited above, he *reflects* directly on his name in a number of different ways.[20] One of the most salient examples of this reflection on the name is found in a collection of texts grouped under the title *La Langue de l'Autre*. This work contains a response to Jacques Derrida's *Le Monolinguisme de l'autre*, a text inspired in large part by Khatibi's bilingualism. Khatibi highlights the fact that his reply constitutes a "testimony" *in his name* (29).

In Khatibi's analysis, the name is a necessary prerequisite for the signature. His comments on his first poems in *La Mémoire tatouée* indicate that these published works remained *unsigned*: "Thanks to my older brother, I was bifurcated at one point when I went toward the modern Arabic novel. At this time, my first poems in Arabic were born. Let's bet that they belonged to my own notion of the wind, since *I didn't sign them*" (98; my emphasis). This assertion that his "anonymous" publications do not carry a signature brings us back to Khatibi's question about the nature of a "pseudonymous signature" in the quotation above. Khatibi draws from the work of Jean Starobinski to explore the consequences of taking a pseudonym. His reading leads him to conclude that adopting a pseudonym means making a break not just with famil-ial and social origins, but with *all others*: "Employing a pseudonym not only marks a rupture with familial and social origins; it constitutes a rupture with others. Our identity, which attaches us to our name, also makes us hostage at the same time to foreign consciences; it leaves us defenseless before public judgment" (*La Langue* 40). While this break with family and society may seem dramatic, leaving behind externally imposed constraints carries the po-tential for liberation from a judgmental public and from the imprisonment of the name.

The negative possibility of being misunderstood and stereotyped because of the name one bears is a particularly great risk for writers like Khatibi, whose name stands out because of its "foreignness" to a French readership: "Fear of being misunderstood, shut up, walled in, retained in a first and last name the law of which you contest without knowing why" (*La Langue* 41). Khatibi has an intimate understanding of this widespread fear of being "shut up" inside a name, unable to truly contest a law that works in indecipherable ways against the name's bearer. Such confinement within an appellation not only means the inability to communicate, but also the inability to move about.[21] Movement (metaphorical and literal) is often restricted to Arab sub-jects whose identities are bound to a name. Despite this fear of forced enclo-sure, Khatibi maintains that he never sought to change his name in his work: "That said, as an author, I never dreamed of changing my name after my teenage years. . . . *The hyphen* between my 'Moroccanness' and my 'French-ness' as a scribe is found in the translation of my first name and my last name, substituted for another" (*La Langue* 41). The translation of his name contains the two *competing* and *complementing* aspects of his personal makeup; his "double belonging"—to Moroccan *and* French cultures—is present in his name. Though he has not altered it on his own, Khatibi's name has under-gone change in its transliteration in French. His double, even multiple, iden-tities speak out through the "hyphen" in-built in his name.

The Improper Name

To turn to the case of Assia Djebar, just briefly, it is noteworthy that the writer's chosen name could not be considered "typically French," since both her first and last name contain sounds that are spelled and pronounced in ways distinctly "foreign" to the French linguistic system.[22] Not only does As-sia Djebar neglect to conceal her place of origin in her pseudonym, she goes so far as to *claim* her birthplace and *tout* it in her very name. In addition, by choosing "Assia" with its feminine ending as her first name and opting for

"Djebar" as her surname, this writer decided upon a name that left little question as to her sex. Unlike George Sand and George Eliot, famous women
who wrote under "masculine" pseudonyms, Assia Djebar did not attempt to
take on a man's first name. Both the Arabic tradition from which she comes
and her "status" as a "woman" are conveyed in the new appellation. Just as
Cixous claimed her unusual heritage in retaining her father's last name, so
Djebar held onto her distinctive roots *even as* she changed names.

Assia Djebar's *nom de plume* therefore does not appear to be subversive at
first glance, but a closer look reveals that she does indeed "play" with gender
differences and with her "origins" in opting for this particular appellation
rather than another. It is typical in Maghrebian society for *men* to be named
after the attributes of Allah. In the case of Khatibi, "Abdelkébir" is a given
name that reflects an aspect of God's character. What is striking about Assia
Djebar's idiosyncratic name choice is that she didn't hesitate in choosing the
source of her name. She didn't take her time deciding *where* to find one of her
two adopted names, but immediately asked her fiancé to recite the names of
Allah. "Djebar" is a name that could have belonged to a man; it is also a
name that she could have *come by* thanks to a man, either a father or a husband. But this surname is unusual because she opted for it on her own. Instead of relying on someone else, *she* determined what she would be called,
and why. This action of deliberately choosing her name—along with its de-
notations and connotations—stands out in contrast to the personal story of
Khatibi, who accepted externally imposed names.

Names in Islamic tradition carry meaning, as we have seen in the example of Khatibi. In her work, Djebar is careful to underscore the significance
of various names, so that the message contained in the appellation is not lost
in translation. Examples of this process abound in Djebar's French texts: the
narrator of *Vaste est la prison* repeatedly updates the reader on the meanings
of names that influence the characters who bear them: "Aichoucha, literally
'little life' (278); "Hania, which means the peaceful or the pacified' (318).
While Assia Djebar's own name never figures into the autobiographical text,
some critics have argued that she slips it into the written work in clever ways,
such as including a quotation from Hölderlin on the continent of Asia, or referring to women ancestors whose names resemble her given first names of
Fatima-Zohra.[23] While this textual play with the name is an important presence in Djebar's *oeuvre* (whether it is intentional or not), I will argue in the
next chapter it is not the *only* illustration of textual play with the name. Djebar has found an innovative and complex way of *signing* her works, *without
the name*, but *in "the" name* of a recurring narrative voice belonging to *Isma*.

Djebar's attuned sensitivity to names exhibits itself in numerous textual passages, but one stands out with respect to the *music* of a particular name. In *Les Nuits de Strasbourg*, a character with an uncertain genealogy seeks to unravel the mystery behind her given name. Irma has believed for years that her parents were Jews who perished during the Second World War and that a kind stranger had claimed her as her own in order to save her from the same fate. As she tracks down this person to whom she owes her life, Irma discovers the truth that this woman—whose precise national identity remains a mystery to her—was her biological mother, and that she herself is not Jewish after all. When the woman resists a meeting with her, Irma makes clear what her true motivations are: "What was I asking of the unknown woman, the renegade: simply that she say aloud my first and last names—or simply my first name: in French, German or Alsacian! If only she had spelled it out in front of me, the overwhelming emotion I would have felt would have made up for the essential!" The mother supposed that the abandoned daughter would ask her to dig up a regrettable past, to uncover the circumstances of an unwanted birth. She feared that the daughter would ask for the name of the father, but such was not the case: "I only sought my name, or first name, but spoken by her voice, in the initial tongue, that of birth, of love, or simply, alas, that of emptiness" (304).[24]

The complex workings of naming in the case of Assia Djebar, including the adoption of different names according to varying circumstances of life and writing, are obviously not unique to her situation. What sets her apart from the other writers in my study is her choice of a new name under which to write. "Assia Djebar" is a pseudonym that she adopted upon the publication of her first book when the writer was not yet twenty years of age.[25] A name change, whether paratextual or textual, cannot be passed over lightly: it is never innocent. Such transformations carry obvious weight in specific textual instances in the works of both Cixous and Khatibi, as well as in a number of other compositions by Maghrebian-born writers.[26] These writers are incapable of assigning names to characters—or to books—without demonstrating an acute awareness of the gravity (and the humor) of the act of naming. Since they have been subject to labeling related to their own names, this personal consciousness translates in distinct ways when they put the proper name into textual play.

From Given Names to Giving Names:
For the Sake of Names

Assigning names to characters is a daunting task, a serious challenge to any writer. Nancy Huston, Sebbar's correspondent in the earlier-quoted *Lettres parisiennes*, explains in an essay that theorist Roland Barthes was attracted to the idea of writing fiction, but denied his impulses because he could not give *names* to characters. This intimidating undertaking was apparently the first and single greatest impediment to creative writing for him: "Barthes himself dreamed of novels, but stumbled from the moment the first obstacle presented itself in his path: how to bestow proper names on his characters and, following that, pretend to believe? Is it possible to trick oneself to this degree? [. . .] He gave up fiction. Yes: no matter what we say, a novel requires an act of faith, *is* an act of faith" (*Nord perdu* 49–50).[27] The emphasis Huston places on the "faith" involved in giving names to characters in novels harks back to the divine nature of naming. To name is synonymous, particularly in literary creation, with bringing into being. The act of naming is one before which every writer flinches, primarily because of the responsibility inherent in this act. In autobiographical writing, this act becomes especially contentious because of possible recognition and expectations of veracity to which writers must be true. The autobiographical nature of Hélène Cixous's writing makes the question of names a particularly sensitive issue, and the ways she both inserts names into the text *and* avoids naming become especially significant.

If coming to terms with one's own name presents a challenge, as we have already seen, then bestowing names on others is often even more difficult. This could be, in part, because in order to address the other, in order to find a name for the other, the writer must *already be named*, according to Judith Butler:

> And yet, the one who names, who works within language to find a name for another, is presumed to be already named, positioned within language as one who is already subject to that founding or inaugurating address. This suggests that such a subject in language is positioned as both addressed and addressing, and that very possibility of naming another requires that one first be named. The subject of speech who is named becomes, potentially, one who might well name another in time. (29)

Writers who waver when naming themselves, who have a hard time *assuming* a name in the written text, may encounter a particular challenge when it comes to giving names to others. Hélène Cixous highlights her own incapacity to name in *Photos de racines*:

> I cannot manage to give names to the characters. It's a blind spot; it resists so much, it's so complicated. I have explanatory hypotheses, but they do not satisfy me. At times I tell myself I have a true inhibition. That the force or the

capacity of nomination has not been given to me. It is so profound, so obscure, it's as if I came back to the interdiction of the Jews: you will make no idols. Each time I write a text, I find myself grappling with this. I loathe all the names, they seem to me like violent appositions. I have a suspicion: perhaps I do not want to detach the characters from myself? However I do not have this problem in theatre. To name, I say to myself, is presumptuous. How could I dare give myself the (divine) right to put people into circulation? (75)

Cixous also has trouble giving titles to her works. Like the proper name of a character, the proper name of a book is undeniably important for a variety of reasons; but it is not a consideration of its importance that gives the author pause, in her own words: "That is why my books have no titles. Giving a title is an act of appropriation. The books for which I am the scribe belong to everyone" (142). Cixous does not refuse to *sign* her works, with one notable exception;[28] she is ultimately responsible for their contents. But she rebels against claiming "ownership" of writing that is put into circulation and thus belongs to everyone.

Cixous's hesitancy to attach names to characters may provide the impetus for her habit of applying multiple names to refer to one person in the text. Providing many names for the same character and playing linguistically with these appellations is a trait of Cixous's writing that I will explore in the next section of this chapter. Cixous's reluctance to name others may also be seen as a reflection of her reluctance to name herself. As she maintains in the continuation of this discussion on naming found in *Photos de racines*, Cixous does not *really* name herself when she writes either: "What one sees in my texts is not the result of a desire to attract attention, not at all! It's a compromise. It is what I have succeeded in obtaining of myself. Fictive appellations. A false name. A mask. A mask-the-real-name" (75). Her many "fictive appellations" for herself and others significantly alter the autobiographical enterprise; one cannot help but wonder why characters who represent living people outside the text should wear multiple masks.

Mixing Life and Art

Cixous often mixes "real" and "fictive" names in her unusual textual creations. Indeed, combining historical figures, biblical characters, and her own ancestors in a single publication is an innovative aspect of much of her writing. Such "unexpected bedfellows" can be found in the very title of a recent publication, *Benjamin à Montaigne*. While the proper names on the cover of this book are subject to multiple interpretations, it becomes clear that Benjamin is the first name of a nearly forgotten relative on her mother's side of the family, and Montaigne is a literary precursor from whom Cixous has drawn much inspiration. The considerable time lag separating the two individuals (Benjamin lived in the twentieth century and Montaigne in the sixteenth) does not stop them from coexisting in these pages; their temporal disjunction only mirrors the textual jumps in time, as Cixous explains in a radio interview for a France Culture program titled *Du Jour au lendemain*: "this takes place in 1930, 1880, 1580; the text travels also from one century to another as it makes visible certain themes that are eternal for us human beings" (Veinstein).

With respect to the same book, Cixous makes a startling statement that bears directly on the real/fiction debate in literary creation.

> Let's also emphasize 'fiction.' [. . .] In this case, two old sisters bear names that are fictional so that it will be clearly understood, if it's possible, among us all, that I am not making reference—that the text is not making reference—to real characters that would be precisely, strictly autobiographical, but instead to throwbacks [*envoyés*] of biography. (Veinstein)

It is not uncommon for Cixous to emphasize the fictive nature of her writing.[29] Her public spoken reflections often accentuate the distance between life and art, between "correspondents of biography" and "real people," in a loose translation of the terms she employs above. But these comments on *Benjamin à Montaigne* stand out because of what they seem to imply about her other texts: if the two old sisters have fictive names in this particular work, then what does it mean when they carry their "real" names in other works? Does Cixous intend for us to read differently when characters' names coincide with their function outside the text? Are we to conclude that every time the "true" mother's name appears in print, the writer is making reference to her real, flesh-and-blood mother?

It is significant that Cixous uses names to illustrate her point in this interview. Since the time constraints of the radio necessitate quick responses to loaded questions, Cixous has recourse to an obvious example to underscore an important lesson in reading: there is a distinction between lived existence and textual representations. The reader should not assume that the writer is making reference to her life always and completely. But the reader should also avoid concluding—in the other extreme—that the writer's life is totally separate from her writing. Cixous's work, while largely based on and intertwined with her life, remains art: the two are not mutually exclusive, nor are they completely synonymous. To communicate—in the space of a quick sound bite—the fact that her autobiographical text should not be termed "real" but instead should be conceived of as "fiction," she heads to the foremost example of identity and asserts that the indefinable nature of the text depends on its names. What Cixous doesn't have time to address, and what she may be hesitant to divulge, is something she nonetheless hints at: the name games she constantly devises in her corpus complicate the picture. Not only do the workings of names disrupt such absurd binary divisions as real and fiction, life and art, they also call attention to the inadequacy of definitions, and the complexity of identity: "This is one of the big questions of this text. How does one (un)define oneself [s'in/définit]? One does not define onself, one (un)defines oneself. One moves along from definition to definition when one is carried by the winds of history" (Veinstein).

It may be true that the two elderly sisters' names are not their real names, since Hélène Cixous's mother is called Eve and her sister, Rosy. But it is also true that the names they are given as characters in *Benjamin à Montaigne* belong to the family, and readers will recognize the two appellations from another text, *Osnabrück*. In this earlier quest for roots, the narrative voice explores her genealogical heritage in conversation with her mother at various moments in the text. There is considerable confusion about the identity of a particular family member, an aunt whose name is either Selma or Jenny; it turns out that there were two separate aunts who carried these two names, but "who was who" is never ascertained, and certainly never clearly explained.[30] Leaving their identity up in the air, the narrator revels in the confusion, letting the family legend remain hazy and undefined.

Adopting Names: Change and Meaning / Change in Meaning

Cixous's theoretical reflections and novelistic themes reveal that names wield the power to command lives. People have a tendency to "take on" their names, to conform their behavior to their appellation. In his analysis of Hélène Cixous's written production, Jacques Derrida draws inspiration from her work to reflect on the ways in which we become our names:

> But to make a name is as much to produce an appellation to which the other responds as it is to transform oneself into a name: I make a name, careful, you're going to see, like an animal that rolls itself in a ball, my body mime and produce the name by becoming the name, when I take upon myself, in myself, the traits of the name. I make a name, I make it, produce it, make it respond, imitate it and become, always by substitution [. . .] I am his/her name [son nom],

I am the name that I make, etc., I give it to myself, I add myself to it, I give myself over to it as if enchanted. ("H. C. pour la vie" 93–94)

"Making a name" for oneself takes place on a very literal level, according to Derrida's analysis. Establishing one's name through writing, as Cixous has done, means more than making others familiar with one's name through meritorious literary activity. It means making a name that the self comes to inhabit; "making a name" is thereby a determining act because the bearer of the name *transforms herself* into that name, "producing" it, "imitating" it, and "becoming" it. This transformation of self into the name that entails the adoption of the traits inherent in the name takes place both outside *and* inside the text.

Hélène Cixous points out repeatedly that names play indubitable roles in shaping their bearer's destiny.[31] But she often does so in an ironic, playful way, as in *Osnabrück* when the narrative voice declares that her mother's physical resilience against aging is not due to good genes or healthful practices, but constitutes instead a faithful reflection of her name:

My father called her Totote. When was she named Totote? . . . My father calls her Totote. It's a name that is pronounced with joyful baritones. . . . Totote is a comic strip heroine. That explains why she doesn't age. Like all such characters, she only has a single age in all books. Time passes and she stays. (51)

The narrative voice reasons, with humor, that her mother cannot age because her nickname belongs to a comic strip character. Like all of these artificial creations drawn in the comics, "Totote" is forever fixed; unsusceptible to the ravages of time, she keeps on ticking. Thanks to her (nick)name, she is eternal. This somewhat simplistic reflection echoes the common theme in literature of immortalizing the name of a loved one through great writing. While people inevitably perish, seminal works of writing have the potential to go on and on, influencing future generations indefinitely. The reflections on the mother in Cixous's text can be viewed as a metacommentary for Cixous's oeuvre, in which the mother continually appears as a central character who doesn't seem to age, who, in spite of the passage of time, *remains*.

Calling Names: The Wounding of Proper Names

While receiving a good name can inspire a person to "realize" that name by remaining true to its meaning and reaching various goals in accordance with its "destiny," being assigned a *bad name* can also have an impact. Being called a bad name is often an unforgettable experience that carries lasting negative implications. Cixous is a writer who is particularly aware of the harmful effects of bad naming.[32] In her many reflections on the mother's name in *Osnabrück*, the most cutting remarks are made in response to the pet name the father coined, "Totote." In the narrator's analysis, this appellation had a detrimental influence not only on her parents' marriage but on their entire family: "You cannot call a woman Totote without one killing the other, man woman, marriage passion, wife husband without counting the children" (53). Nicknames are not innocent; calling someone by an unflattering name can lead to devastating consequences. And the person named is not the only one damaged by the injurious appellation; loved ones and family members can also suffer under the onus of a bad name.[33] This point reinforces Derrida's claim (cited earlier) in his work on hospitality that "a proper name is never purely individual." Those who name and those who witness the name are affected by it as well.

Cixous grew up in a multicultural environment in Algeria, and exposure to people from different cultures and languages in this society made her acutely aware of the importance of names in addressing and referring to others. Showing respect for people as individuals is of the utmost importance to this woman who experienced and witnessed prejudice on many levels in the colonized environment of her childhood. The tremendous political currency of "name-calling" is highlighted in recent autobiographical texts that return to the place of Cixous's early years. A striking scene of accusation and judgment is found in *Osnabrück*, when the narrator puts her mother "on trial" for referring to an Algerian woman in a prejudicial manner:

> You said, 'the fatma,' I say, severe [. . .] I accuse my mother of having said 'the fatma' in front of a circle of guests. [. . .] You know that the term 'the fatma' is willed with scorn, I say. You lived in Algeria, I say severe to the German my mother. [. . .] 'The fatma' is a colonialist expression. *Pieds-noirs* called all women the fatma. I will not allow this word in the mouth of the midwife the German my mother. (112)

The narrator accuses the mother of verbally disrespecting a woman and reminds the mother of the *gravity* of her nominal blunder. In attributing a widespread Algerian name to this individual, the mother not only completely effaced the woman's individuality by clustering her with other women of her racial makeup; she committed an unthinkable sin by turning the proper name into a common name with the use of the definite article. This objectification of a person is completely unacceptable to the narrator, particularly in light of the colonial history in this country. The French "colonizers" refused to acknowledge the differences among the individuals they colonized by applying an easy name to refer to all of them. "La fatma" is a revelatory term; it exposes an attitude of complete indifference toward the colonized peoples.[34] This "colonialist" expression and the prejudices it conveys are anathema to Cixous's writing project, which seeks to respect the proper name as much as possible.

Cixous is aware that "misnaming" this woman is a significant act that reflects a universal "colonial" desire to name the conquered and thereby gain mastery.[35] According to Derrida, the process of naming is inherent to all culture: "All culture is originarily colonial. In order to recall that, let us not simply rely on etymology. Every culture institutes itself through the unilateral imposition of some 'politics' of language. Mastery begins, as we know, through the power of naming, of imposing and legitimating appellations" (*Monolingualism* 39). The politics of language common to every culture is especially applicable to personal names in colonized Algeria. Colonial naming assumed tremendous importance in this part of the world, as in other colonized territories, because a name established one's status and determined everything. Sociologist Pierre Bourdieu explains that his last name made him the butt of jokes and the recipient of derogatory remarks during his childhood, but his surname did not ultimately serve as an impediment to his success as a French intellectual.[36] The same could unfortunately *not* be said for the "fatmas" of Algeria.

The attempt to unveil and thereby correct the mistaken application of the name "Fatma" to all Algerian women serves as an important microcosm of Cixous's work. Names are sacred to this writer because, as the following quotation reveals, they are often synonymous with *life*:

> There is no small crime more hurtful for me than to catch myself forgetting the name of a person who greets me. And the worst is that if I ask them what their name is, I execute them in their eyes. But I didn't want to kill the appearance of the person! (*OR* 21)

The small crime of forgetting someone's name suddenly becomes a symbolic "execution" when the narrator finds herself obliged to ask the person what his or her name is. Aware of the terrible pain she is inflicting by demonstrating ignorance with respect to the other's name, the narrator agonizes over the "mortal" wounding caused by this loss of memory. If we can view names as equivalent to life, the fact that the narrator is unable to name the individuals who greet her may mean that they are *dead* to her. Since she has forgotten their names, they may assume that she has forgotten *them*. But a haunt-ing episode of a mistaken name found in Cixous's novels and critical essays reveals that a name and a person may not always be the same, that one may well know a person without possessing (correct) knowledge of that person's *name*:

> What remains of "Aïcha" who has been dead for a long time: volumes and vol-umes. Art, "Algeria," as the caressing name of the untouchable. [. . .] I loved the touch of the name Aïcha, nothing sentimental, all sensual and infantile. And it turns out that she wasn't named Aïcha and that not one of us knows whence came this name that was not hers and not one of us now knows who among us learned this from whom and how. At present we all know that Aïcha was really named Messaouda. But too late [. . .] *we who took care, my brother and I, to stop the family from ever committing an aggressive act against proper names* like those that were always carried out by others, we who did not tolerate any mis-take in the house. (*Les Rêveries* 91, 93; my emphasis)[37]

Despite the protagonist's efforts to never commit any error in referring to other people, despite her immense respect for the names these others bear, she discovered too late that an important woman from her childhood was not named "Aïcha." Upon the discovery of this monumental mistake, the narra-tor remembers her horror. She, who had so vehemently chastised her mother for calling the cleaning woman "Fatma" instead of "Barta," the woman's real name, was suddenly found guilty of the same crime of *misnaming*. But this "sin" was not deliberate, nor was it motivated by a lack of interest in the per-son misnamed. How the wrong name became unilaterally established among the family members is a mystery; what matters is that this dear person was harmed by multiple, innumerable instances of being called by the wrong name.

This remarkable mistake, which is also referred to in "My Algeriance," communicates a truth that may go *beyond* the strict boundaries of the name.[38] Whether Aïcha was her *proper* name or not, it *became* the woman's name in dealings with the Cixous family. It was their way of calling her, and she quickly learned its purpose of designating her in their household. It therefore functioned as an effective appellation in a specific context. Whether Mes-saouda felt personally "aggressed" by this change in name is unknown; she may have found it humorous at first and then adapted with little trouble. She may have seen the affection of those who called her "Aïcha" and she may have even become fond of this name because it was unique to her relations with these people who loved and respected her. She therefore might have embraced this new name, and she could even have viewed it as *revelatory* of her, characteristic of her interactions with particular people who know her under this particular name. This mistake begs the question of the ultimate importance of the name. Did the young protagonist *know* the woman she called Aïcha? She may feel that she betrayed the woman for years when she finally discovers she was mistaken about the woman's nominal identity, but it seems unlikely that the protagonist would have had better relations with Messaouda if she had called her by her given name. In the end, the *person* matters more than the *name*. And, in the final analysis, the name *actually used* to refer to and address the person may acquire greater significance than the "real" name.

Losing the Tag: Of Namelessness and Orphans

Abdelkébir Khatibi, in his poetic *Amour bilingue*, does not mention his proper name once, in contrast to the reflections on the given name found in his first novel, *La Mémoire tatouée*. In the later text, the anonymous narrator celebrates the "unnaming" that is enacted through telling his story: "Whereas, I name myself in two languages in unnaming myself; I unname myself in telling my story" (*Love* 79). The forgetting of the name deplored in Cixous's narrative commentary in OR is therefore *embraced* in Khatibi's text, where leaving names behind is a liberating gesture: "What fascinated him, attracted as he was by the no-name, was this utopia and this void which, erasing their sources, wanted to be this grace of the unnameable, this charm of forgetting" (*Love* 27). The act of "unnaming" himself brings the narrator great joy, but this joy does come at a price, for it means a rupture with the past. It means going *against* destiny, living *against* the name: "I lived opposed to my name, I loved against myself, so that nothing of my wild imaginings would remain" (*Love* 79).[39] If names are influential, if people have a tendency to "take on" their names, then Khatibi's textual enactment of "unnaming," his written example of a man who engages in a powerful experiment that consists of going "against the grain," *against the name*, and refusing all appellation, maps out the possibilities for those who want to resist the determining power of names. Living in opposition to naming is a noble enterprise, but one has to ask if it can really work.

The narrator is not the only protagonist to undergo this process of "unnaming" in *Amour bilingue*. The woman he loves is also subject to the benefits of this delightful forgetting of her genealogy, this complete break with the past marked by the loss of name. But the effects of this radical namelessness may not be entirely positive, as the male protagonist's worries suggest: "Sometimes she forgot her own given name. How did this loss affect her?"

(*Love* 27). The man is right to be concerned, for the woman experiences a sudden need to return to her former self, in a sense, by taking back her name and claiming it finally as her own:

> At the moment where the incomprehensible seemed to have subjugated her, she brusquely took back her own name, her disfigured given name. This was a disconcerting ordeal. But to seize her title with such speed soothed her soul. She said "yes" to her name. That was the moment of blessed grace, this glorification of her truth. . . . An appeal to pure reminiscence was not accorded her by this naked violence, but she named herself with assurance. (*Love* 105)

This complicated passage may seem at first glance to condone the "*reprise du nom*" as a return to "truth" since, as philosopher Françoise Proust puts it, "the truth of a thing is its name" (218). But the conclusions one can draw from this significant renaming are multiple, since taking back the name does not, *cannot* entail a smooth return to how things were. The given name is "disfigured," it has therefore been altered and is not entirely recognizable. While it is "soothing" to reaffirm the name, it is not a "pure reminiscence" but rather an impure memory that emerges through the "naked violence" of this act. This return to a lost name is "disconcerting" because it does not mean an unmitigated return to the past, and the future remains uncertain, as the narrator's query reveals: "After she took her name back, what then?" (*Love* 105). Rather than constituting a definitive ending, the act of self-naming, even if it is self-renaming, is merely a start. What matters is that the woman has *chosen* this name, she has come full circle to *embrace* her original appellation, she has *adopted* the name that was initially hers, just like Hélène Cixous when she published her first texts. This act, far from being a conclusion, is instead a beginning. Re-adopting the name generates new life and new possibilities, recuperating the former not in order to return to the old but to embark on the new.

Jacques Derrida's opening contribution to the May 2003 colloquium on Hélène Cixous's œuvre at the Bibliothèque nationale de France provided the title for the three-day event: "Genèses Généalogies Genres." As a close friend and reader of Cixous's writing from the very beginning of her career, Derrida knew the importance of family and name in her work: "it's also a dramaturgy of the family, of origins, birth, and the filiation of the name" (*Genèses* 16). He was also aware of the preeminence of one particular name: "Georges, a first name as aleatory as destined" (18). In Derrida's analysis, this first name of her deceased father was decisive, and its recurrence in various texts is revealing, as the name of her son, also departed, and—as homonym—in Gregor ("a being of letters [*un être de lettres*]" 25), a character from *Manhattan: Lettres de la préhistoire*. Derrida's comments focus on the letter G, picking up on a cue from this work of fiction, in which Cixous plays (literally and figuratively) with this letter: "and by misfortune he accidentally comes across somebody in the elevator who takes him at his word, at his letter G and that's the end for the moment of his freedom here he is obliged to Play the Game of the Player [G *de Geu de Geouer*]" (221).[40] Derrida shows his ear to be in tune with the resonance of what the text's narrator terms "la coïncidence des noms" (*Manhattan* 16), providing his own neologism for the "first names in G": "*Symphométonymie*" indicates that these names play off each other spatially and temporally, not only through the eye, but through the ear as well.

The title of the colloquium at the BnF came as no surprise to those who know of the importance of the name in Cixous's texts. The name is a question of genealogy, of coming from somewhere and someone, of having a lineage, a heritage, a traceable genesis, a (familial) home. Given this context, it is significant that in the work of Hélène Cixous, as in the writings of Abdelkébir Khatibi and Assia Djebar, the figure of the orphan occupies a special place. A being without definite, known origins is one that suffers from this lack, but who also benefits from the freedom of ties that such a lack provides, from the liberty of playing out the multiple possibilities of source, of "genesis," and tapping into all the opportunities of becoming. In an early text, Cixous praises in an abstract manner the idea of self-generation far from family roots, distanced from genealogy: "There is a tropical, colored country where a race of young orphans grows of iself, with the strength of their roots. They give themselves source, orientation, future. Without any immediate relation to a genealogy, since it has forever been untied from family knots" (*Souffles* 18). Later in the same text, Cixous celebrates the dawning of a new day, free from old names tied to father and mother: "Mother of, father of, the old names make us turn in circles. Enough lost, enough time searching behind 'father' who will be. Of father there is nothing, and of mother hardly more except all that one forgets? The named fathermothers exit! And let the day begin, alone, without propitiatory sacrifice!" (215).[41]

When Cixous speaks favorably of the status of young "orphans" in *Souffles*, she does not appear to focus on the Greek etymological meaning of the term as "bereaved." Her emphasis is on the gains of giving oneself genesis, direction, and future, not on the loss inherent to orphanhood; she places the accent on *beginnings*. Orphans abound in the writings of Djebar and Khatibi, and their texts reveal that in Maghrebian societies, "orphan" is a term that applies to anyone who has lost a loved one, and thus extends to include a very large number of people. Despite its widespread application and its negative connotation, Khatibi clings to the figure of the orphan as a positive image in a number of texts, especially the indecipherable *Le Livre du Sang*. In a poem entitled *Le Lutteur de classe à la manière taoïste*, Khatibi insists that he goes against the trend of embracing identity and searching for origins by upholding the virtues of the status of "orphan": "everyone cherishes identity / everyone seeks the origin / as for me, I teach orphan knowledge" (14). Orphans know that roots can hold you down, cut your wings, and prohibit the movement (metaphorical and physical) that allows for multiple identities, and multiple names.

Naming Multiplicity

Prior to the woman's return to her given name in *Amour bilingue*, she *is given* names on many occasions by the man who loves her. In order to show his affection, he bestows a number of continually changing, inventive names upon her. He literally showers her with appellations:

> Thus he speaks to her in an intimate manner, in the second person singular, using a multitude of given names that he had transformed over the years. The desire to baptize her every time he was overcome with tenderness. Was he trying in some obscure way to make her lose her own first name? Why was he so determined to keep the privilege of naming her in this definite, casual, and terrible way? (*Love* 25)

The man's desire to name the other in this passage reveals a general human tendency to label, to classify, and to fix things by providing them with names. This Adamic assigning of names is the very act against which writers such as Khatibi and Cixous usually rebel. As we have seen, they often highlight the fictive nature of the names they hand out and express their reluctance to give names to characters because they don't want to pigeonhole, stereotype, or even *define* in a very general way the beings evoked in their novels. Instead of providing his beloved with a single, immovable name like Cixous's father who inexorably calls his wife "Totote," the man in *Amour bilingue* calls the woman by many names, always seeking a new term with which to "baptize" her. This is an ambiguous process, as the narrator's questions reveal. The purpose and the outcome of this naming are not certain, but the desire to give multiple names, particularly to a loved one, is widespread.[42]

In a poignant passage from *Osnabrück*, the narrator reveals a childhood wish to be given nicknames. She reveals that her mother has never called her by the terms of endearment that she hears other mothers employ in front of their children. Her longing to be called, to be lovingly evoked in multiple ways and in varying tones, reveals a deeper desire for maternal affection: "Call me my angel, my love, call me my little duck I would like my pearl my little bit of silk my coffee bean [. . .] call me my ribbon my bunny my lamb in the straw, my love, call me darling and you'll have me" (171). In *Le Jour où je n'étais pas là*, Cixous relates the experience of a mother who calls her first baby boy by a number of appellations; it is the unfortunate tale of an infant she tried to save with names: "She calls him. She puts her hope in the name. [. . .] She will hold him up in the stitches [*mailles*] of names from Antiquity: solid, assured, faithful, these secret and sacred names" (55).[43] What is crucial is that the names the child receives are not put into existence "on paper;" they are not legal appellations that serve for purposes of official identification. Rather, they are situated in a realm far from administration, at a distance from bureaucracy, out of the reaches of the law.[44] They are located on a level of sound, of intonation, of music, and instead of meeting the eye, they are meant to touch the ear: "She calls him. The names do him good. They provide his ears with minuscule wingflaps. She has the impression that the little one sends to her ears minuscule sounds of caressing names. It's because now he is called. Sometimes Adam, or Georges, or Lev" (*Le Jour* 56). While the names are important ("strong" names with histories—biblical, familial, or otherwise—are meant to bolster her son), the way they are pronounced is nearly as significant. Giving her son a number of names, each filled with possibility, opens up his path to multiple futures.

Their particular occupation, as writers, means that the proper name these individuals bear is often *multiple* in nature, since it refers to the "author" whose name appears on the cover of the book and comes to designate the ensemble of works composed in this name, the "narrator" whose voice often expresses in the first person the thoughts and feelings of the writer, and the "protagonist" who plays the role of the main character in the written work, not to mention the important "referent" for all of these textual terms: the real person, the living being *behind* the name. The same name can be used for "author" and "person," and this creates some confusion, as Derrida's comments on Cixous reveal:

> She is Hélène Cixous, as we call her, as she calls herself. But is she, Hélène my friend in life, for life, Hélène who is here before me and among us? Or rather her homonym Hélène Cixous, as we call her, the signing author of an immense œuvre, of which the world and the rumbling of the world ring out, the address, the origin, and the destination of so many all-powerful letters of which I am only about to speak? ("H. C. pour la vie" 29)

Speaking of a person who is also an author is difficult, because the proper name is shared by the living being and the collection of works. Derrida insists again later on the vacillation between person and œuvre when he evokes "her very name, the homonym between Hélène Cixous and Hélène Cixous, the double between her life and work also" (65).[45] "*Corps*" and "*corpus*" are separate entities, but since they have in common the proper name, there is a tendency to conflate the two, to forget that the proper name itself, even when it remains the same, is multiple: it refers to different roles, it is assigned to different *bodies*.

Playing "Properly" Within the Text

According to Hélène Cixous, the proper name is inevitably at work in the written text. Writers may not always be consciously aware of the myriad ways they insert the name into their work, but the name is present nonetheless. Cixous's comments on writing in the 1990 Wellek Library Lectures at the University of California, Irvine show that, as a voracious reader and writer, she is attentive to the "textual effects" of the proper name:

> The signifiers of our great writers work on us; the common proper name, the proper common name affects us, as readers, and especially the one whose name it is. We must all deal with the unconscious effects of our proper name. We find this aspect of language's intervention in our destiny on the flesh of our imagination. We work on writers whose names are bearers of textual effects. That doesn't mean I am attracted by authors whose names are at work in the language but simply that there aren't any names which don't produce such effects. This includes names that are seemingly insignificant, such as mine for example, an impossible name, but which has always produced signifying effects. Genet constantly puts his name to work in the French language. Entire works were born from his name. There is *corneille* (crow) in Corneille's texts: the bird, the relation to elevation, to flying, to a certain type of bird. If we take up Leviticus again, we will find all kinds of crows. Racine must translate the effects of roots (*racine*) in all his texts, especially the roots (*racines*) of the heart. In other words, I am only referring to the root (*racines*); since the proper name belongs to the order of roots, it is the lightest and most intangible root we have. It roots us, in language and beyond, without our knowing precisely where. One author whose name was not without signifying effects—of which he was perfectly well aware—is Kafka. In German, *Kafka* means *chouca* = *corneille* (crow). He knows it, plays with it, inscribes it. (*Three Steps on the Ladder of Writing* 145)

Cixous maintains that there is no such thing as a writer whose name does not produce signifying effects in the written text. The names within—through their play with meaning, as well as with sound and word associations—"echo" the proper name outside the work, on its cover and elsewhere. It is important to note that there is a certain fluidity present in the play between the "inside" and the "outside" of the text. Ignoring the strict borders that distinguish what Gérard Genette has called the "paratext" from the actual "text" creates a game of recognition between the external and the internal.[46] The textual effects of the proper name are varied, often subtle, and always far-reaching. The results of the proper name are not always clear, but somehow the name "roots us," even if we are not sure where. What matters is not finding one's roots for good, or establishing roots for eternal security and stability; the most important effects of the name are to be found in the word "play," a word that indicates performance, flexibility, and movement, without taking itself too seriously.

It is no surprise that Cixous should point out the predominance of the proper name in the works of writers like Corneille, Racine, Genet, and Kafka. Her personal literary production is rife with creative uses of the proper name. Her own name is inserted repeatedly into the text, but not always in predictable places. She slips her surname into a list of uncapitalized surnames in the following passage recalling her childhood in *Les Rêveries de la femme sauvage*: "The professor called out our names and we responded cixous drif khaled lakdari present, everybody can testify to it" (152). The roll call at school is a significant moment for the young protagonist in this autobiographical text; the inscription of her name here alongside those of her closest girlfriends, all in lower case letters, reenacts the fusion that occurred between these four young people. During their formative years as students together in Algeria, these girls not only maintained their individuality and preserved their singularity by holding onto their distinctive appellations, but they also joined to form a foursome, bearing a "common name" conglomeration of the four last names. In this passage, Cixous has inscribed her last name into the written text in a subtle way, transforming it *orthographically* by dropping the capital letter and altering it *contextually* by placing it next to the names of others and thereby merging with them into a multiple entity comprised of distinctive, *named* persons.

This practice of playing with names in creative ways to form new configurations is crucial to Cixous's writing practice, as Derrida points out in his comments on the "braiding of the name" in her work:

> Naming herself already, this braiding of the name [*cette tresse de nom*], the proper name and the common name, she does what she says she is, the poetic operation of writing that makes the event and allows it to come. She interweaves the most singular writing, the very operation of the text and what it

does, the text, in making the name (the text is a braid, a material interstitch-
ing other threads); she interweaves the braid that is the text with the braid
that the text names, indeed, "la tresse de nom," but also, in the passing of this
braid, the most idiomatic and irreplaceable that exists. ("H. C." 85)

Derrida has picked up on Cixous's own term "tresse de nom" in order to examine the ways she interweaves proper and common names into the various
portions of the text. The unique combinations she creates through this intertwining makes her writing the most "idiomatic" and "irreplaceable" possible, in Derrida's analysis. In OR, les lettres de mon père, the importance of "la
tresse de nom" to Cixous's writing is clear: "But everything begins with the
proper name. I desire you and I keep you and I hold you solidly above nothingness, I pull you out of the ditch by the braiding of the name [la tresse de
nom]" (21). The narrator in this passage insists that everything starts with the
proper name. Preservation from nothingness is dependent on the name; the
first-person voice asserts the idea that if I desire you and "keep" you, it is because of the name. But the name that saves is not a singular, unchanging
name; it is a name that has been reshaped, re-formed, remade. Braiding the
name means *mixing* it, in a hands-on activity that alters the original form
without transforming it altogether. The very title of this book contains a portion of a proper name. Her father Georges is represented in the letters OR;
the "tresse de nom" is already at work, even in the paratextual apparatus. Particularly in Cixous's writing, a title is not only the "proper name" of a book,
it is also a group of words that often contains proper names of people and
characters within it.[47]

When Cixous inserts her own proper name into her fiction, it is seldom to
reflect on it as she does in theoretical texts. The novels contain few references to the name; the name is not highlighted but quickly passed over, and
the naming of the self isn't "initiated" by the narrator. It is always another
character that pronounces her first or last name. For instance, the young protagonist overhears her father speak of her: "My father said. I heard. 'She,
Hélène, no,' he said. I was named" (Osnabrück 174).[48] In a separate instance,
her name is uttered by her mother's fictional character, Selma: "'It's for
Hélène. For you I have yogurt.' 'But I already had yogurt this morning,' says
Jennie. 'I set aside this plum for Hélène, says Selma'" (Benjamin 162). In
these two textual moments, it is almost as if the daughter is called into being
by each of her parents: their nomination means her creation. *She is* because
she is called. In a different example, a man addresses her mother with his
grievance and designates her by name: "People would go to him and recount
extremely mixed-up stories, he had had it, he called me in, he said to me

Madame Cixous yet again 'an Arab story,' I've had enough!" (*Les Rêveries* 97). This textual moment creates confusion on the part of the reader who is initially unsure to whom the last name refers: the mother or the daughter, the person or the author? The insertion of the surname in the book's pages—and the appellation's possible reference to more than one character—sheds doubt on names as clear designators of their bearers. Thowing into question that which we take for granted is one of the results of the name game in these written works. These examples reveal that the full name is seldom present in Cixous's fiction: she is either "Madame Cixous" or "Hélène," and perhaps she is both, but the reader still *does not know her name.*

In "La Venue à l'écriture," the writer adopts the tone of her detractors, playing with their criticisms:

> Besides, what is your principal name? The public wants to know what it's buying. The unknown just doesn't sell. Our customers demand simplicity [*du simple*]. You're always full of doubles, we can't count on you, there is otherness in your sameness. Give us a homogeneous Cixous [*Faites-nous du Cixous homogène*]. You are requested to repeat yourself. Nothing unexpected. A minimum of change for us. Halt! At ease. Repetition! ("Coming" 33)

Cixous is "right on the money" with these humorous words, for she goes directly to the financial point: the name is a marketing device, and the literary product, for all of its noble virtue, is ultimately meant to sell. The public must be satisfied with the commodity, and her name itself is transformed grammatically (with the use of the partitive) into a manufactured item, a piece of merchandise that can be ordered as desired. She is also "right on" when she insists on the desire many express to find reiteration in her work. What they find instead, from one Cixousian text to the next, is "reiterability," resonance that meets with dissonance, music that takes off on improvisational phrases and never says exactly the same thing in exactly the same way. What she shows her readers textually is that self-sameness is not "simple," that all of us bear multiple names, and that autobiographical texts constitute the premier place for playing them out.

Signing Off

If Cixous seems to have contradictory impulses with respect to names, wishing at once to preserve them from disrespectful use—and, more importantly, from oblivion—*and* free them from their charge (of connection, ties, obligation, and the past), this is largely because of the qualifying term, *proper.* The writer addresses the problematic question of ownership, of appropriation, of possession, indicating that her texts are not *hers* alone: "I want to paint our subterranean soul. There are already words. But not yet proper names. Here, by the way, before, nothing is proper, nothing is of its own. This is why my books have no titles. Giving a title is an act of appropriation. The books for which I am the scribe belong to everyone" ("Writing Blind" 142). The final sentence in this quotation is crucial, for it reflects Cixous's unique perception of authorship. As author, she doesn't claim to be the sole proprietor of the ideas and expressions in her written work; rather, she considers herself a "scribe" who is carefully attentive to the world around her (and within her), taking down copious, scrupulous notes that draw their inspiration from these sources for which she does not claim credit in the usual sense.

The hesitation to claim ownership is partly a gesture of generosity that is in line with Cixous's goals as a writer attuned to injustices and committed to their denunciation, but it is also a general statement of recognition: it is not always easy to determine the sources of thoughts, of inspiration. As a young writer dealing with self-doubt and feelings of being an "imposter," she specifically questions what it is she has effectively stolen, wondering where the lines of ownership are drawn: "False signatures you're using there [*Imposture de mes signatures*], I told myself not long ago. 'Thief!' 'Me, a thief? But who's being "robbed"?' What belongs to whom? [*Où est le propre?*] ("Coming" 46). The conception of complete originality is thwarted when Cixous intimates that sometimes a writer ends up quoting herself: "On the sly, I stole myself. Don't repeat it!" (46). If she did nothing but quote herself, and if one text after another proved to be in precisely the same pitch, then she obviously would escape the criticism of not creating an œuvre characterized by homogeneity. But if critical voices clamor for a "Cixous homogène," it is because she does vary from work to work, often picking up on the same themes but providing new variations.[49]

In "La Venue à l'écriture," Hélène Cixous returns to the beginning, to a time before names: "In the beginning, I adored. What I adored was human. Not persons, not totalities, not defined and named beings. But signs" (9). In these brief, laudatory phrases, the writer points beyond the limits of names and indicates her preference for the less decisive signs. Much later in the same essay, the writer reveals that names, tending toward possession, are improper to living beings: "For a long time now, the names that are only right for the urge to possess have not been right for naming the being who equals life" (44). In her view, multiple names would be required for a single person, but all the names in the world would not meet the challenge: "All the names of Life suit it [*lui vont*], all the names put together don't suffice to designate it." At the May 2003 colloquium in honor of her work at the Bibliothèque nationale de France, Jacques Derrida accentuated the *"indécidabilité"* of Hélène Cixous's œuvre as *"sa signature propre."*[50] Resisting all labels, defying all attempts at categorization, the writer and writings that bear her name are indefinable:[51] therein lies their strength, their *"pouvoir infini,"* to play back the words of Derrida. Her "proper signature," even after she has reached the end of her writing career, will be characterized by infinite possibility: "When I have finished writing, when we have returned to the air of the song that we are, the body of texts that we will have made for ourselves will be one of its names among so many others" ("Coming" 44). The proper name, the heading for an immense œuvre, is ultimately not a question of individuation and property. It is instead a question of others, of their song, and a resonance that transcends the single life and its time: "Hélène Cixous isn't me but those who are sung in my text, because their lives, their pains, their force, demand that it resound" ("Coming" 47).

Notes

1. The French text makes it clear that the student is male. This gender assignation makes the use of the adjective *"trompé"* especially interesting, since this word is often used to describe a man who has been cheated on. This passage certainly resonates with this interpretation: the man feels that the woman has been "unfaithful" and he chides her for it. To take the metaphor further, the "legitimacy" of her "offspring," her textual production, is put into question as a result of her infidelity.

2. In a short story with an autobiographical bent, Sebbar reveals that her name was never well received, even when she was just a young girl in Algeria. Her childhood friends' impressions were negative, and Sebbar was the object of considerable skepticism, even scorn, because of this troublesome appellation: "It is bad to be called Leïla SEBBAR, to have Arab first and last names when one has a French mother. . . . It's high treason. . . . And besides, SEBBAR is a strange name, not French of course, but not really Arab either. An Arab name is with BEN, naturally, they say . . . I will learn later, reading the Koran translated by André Chouraqui, that my father's last name, SEBBAR, is the 99th name of the prophet Mohammed" ("Les Jeunes filles" 194–95).

3. The student's assumption that a person who is not fluent in Arabic is incapable of accurately representing Maghrebian society (or the situation of Maghrebian immigrants and their offspring in France) is fundamentally misguided, in my view. The concern for "legitimate" representation of Arabs in literature is certainly valid, but excluding anyone lacking proficiency in Arabic is not only harsh, it places an unnecessary restriction on those who are "legitimately" authorized to write about Arab peoples. Sebbar's personal experience as a child in Algeria would work as a counterargument to guarantee the "legitimacy" of her writing enterprise and her representa-

tion of the particular problems that plague those at the margins of Algerian and French society.

4. In *La Blessure du nom propre*, Khatibi declares that proper names should be disrupted in the text: "We must therefore displace the Hindu saying, 'your proper Name is your destiny,' by no longer considering the question of identity as a divine fatality, fixed at a center and an origin, but by playing with the proper Name according to the crystal of the text: this reflection of being that transforms itself as it combines with the paging through of meaning" (14).

5. In the famous "autobiographical pact" conceived by Philippe Lejeune, the proper name found on the cover of as well as within the book (as narrator and protagonist) creates specific expectations for truth and veracity for both writer and reader. According to this understanding, it is the name that serves as the ultimate reference point for determining reliability and genre.

6. In a footnote from her book on immigrants in France, Mireille Rosello refers to the specific situation to which Cixous responded most actively, and to the theatrical production that this intervention inspired: "After being expelled from the first church they occupied (Saint Ambroise), the 300 undocumented African immigrants, who had been relatively ignored by the media, found refuge in the Théâtre du Soleil at the Cartoucherie, and after leaving the Church of Saint Bernard, they returned there. In 1997, the guiding spirit of the Théâtre du Soleil, Ariane Mnouchkine, put on a 'creative creation,' the play *Et soudain, des nuits d'éveil*, which retells the sans-papiers's story as a tragic adventure of Tibetans, in collaboration with Hélène Cixous and Jean-Jacques Lemêtre" (*Postcolonial Hospitality* 181).

7. This praise of "unnaming" is reminiscent of Cixous's poignant imploring of her friend to "de-name" herself, to be free of all encumbrances: "But, my friend, take the time to unname [*dé-nommer*] yourself for a moment" ("Coming" 49). It is no accident that references to time surround the coined verb *dé-nommer* in this quotation, I would argue, for names are inextricable from time. Both names *and dates* are required on legal documents, for instance, in part because names are subject to change.

8. While she has chosen in theoretical texts like "La Venue à l'écriture" and "Mon Algériance" to underscore the importance of her last name in directing her toward a career as a "scribe," various subtle comments culled from diverse texts in her oeuvre reveal that her first name also played a role in this movement toward writing. Hélène Cixous's first name came from her maternal great-grandmother, Helene Jonas, maiden name Meyer. While little is known about this ancestor, there is a curious detail that stands out, an anecdotal history that is a "telling" part of the family's past: in the years preceding the Second World War, this Helene possessed the only telephone in the city of Osnabrück. The writer takes this object to be her gift, to be her legacy, handed down from her namesake: "This absolute telephone is my heritage. I hold it from Helene Jonas maiden name Meyer my ancestor I tell myself. I am the result of the telephone of Helene née Meyer, nobody else with a phone in Osnabrück but my great-grandmother, no one to call but God as she waited" (*Osnabrück* 132). While references to telephones abound in her texts, the most significant may be in

"Writing blind," an essay in which the writer acknowledges her debt to this apparatus: "I owe books and books to the telephone and I will give at least one back to it" ("Writing blind" 142). Her indebtedness stems from the fact that the apprenticeship of giving and receiving phone calls has taught her to privilege sound over sight in the writing process: "I admit my work is of acceptance my principal organs are: my ears which are spacious extensible velvety of the necessary size, courageous also never closed and my eyes which are other ears" (142). Over the phone, the writer's heart is engaged even if her interlocutor is out of view: "The rest, heart above and heart below, is connected to the telephone exchange. I catch everything by the ear, the murmurs, the most enigmatic phrases and the angers also" (142). Another obvious "namesake" that her own great-grandmother did not know of was "l'Hélène grecque," as Cixous called this historical figure at the May 2003 colloquium at the BnF: "I was not persecuted by the character . . . a second Hélène, that of Faust, gave me pleasure." Even if she wasn't persecuted by the Greek Helen, she knew of her and the connection to her own name is clear in such feminist texts as "Unmasked": "But that's all Helen's fault, say the Bibles. [. . .] Ho! Mad Helen, who single-handedly destroyed so many lives in Troy" (*Stigmata* 135).

9. That Derrida should demonstrate an interest in Hélène Cixous's choice of a name should come as no surprise given his personal history. "Jacques" Derrida was given the first name "Jackie" when he was born. His legal name remained "Jackie" throughout his life, even if the works of his enormous corpus all bear the name "Jacques Derrida." Derrida explains that, when it was time to publish his first trio of books in 1967 (*La Voix et le phénomène*, *L'écriture et la différance*, and *De la grammatologie*), he couldn't use his given name for these serious works of philosophy: "Jackie, ça ne fait pas sérieux" (personal conversation). Cixous, in *Portrait de Jacques Derrida en Jeune Saint Juif*, evokes the first name Derrida abandoned when he entered the publishing world by fictionalizing a conversation she remembers having with him (29).

10. The fact that Cixous turned to her maternal lineage when seeking a name takes on new light in France today, given recent legal transformations that allow for considerable flexibility when choosing a child's name. This break with tradition is synonymous with a desacralization of the heretofore revered "name of the father" in French history. During her air time for the radio station *France Culture*, Julia Kristeva has reflected in clear, simple terms on the symbolic consequences this new law will have on memory for families and societies: "What would happen if the mother could also transmit to her descendants her own *patronyme*, as a symbolic indication, a mark of filiation, an inscription in memory of ancestors?" (110).

11. Cixous evokes this autobiographical moment in her essay on Jacques Derrida. In this creative, playful text, her reflections take an unexpected twist—and turn— when she likens her refusal to cut her nose to a circumcision (in reverse): "It's always the né as you know. Or the *nez* [nose] in French. My too-long too-big nose my oversize appendage and childhood fear. Chop it off, says my mother. I was fourteen at the time. And I almost did. True this is a scene with two meanings, a double circle mov-

ing in opposite directions. I was about to have my nose trimmed, I didn't do it. I was afraid of running away from my signifer, my né-Jewish too big too long nose, my tip of an organ my father. In this way I had myself circumcised in reverse by refusing the operation. There are more kinds of circumcision than we think" (*Portrait* 74).

12. Cixous tries to decipher this unusual, idiosyncratic surname, and finally learns that it may be Berber. She does not uncover its trajectory, however: "Then slowly very slowly through our surprise a rumor rose to my ears: one day someone tells me: Cixous is an Arab name. Arab? Then the rumor left again. To return in a firm tone: some Berber friends recognized the barbarian duckling. Cixous, they say is the name of a Berber tribe. How, by what story of love, of conversion, of war, of passion, how my formerly Spanish family was or how it became or ceased to be Berber—only forgetfulness knows" ("My Algeriance" 157).

13. Jacques Derrida, in the midst of a discussion of identity and language, briefly provides the dates and circumstances of "the withdrawal of French citizenship from the Jews of Algeria" (*Monolingualism of the Other* 16): "In October 1940, by abolishing the Crémieux decree of October 24, 1870, France herself, the French state in Algeria, the 'French state' legally constituted (by a Chamber of the Popular Front!) following the well-known act of parliament, this state was refusing French identity to—rather, taking it away again from—those whose collective memory continued to recollect" (17).

14. In these comments from "In October 1991. . . ," Cixous makes light of her name, indicating that she has found peace with this appellation on a personal and professional level, and acknowledging the significance and necessity of this name as a heading for her œuvre: "Who still lives and answers in my name? I don't know. If my name wasn't there, my famous unpronounceable name, to which I have finally reconciled myself, if there was not my name to go ahead of me and replace me, make me in my absence, fill in my gaps, if there was not a you/roof ['*toi(t)*'] when I'm not there, and if there was not my shadow, it would be a fine catastrophe" (89).

15. In a series of radio interviews conducted by Pascal Amel for France Culture, Khatibi responds to questions about his name, situating his birth historically and geographically: "Yes, I was born at the beginning of the Second World War. That's the background. The war in a country that was colonized, 'protected' by France, in a little town called El Jadida" (*La Langue de l'Autre* 71). It is during these interviews that Khatibi indicates that the name he received at birth influenced his life work, just as Cixous's name may have destined her for writing: "I was born into this symbolic grain, into this attribute that is the greatness of Allah. It's a heavy attribute to carry! I was born to the world and to my name at the same time, the day of the religious festival of sacrifice. This festival directed me toward writing, toward narrative. Something was forever engraved in my destiny" (72).

16. In "My Algeriance," Cixous addresses circumcision in the Jewish context, referring to it as "the ineluctable and intolerable election that nails the Jewish boy's body to an identity he has not chosen" and thereby insists upon the *forced* nature of this corporeal change that male children must undergo (158). Cixous, as a woman,

was not subjected to this involuntary cut, this undesired "tattoo," unlike her brother: "And I who was not a Jewish (and tattooed) man, I understood this revolt. I, who had not been marked by the knife, and whose body had not been decided before me, I could choose" (159).

17. In his analysis of the proper name in Moroccan literature, Marc Gontard draws the following conclusion from the opening passage of Khatibi's autobiographical *récit*: "It is this 'tattoo' of 'memory' through the proper name, sign of a spiritual identity [. . .] with this insistence on the theophorous first name: Abd-el-Kébir (servant of the Almighty) that [. . .] inscribes religious identity into the propitiatory function of denomination" (80).

18. Khatibi revisits the changing of his name in *Amour bilingue*, where he provides further commentary on this transformation: "Between a first name given by god and a family name given me by my elder brother, after my father's death. The funniest part of the whole business, I admit, is that a local official thought it advisable to amputate one letter from the family name without anyone's permission. What a waste!" (36). The use of the verb "amputate" is important here, for it carries with it the idea of corporeal truncation: cutting off a letter is like amputating a limb. It marks the permanent removal of a crucial part of the body. The name has been forever altered, the wound is indelible.

19. This practice of changing names to encourage assimilation in national contexts has a long history in Europe. In 1928, Mussolini decreed the "Italianization" of all names from the Italian Tyrol and, in 1959, Todor Zivkov ordered a similar "Bulgarization" of minority names, especially Turkish ones. Nationalism, according to a recent publication titled *Le Patronyme, histoire, anthropologie, société*, inspired such changes in order to erase all trace of foreign origin. In France, following the passing of the law on naturalization in 1927, the "Frenchification" of names became a right. This "right" creates complex problems for peoples from elsewhere who want to preserve their heritage but who also feel a need to integrate themselves, to "fit into" the society they live in. The social stakes of the name are high; dissimulating one's roots in a place where an Arab name creates immediate xenophobic suspicion can be an important act for finding employment, securing housing, and receiving respect in public, on the one hand. On the other, the "liberty" of changing one's name can quickly run the risk of betraying one's origins.

20. Khatibi often "signs" his works by including a number of references to the holy day on which he was born and by evoking the sacrifice that this date commemorates. In the following passage, Khatibi recalls the sacrifice and goes further, to underscore the fact that the act did not take place: "Raïssi, think now of Abraham, the friend of God who asked him for his son as ransom. Or else, think of this: God gave him Isaac as a substitute for Ismael. Yet Abraham had asked for neither ransom nor a substitute. Then he obeyed. God then substituted the ram for the son" (*Pèlerinage d'un artiste amoureux* 113). This version seems to serve as a corrective to the "cry" associated with his name in this self-reflective moment from *Le Livre du sang*: "The music of Islam beats in this way, for ears turned toward Mecca, catching from afar, in the slit-

ting of the throat of Abraham's son is MY NAME INCARNATE, a formidable cry, sustained from century to century, from millennium to millennium" (64).

21.   In *Le Passé simple*, Moroccan writer Driss Chraïbi addresses the name in a humorous passage about a taxi driver who has bought a (French) name and nationality from a visitor to his country. The chauffeur effectively acquired a new identity through the sale of his sister to a foreigner—since the French tourist's aspiration was "the Arab woman. I gave him my sister and he delivered this card to me" (68)—and has thereby escaped the rigidity of a nominal system that encases and encloses him in a "prefabricated" name: "He told me he was named Jules Césaire. Faced with my surprise, he explained himself: 'So what? Because I'm Arab I have to have a prefabricated name like Ali ben Couscous?'" (67). This name change (and the citizenship that "legalizes" it) carries with it definite advantages: "He benefited from a citizenship that allowed him to sweep away everything in front of him: traditions, chains" (69). Changing names, for this Arab driver, is an act of liberation.

22.   Djebar's adoption of a pseudonym that is undeniably "un-French" differs from other pseudonyms by Francophone writers. In a review for *Le Monde* of a book by Chinese-born François Cheng, Josyane Savigneau underscores the *very* French nature of this chosen first name: "he chose for himself the most symbolically French first name."

23.   Ernstpeter Ruhe has interpreted the epigraph taken from Hölderlin containing the word "Asia" as a subtle reference to Djebar's first name, Assia. Anne Donadey has referred to the insertion of her ancestors "Fatima" and "Zohra" in the text as echoes of Djebar's original appellation: "The fact that Djebar reveals the given name of her relative, Zohra, exemplifies the double act of unveiling/veiling, which is for her the necessary condition of writing an autobiography. The unveiling of her relative's name functions at the same time as an unveiling and veiling of her own. 'Assia Djebar' is a pseudonym; her real first name is Fatima-Zohra, which is never revealed in her novels. The double first name links her, not only to her ancestor, but also, symbolically, to one of the two nineteenth-century women mentioned in *Fantasia*, Fatma, whose fate was transmitted by a French text, as well as to the Prophet's daughter, '[c]elle qui dit non à Medine' [the woman who says no to Medina] (*Loin* 68)" (*Recasting* 61).

24.   Hélène Cixous's commentaries on her first name are remarkable for their emphasis on the sounds of the mother tongue and the proper pronunciation of this appellation: "I love my mother tongue—but which one—to begin with it *heaves*, it *haspirates*, it *rasps*, it calls me enticing me, it *c*hatches me, it *h*ails me, it *h*élène's me, it holds me back and drags me with this imperative H, the breath of YaHaweh himself, it cannot be disobeyed, it gives me the impetus and the summons out of this H that inaugurates me and does not exist in French, but in Arabic-German it aspirates the turmoil [*émois*] along its path. [. . .] My first name is German, the French language swipes it from me" ("The Names of Oran" 187).

25.   For an in-depth analysis of Assia Djebar's pseudonym and its implications for her work, see Alison Rice, "The Improper Name: Ownership and Authorship in the Literary Production of Assia Djebar."

26. *Talismano* by Tunisian Abdelwahab Meddeb constitutes one of the most striking examples of calling attention to the proper name in a Francophone novel. This work of fiction is the focus of "Incipits," an article in which Khatibi quotes extensively from Meddeb to illustrate his points on the name (specifically in Arabic), its significance, and the inadequacies of its translation (into French). A more recent example of proper names, their importance, and their capacity to be misunderstood in France is found in the vivid opening passages of *Vivre me tue* by Paul Smaïl (a pseudonym).

27. In spite of his hesitations, Barthes did compose a fictive work in 1975 whose title exposes its autobiographical bent: *Roland Barthes par Roland Barthes*. In his metatextual comments he underscores the *absence of proper names* in this work: "The substance of this book, ultimately, is therefore totally fictive. The intrusion, into the discourse of the essay, of a third person who nonetheless refers to no fictive creature, marks the necessity of remodeling the genres: let the essay avow itself *almost* a novel: a novel without proper names" (120).

28. It is ironically interesting that the one form of writing that does not pose a problem for naming is theatrical, according to Cixous's account above. A recent development may indicate that she no longer subscribes to this point of view: after years of collaborating with Ariane Mnouchkine at the Théâtre du Soleil, a new spectacle played to sold-out audiences during the months of May and June 2003 at the Cartoucherie of Vincennes. Officially billed as a "collective creation," this work differed from earlier such creations like the 1997 *Et soudain, des nuits d'éveils*, presented as "a collective creation collective in harmony with Hélène Cixous." In an unprecedented move, the playwright opted not to sign her name to *Le dernier caravansérail (Odyssées)*, even if she left her mark on the program in the form of questions: in her article for *La Quinzaine littéraire*, critic Monique Le Roux gives us an insider's glimpse into "Hélène Cixous's interrogations in the (unsigned) program." René de Ceccatty sees this "extreme situation" of "the absence of a signature" as fitting in with the trajectory of Cixous's literary production, as he stated during the colloquium of May 2003: "Cixous has never finished her books; they constitute a flow." In De Ceccatty's opinion, the absent signature is emblematic of Cixous's œuvre: "unmasterable, inexhaustible."

29. In *Manhattan*, Cixous flirts repeatedly with the fictive nature of the text and its unsteady relation to the "real" past it depicts: "I know absolutely nothing about the actor who played the character of G. Is the actor more real or less real than the true character?" (222). The reality of this ghost from her part is constantly called into question, especially since the very name by which she knew him was invented, improvised on the spot: "He thus lived a life under the law of the name that he had given himself instead of the name he had been given and therefore under the law of Gregor as proper and proprietor of his thoughts [. . .] completely replaced by him, Gregor, that he had improvised from one moment to the next" (175–76). Despite his credible name, this character is nothing more than a figment of fiction: "for the set they put up New York they took as an interim representative a character as strong as

fiction, an imaginary substance as unreal as Gregor Samsa" (215). In these quotations, life is a work of art, indeed: it is a theatrical play. In *Photos de racines*, Cixous's interlocutor Calle-Gruber asserts that she thinks the writer "would like [. . .] names that can be torn, like the tissue of the novel which can be torn. Names that are not quite 'for real,' that can play with the rest of the text, that can have the same suppleness, the same fluidity as the text. That do not lead to a psychologization of the story. In this case you would be attempting to avoid being cornered in a certain realism that the proper name immediately imposes" (76).

30. Two brief quotations from *Benjamin à Montaigne* reveal the reigning ambiguity of the two aunts' identities: "'Who told you about Selma?,' my mother cried out. 'Aunt Jenny, not Selma. She was the fat one.' 'It was Jenny?' 'Jenny not Selma! Jenny!' 'You said Selma!' 'I said Jenny'" (142); "'Which one was Selma in the end?'" (149).

31. In a response to a group of papers at the May 2003 colloquium in her honor at the Bibliothèque nationale de France, Cixous stated her consciousness of the tremendous influence of names, of "the extent to which everything depends on the name."

32. Cixous not only demonstrates an awareness of the noisome effects of "bad naming," she recognizes that naming in general can be considered negative. In the following passage, the name comes between her and her anonymous telephone partner. Instead of creating a deeper connection between the two speakers, the name serves to distance one from the other, introducing singularity and differentiation into a conversation that marked a true meeting of minds and emotions: "To return to my ghostly, totally invisible and unfigurable partner, but who was a voice, at the end of our conversation during which we had only one name for two voices and it was mine and we were both united under this name that held us like a parasol, I thought I ought to ask her name before separating; but perhaps I shouldn't have. What is your name I say most softly but in spite of the softness it was nonetheless the small wound of separation and I had not wanted it. And with timidness she went back into her name and turned it toward me as if she felt encloistered behind the door. And so out loud I said her name, she said that she did not have one and I said that no one had one, there are only words and phrases with hands and lips tears in the eyelids while names are exposives, it ought to be possible to disarm them, and that they are proper and pride and aggression, it is the names, I say, that should be chased off like honorary excrement, and I said her name softly to her to take her by the hand with vigor and bring her back under the two-voiced parason. And when we interrupted our adventure we were together again" ("Writing Blind" 142).

33. The use of the word "injurious" here, as well as the conception of naming as "action," recalls the work of Judith Butler's "On Linguistic Performativity" in *Excitable Speech*. Butler refers to the "history" of injurious names, calling attention to the important fact that names do not emerge in a vacuum; they are tied to specific instances of naming and carry with them an entire time line, an evolution that reveals multiple occasions of naming: "Clearly, injurious names have a history, one that is invoked and reconsolidated at the moment of utterance, but not explicitly told. This is not simply

a history of how they have been used, in what contexts, and for what purposes; it is the way such histories are installed and arrested in and by the name. The name has, thus, a historicity, what might be understood as the history which has become internal to a name, has come to constitute the contemporary meaning of a name: the sedimentation of its usages as they have become part of the very name, a sedimentation, a repetition that congeals, that gives the name its force" (36).

34. In her book on Leïla Sebbar and Assia Djebar, Rafika Merini calls attention to a particular passage in Djebar's *L'Amour, la fantasia* and highlights the use of the name "Fatma." Merini reads this name as a reference to the French tendency to call all Maghrebian women by this common proper name. She also identifies this tendency as potentially blasphemous: "Unconscious perversions occur, escaping the notice of even as well trained an eye as that of Djébar (sic): she uses the colonial name of the symbolic woman's hand, the five fingers of which ward off evil on many breasts and doors (in the form of charms or doorbells), although it can only have been intended as another attack on the 'inferior,' if not 'non-existant' culture of North Africa as the colonizers saw it. This French name, 'Fatma's hand,' not only implies that all Maghrebian women are called Fatma, and are, therefore, indistinguishable from each other, but also that the Prophet's daughter's name can be taken in vain by them with impunity" (97).

35. Naming is of course not limited to people, but involves places as well; streets, public parks, and monuments often undergo name changes under new political regimes. Djebar's *La Disparition de la langue française* reveals that the departure of the French from Algeria resulted in a process of renaming that strikes the principal protagonist when he returns after a long absence: "And as he drives toward the east, worry begins to stir in him; like billiard balls, the names changing the arteries slide: French names of yesterday (Cat Street, Eagle Street, Stork Street, Swan Street, Condor Street, Bear Street), and those that come to him right away in Arabic (Palm Street, Fountain of Thirst Street, Tanner Street, Butcher Street, Pomegranate Street, Princesses Street, Street of the Destroyed House)" (68).

36. According to an article entitled "Class Neuroticism" ["La névrose de classe"] written by Emmanuel Poncet shortly after Pierre Bourdieu's passing, the eminent sociologist claimed to be the victim of "class racism" during his adolescence because of his "peasant" name (2).

37. The ardent insistence on the housekeeper's name in this passage is called into question later in the text. The mother claims that this enigmatic woman was neither "Fatma" nor "Messaouda": "I retained Maria my mother said, the true name I never knew, it wasn't Barta, maybe Faria I don't know, a cleaning woman for whom I did a lot of good. . . . I myself introduced this misfortune called 'Maria' in my house, I opened the door and she hadn't even knocked" (*Les Rêveries* 165). The continual *mise en question* of the real name of this cleaning woman mirrors a difficulty of incriminating this elusive character. If her name is not even clear, how can one bring the woman to trial for her crime? Names are necessary in order for legal retribution to take place. The constant calling into question of this woman's identity shows that

she ultimately escapes the order of the law and can get away with her wrongdoing without facing judgment. A similar vacillation in names can be found earlier in this text, but with different consequences: "either Idir or Kader says my brother it's Idir I say but maybe Kader, who rocks gently between two names" (156). The uncertainty of this sympathetic character's name is much less serious; he evokes a fond memory among the siblings who knew him and his "real" name is not crucial to their remembering.

38. In this reflection from "My Algeriance," misnaming is viewed as reappropriation, a wrong that is only now being righted: "Whereas all maids in Algeria were called Fatma. But not us. Aïcha was unique. Until the day, very late, after independence, when I discovered: Aïcha was named Messaouda. What? And for twenty years we had kept calling her Aïcha? That's right. There had been I know not what initial error, a parapraxis and Messaouda had docilely let herself be expropriated and reappropriated. She had not dared. We who had wronged her and Fatmatized her for twenty years" (157).

39. Whether "living opposed to the name" is the same thing as "unnaming" the self is not entirely clear. I am arguing for a synonymous relationship in an ideal setting. If one chooses simply to live in opposition to one's name, one is reacting to the name and rebelling against its dictates. In this case, the person is just as determined by the name as if he or she conformed to the name. In contrast, "unnaming" represents the ideal manner of living in opposition to the name since it leaves the logic of the name entirely and operates in another realm, that of the unnameable, where names are irrelevant and unnecessary and therefore do not retain their "determining" qualities to influence a "destiny."

40. This is only an example of a number of instances of textual play with the letter "G" and the names it is associated with: "the letter G; the connection between the names: the tenderly loved elements of the Georges and the unrecognized name of Gregor; the impossibility for me to say the words I have in 1964 and all the other angel-words in *j'ai, gé, jet, gel*, etc., I always tried instinctively to avoid all bothersome contact with G but the letter is disguised everywhere in the French language" (*Manhattan* 121).

41. Cixous analyzes the work of Joyce in the context of modern medical advances that render the mother's biological status as uncertain as the father's. Cixous underscores the unsteady nature of both motherhood and fatherhood in our times: "But what is a mother? And a father?—That is the enigma. Enigma through which Joyce is going to set the thinking on genealogy reeling. After all, one can also imagine a new secondhand mother or father; one knows that the stability of the reference to the mother, in opposition to the instability or to the improbability of paternity of which Freud spoke, has foundered over this last decade since a mother has become potentially replaceable and fictitious, surrogate" (*Stigmata* 106).

42. The close tie between names and time insisted on in passages from *Amour bilingue* indicates that names can (and do) evolve with the passing of weeks, months, and years. Rather than remaining stable indicators of fixed identity, names naturally

transform themselves, even in subtle ways, in response to external factors. It is common, of course, for name changes to take place according to various stages of life, especially for women who in many cultures are expected to change their name upon marriage. The possibility of several marriages thus carries with it the possibility of several name changes for women. Abdelkébir Khatibi writes of a woman who changed name and even religion when she wed a relative of his; this seemingly effortless change was reversed upon divorce: "One of my relatives loved a Jewish woman. They were married without scandal. She changed her religion and her name, she took them back when they were separated. These were like a vestment, a symbolic ornament whose color and perfume changed with the seasons of the body" ("A Colonial Labyrinth" 5–6). This transformation from Jewish to Arab (name and faith) and back again recalls the change in name and faith effected by characters in *Les raisins de la galère* by Tahar Ben Jelloun. Despite very different beliefs and practices, there are similarities between these two immigrant groups who find themselves excluded from mainstream society in France.

43. In *OR*, Cixous makes reference to a recurring biblical figure in her text, illustrating what is echoed in this passage on her own son: calling names has the power to give life, and can even bring back to life that which has already passed away: "If Jesus had not called Lazarus by crying out his name with a strong voice, Lazarus! Come out! Come here!" (23). In this same text, a cat disappears precisely because no one has known how to call her; remaining depends on being called: "Misfortune to the creature that is not begged to live according to the name of his name. I met, briefly, very briefly, the case of a cat that didn't have a name!" (22). *OR* is not the only text to indicate that it would be difficult to overestimate the importance of calling someone by name(s): "Since nobody called me, my name fell into disuse" (*Un vrai jardin* 12). As in the case of Jacques Derrida at the end of his mother's life, keeping the name alive means speaking it; iterability is crucial to keeping the name: "She no longer says my name. My name is no longer" (*Jacques Derrida* 55).

44. Cixous evokes the importance of names in relation to law in her theatrical retelling of the story of Joan of Arc: "Who is responsible? Identification. For every subject / A clearly identified responsible person. / What I want and what I do not have / Names are names / The person, the status. No facsimile / Decline who is who and who does what" (*Rouen* 63–64).

45. In an interview with Sophia Phoca, Cixous indicates a desire to keep her work at a distance from her person: "This is really what a writer can wish. To have become a pure writing-being and not to be re-appropriated as a person 'in reality' which is very dangerous and totally deceptive. I'm always extremely wary in this regard. So I'm happy when people treat me as text, which I think is closer to the truth" (10).

46. Genette provides an explanation of the paratext as that which surrounds the text, presents, and accompanies it, in *Seuils* (7).

47. Derrida has pointed out that each book title is in essence a "proper name." He has also taken care to underscore the importance of proper names in the titles of Cixous's books. The number of occurrences of proper names in titles is striking, even

in "partial" form, like in OR: "Each book has a history. [. . .] And that's why with her you always must begin again. Each book has a proper name. It would be murder to speak of it only as metonymy, to call it by name or by the name of another. For a metonymy can also kill. Each book has a proper name, each oeuvre is a proper name, indeed a filiation of proper names, even there where the name, whether the first name or last, does not appear, as it appears on the other hand in titles like *Le Prénom de Dieu* (in the singular) (1967) or *Prénoms de personne* (in the plural) (1974) or *Révolution pour plus d'un Faust* (1975), *Le Nom d'Œdipe* (1978) . . . OR is obviously a part of a proper name, of so many proper names, beginning with Georges" ("H. C." 74–75).

48. Being hailed by the first name "Hélène" is a frequent occurrence in various texts, notably *Osnabrück* and *Benjamin à Montaigne*: "'Hélène?' Calls the voice that hails me, strongly haspirating me hey there! I began thus as a German sigh" (*Osnabrück* 182); "'Hélène,' shouts my mother" (*Benjamin* 47).

49. While each text is different, the same "musical" signature can be found throughout, as Cixous asserts: "So for each text, another body. But in each *the same vibration*: the something in me that marks all my books is a reminder that *my flesh signs the book, it is rhythm*. Medium my body, rhythmic my writing" ("Coming" 53, my emphasis). Derrida addresses Cixous's "genealogical signature" in this way: "Thus every book is absolutely alone, it is a beginning as absolute as a proper name, even if, however, a huge echo chamber and hall of mirrors, the labyrinth of so many inter-mingled threads make these books solitary and irreducible one to another, through so many generations, *a single genealogical and elementary signature*, that is to say bigger than itself" ("H.C." 75, my emphasis). For an insightful analysis of the contemporary phenomenon of serial autobiographies among women writers, see Leigh Gilmore's *The Limits of Autobiography*. In her treatment of Jamaica Kincaid's work, Gilmore makes a statement that is also applicable to Cixous's corpus: "Serial autobiography permits the writer to take multiple runs at self-representation, more as a way to ex-plore the possibilities within autobiography than to produce a single, definitive solu-tion to the problem of representing identity" (103).

50. "There, in this example of undecidability that we could multiply to infinity in Cixous's work more than anywhere else, as if that were her own signature and one of the multiple secrets of several of her geniuses. . . ." (*Genèses* 26). Placing the affir-mation of Cixous's "own signature" next to the words "comme si" is a meaningful combination of terms, for it evokes Cixous's analysis of "comme si" as *his* signature (*Portrait* 13). This *rapprochement* of the two signatures hints at the interaction that has contributed to each of these two *œuvres* from the outset.

51. Peggy Kamuf describes the signature as located at the border between self and work, an interesting articulation of the relations and disconnects between name and œuvre: "A signature, however, is not an author or even simply the proper name of an author. It is the mark of an articulation at the border between life and letters, body and language. An articulation both joins and divides identity with/from difference. A difference from itself, within itself, articulates the signature on the text it signs" (*Signature Pieces* 39–40).

PART ONE

ASSIA DJEBAR

CHAPTER TWO

~

Religio: Re-thinking and Re-linking Cultural and Religious Tradition

Music is a belief.

—Hélène Cixous, *Vivre l'orange* (1989)

My life is a continent that only a narrative comes close to. [. . .] I must have a melody—first a hum, *cantus obscurius* of the mother tongue that is still insignificant, a substantial, nourishing presence—to appease the evisceration of time by time. Song, *mélos* is tied to memory.

—Pascal Quignard, *La Leçon de musique* (1987)

Assia Djebar's literary production is filled with references to a belief system with foreign resonance for many of her French-speaking readers. In works ranging from the collection of short stories titled *Femmes d'Alger dans leur appartement* to the elegiac remembrances of deceased fellow Algerian intellectuals in *Le Blanc de l'Algérie*, Djebar can hardly evoke Algeria without referring to the religion that has held sway in her native land for centuries. Rendering the customs and traditions of this particular faith in written works most often destined for an audience from a different background, Djebar engages in a textual translation that remains respectful to her heritage, but with a certain distance. Rather than expressing a firm adherence to the Islam of her homeland, she communicates the ways in which nearly every aspect of life in Algeria is impregnated with its beliefs. Her goal is thus not to grapple uniquely with questions of faith on an abstract level, but rather to transmit the ways faith is an integral part of existence in her country on a practical

89

level. From the words and expressions in Algerian dialectical Arabic to the rhythm of the days, weeks, and months, practically everything is dictated by Islamic belief. In her renditions of its presence, "religion" in the writing of Assia Djebar occupies a position that is at once "cultural" and "intellectual" *and* "spiritual" and "personal."

The adjective "autobiographical" has often been applied to Djebar's writing of late, with an emphasis on the unfinished "Algerian quartet" as the apex of this writing. But little attention has been paid to the question of religion in her work. While it is undeniable that complex issues of identity and identification are closely related to the oft-cited themes of language and blood ties, it is my argument that belief systems, with the customs and mindsets that they form and inform, are also indispensable to a person's makeup. I think it would be a mistake to overlook the portrayals of and references to religion in Djebar's written work, for the communication of this aspect of her personal background is crucial to her autobiographical enterprise.

Understanding who Djebar is, as a writer and a protagonist, as a textual creator and a textual creation, depends upon a comprehension of the role of religion in her native country in general and her familial and communal culture in particular.[1] Partly because the text most focused on Islam and its historical roots, *Loin de Médine: Filles d'Ismaël* constitutes a divergence from such openly autobiographical novels as *L'Amour, la fantasia* and *Vaste est la prison*; it has not yet been considered as a work that reveals personal aspects of its writer. In this chapter, I will examine religion in *Loin de Médine* in order to demonstrate that this text is an essential component of Assia Djebar's corpus. I contend that it is complementary to a series of works that reveal a complicated, composite image of this Algerian-born writer.

A few recent scholarly studies turn their attention to the presence of Islam in Assia Djebar's writing, two of which deserve special mention here. John Erickson's *Islam and Postcolonial Narrative* dedicates a chapter to Djebar, drawing from the critical analyses of Winifred Woodhull and Anne Donadey in its treatment of language and autobiography in *L'Amour, la fantasia*. While the book's title indicates that Islam is at the center of this study, Erickson focuses mostly on women's customs and possibilities (or impossibilities) for speech, rather than directly addressing religion and its role in Djebar's texts. In contrast, Mireille Calle-Gruber devotes significant space to *Loin de Médine*, a work that deals explicitly and extensively with the sources of Islam and the religion's early history. In *Assia Djebar ou la résistance de l'écriture*, Calle-Gruber judges this novel to be a crucial development in the writer's career, underscoring that the emancipation of women affirmed in *Loin de Médine* occurs *within* Islamic tradition rather than outside, or in opposition, to this religious background. While this work may take risks in its goal to emancipate people—particularly women—from what Erickson has called the "strictures imposed in the name of the Word,"[2] it does not do so with utter disregard. For the *religious* tradition of Islam is also the *cultural* tradition of her people, and Djebar treads cautiously when dealing with these precious roots.

As my title indicates, the word "religion" comes to us from the Latin *religio*, a term that remains untranslated, and perhaps untranslatable, if we are to take to heart Jacques Derrida's rhetorical question: "Et si *religio* restait intraduisible?" ("Foi" 43). In "Foi et Savoir," a text examining religion in connection to the contemporary phenomena of "Latin" and "globalization," Derrida explores the two possible etymologies of *religio*: either from *relegere*, "from *legere* ('harvest, gather'),'' or *religare*, "from *ligare* ('to tie, to bind')," the meaning of *religio* has been hotly contested and has given rise to two camps ("Faith" 71). To put a complicated disagreement in simple terms, Cicero's texts support an understanding of *religio* as *relegere*: "bringing together in order to return and begin again; whence religio, scrupulous attention, respect, patience, even modesty, shame or piety"; whereas the writings of Lactantius and Tertullian find favor with *religio* as *religare*, an etymological origin Émile Benveniste attributes to Christian invention: "linking religion to the *link*, precisely, to obligation, ligament, and hence to duty, to debt, etc., between men or between man and God" ("Faith" 73–74; translation modified).[3] Derrida finds an important link between these seemingly disparate understandings of *religio*: "In both cases (*re-legere* or *re-ligare*), what is at issue is indeed a persistent bond that bonds itself first and foremost to itself. What is at issue is indeed a reunion [*rassemblement*], a re-assembling, a re-collecting. A resistance or a reaction to dis-junction" ("Faith" 74). Derrida focuses on Benveniste's proposed translation, "*recollecter*," to point to other possibilities of interpretation: "'Benveniste [. . .] glosses it thus: 'return for a new choice, return to revise a previous operation,' whence the sense of 'scruple,' but also of choice, of reading and of election, of intelligence, since there can be no selectivity without the bonds of collectivity and recollection" (74). This conception of *religio* as "recollecting" from the past, as choosing and selecting in connection with community and memory, is appropriate to describe the writing of Assia Djebar.

Djebar's treatment of religion serves to loosen it from strict interpretations that don't allow room for deviation from accepted patterns of behavior. She is respectful toward the Islam of her ancestors, but she is not blindly subservient to it; her texts are critical in their reaction to scriptural variations that form the basis for law and customs. In many cases, she exhibits a certain skepticism toward established practice and returns to the sources of tradition to discern a truth that comes from careful study, rather than blanket acceptance of imposed rules. But this stance does not prevent Djebar from identifying with her background, and the physical movement in her personal itinerary away from her native country and mother tongue to Western universities and publishing houses does not mark a clean break with her past. While her ties to her religious tradition may be slackened, they are not cut completely, and the act of "recollecting" religion in written work is ultimately one of preservation. Djebar remains attached to what is good in her religious upbringing, while leaving behind the components she considers objectionable. In this way, instead of opting to "lose" her religion in the sense of the idiomatic expression, she sets out to *choose* her religion, making informed decisions that involve eliminating negative (r)evolutions and preserving what is best about the belief system. This process involves selectivity, for Djebar is in essence engaged in *selecting* religion in her writing. If religion can be seen in a sense as an explanation of the world, or as a sort of "rulebook" for living, Djebar rewrites the book "*à la carte,*" all while filling in some of the obvious gaps in the official tome. Her examination of the original, originary texts of Islam allows her to determine what has been distorted in religious practice and to correct some harmful misreadings. In *Loin de Médine,* she provides a much-needed new, updated version of the earlier works, bringing them into their time, so to speak. It is important that this daring treatment of religion takes place in French, her language of writing.

Many autobiographical writings follow the model of what we could call the "conversion narrative," the prime example of which can be found in the *Confessions* of Saint Augustine. In this as in many texts that follow, there is a clear "before" and "after" into which the life story can be divided. In the case of Assia Djebar, the transformation is not religious, as it was for her predecessor; her conversion arguably takes place on a *linguistic* level. As a young girl, she "converts" to French, but the acquisition of this tongue is not a sudden occurrence that can be attributed to a single date. Her exposure to French begins early in her experience, and the language slowly, gradually gains place within her. The fact that her childhood years in French school overlapped with her training in Arabic at the *école coranique* serve to further blur her "coming to French" so that in her personal history there is no clear break, no significant rupture that can be seen to separate the "before" from the "after." As Djebar often affirms, *L'Amour, la fantasia* is a story of language as much as it is a story of her life. The two are so tightly intertwined as to be inextricable; the "before" and the "after" are mixed. Her experience therefore does not measure up to the linear, chronological accounts of lives found in canonical texts of the autobiographical genre, it does not fall in step with those who have gone before her. She is exposed to French irregularly, both in school and outside of it since her father is a teacher of the language and her mother learns to communicate in the foreign tongue as well. Her interaction with the French language is marked by temporal disruption, indeed by disjunction, as in the phrase that resounds throughout *Spectres de Marx* by Jacques Derrida: "this time is out of joint."[4]

In a speech delivered during a colloquium on "Francophone Voices," Djebar expressed a certain reticence to embrace what she called "this ambiguous notion of *francophonie*." To explain this hesitation, she took a moment to address her complex constitution, reflecting on the multiple factors contributing to her personal idiosyncratic makeup. These reflections were careful to address her relation to her native country, particularly with respect to religion. As the following quotation reveals, Djebar considers herself to be a Muslim with respect to *culture* much more than with respect to *faith* or *practice*: "I am [. . .] of Algerian [. . .] or even Muslim sensibility when Islam is lived more as a culture than as a faith or a practice" (*Ces voix* 26).[5] The distinction Djebar establishes between culture and belief is crucial to understanding her approach to Islam in her texts. This religion is often relayed as a cultural tradition, but not always. Occasional moments of "slippage" reveal some regret with respect to this faith. Various narrative voices lament the unrealized possibilities, the overlooked potential of a religion that has in some ways been misconstrued, miscommunicated, and, importantly, mistranslated. Just as she translates her *self* into textual form in her autobiographical works, so she translates her religious heritage into a different language. These intricate literary translations are not the equivalent of sociological reports on the "other" culture that her Algerian homeland represents for many "Western" Francophone readers. Rather, they are artistic compositions that render the tensions and dissensions of a woman whose "Muslim sensibility" continually comes into contact with her activities as an intellectual and a critic in the "Francophone" arena. Holding these forces at bay is a complex task that requires Djebar to find a personal definition of her relationship to her religion. If the title of a recent article by Dominique Vidal is correct, if France is indeed a country made up of "*sans-religion*," then it is especially pertinent that those living on French soil should put into question the religion of their ancestors. In spite of the "secular" nature of contemporary France, Jocelyne Cesari maintains that Muslim immigrants and their offspring generally refuse to release their ties to Islam, even if they no longer observe every religious interdict: "Muslims who deny Islam? No, that would be to deny their history, their identity. Atheists? Even fewer. Everything is a question of criteria: one is born a Muslim and one remains a Muslim, even if one eats pork and doesn't respect the five pillars" (*Le Monde diplomatique*). The adjective "*musulman*" is, in the view of this academic, "*polysémique*."[6] In Djebar's treatment of Islam and her own relation to this belief system, the multiple meanings of "Muslim" faith and practice are revealed. She makes it clear by her own example that many aspects contribute to what she calls her "*sensibilité musulmane*," that this sensitivity is complicated and multiple, indeed "polysemic," and that it is often concentrated on a cultural, rather than religious level.[7] According to Cesari, author of *Musulmans et républicains*, it is not uncommon for young Maghrebians in France to identify more closely with the cultural side of Islam at the expense of strict religious observance. Djebar is therefore not alone in this regard.

What is singular about Djebar's work is her subtle portrayal of Islam in various texts and in different forms. She does not present the strand of faith as it is practiced in her native Algeria as universal; rather, she underscores the lack of uniformity among Muslims in other Arab countries, and throughout the world.[8] In recent publications, she demonstrates a special sensitivity to other religions as well. Since Djebar is quick to notice the interpenetration of various faiths and practices, the interaction of the three Abrahamic faiths—Islam, Christianity, and Judaism—both in the Maghreb and in Europe occupy a central role in works from *Les Nuits de Strasbourg* to *La femme sans sépulture*. No religion exists in a vacuum, as Djebar's writings demonstrate, and her careful attention to contextualizing faith and practice with respect to geographical location and time period is important to her literary project.[9] Her reliability as a historian whose writing practice is grounded in research is indispensable to the credibility of what Calle-Gruber refers to as a "*réinterprétation critique*" of the "*Livre*" in works like *Loin de Médine*. Indeed, "critically reinterpreting" canonical texts is precisely appropriate to describe Djebar's unique method of re-reading and re-writing cultural and literary tradition.[10] This chapter aims to decipher how this "reinterpretation" of the religion of her homeland at once respects and disrupts that religion, ultimately "loosing" it from rigid readings that have potentially harmful results. When religious tradition is explored as cultural heritage, it is much easier for the writer to escape the trap of fanaticism, a very real threat in Algeria in recent years.

Loin de Médine: "Reste la musique"

When she set out to write *Loin de Médine: Filles d'Ismaël*, Assia Djebar was an impassioned woman on a mission. Her timely goal was to unearth the roots of a religion that was posing a particular threat in the Algerian capital in October of 1988, as she explains: "Without taking myself for Cassandra, it was easy to predict that, in the following year, the fundamentalists would come back to the center of the political sphere [. . .] resolved to impose their caricatured vision of an Islam without origins" ("Idiome de l'exil" 16).[11] The pressing nature of the present situation provoked the historian to plunge into the past to discover the crucial early period of Islam at a moment when extremists were about to wreak havoc in Algeria: "I returned to Paris and, in order to keep from breaking down, I decided to confront the origins of Islam, armed only with my experience as an historian. [. . .] Suddenly, I began to live in Medina in 632 A.D." (16).[12]

In *Simorgh*, Algerian poet Mohammed Dib points to the need for just such a return to the beginnings of the religion's history: "Islamic States that officially proclaim themselves as such are the emanation of a narrow and regressive dream: that of the return of a poorly known History that never took place nor was written, even during the first centuries of Islam" (98). Dib's assertion that the early period of Islamic history is not widely known or understood, even among practicing Muslims, underscores the importance of Djebar's project. In contrast to the political concerns and power issues of Islamic States, her look at early Islam is a *disinterested* one: she takes great interest in the subject matter *for its own interest*, not for some personal gain. Her work is pertinent to the present, and certainly filled with emotion, but it is ultimately intended to be an *intellectual* endeavor, as the writer explains: "The multicolored richness of an original text, its rhythm, its nuances, and its ambiguities, its very sheen [*patine*], in a word its poetry, the only true reflection of a period, spurred my will to *Itjihad*" (*Loin* 8). In a footnote, Djebar provides the following definition of the word she has placed in italics in the text: "*Itjihad*: intellectual effort for the search of truth, deriving from djihad, interior struggle recommended to every believer." The search for truth in this text takes place therefore in a rational, logical manner, but this intellectual "distance" does not preclude the heart, as the etymology of *Itjihad* demonstrates. The intellectual effort to reach the truth stems from an intimate "battle" that is the lot of every believer.

The exploration of Islam's roots in *Loin de Médine* is not simply the work of a curious historian, despite Djebar's training in this academic field. When she embarks on a quest for the origins of this faith, Djebar is equally engaged in a personal pursuit of her religious heritage. The texts she relies on to complete her project were composed well over a thousand years ago in Arabic, and deciphering their meaning requires an intense translation on a number of levels: cultural, temporal, and linguistic. Djebar's close reading of the

Qur'an, the sacred book of Islam, is complemented by and largely dependent on detailed examination of works by chroniclers who were present at the emergence of the Muslim faith. And she could not have completed this difficult project alone, as this word of acknowledgement reveals: "I insist on thanking the Arab poet Nourredine El Ansari who helped me in my confrontation with the language of the chronicles" (*Loin* 8). Djebar's immersion in these texts at the time of her study was complete: "I plunged into the deciphering, word after word, chapter after chapter, of the Arab chroniclers Ibn Saâd and Tabari. I needed to hear thus in my mother tongue, in its timbre, its rhythm, and its sobriety, in its holes [*trous*] as well." ("Idiome" 16). The noun "*trous*" in the plural returns frequently in Djebar's comments on her research into this period of history, particularly with respect to women. In her view, such gaps in the narrative are significant, and seldom accidental, as communicated in this provocative footnote from *Loin de Médine*: "For [in the case of] these 'holes' in the Persian version with respect to Abou Bekr's wife Esma (like those regarding other women), there is reason to ask oneself if they are there by accident" (216). Locating—and filling—what Djebar calls the "holes," the omissions or the silences, in these original texts is what leads to the rich resulting composition in French.

The translation she effects in her written work in general, and in *Loin de Médine* in particular, is dependent on an *aural* comprehension Djebar draws from the printed page. In deciphering the chroniclers' accounts before her, she has ready recourse to the oral aspect of her education in Qur'anic school during her early childhood. As she demonstrates in her autobiographical writings, learning to read and write in the language of the Qur'an meant training her mouth and *ear* as well: "Stumbling on, swaying from side to side, care taken to observe the different tonic accents, to differentiate between long and short vowels, attentive to the rhythm of the chant; muscles of the larynx as well as the torso moving in harmony" (*Fantasia* 184). In her personal religious experience, she insists that *sound* was the crucial element, wielding much greater power to produce an effect—or an affect—than sight: "A young girl's introduction to religious observance itself can only be through sound, never through sight: no office in which the disposition of people, the code prescribed for costume and posture, the ritual hierarchy would strike the sensibility of the female child" (169). Rituals involving clothing and position leave her indifferent as a child. In her early years, real religious emotion is evoked otherwise, entering into the body and mind through a different channel, through another canal, through an *opening* that is much more sensitive in Djebar's anatomy.

In *L'Amour, la fantasia*, the young girl in the autobiographical segment titled "Troisième Mouvement: La complainte d'Abraham" is initially moved
by religion due to a special radio program in honor of a particular date: "My
first stirrings of religious feeling go back much further: in the village, for
three or four years running, the day of the 'feast of the sheep' was heralded
by 'The Ballad of Abraham'" (*Fantasia* 170). On the chilly winter mornings
in the time of this yearly commemoration, the girl's mother regularly turns
on a special piece: "The programme in Arabic invariably involved the same
record in honour of the holiday: a performance by a celebrated tenor which
included a dozen or so verses telling the story of Abraham and his son" (170).
It is the specificity of this *musical* medium of communication that elicits the
girl's response. In her experience, *song* transmits the message of the celebration much more effectively than other forms of religious instruction, to the
point that Djebar concludes that this regular listening exercise is solely responsible for creating within her a "sensitivity" (tied) to her faith: "It was listening to this ballad every year throughout my childhood that formed, I
think, my feeling for Islam [*une sensibilité islamique*]" (170). The annual
rhythm of this special occasion of remembrance becomes ingrained in the
young protagonist, entering into her body and mind for good.

It is undeniable that the import of the song, that the story it imparts plays
a key role in capturing the young girl's attention to such an extent. This is
one of the most gripping tales of all time: "I hung on the opening words of
the Biblical drama but I do not know why the song evoked such a passionate
response in me: the progress of the story to its miraculous ending, each character whose words brought them so vividly to life, the burden and the horror
of Abraham's fate which weighed so heavily on him as he was constrained to
conceal his anguish" (*Fantasia* 171). But the manner in which the story it
told is of equal, if not greater, importance in touching the girl's emotional
(and physical) core: "It was as much the texture itself of the song—the var-
iegated pattern of the phraseology—as the melancholy of the singer's voice
(making me curl up more tightly under the sheets) which cast such a spell
over me: the unfamiliar terms, the reticence of the Arabic dialect" (171).[13]
This early experience with music and its capacity to create deep emotion left
an indelible mark on Djebar as a writer. What remains in her memory, what
persists despite the passing of the years, is the music. The songs and their
messages are firmly embedded in her mind: "There remains music" (169).

In *Loin de Médine*, Djebar employs her finely tuned ear to the task of re-
reading and re-writing the stories from the beginning of Islam. Listening to
the original tongue in the language of composition is the key to finding the

voices that have been erased from the official soundtrack: "Listen to the sound, the rhythm, [. . .] then retrieve, thanks to the 'holes' in the first narrative (difficulties emerge because of both the language and the occasional ambiguity of the original text), retrieve therefore this feminine memory [. . .] to give life thus . . . in French!" (*Ces voix* 53). It is her attention to the uncertain aspects of the writings, it is her desire to delve into the difficult ambiguities of the works under study, that enable Djebar to do more than simply *locate* the missing voices. Thanks to this painstaking grappling with the absences in the text, she *gives life* to these voices in literary form.

Current affairs in her native country stand out in stark contrast to Djebar's lifegiving project; a considerable number of Algerian intellectuals have perished at the hand of assassins. According to Djebar's account, these murderers move to abolish every possible deviation from established Islamic thought: "They are Algerian murderers, instrumentalized by so-called fundamentalist propaganda, in the name of a political Islam that enabled a new religious Inquisition, worthy of the one Catholic Europe experienced at the end of the Middle Ages. They are the murderers of writers and journalists who said in their own way, in my country: 'Everything must go!' ['*Tout doit disparaître!*']" (*Ces voix* 244). When Djebar likens the actions of contemporary Islamic fundamentalists in Algeria to the persecutory measures of Catholics in medieval Europe, she brings together more than two different time periods. She effectively juxtaposes two different religions and demonstrates that one is not inherently more violent than the other.[14] Instead, religion in all forms is prone to violent misunderstanding when the *letter* is emphasized at the expense of the *spirit*. Respecting the holy text of the Qur'an does not mean exacting a strictly *literal* interpretation of its contents, but instead remaining faithful to its message.

The dangers of taking the written word out of context are clear in Djebar's native country. Having lost a number of close friends and acquaintances to various "*fous de Dieu*" opposed to individual freedom of thought and expression, Djebar is fully aware that misinterpretation of the Qur'an and Islamic tradition can lead to unthinkable inflexibility and murderous actions.[15] In light of this situation, the French language loses its problematic status as the idiom of the colonizer[16] and takes on a liberating potential as a "neutral" lens through which to re-view the tenets of Muslim faith and practice. Just as the French language has provided Djebar with freedom of movement in her personal life, so Djebar finds freedom from the religious weight of the language of the holy text and its history ("Arabic remains thus the language of liturgy, of the Qur'an") in French, a language situated "*hors de la componction religieuse*": "[T]hese women of History inscribed themselves, body and voice, in my text, precisely because the neutral language—outside Islam for the time being—gave them its dynamism, its freedom, the fulcrum of the fictional wheel turning incessantly within me" (*Ces voix* 52).

The differences between the two languages Djebar studied in her early life—at the Qur'anic and French schools she attended prior to the age of ten—play themselves out in corporal and spatial terms. According to her autobiographical account, studying the written Arabic of the Qur'an led to *enclosure* whereas studying French led to *exposure*: "And when I sit curled up like this to study my native language it is as though my body reproduces the architecture of my native city: the medinas with their tortuous alleyways closed off to the outside world. [. . .] When I write and read the foreign language, my body travels far in subversive space" (*Fantasia* 184). This interpretation of her personal linguistic situation transfers easily to the situation of her historical study of women in Islam. Restoring the lost stories of these forgotten women is only possible in the language of movement, travel, of open (and subversive) space. Djebar's own analysis reveals that the "exterritoriality" of this "neutral" linguistic space is crucial to her project of re-reading and re-writing the sacred moments of early Islam. This second tongue, free from prejudice and pre-fabricated formulas that close themselves off to multiple interpretations, brought Djebar to the point of literary creation. Translating these early moments of Muslim history into French quite naturally entailed bringing back to life, indeed *resuscitating*,[17] the women whose absence in the official versions is striking. The "territory" of the French language was thereby essential to this undertaking: "I gave myself over to this reconstruction, this reanimation with my enlivened imagination, an imagination rooted indeed, but certainly not entrapped" (*Ces voix* 53). The roots are still there, but they prove to be malleable. In her comments on the liberating potential of the French language in rewriting Islamic history, Djebar embraces the incessant turning of what she calls the "fictional wheel" within her.

It would be difficult to overestimate the importance of fiction in her work, as this mode of writing allows for imagination and creativity in literary production. The opening paragraphs of the *avant-propos* of *Loin de Médine* explicitly treat of the genre chosen for this collection of stories: "I called this set of narratives, scenes, and visions at times a "novel," nourished by the reading of several historians from the first two or three centuries of Islam (Ibn Hacham, Ibn Saad, Tabari)" (7). The glaring absence of women in the chronicles of this critical period of a burgeoning new faith propelled Djebar to restore them to their rightful place in history, and to adopt a specific literary form to do so. As the first-person narrative voice explains, fiction is essential to collective memory: "fiction, filling in the gaps of collective memory, proved necessary to the putting into place [*mise en espace*] that I attempted, in order to reestablish the length of the days I wanted to inhabit" (7). Putting women back where they belong, geographically and temporally, is an undertaking that calls for fiction.

The Theatre of Islam

Djebar goes on in the *avant-propos* to address the "theatrical" aspects of this staging of early Muslim history: "Several voices of *rawiyates* interrupt this reconstruction, weaving the behind-the-scenes of this first Islamic theatre, as if contemporaries—anonymous or known—were observing the wings in such a way that, as soon as Muhammad disappeared, the stagings of power seek, confuse, and replace each other" (*Loin* 8). The seizing of power that characterized early Islam has not ceased with the passing of time, as the very urgency of this writing makes clear. But referring to this important period of religious history as a "theatre" could be seen as heretical, since such an evocation appears to underscore the "staged" aspects of the events and the "created" traits of the early characters whose "coming to life" before the spectators is dependent on a script. Djebar is indeed treading on sacred territory when she uses the theatrical metaphor for the events of early Islam, but she does so with the purpose of highlighting the selective nature of any account of past events; this reference to the theatre demonstrates her own role as a "playwright" revisiting the happenings of history and seeking to bring them new life in the form of art. The distance—temporal and emotional—separating her from the events she depicts is underscored through her reference to the theatre. Making mention of the theatre is crucial, for it restores to Islam something that the religion has been missing. As she claims in *Ces voix qui m'assiègent*, Islam has denied itself the theatre, and Djebar's recent creative production has sought to restore to this religion this right to representation.[18]

Loin de Médine is not the only work in which the narrator boldly embraces the power of fiction to restore the past. Assia Djebar's most recent novel, *La femme sans sépulture*, boasts at once of faithfulness to historical sources *and* of liberties taken in the written recomposition of history. A key passage in the *avertissement* highlights this apparent dichotomy:

> In this novel, all the facts and details of the life and death of Zoulikha—heroine from my childhood town during the War of Independence in Algeria—are related with attention to historical faithfulness or, I would say, according to a documentary approach. Nonetheless, certain characters that frequent the heroine, particularly those presented as family members, are treated here with the imagi-

nation and variations that fiction permits. I dipped limitlessly into my artistic freedom, precisely so that the truth of Zoulikha would be illuminated further, at the very center of a large feminine fresco, following the model of the ancient mosaics of Caesarea in Mauritania (Cherchell).

The first-person voice hereby warns the reader of the "artistic freedom" present in this historical reconstruction that upholds the noble purpose of shedding greater light on the *truth* of the novel's heroine. The fidelity of the account, in this view, should not be compromised by the accompanying bits of fiction. To the contrary, it is enhanced by the workings of imagination, by the *variations* in this text. The interplay of these various strands of possibility ultimately render a greater truth than that of a simple historical report, of a documentary. The historical report serves as a starting point but its truth must be given substantial depth and breadth, brighter color, in order to better perceive the pieces that combine to make up a "large" truth, like that of the "feminine fresco," of the mosaic in her ancient native town.

Seeking truth in variation is a tradition in Djebar's family. She is not the first to discover the capacity of variants to provide a well-rounded version of monumental events. In her childhood, according to an autobiographical moment recalled in *L'Amour, la fantasia*, Djebar is moved by the multiple versions her aunt evoked of the life of the figure who is undoubtedly the foremost pillar of Muslim faith: "[A]n aunt used to recount the life of the Prophet, with many variations [. . .] inspired the same emotion in me" (*Fantasia* 171). This early exposure to a number of possible readings of a single life story opened Djebar's eyes to the multiple components of biography, as well as to the multifaceted nature of reading and writing. When she set out in *Loin de Médine* to re-read and re-write her own cultural and literary tradition, anchored in the religion of Islam, she drew from this familial practice of exploring possibilities and allowed her imagination to go full throttle. Refusing to rein in speculations and suppositions, she instead gave them sovereign status, allowing them to reign in the literary work of fiction. Djebar thus does not aim for a narrow truth arising from a strict interpretation of historical religious sources, but instead gives place to a broad understanding of possible variations on a theme.

Contrapuntal Reading and Writing

The musical metaphor for Djebar's writing can be carried further with the help of a concept elaborated by Edward Said in *Culture and Imperialism*: contrapuntal reading. The reading Djebar enacts through a critical lens in *Loin de Médine* is an effective example of Said's term: "[C]ontrapuntal reading must take account of both processes, that of imperialism and that of resistance to it, which can be done by extending our reading of the texts to include what was forcibly excluded" (66–67). When Djebar pays particular attention to the silences, to the omissions in the different accounts under study, she is engaging with the texts in ways that echo Said's definition: "In reading a text, one must open it out both to what went into it and what its author excluded. Each cultural work is a vision of a moment, and we must juxtapose that vision with the various revisions it later provoked" (67). The awareness of the specific moment of textual composition, as well as the time periods of post-dated revisions, is crucial in Said's analysis. Contextualizing the written work is essential to understanding the explicit and implicit forces that shape it.

As we have already seen, Assia Djebar is attuned to historical time, making mention of the precise dates of occurrences throughout *Loin de Médine*, not only according to the Muslim calendar of the official records, but also "in translation," according to the Roman calendar familiar to the French-speaking reader. These detailed references to dates and accurate depictions of the times are in line with the work of a trained historian, and it is no accident that Djebar places this quotation by famed nineteenth-century historian Michelet as an epigraph at the beginning of the book: "There was therefore a strange dialogue between him and me, between me, his resuscitator, and the old time put back on its feet" (9). By placing her unique voice in the mix, Djebar shows that she is not content to engage in a contrapuntal reading without transforming that reading into a *writing*. Bringing time back to life, placing it back on its feet, requires a musical exchange that interweaves a number of voices in a polyphonous chorus.

Said explains the intricate workings of the sort of reading (and writing) Djebar undertakes in her texts. He makes a distinction between a univocal and a contrapuntal reading; the latter takes into account the multiple influences on any single written work and the many possible directions the themes can take:

> As we look back at the cultural archive, we begin to reread it not univocally but contrapuntally, with a simultaneous awareness both of the metropolitan history that is narrated and of those other histories against which (and together with which) the dominating discourse acts. In the counterpoint of Western classical music, various themes play off one another, with only a provisional privilege being given to any particular one; yet in the resulting polyphony there is concert and order, an organized interplay that derives from

the themes, not from a rigorous melodic or formal principle outside the work. (*Culture* 51)

It is important to note the context in which Said defines "contrapuntal reading," for he is writing specifically to the situation of former colonies that, under British and French rule, saw the emergence of fiction with layers of meaning that often escape a "univocal," literal reading. While the period of early Islamic history explored in *Loin de Médine* predates the colonizing activities of the eighteenth and nineteenth centuries, Djebar's text can nonetheless be viewed as a contrapuntal reading practice on several levels. The most important of these would be metaphorical: religion can be seen as a dominating force that has justified a number of invasions and violent wars on North African soil not just in the distant past, but in recent memory as well. The "civilizing mission" of the French colonizers was not devoid of religious fervor; many brought their Catholic beliefs and customs with them in their conquest of this foreign land. But Djebar's "contrapuntal reading" does not simply take place on a "colonizer" versus "colonized" battlefield (or "Western" versus "indigenous," by extension). Her re-reading and re-writing of the early historical texts places at a counterpoint the written accounts of male historians and the oral versions of women. In contrast to men who can read and write, in contrast to Djebar herself whose exceptional personal history has given her these skills as well, these women hold memories in their heads and they share them aloud. They are the ones who, from generation to generation, have preserved families from forgetfulness, and kept tradition intact throughout the centuries. This is the musical combination Djebar restores to writing, bridging the seemingly insurmountable gap between the written and the remembered, between textual history and established practice. Reinterpreting the past means finding the harmony among these different strands that make up tradition.

De la Combattante à la Fugueuse: Fight or Flight

It is Assia Djebar herself who proposes the juxtaposition of the two women I examine in this section, selected from among the dozens who figure in *Loin de Médine*. At the Maison des Ecrivains in Paris in April 1991, the writer singled out two characters as especially worthy of her attention that evening: "the crossing of she who flees [*la Fugueuse*] and she who fights [*la Combattante*], two women who run in the desert, among the three dozen women resuscitated in this Islamic dawn" (*Ces voix* 53). If Djebar discerns the act of running as a point in common that warrants bringing together these two individuals, the focus on this particular activity is not an accident. During a colloquium held five years later, Djebar drew a comparison between running and writing when describing her work: "To write or run? To write in order to run; to remember, and—in spite of onself—not the past, but pre-memory, from before the first dawn, before the night of nights, before" (*Ces voix* 138). Writing is not unlike running, as Djebar intimates in these provocative statements. These endeavors both involve the body, both engage the breath, they require a unique training and the establishment of a certain rhythm in order to reach the finish line. But as the stories of the "Combattante" and the "Fugueuse" demonstrate, very *different* styles of running can prove equally effective. A close look at their depictions will show how the (foot)paths available to women in Islam may head in different directions, and how effective models for women in Islam are not identical.

The chapter devoted to the *Combattante* starts with a bang, thrusting the reader into the thick of the action immediately following the defeat of Mecca at the hands of the Muslim army of the Prophet Muhammad. The title character is active from the outset: "She runs, she runs, Oum Hakim" (133). This young woman is barely eighteen, but she is already married and a mother of two, and her movement is inspired with a purpose. Having obtained pardon from Muhammad himself on behalf of her warrior husband Ikrima, she aims to catch her beloved before he departs for the West. The distance is long, but her courage is great: "She quickly makes a few calculations; she knows the distance to the water's edge. Maybe, if her breath doesn't fail her" (136). The young wife is determined not to slacken her pace for anything: "hardened features, but an even pace, almost mechanical. With the tenacious rhythm of a distance runner" (137). Her mechanical efforts as a distance runner are not in vain, for she reaches her husband at last and he listens attentively to her account. They return together on horseback that very morning, and in a matter of hours Ikrima fulfills the condition of his pardon: he converts to Islam.

While her husband becomes a fervent believer in the religion that has recently dominated Mecca, Oum Hakim does not. For her, what ultimately matters is the ability to live together, in peace. The goal of her footrace was not to see her husband find new faith, but instead to preserve their relationship and their home, as her words reveal on the occasion of their reunion: "they are going to come back together; together they will regain Mecca; Muslim or not Muslim, no matter, it's their city!" (139). While peace is important in her private life, Oum Hakim does not shy away from war, as her nickname indicates. Along with other women from her town, she takes to the battlefield once again, as she did in the past. In her view, very little has changed with respect to the nature of these struggles, even if they are not carried out in the same name.[19] Whether for or against Islam, the *Combattante* is fighting for the same thing in the end: her family and fellow inhabitants of Mecca. She is not unusual in her willingness to take up arms; other women join her in assuming multiple roles in this early history. While it may seem at first glance to be contradictory, their occupations as wife and mother contribute to—rather than detract from—their activity as fighters: "wives, mistresses of the home, but also fighters" (142). Djebar readily refers to the legendary Amazon women in describing the courage and resourcefulness of these women warriors who fight alongside their husbands just as they have in the past, but this time for a different religion.

Oum Hakim's fervor as a warrior is captivating because of her ambiguous relationship to Islam. She fights in the name of this religion, but seems disinclined to respect its tenets. Indeed, she vocally rejects ideas with which she disagrees. In response to a denigrating comment on the "bad life" of prostitutes, Oum Hakim lashes out, insisting that women do what they can to make a living and that perhaps prostitution is preferable to submission to a bad husband (142). It becomes clear through such comments that the combat of this woman warrior extends far beyond the battlefield. If she takes up arms to fight on the side of Islam for the greater good of her people, this does not stop her from resisting certain aspects of Islam. It is in this sense that Oum Hakim falls into the category of *"insoumises"* found in the section title (*"Soumises, insoumises"*); she fits the definition of women who refuse to submit totally and unquestioningly to every imposed rule. Her earlier yielding to the need to convert in order to save her husband does not lessen the impact of her later stance against certain injustices; the combatant knows how to pick her battles.

The emphasis on the "submissive" character of those who adhere to the Muslim faith is crucial at this point in the narrative of early Islam. In a reflection on the meaning of "Islam," Assia Djebar comes back to this translation, underscoring the difficulty of rendering this word in French, and the room for error inherent to such movement between tongues:

> "Islam," they say, is translated—or betrayed—as submission. While we wait for an uncertain rebirth, maybe it is necessary to remind ourselves that in the time when all languages were flourishing, Greek, Persian, Berber, Coptic, and others became mixed in the translation pot, leading to betrayals both written and oral. (*Ces voix* 185)

In this passage, Djebar plays on the well-known Italian adage *"traduttore, traditore"* in evoking the possible betrayal of the original meanings of words and

concepts in Islam at the time of its blossoming. The multiple languages influencing the translations of the written and oral accounts necessarily sully
the "purity" of the religion in the years following its inception: "This *métissage* of blood and languages, of women taken and acquired 'foreign' tongues,
forms the ornamentation for the very clothing of Tradition" (185). Unveiling in this way the mixing of peoples and tongues debunks the myth of a
"pure" tradition and is thus a potentially subversive act. It is an especially
risky move in the context of a religion that so revered the status of the
Qur'an in the original Arabic that any translation was forbidden for centuries
following the book's composition.[20] But this gesture of highlighting the possibility that Islam may not mean precisely (and uniquely) "*soumission*" is also
important because it may open up other approaches to religious behaving
and belonging.

In *Loin de Médine*, the *Combattante* is not altogether opposed to praying. If
she refuses to pray in the traditional sense of the word, this does not preclude
prayer in another sense, as this brief speech shows: "For the moment, I myself will be the combatant for Islam! On the roads of Syria and then Iraq, she
imagined finding in this fashion her own way of praying, of praying ardently:
in the midst of armies and their tumult, ready to throw herself in at any time,
on horseback and with a saber in hand, to die!" (154). This woman of action
proposes an ardent prayer and demonstrates a willingness to sacrifice herself
for the cause. Such complete devotion in combat seems contradictory to her
steadfast refusal to adhere to the tenets of Islam in her private life. It may be
that the *Combattante* possesses a personality that prohibits her from displays
of religious commitment in more accepted manners. The repetition in several passages of the verb "*pouvoir*" to refer to religious devotion may indicate
that some individuals are simply incapable of certain manifestations of faith:
"Yes, in Ikrima's view, she had been a loving wife who could not follow him
in his new faith" (154). This inability to follow doesn't make this devoted
wife any less of a warrior for Islam, as her exploits on the battlefield attest.
Praying in her fashion, this historical figure enacts a different interpretation
of the concept of prayer, demonstrating that narrow rules of appropriate behavior cannot encompass an entire population.

Throughout *Loin de Medine*, we find a contemplation of Islam in its early
stages with the implied accompanying question of how to appropriately "run"
for God. The question is complicated, as numerous examples reveal.[21] The
Fugueuse provides a useful counterpoint to the figure of the *Combattante* because the former runs without hesitation toward the Islamic faith. The young
Oum Keltoum converted to Islam over a period of three years, thanks to an

elderly, freed slave who instructed her in the ways of the Prophet. In order to practice her newfound faith, the ten-year-old child fled her home and family in Medina for the community of believers in Mecca. When she explained to Muhammad and his followers that she was a Muslim who desired to live among Muslims, the reaction was positive, but the Prophet had signed a contract promising the return of any persons belonging to the side of the enemy. To resolve the dilemma, he called Oum Keltoum before him to express herself. Despite her young age, Oum Keltoum was aware of her lot in life and knew precisely how to plead her case convincingly: "Oh Messenger of God, I am only a woman! For you know to what extent the situation of women is still that of the weakest!" (167). The feminist argument was certainly not enough in itself, but in its connection with faith, it proved groundbreaking. Muhammad's response proved that contracts are not inflexible, and that a higher law takes precedence over human agreements: Oum Keltoum was welcomed into the Muslim community. As the narrative voice sums it up, this was the day when God revealed that women should be protected within the Muslim faith.[22]

The exception made for Oum Keltoum, "the first woman Migrant [*la première Migrante*]" (167), recalls an even more eventful overturning of the law recounted earlier in *Loin de Médine*. On this memorable occasion, the Prophet's son-in-law Ali expressed a desire to take a second wife. When Muhammad discovered his daughter Fatima's great chagrin at this news, he found himself at an impasse with a law that transcends that of a simple contract between men: "Isn't that Islamic law: multiple women, fruitful descendence for each 'leader' of the community?" (72). Ali certainly has the right to take another woman into his family, and the narrative voice speculates as to the misgivings Fatima must feel as she protests the "*fatalité*" of this lawful action. Despite the confirmation in the Qur'an of a man's right to take up to four wives as long as he can care for them equally, Fatima holds firm in her refusal. And her father upholds her in this decision. His reasons for denying this marriage are valid, for the proposed second wife happens to be the daughter of his enemy, and therefore the enemy of God (74). But other words from the Prophet's mouth reveal that this decision is more about familial feelings and personal attachment than questions of religion or even politics: "For my daughter is part of myself. What hurts her hurts me! What upsets her upsets me!" (73). This touching demonstration of filial love marks a scene of importance for women in Islam, for Fatima's voice was heard and her wishes were respected, indicating that this belief system has a place reserved for women's expression.

"Putting Down a Revolution":
Disinherited Women in Islam

Djebar is careful to underscore the advances of early Islam in creating rights for women. This is evident in the Prophet's intervention on his daughter's behalf on the question of marriage, as we have just seen. But Djebar's most insistent highlighting of Muhammad's measures on behalf of women is to be found on another question: the contentious issue of inheritance.

The chronology of *Loin de Médine* is complicated, for the collection of stories recounting early Islam do not follow a linear pattern. The prologue announces the unfortunate happening around which the book turns: the death of the Prophet. But the very uncertainty of this monumental occurrence is called into question from the outset: "He is dead. He is not dead" (11). Events preceding and following the moment of Muhammad's passing are not arranged in any clear order, and the narrative voices frequently flash back to actions and words that occur prior to the "present" of the story. It is in just such a textual moment that the reader discovers the important advances the Prophet brought about before his death. According to the official record, Muhammad's daughter pronounced this laconic phrase after she was denied her right of inheritance: "'No,' Fatima accuses, 'you dare to refuse my right as a daughter!'" (79).

The narrative voice embellishes and explains this cursory comment by providing the potential words of Fatima, by giving the unspoken commentary that explains why this right is so crucial: "The revolution of Islam, for girls, for women, consisted first in letting them inherit, in giving them the portion that comes to them from their father! It was through Muhammad that this inheritance was first established in Arab history!" (79). It is ironically tragic that this recent accordance of inheritance to women was undermined so quickly: the Prophet's own daughter was stripped of this right. The revolutionary potential of Islam for women was stifled as soon as Muhammad was gone. The positive version of Islam that the venerable Prophet incarnated disappeared with his final breath, and the distorted version that emerged following his death effected an "about-face" that proved harmful to the cause of women. While the influence of the Prophet would be present for years to come, the physical absence of this holy man gave rise to an Islam unfaithful to his message.[23]

The Prophet's daughter was only the first in an endless line of disinherited women. The text reveals that brothers, uncles, and even sons stripped them of their rightful due.[24] The dominance of men in this religious tradition manifests itself early in its history, and the damage of this disregard for the revolutionary measures of Muhammad extends into the present. In her essay, "To write with no inheritance" ["*Ecrire, sans nul héritage*"], Djebar deplores the current condition of Muslim women in various parts of the world, notably Iran and her native Algeria, where they continue to be deprived of their right to inherit. This situation is in direct contradiction to Islamic law: "Girls, not heiresses. Or rather, from Islamic law in order to overturn it: disinherited" (*Ces voix* 259).[25] Just as Fatima was powerless before the forces that denied her inheritance, so Djebar finds herself incapable of changing women's status around the world. But, just as Fatima found the courage to raise her voice against injustice, so Djebar denounces disinheritance: "Out of powerlessness, I sketch in my way this great misery, source of masked violence" (261). Fatima protested her situation until the very end, pronouncing the word "*non*" with insistence against the law of Medina up to the moment of her premature passing (*Loin* 87). In an essay, Djebar questions whether this early death was not the result of a lack of writing.[26] Since Fatima didn't write, Djebar has recourse to differing versions, to "*variante[s] de la Tradition*" (86), in revisiting this valiant woman's experience. In contrast to Fatima, Djebar *does* write, and her writing aims to restore a heritage—and a history—to disinherited women.[27]

In *Loin de Médine*, Djebar simultaneously shows what Islam has done *for* women and what Islam has done *against* women. The early revolution on behalf of women's rights is unveiled, but so is its reversal. The course of the narration reveals that the real culprit for this turn of events was an inappropriate understanding of the Prophet's words. When Fatima utters the resounding "*non*," she is refuting a *literal interpretation* of her father's words: "Thus she said '*non*,' the beloved daughter. '*Non*' to the first caliph for his literal interpretation of the '*saying*' of the Prophet" (85). When the authoritative voices hold mercilessly to the phrase "*gens de la maison*" and thereby claim that the daughter, the "sole heir by blood and by the personality of the man Muhammad" is ineligible to inherit from her father (86), they are misinterpreting Muhammad's words. Fatima challenges them, asking for proof in the Book that they are right in their actions. She comes up against inflexible responses, but she refuses to give up her fight. In this, she resembles Oum Keltoum, the *fugueuse* whose flight brings her right to Islam, but whose flame for the faith is not characterized by a passive acceptance of its rules. Her knowledge of the scriptures, and her rights, are evidenced by the actions and words she adopts without hesitation.

Oum Keltoum finds refuge in Islam because she knows its regulations and her rights. When her second husband does not meet with her approval, she is aware that she can lawfully leave if he repudiates her. This is the freedom her religion accords her: "I am Muslim! If I still desire to leave, it is because I do not accept Zubeir as my husband! Islam is the opposite of constraint!" (176).[28] In this second marriage, she does not find the *"amour et ferveur"* of her first conjugal relationship (171), and she therefore finds a way out.[29] For her, Islam is indeed the opposite of constraint; it is a faith that gives her a great deal of room for movement. Djebar is always quick to speak out against constraints of all sorts, and her defense of movement is connected to freedom of thought, as she claims in an interview for a 1992 television documentary produced by Kamel Dehane: "Every thought is a thought of movement." This praise of movement and its liberating capacities elucidates the special place the *combattante* and the *fugueuse* occupy in Djebar's text. The activity of running unites their efforts, even if the running they engage in heads in slightly different directions.

The women of *Loin de Médine* provide a panoply of models for behavior, and their presence in this text transforms it into an exemplary piece of Assia Djebar's varied autobiographical practice. Not only does the writer insert herself into the work through narrative textual interventions, but she is also active through *projections*. Women such as Oum Hakim and Oum Keltoum, as well as Fatima herself and even her mother Aïcha, represent ways of exploring the self.[30] In her published lectures and essays, Djebar employs recurring words and expressions to describe the characters and actions of the women she admires and valorizes. In these forebears, Djebar finds inspiration for her own life, but she isn't content simply to *take* from them; she *endows* them with some of her own greatest qualities and abilities as well. Djebar projects herself into her characters and thereby engages in a very autobiographical writing that disperses characteristics of the self and attributes various personal traits to others. For instance, the insistence in *Loin de Médine* on Fatima's adamant pronouncement of the word "non," the repetition of this important term of resistance, finds its undeniable echo in the reflections of Djebar on her own repeated adoption of the word "non."[31]

If the *Combattante* and the *Fugueuse* are especially significant figures in Djebar's view, it is because their activity resembles her own. In *Ces voix qui m'assiègent*, Assia Djebar yields a personal reflection on the writing process. Djebar establishes a link between running and writing in connection to memory, as we have already seen. She later determines that her writing not only remembers the past, but encompasses time in other directions as well: "Thus goes the race, the time of a novel, or a narrative, or a short novella. To write or run. To write in order to run. To run and to remember. Forward, backward, what would be the difference?" (150). The complex chronology of Djebar's texts bear witness to her affinity for time travel, and to her vast historical knowledge of the past that contributes to her rendering of the present. The "time" of the written piece—the "temporality" of whatever genre of composition (novel, *récit*, or short story) she has chosen—often moves at a quick pace, in Djebar's analysis. She likens her writing to the movement of a messenger on horseback [*une écriture de coursière*]: "to write with a breath accented by bounds, lunges, pauses" (*Ces voix* 138–39). The rhythm of the text is characterized by a lively clip, often communicating an urgent message inspired by pressing current affairs.[32] The need for speed of transmission is complicated by the "doubt" expressed in Djebar's words. Perhaps her own uncertainties regarding the content of her message have an influence on the speed of the writing and the temporality of the account.[33] This passage indicates that when she relates the faith of her familial and cultural tradition, Djebar may also be communicating her innermost doubts about this religion. Neither fighting on its behalf nor fleeing it entirely, she is questioning the beliefs and practices from which her writing emerges.

In her acceptance speech on the occasion of the German literary prize awarded on 11 October 2000, Assia Djebar introduces herself to her audience at the Paulskirche of Frankfurt in the following manner:

> I would like to present myself to you simply as a woman-writer, from a country, Algeria, tumultuous and still torn apart. I was raised in the Muslim faith that has been in my family for generations, a faith that has shaped me emotionally and spiritually, but which I admit I must confront, in part because of the interdicts from which I cannot yet separate myself completely. ("Idiome" 9)

This public presentation of her person immediately addresses the complicated relationship Assia Djebar entertains with the faith of her ancestors. It is significant that she evokes this religion in the context of an award known in French translation as a "Prix de la Paix," for violence has been carried out in war-torn Algeria for centuries in the name of Islam. Djebar demonstrates that there is a struggle taking place within her, that she herself is deeply conflicted with respect to Islam, this religion she sees as filled with interdicts. Despite her steadfast resistance to these restrictions, she cannot dissociate herself completely from her background. Nor would she want to: the Muslim faith of her family is undeniably a part of her, it has shaped her emotionally and spiritually.[34] The emphasis in the above quotation on the affective and spiritual ties to Islam indicates that, despite her intellectual approach to religion in *Loin de Médine*, there is a deeply emotional quest in Djebar's work for a religious reality on a different level.

In various brief moments of re-reading and re-writing Islamic history and tradition, Djebar provides a glimpse of religion as she would like it to play itself out in individual and familial settings. Far from a battlecry, religion in these cases would constitute a personal cry for understanding and sharing between people. Instead of a pretext for violence and intolerance, religion in Djebar's view should be a place for love and acceptance. This open space is where she discerns its roots and where she draws her inspiration. If her writing can be characterized by the word "*contre*,"[35] it is writing *against* wrongdoing perpetuated in the name of any faith. For her, faith should bring people together rather than tear them apart.

The privileged figure for the unifying potential of religion is found in the monogamous heterosexual couple in Djebar's work. This twosome is featured in the pairing of the Prophet's daughter Fatima and her beloved Ali in *Loin de Médine*. In Muhammad's own words, their mutual love for the Prophet brings the husband and wife together even in times of disagreement: "they each love the Prophet, both coming together thus in this love" (69). In Djebar's reading, the religion of Islam can be seen as originating in this figure of love between two individuals:

> When the Prophet first started having visions, he returned one day from the cave so upset that, in her words, "they made him weep"; and as she spoke she almost burst into tears herself. "To comfort him, Lalla Khadija, his wife, sat him on her lap," my aunt explained, as if she had herself been present. "So," she always concluded, "the very first Muslim, perhaps even before the Prophet himself, may Allah preserve him! Was a woman. A woman was historically the first to adhere to the Islamic faith, out of conjugal love," according to my relative. (*Fantasia* 171–72)

The aunt's version of events puts a different spin on early Islamic history. The affectionate relationship between Lalla Khadidja and Muhammad gave the Prophet the comfort and strength he needed in the early stages of his faith. He was won over to Islam because of his wife's devotion, to him and to his faith.[36] This account initially shocks the young listener who is unacquainted with open manifestations of love in her native Algeria.[37] But it touches her just the same, inciting within her the same emotion she felt upon listening to the baritone voice sing of Abraham.

In *Loin de Médine*, a foreigner laments the Muslim faith to which she has converted. She regrets that this new religion is such a far cry from the environment of her homeland, where the music of children and women can be heard: "'If only Islam were enveloped in the songs of children and woman,' she sighs, 'how I would have demonstrated a throbbing faith, like an amorous passion! That would have eliminated the distance between my hometown!'" (*Loin* 194). If only Islam had been slightly different, if only it had resembled a song, then this new believer would have expressed such passionate love for her faith. The regret in this woman's experience is the regret found elsewhere in Djebar's writings about religion. The intertwining of the themes of music and love in her reminiscence of childhood awe is important, for these are the components of meaningful religious experience for her. Oum Keltoum's flight from home and family was inspired by pure love of Islam: "you left solely for the love of God and his messenger, solely for the love of Islam!" (*Loin* 169). The glowing message of Muhammad's exclamation clashes with Islam in the centuries following the extinction of the Prophet's voice; Islam turns away from love to focus on submission, according to Djebar's account in *L'Amour, la fantasia*.[38] Her aunt's story of deep love and devotion between the Prophet and Khadidja is what gives the young protagonist a desire for Islam. It is a belief in this sort of love between people, in a love that serves as a model for reconciliation and overcoming differences, that perhaps motivates her to turn to the theatre of Islam, to put on stage the early actions that are filled with ambiguity and possibility. As a girl, the narrator is moved by the story of Muhammad's tender tears in remembrance of his wife when he hears the sound of footwear that resembles that of his deceased spouse: "The story of the sound of sandalled feet would bring on a sudden yearning for Islam. A longing to embark as on a love affair, a rustling catching at my heart: with fervour and taking all the risks of blasphemy" (*Fantasia* 172). In Djebar's written work, affection and emotion are restored to a place of privilege in the Islamic narrative. Putting an emphasis on these aspects of the religious experience effectively places religion on a different plain. She moves away from laws toward love, sometimes at the risk of blasphemy.

The Return of the Religious

Assia Djebar's turn to religion in her written work is not limited to *Loin de Médine*; comments on Islam are abundant in *Ces voix qui m'assiègent* and they find their way into a number of other texts as well, from *Oran, langue morte* to *Les Nuits de Strasbourg*. This attention to faith and practice is hardly surprising for several reasons. First, as we have already seen, the context in Algeria following Independence in 1962 is filled with heavy religious implications. As an article by psychologist and sociologist Fethi Benslama indicates, identity cannot be understood apart from religion in North Africa: "[T]he explanation of the phenomenon of identity is based on a notion found in a number of texts on Algeria: *the instrumentalization of religion.*" Benslama is intent to uncover the ways in which Algerians have become accustomed to "the use of religion for ends that are different from its intent, namely, the political conquest of power" (38). As a writer from Algeria, Djebar can hardly ignore the importance of religion as a political instrument in her country.

It is also not surprising that Djebar should "re-turn" to religion in her writing because of the larger international context in recent times.[39] If religion can be said to be making a comeback in the Algerian political scene in the last twenty years or so, this trend is indicative of a larger move in a number of countries, and the publications of scholars such as Gianni Vattimo and Jacques Derrida address the phenomenon that has been called the "return of the religious" in the form of various fundamentalisms around the world, as Derrida explains: "What one calls 'return'—and this is not limited to Islam, far from it—distinguishes itself through the appearance of 'fundamentalisms' or 'radicalisms' that are aggressively 'political'" (*Papier machine* 342). This return of the religious coincides with another worldwide phenomenon known as globalization, and the two are far from mutually exclusive. In "Foi et savoir," Jacques Derrida coins the word *mondialatinisation*, or "globalatinization," and refers to the compatibility of the turn to religion in an age of technology that permits rapid travel and instant communication through a variety of means.[40] Derrida elaborates his notion of *mondialatinisation* as a largely linguistic phenomenon that emanates from the United States, a country that exports religious concepts in a language that draws much from Latin. Countries with no ties to Christianity have incorporated into their politics words and concepts that emerge directly from this belief system. Because of this very particular influence in the world at present, the term "return of the religious" can be extended to include a number of broad understandings of religion:

> For everything that touches religion in particular, for everything that speaks "religion," for whoever speaks religiously or about religion, Anglo-American remains Latin. *Religion* circulates in the world, one might say, like an *English word* [*comme un mot anglais*] that has been to Rome and taken a detour to the United States. Well beyond its strictly capitalist or politico-military figures, a hyperimperialist appropriation has been underway now for centuries. It imposes itself in a particularly palpable manner within the conceptual apparatus of international law and of global political rhetoric. Wherever this apparatus dominates, it articulates itself through a discourse on religion. From here on, the word "religion" is calmly (and violently) applied to things which have always been and remain foreign to what this word names and arrests in its history. The same remark could apply to many other words, for the entire "religious vocabulary'" beginning with "cult," "faith," "belief," "sacred," "holy," "saved," "unscathed" (*heilig*). But by ineluctable contagion, no semantic cell can remain alien, I dare not say "safe and sound," "unscathed," in this apparently borderless process.

Globalatinization (essentially Christian, to be sure), this word names a unique event to which a meta-language seems incapable of acceding, although such a language remains, all the same, of the greatest necessity here. (66–67)

When Assia Djebar addresses religion in her work, it is clear that the vocabulary of her "Latin" tongue of composition wields an influence in her writing. She often employs words such as "carême" instead of "Ramadan," for instance, translating the concept of fasting into the terms of another belief system that has a similar, but different, tradition.[41] The "leveling" inherent in this dominant trend of Latin/Christian influence is disquieting, and while Djebar certainly has incorporated many of its words and themes in her writing, she has not allowed this trend to wipe out the particularities of the history of her country and her person. She has successfully circumvented the obvious inherent risk of *mondialatinisation*: the erasure of specific traditions in the name of a larger "religion."

In Djebar's *La femme sans sepulture*, the narrator returns to her hometown of Cherchell after years of absence. The visitor interacts with several women as she delves into the life and death of Zoulikha, a heroine whose bravery during the Algerian War is legendary. In the postwar context of the narrator's inquiry into Zoulikha's experience, the question of religion inevitably surfaces, notably in the form of a *song* the narrator learned as a child whose words contain an important message: "We have only one language, Arabic / We have only one faith, Islam / We have only one land, Algeria!" (71).[42] Zoulikha's daughter, Mina, is the narrator's companion on memory lane, and her reaction to this song bears witness to an awareness of the limited view this *comptine* conveys: "'Me too,' interrupts Mina, 'I came to know this hymn, several years after you. I found it . . . a bit reductive, at the end, the rule of 'three times one.' Islam being the third of the monotheisms, do we absolutely insist on tripling the sacrosanct oneness?" (71). This character realizes and calls attention to the fact that Islam is not the sole monotheistic faith, that it is instead one of three religions that profess belief in one God. The problem with the little song is that it adheres to a unity that is false in nature, as the narrator's subsequent reflection reveals: "The game of threes, on the same earth: three languages, three religions, three heroes of the resistance, isn't that better?" (72). Plurality characterizes the Algerian land; languages and religions coexist in this varied territory, and any evocation of one tongue, one faith, and one land is illusory at best and prejudiced at worst, as the narrator's words show.[43]

The content of *La Femme sans sépulture* demonstrates in subtle ways that when various traditions exist side by side, they have an influence on each other. The most salient example is found in the comments surrounding the death of the story's heroine, Zoulikha. The title of the work alludes to the importance of a tomb and the lack thereof; the woman's body disappears after her passing and this causes her family great pain. According to Islamic tradition, the body of a loved one is to be buried after death.[44] The textual speculation is that a young male admirer saw to it that Zoulikha's body was honored in accordance with her beliefs. Since a proper burial is of great significance in her faith, her daughters and other loved ones will rest more easily with the assurance that Zoulikha was given a ritual interment.[45] But Islam is not the only influence in the textual account of the events at Zoulikha's death; Christian imagery is also present in this book, especially in the phrase "crucifixion sans croix!" that refers to her brutal end at the hands of her torturers (203).[46] Another evocation of Christ is to be found in the figure of a devoted follower crying at her feet.[47] The reader of this text might begin to wonder if the "hagiography" to which Zoulikha makes reference would be in the Islamic or in the Christian tradition (210). And one would have to wonder if, in the narrator's eyes, the distinction really matters after all.

In *Loin de Médine*, Assia Djebar addresses the influences and interactions of Christianity and Islam, with a focus on the maternal figure. She explains that the revered role of the mother in Catholicism inspired a backlash at the time of the emergence of Islam: "The theme of maternity had been so glorified, so celebrated during the preceding seven centuries of Christianity, that it seems normal that it receded then" (215). Djebar thus demonstrates in her historical study that religions do not remain indifferent to each other, that they adopt certain attitudes not only as similar to, but as different from the other faith. Some practices emerge in reaction to others, in order for a religion to distinguish itself from another. If the role of the mother assumed relatively small importance in the early years of Islam, such is not the case in current times, as the narrative voice makes clear: "the mother, nonetheless, is absent. This role, overvalued today in the experience of the male Muslim, was nearly evacuated" (215). An awareness of the setting that framed the events of Islamic early history allows Assia Djebar to place things in perspective over time.

Questions of faith, ritual, and religious observance inevitably come to the forefront at key moments in life's course. Birth, marriage, and death provide an occasion for religion and tradition to surface with acute pertinence. When a loved one passes, suddenly the questions of religious belonging, of communal practice, of respect for familial custom and ancestors' tradition resurge with newfound application. This is the case in Hélène Cixous's recent works of autobiographical fiction, particularly *Benjamin à Montaigne* when the narrator engages in a discussion with her aging mother about what is to happen upon the latter's death. The prospect of a Jewish ceremony is utterly scandalous in the eyes of the daughter: "I entered into my mother's house the 13th of February without glancing at the place and I was struck: no rabbi! It's a contradiction and a denial of your negative beliefs" (203). If the mother does not have any religious convictions, then she should not approve of a specifically religious burial service, in her daughter's opinion. In response to her daughter's outrage, the mother insists that this desire for a rabbi is a gesture of respect for her own father.

Belonging to the Jewish tradition is much more a question of faithfulness to loved ones and their culture than it is a question of religious belief, in Cixous's text. The daughter finds her mother's reasoning devoid of rationality, but she is not comforted by the fact that logic is on her side: "I wanted to have reason on my side, my faithless mother had faith on her side [. . .] it's out of love for you Selma that I give in to your double stupidity, I thought in pain. Faith can therefore exist there where there isn't any, and faith can falter where it exists?" (203–4). Faith is not a question in this instance of inner conviction but rather one of outward action, and it is the crucial occasion of death that brings the greater issues to light. The narrator laughs at the prospect of the dead showing respect to the dead: "The respect the dead show toward those who are already dead doesn't mean anything to me, but meaning doesn't hold any importance" (204). What really matters upon death may be less rational than one would think, as a short story by Assia Djebar reveals.

In "Le Corps de Félicie," a short story at the heart of a collection titled *Oran, langue morte*, a Frenchwoman named Félicie passes away in her native land and her children are left with the difficult task of arranging for her burial. Their dilemma stems from the fact that Félicie spent a number of happy, fruitful years on Algerian soil, and her beloved husband Mohammed is buried there. As the children reflect on how to deal with this situation, they recall that some Algerians had found their mother to have distinctly Muslim qualities, despite her Catholic beliefs. These friends employed a specific word in Arabic to refer to her goodness: "a specifically Muslim quality: *nya*, something like 'good faith'" (255).[48] Félicie's "good faith" may have contributed to a successful marriage that straddled the borders of language, culture, and religion that could have separated her from her significant other. Their marital union is an example of how love between couples can transcend differences, a recurrent theme in Assia Djebar's writing. But at the significant moment of her death, Félicie's children find themselves at an impasse, with no easy answers to the questions of religious identity that will determine her fate. If she is to be placed alongside her husband in Algeria, she must be declared a Muslim. No Christian or Jewish bodies are allowed in the cemetery at Béni-Rached (305). Naturally, such a declaration provokes some controversy among her children, some of whom deem it preposterous to change religions after an entire life of faithfulness to a certain tradition: "*Mman* has not denied her first faith!" (307). When one child lauds the mother's good heart as that of a Muslim: "My mother who had only done good had the heart of a Muslim!" (306), another defends her Catholicism and claims that this belief system is just as worthy: "*Mman* had a Catholic heart, with the Virgin and the little Jesus. . . . That's not less good, is it?" (306). This clash over religion could effectively preclude any hope for a solution, but Félicie's children seem to be of one accord when it comes to their mother's final resting place.

There is no question but that Félicie should be buried next to her husband in Algeria, that she should return to the man and the land she loved dearly. Religion proves to be merely a formality in the larger scheme of things. Words such as the following affirm this decision: "Considering Félicie a 'Muslim' is only a formality" (306).[49] When a voice asks what Félicie would have said if asked to pronounce the *fatiha* in order to be buried alongside her husband, the rhetorical question goes unanswered, for during her lifetime Félicie placed her loved ones above religious fidelity. In the name of her love for Mohammed, for instance, she consented to wear a gift he had given her years earlier. This present of a necklace containing a golden Qur'an in calligraphy saved Félicie's life in Oran at the moment of the country's independence from French rule in July 1962. It protected her from the "vengeance" of angry "Muslims" against the "Christian" conquerors of their territory. It does not seem as problematic that Félicie should be declared "Muslim" at her death, given this earlier "religious" concession for the love of her husband. The obligatory acquisition of a Muslim forename that accompanies her new adhesion to Islam places her on a parallel with her children, all of whom bear two first names, one of Muslim origin and the other from the French. According to a grandson, Félicie will be able to choose between the two as the mood strikes: "my grandmother is finally going to be able to act like all her children: she now has a Muslim first name and a Christian one, and she can choose between them, depending on her disposition!" (310). If it is at death that the hidden questions of religious adherence come to the surface, it is also at death that their relative importance becomes clear.

In Assia Djebar's treatment of religion, I would like to suggest that a complex process is under way. One of the great dangers of the "return of the religious" in Jacques Derrida's understanding is the relativism, or relativization, of the Abrahamic faiths, an ecumenical movement that aims to reconcile all "sons of the same God." This danger may not be as pernicious as the "radical destruction of the religious" in the form of fundamentalisms, but it may be just as threatening to valued democratic freedoms: "It must be said as well that, faced with them, another self-destructive affirmation of religion, I would dare to call it auto-immune, could well be at work in all the projects known as 'pacifist' and ecumenical, 'catholic' or not, which appeal to universal fraternization, to the reconciliation of 'men, sons of the same God,' and above all when these brothers belong to the monotheistic tradition of the Abrahamic religions" ("Faith" 78; translation modified). Djebar is careful in her writing not to relativize in her references to Christianity, Judaism, and Islam.[50] She is critically aware of the differences among these traditions, both in their scriptural foundations and in their evolution and practice. While she may bring out some of the similarities among these faiths in her fiction, she does not place them on the same level, but instead insists upon their differences. She is not naive in her presentation of these differences; she understands that these various belief systems have in many cases emerged from common roots, and that differences ranging from geography to history have led to diverse ways of life and differing worldviews. What is crucial in her treatment of religion is the distinction that Jacques Derrida insists upon in his reflections on the topic: "I think it is necessary to distinguish between faith and religion" (*Papier machine* 343). Djebar does not place her personal beliefs and doubts into the mix; she makes it clear that her investment in the topic is cultural rather than spiritual. Not only is her personal faith not in question in the text; it is entirely irrelevant. She does not engage in "soul searching" in her written work.

Keeping Secrets: Assia Djebar, *"marrane à son insu"*

In a number of critical and autobiographical texts, Jacques Derrida has referred to himself as a *"marrane,"* harking back to his Spanish roots and highlighting his Jewish heritage. The figure of the Marrano suits him precisely because of its secrecy: these Jews *claimed* to have converted to Christianity, but in truth they continued to practice their religion undercover. Like many other Jewish families, Derrida's ancestors fled Spain for North Africa in the fifteenth century. Assia Djebar's forebears followed the same general trajectory, also under duress for religious differences: "My family's city, the former Caesarea, was repopulated by hundreds of Moriscos, the people who were expelled en masse in Cervantes's time, in a final and profound bloodletting inflicted by Spain on itself at the beginning of the seventeenth century" (*Vast*

173–74). Their faith was also that of the "other" in Spain, and they were forced to keep it hidden for generations: "bringing with them the Mohammedan faith that for three or four generations, since 1492, they had been practicing in secret" (174). The hazards of history led to her family's establishment on the soil that later became known as Algeria, and all so that they might profess their faith in peace.

The word attributed to her Spanish ancestors who crossed the sea is a provocative one: "*transfuges*" (169). This term often carries a pejorative connotation, making reference either to a warrior who abandons his flag to join enemy lines, or in a broader sense to anyone who abandons an original position and thereby changes sides, whether in a political or religious arena. Their displacement from the Iberian peninsula to the Maghreb was undoubtedly characterized by flight, faithful to the Latin etymology of the word *transfuges*. But the idea of abandonment contained in its evolved form in French hardly seems appropriate to describe the movement of Djebar's family. While they did give up their homeland, they did so with a greater goal in mind: preservation of a religious tradition. Holding onto their beliefs was the motivation for fleeing; changing geographic location was intended to provide continuity in faith and practice. What had been perpetuated in secret might now be brought into the open. What had been celebrated quietly in the dark might now be trumpeted boldy in the light.

With the French conquest of Algeria in 1830, the hopes for unmitigated expression of religious belonging were once again dashed. In *Vaste est la prison*, the narrative voice reminisces about her interactions with other children as a young child, a recollection tarnished by her mother's removal of an important item of jewelry, her amulets (287). This gift from her deceased paternal grandmother was indeed much more than a hidden necklace; it provided protection. But the mother insists that the daughter would not want others to discover "these magical squares and triangles" (*Vast* 295). The daughter claims that the other girls wear crosses around their necks in plain view, and insists that her covered treasure has such great significance that it should not be removed: "But still! It's the writing of the Koran!" (295). But these protests fall on deaf ears, and the mother remains insistent, warning that the punishment would be great: "They would call me a pagan, me, the one who was native [*indigène*], there with all the French girls, me the Muslim [*musulmane*]!"[51] The forced removal of this deeply symbolic item constitutes an irreparable loss: "it was my mother who, caught up in a fit of rationality, took this first writing away from me" (296). In this pivotal scene from her childhood, the writer explains not only how she was deprived of the written form of her mother tongue, but how she was stripped of the tradition to which this language was connected. The ridicule that threatened to accompany any sign of religious belonging provoked the removal of the secret itself.

Even if all external signs are free of religious import following the removal of the amulets at the age of five or six, the inner taboos of Djebar's tradition remain with her long into the future. Her background makes her uncomfortable with touch, with physical proximity even in the most ordinary situations. She reacts with even greater apprehension at the age of twenty or even thirty when she comes into contact with the "*familiarité facile*" and "*neutralité apparente*" of mixed-sex interactions in accordance with "*les usages occidentaux*" (*Vaste* 286–87). Open expressions of affection are a shock to her instinctive sensitivities as a prudish "oriental" coming for the first time into contact with the "secret" world, in Djebar's words. In a curious reversal, *Vaste est la prison* shows the Occident to be filled with mysterious "secrecy" that the "Oriental" woman wants to uncover.[52]

Despite her wide-eyed interest in the "liberated" customs of the Western world, Djebar is restrained from complete freedom of action in her personal life. Alone in an elevator with a younger man with whom she is smitten, she is unable to speak or move: "still paralyzed by taboos" (*Vast* 93). A large portion of her paralysis is due to her husband who has kept her in the position of an "Oriental," in contrast to the Westernized in Algeria: he was responsible for her "*complexe culturel*" (50). What Djebar terms her "cultural complex" is more easy to identify than it is to discard; indeed, it took her twenty years to get over her inhibitions, according to her autobiographical account. Ridding herself of taboos with respect to certain customs, such as segregation of the sexes, does not necessarily translate into other areas of life. In a moment of extreme agitation, the infatuated protagonist of *Vaste est la prison* impetuously calls out to God: "A while ago I had said the *fatiha*, [. . .] as if Allah alone, in the darkness of that corridor on the sixth floor, had protected me—or imprisoned me, I didn't know which—I acted as a woman in love who finally has only the magic of religiosity to cure her" (*Vast* 44). The mother, upon removing her daughter's sacred necklace, mentioned magic in negative terms and made a "rational" decision. Years later, the daughter has not entirely rid herself of "the magic of religiosity"; to the contrary, it surfaces at the times that seem to matter most, in the moments of deep emotion and significant action. But despite their importance, these instances of return (to/of) the religious are often kept secret.

In *Vaste est la prison*, we find first-person commentary on various sequences surrounding the filming of *La Nouba des femmes du Mont Chenoua*, a cinematic work of fiction containing many autobiographical details. In the presence of her technicians, Djebar serendipitously discovers a plaque bearing the name Malek el-Berkani—one of her ancestors who fought against the French invaders in 1871—this is how the writer and filmmaker describes her response: "I let my imagination go; I smile. Must not tell the crew that I am, through my mother and my mother's father [. . .] the direct descendant of this combatant" (Vast 331). Instead of calling attention to her genealogical connection to this fighter, she keeps the information to herself. Instead of boasting aloud of this lineage, she holds her tongue. This delicious bit of familial history will remain quiet at this time, even if she cannot help but feel proud of this past that is at once *hers* since she is a blood relation to the hero and *not completely hers* since she was not yet born at the moment of his exploits. In *Apories*, Derrida refers to the temporal complexities that are an integral part of the *marrane's* experience:

> Let us figuratively call Marrano anyone who remains faithful to a secret that he has not chosen, in the very place where he lives, in the home of the inhabitant or of the occupant, in the home of the first or of the second arrivant, in the very place where he stays without saying *no* but without identifying himself as belonging to. In the unchallenged night where the radical absence of any historical swiftness keeps him or her, in the dominant culture that by definition has calendars, this secret keeps the Marrano even before the Marrano keeps it[. . .] Thanks to this anachronism, Marranos that we are, Marranos in any case, whether we want to be or not, whether we know it or not. Marranos having an incalculable number of ages, hours, and years, of untimely histories, each both larger and smaller than the other, each still waiting for the other, we may incessantly be younger and older, in a last word, infinitely finished. (*Aporias* 81)

In Derrida's analysis, Marranos have at their disposal countless ages, innumerable histories, and the resulting "anachronism" is a stroke of luck. In response to the dominating power that controls the calendar, the secret that the *marrane* possesses (without having chosen it) provides its holder with *alternative* measures of keeping time. The dissimilated practices and the hidden tongues that have been transmitted through the years, from one generation to the next, are indeed a gift to the marrane, who can counter the clock of dominant culture with the beat of a different drum: "for this friend at least, what I am attempting to do is bring his last breath back to life [. . .] I, however, am only capable of raising familiar ghosts [*fantômes familiaux*]" (*Vast* 342–43). The narrative voice reveals the possibility of reviving ghosts in written texts, but this resuscitation may not be limited to the printed word, as Derrida insists: "There are still sons—and daughters—who, unbeknownst to themselves, incarnate [. . .] the ventriloquist specters of their ancestors" ("Marx & Sons" 262). When Djebar recounts her instinctive recitation of the *fatiha*, she just may be revealing the sort of incarnation Derrida has in mind.

When, as a film director in her native land, Djebar stumbles upon the resting place of her celebrated ancestor, she gives herself over to reflection: "At my feet, while I sought an image in the sky, my ancestor must have been disturbed by my incongruous presence, especially by my being oblivious to his resting-place, the place where he was buried" (*Vast* 331). The convergence of past and present, of her predecessor's place in the ground and her own focus on the sky, makes this an opportune moment for critical inquiry into her artistic project(s). Stirring up the dead and digging into the past, Djebar may at first glance appear to be doing an injustice to her ancestors. But her filmmaking and writing endeavors constitute, on the contrary, a faithful and reverential return to the truest sources of her innermost self.[53] Many ingrained patterns of thinking and behaving have come to her without her conscious awareness, and only the active quest for the past will bring into focus the dispersed truth that has occluded Djebar's own secrets: "to the condition of a sort of Spanish Marrano who would have lost—in truth, dispersed, multiplied—everything up to and including the memory of his unique secret" ("Faith" 86).

If the potentially derogatory term *transfuges* is used in *Vaste est la prison* to refer to the writer's ancestors who fled their native Spain, it is in part because the writer fears that the Andalusian culture of her forebears stood to lose a great deal in transit. Indeed, the customs and costumes of Grenada and Cordoba gathered dust quickly, even before her mother's birth in North Africa: "What was this legacy that she inherited and what did she transmit to me of this memory already covered in sand?" (*Vast* 174). But one thing has survived the trip, one aspect of this civilization has weathered the geographical relocation, one cultural element has withstood the test of time: music. Even when all visible signs of this heritage have disappeared, this audible trace remains, and the music of the past provides rhythm and melody for the present: "Thus I spent the summers of my early childhood surrounded by women who sang or embroidered. These odalisques young or old of a city closed in upon itself, where only the lute could complain out loud, passed on to me this still flickering light from the women's Andalusia that sill provided us with a little nourishment across the centuries" (*Vast* 175). Impervious to space and time, music remains, perhaps the deepest secret of all.

Religion, Feminism, and Context

When Djebar treats of religion in her writing in French, she is embarking on a journey, engaging in translation in its etymological sense of displacement, of moving, of going from one society to another, not only in words but also in mindset. For the society of her upbringing, and the setting for much of her work, is influenced by Islam.[54] Muslim societies in North Africa are characterized by a language impregnated with religious expressions, as Abdelkébir Khatibi's comments in *Amour bilingue* demonstrate: "In my country (?), there's a ceremony of the answer without a question: proverbial speech, empty maxims, unpronounceable ritornello. Spell this: there is no God but Allah" (80–81). Even if Khatibi has left behind the beliefs of his society, the sayings and customs of his native environment are still a part of him: "Living without belief: perhaps, but what became of the spirits, the phantoms, and the angels of his mother tongue? He thought of the superstitious talk of his childhood and of his illiterate mother" (43). It is significant that Khatibi makes reference to his mother in his contemplation of belief; Djebar carefully aligns religious transmission on the side of women in various textual explorations of faith and practice in the Maghreb.

Daily religious life in the Muslim family depicted in Djebar's work is regulated by women whose cultural role is to retain and share the appropriate words to preserve tradition.[55] This responsibility in itself is not negative, but it carries with it negative consequences. Djebar explains that the role of perpetuating memory hides the claustration of women in this society:

> This function of the spokesperson [*porte-parole*], or rather the memory-holder [*porte-mémoire*] covers up the enclosure of women in space (the tendency to immobilize them, and at the same time, to wrap them, envelope them, bury them . . .). This tendency to asphyxiate the body pushes women to the only possible translation: to put up with life through song, lamentation, incantation by the voice which alone is liberated. Yes, make of the voice—that comes out powerful, bitter, vengeful, stripped, or simply naked—the only immediate consolation. (*Ces voix* 74–75)

Women in Maghrebian society are immobile. They are assigned the role of "carrying" familial and religious memory, and they carry it as they carry children. Its transmission is dependent on them, but this job of "*porte-mémoire*," of holding memory, effectively holds (and holes) them in, restricting their movement and thus their freedom. The noble goal of serving religion puts them entirely at the service of a religious society that has deviated from its initial purpose. The subjugation of women in this society is not in accordance with religious precepts, but with their distortion.

Women in Djebar's native culture are relegated to the realm of orality; they are traditionally denied the privileges of men, as Djebar makes clear in an article whose title evokes wars of language, "French as booty" [*Du français comme butin*], but whose content reveals the realities of the war between the sexes in traditional Magrebian society: "To write in the foreign language almost becomes an adulterous act outside the ancestral faith. For the taboo in Islam spares males in this case; what's more, it valorizes them" (*Ces voix* 70). The relationship to language, and more specifically to writing, is quite different for men than it is for women in Islam.[56] If Djebar has had to "question herself doubly" because of her liberation from claustration thanks to the French school system, it is because her culture is so different from her education.[57] The most alienating gesture, the movement that forever removes her from her background, is the choice to write. This irrevocable decision is in direct defiance of religious tradition: "Speaking outside the matriarchal warmth, outside the refrain of Tradition, outside 'faithfulness,' when this term is taken in a religious sense, writing in the first person singular and of singularity, with a naked body and a voice hardly changed by the foreign timbre, makes us confront all the symbolic dangers" (70). Assia Djebar runs a personal risk when she writes in the first person singular in French. She creates an insurmountable distance between herself and the matriarchal warmth of the Tradition of her home, but she does so for the greater good of the very women from whom she becomes estranged.

Feminist scholars have exhibited vastly different reactions to Djebar's response to women's position in Islam. Winifred Woodhull is critical of the fears expressed in Djebar's texts, though she concedes that these fears are "well founded" due to "religious conservatives' recent victories in Algeria" (86). Woodhull favors the "construction of international networks in which feminism's relation to other struggles can be defined within specific historical, geopolitical, and cultural contexts, and in which languages of revolt can challenge hegemonic discourses, including those of First-World feminism" (87). In the eyes of Mireille Calle-Gruber, the work of Assia Djebar does not fall into a dichotomous relationship that posits first-world feminism against an inferior Third-World version. To the contrary, the very genius of Djebar's writing project is that it avoids such divisions by seeking to emancipate women from an enslavement that is anathema to the laws of Islam:

> The writer elaborates a singular feminism in her œuvre: she doesn't imitate Western feminisms, nor does she copy their vindications and strategies; she

does not place the emancipation of women and Islam in a facile dichotomy; she refuses the refusal of her own culture and affirms the demand—much more exorbitant—for a feminine freedom inscribed in the laws of Islam. (*Assia Djebar* 151)[58]

Djebar's feminist criticism of Islam is powerful because it remains within the context of the religion and exposes its truth. Vindicating the rights of women *inside* this faith tradition requires returning to the texts of importance and rereading them. When she sets out to rewrite them, she provides a "countersignature" to the original in the Derridian sense of the term: "a countersignature has its own say in the course of and beyond a passive reading of a text that precedes us but that we reinterpret, as faithfully as possible, by leaving a mark there" (*Papier machine* 373).[59] Djebar countersigns the early texts of Islam, leaving her mark on careful reinterpretations of these initial works, all while remaining as faithful as possible to their message.

Countersigning (with) the Name

In her autobiographical works, Assia Djebar does not insert her own name, the pseudonym she chose for the publication of her first novel, the heading under which she composes her œuvre. But if this name by which she is now known—in public and in private—is not included in the written work, Djebar does frequently employ *another name* with unique resonance: Isma. In *Oran, langue morte*, this character introduces herself in epistolary form with the following affirmation: "Therefore I, the friend of exploded, dislocated, effaced Nawal, I introduce myself: Isma. 'Isma': the name, but what name, rather the seeker, my name, or that of the other. Isma the other. Isma then, that's enough, along with an indication of my age, and on the first meeting" (78). This is not the first time Djebar employs this name in a text; readers will easily recognize the character from the second volume of the autobiographical quartet, *Ombre sultane*. In this novel composed in two voices, one of the women describes herself in this way: "I no longer have a face or possess a veil; 'Isma,' I scatter my name, all names" (*Sister* 12). In the third volume in the autobiographical series, *Vaste est la prison*, Djebar returns again to the narrative voice that carries *le nom*: "Even now, three-quarters of a century later, I, Isma, the narrator, the descendant through the youngest daughter, do not know" (*Vast* 234).[60] The insistence in this passage on the equivalence between the name "Isma," the narrator, and the "*moi*" is clear. As Djebar admits in an interview for the television program *Droit d'auteurs* aired on 30 March 1997, this special name plays an important role in her work:

"Isma is a bit autobiographical. [. . .] When I say 'Isma,' I'm expressing the personal side."

Isma, this personal appellation, is a variation on "Esma," a name that goes back to early Islam. The autobiographical self finds its inspiration in the roots of this religious tradition, for this chosen name comes with a history. "Esma" is frequently evoked in *Loin de Médine* in reference to two different women in early Islam, Esma bent Abou Bekr and Esma bent Omaïs. These two individuals emerge at various moments in the text, and sometimes their respective identities blend together. It becomes difficult to tell them apart since they are not always mentioned by name; instead, they are referred to by one of the multiple traits by which they are known. The older of the two Esmas, for instance, is the inspiration for two separate chapters, "The Washer of the Dead" and "She with Tattooed Hands." At first glance, it would be easy for the reader to mistakenly assume that the one who washes the dead is not the same as she with tattooed hands; but Esma is indeed described by both of these short phrases.

Very little is known about this person from the official account, but the narrator manages to paint a portrait of a well-rounded woman with many positive traits. Esma has an elegant soul (219); she is quick to comfort and care for others (223); in the same vein, she is eager to console those who are suffering (231); she is especially tender and helpful to her husband (233); she is a good listener (232); she is maternal (234); she is a devoted companion and caretaker (235); she is a healer (237-38); she is no stranger to the experience of death (225); she has known three men in marital relationships, and has found happiness (239); she has not remained in one single location, but moved about on more than one occasion (223); she is firm in her conviction and faithful in her word (236). Esma's storied life has given rise to multiple names that combine to defy categorization and transcend borders: "Esma 'washer of the dead' or 'woman of the sea,' Esma 'she with tattooed hands,' manages to stay on the invisible border" (237). This woman is the living example that contradictions can coexist without ruling each other out. "Magician and such a fervent Muslim—again the only one to assume the contradictions that threaten, that will appear; the only one to go beyond them" (223). This is why Assia Djebar has found in Esma a perfect model for inscribing herself into the text.

The historical figure of Esma allows Assia Djebar to write herself into *Loin de Médine*. The similarities between this woman and the writer, between the chronicler's account and Djebar's life trajectory are significant. And the most important work is done by the writer's imagination. What makes Esma such a compelling figure in this evocation of early Islamic history is the fact that the traits she shares with the narrative voice are not explicit. Assia Djebar slips her person into the text in subtle ways that elude the discernment of many readers and critics. This work has not been categorized as "autobiographical" by any account, but the evidence of autobiographical elements is undeniable, from the obvious description of Esma as a "listener" [écouteuse] to the more subtle reference to the meaning of the first name "Assia": "consolatrice." In a figurative manner, Assia Djebar is undoubtedly thinking of herself when she employs the term "laveuse des morts," for her writing of her Algerian compatriots in works like Le Blanc de l'Algérie, is a way of treating the dead with respect and honor. Djebar can certainly refer to herself as "celle aux mains tatouées," for her writing project means dipping her fingers deep into ink that stains, but that preserves her people and their memory from oblivion. Bringing back Esma in the written text means inserting herself into the work in an effort to translate tradition and preserve religion from the injustices of time. Restoring love and music to the narrative of Islam, bringing back the stories fitting for great theatre, leaves an indelible imprint not only on her hands, but on the printed work: "The red color of these fingers concentrates the intensity of these goodbyes, their gravity" (218). It is through writing that Djebar effectively looses religion from oppressive ties that bind. It is through careful choice that she "recollects" the past, that she gathers memories ancient and recent to select what is well founded and worthy of the future. It is through thoughtful re-thinking of the past that she re-connects current cultural practice to historical and literary precedents, and re-links Islamic community to its religious roots: religio.

Notes

1. In an article titled "Tradition and Transgression in the Novels of Assia Djebar and Aïcha Lemsine," Silvia Nagy-Zekmi highlights the relation between identity and tradition. Her approach focuses on religious teachings and seeks to rectify prejudiced depictions of religion in a Third-World context: "Tradition has been portrayed as a negative force when it comes to the Third World" (2).

2. In his introduction on the way new discourses are created from old in not only Djebar's "postcolonial narratives," but Tahar Ben Jelloun's, Abdelkébir Khatibi's, and Salman Rushdie's as well, Erickson makes the important assertion that while all four of these writers are "to varying degrees, believers in the Islamic (Sunni) faith system and, moreover, draw willingly and strongly upon Western culture, literature, and thought [. . .], in strikingly different ways, their writings refute or clash with certain of the strictures imposed in the name of the Word" (2).

3. This link between people is identified by Hélène Cixous as one of the "religious" aspects of theatergoing, and she admits that is it precisely this element that

pushes her away from the collective experience of attending plays: "I avow that The-atre is a form of religion. I mean to say that what we feel there together, in the *re-ligere*, the tying together, the gathering of emotions. I say 'I avow' because that is one of the reasons why I resist the call of the Theatre: because of anti-religion. Because of a need for individualism" ("Le lieu du Crime" 256).

4. The importance of heritage, and of putting heritage to good use by "borrowing" from the past, is central to Jacques Derrida's reflections in *Spectres de Marx*. As we shall see, the question of inheritance is a major concern of Assia Djebar's, as demonstrated by her quest for familial roots in the context of her religious and cultural heritage. The more "out of joint" her experience is (due largely to French colonization), the more she seeks to uncover her past: "The paradox must be sharpened: the more the new erupts in the revolutionary crisis, the more the period is in crisis, the more it is 'out of joint,' then the more one has to convoke the old, 'borrow' from it. Inheritance from the 'spir-its of the past' consists, as always, in borrowing. Figures of borring, borrowed figures, fig-urality as the figure of borrowing. And the borrowing *speaks*: borrowed language, bor-rowed names, says Marx. A question of credit, then, or of faith" (*Specters* 109).

5. In his novel *Pèlerinage d'un artiste amoureux*, Abdelkébir Khatibi depicts an en-counter with a man in the port town of Algiers whose words reveal a similar "multi-ple" belonging at the time of colonization. The character makes it clear that religion is separate from the government, that there is no connection between "church" (or "mosque") and "state" during this period of French rule: "Am I Muslim? Am I Al-gerian? Am I French? All three [. . .] France—and therefore Algeria—is a secular state" (47).

6. This multifacted nature of Islam stands out in contrast to Catholicism, accord-ing to Jocelyne Cesari in *Le Monde Diplomatique*: "The leveling machine of the Re-public reduced Catholicism to the dimension of confession. Despite the French gov-ernment's efforts to organize it, Islam will never be a simple religious practice."

7. When Adlai Murdoch addresses the "paradox underlying postcolonial identity-construction" that Djebar confronts in her autobiographical work, he highlights "the problematic legacy of a bicultural heritage" (87) without mentioning the religious component of the culture of origin. I contend that Djebar's "bicultural heritage" is complicated by the religion of her "first" culture as it encounters her "second." Mil-dred Mortimer picks up on this essential aspect when she includes religious details of Djebar's background and the creation of "Djebar's autobiographical self" in her analy-sis of *Ombre sultane*: "Awakening in her father's library, a room containing his Mus-lim prayer rug and French texts, Isma identifies with a parent who, like herself, ne-gotiates between East and West, and pays tribute to her father, the teacher who launched his daughter on a bicultural journey that resulted in her appropriation of language and space."

8. As we will see shortly, the very hostile environment of her native Algeria in current times contributes to Djebar's refusal to accept Islam in *all* its current forms. Indeed, she doesn't throw out religion, but tempers it, tones it down, interprets and revalorizes it in the face of the misuse and abuse that mark current history.

9. This contextualization is especially needed when it comes to Islam, as Edward Said has noted in *Covering Islam*. Quoted in a provocative article for *Le Monde diplomatique* titled "Islamophobie," the following words refer to the danger of forgetting history: "When one speaks of Islam, one eliminates—more or less automatically—space and time" (41). Djebar's work can be seen as a corrective to this tendency, since it puts place and time at the forefront of its concern.

10. Re-reading the foundational texts of Islam often means reading *otherwise*, as Khatibi makes clear in his letters to Jacques Hassoun. For Khatibi, reading the Qur'an does not have to be a theological or mystical act, nor does the reader have to be situated within the strict binary division of believer versus nonbeliever: "One can therefore read the Koran otherwise than theology or mysticism. And what is put into play in these three forms of monotheism is how the sacred message interpellates us today, whether one is a believer or not or beyond all opposition between belief and atheism" (*Le même livre* 163). Khatibi is interested in sacred texts and contemporary religious practices as an intellectual, not as a "believer": "It's the arrangement of imaginary forms that occupies my mind, and not religion as such" (163). Hélène Cixous's approach to texts with religious significance is similar with respect to the imaginary, but she views the Bible as a literary source among others, located *outside time*: "Lévinas has always belonged for me—from the beginning and without question—to a universe not without a past but situated in an undated country, without a home, outside time, and where I rediscover the works of German literature, the Bible, a number of sources" ("A la source" 51).

11. Djebar takes issue in this statement, and in her work in general, with fundamentalist misinterpretations of Islam, not with Islam on the whole, an important distinction that is frequently explained in critical analyses of the situation in Algeria, as in the following comment: "It is [. . .] a mistake to assume that Islam is necessarily or latently fundamentalist or to believe that religion is the origin or cause of the kind of crisis and the horrors that are happening in Algeria today" (Venn 86).

12. It is of significant note that the date Djebar cites as her "location" during the time of research and writing, the date that coincides with the dawn of this religion ("*aube islamique*," *Ces voix* 53), is on a chronological scale that matches a different faith system. Christianity and Islam interact and intersect at numerous points in her study; the histories of these different Abrahamic religions intertwine at crucial moments. But it could be argued that their different calenders cause for a permanent disjunction, recalling once again Derrida's citation of Hamlet in *Spectres de Marx*: "This time is out of joint." The calendars follow a different rhythm, they count in different ways, and they provide different perspectives on the passing of time. *Loin de Médine* contains frequent translations of dates, but often translations are omitted, leaving the "Western" reader amiss as to the precise moment of the well-documented occurrences cited in the text.

13. The language of the song is important here, for the dialectical Arabic is not the holy tongue of the Qur'an. It is the spoken language of the people; the fact that the story is related in this way renders it accessible to the multitude of listeners:

"This language which the tenor's art made so simple, was vibrant with a primitive solemnity" (*Fantasia* 171)." When Djebar writes of religion in French, she is able to move completely out of the realm of religious interdicts and into the arena of move-ment and possibility in interpreting religion: "But I navigate this way, without even a *galam* in hand, not even weighted to the Qur'anic slate of childhood, I maneuver, the body mobile and upright, toward the Arabic language bundled in its taboos" (*Ces voix* 184–85).

14. Ethnographer Germaine Tillion makes a similar comparison between religious violence in France and in Algeria over time, emphasizing the role of social class and education in distinguishing among people who belong to different religions. In her view, fanaticism has little to do with differences among religions. See *L'Afrique bas-cule vers l'avenir*, especially page 36.

15. When Djebar's countrymen insist that "everything must go," it is especially the liberty of writing that is targeted, since the right to a literary search for personal truth and error is viewed as a threat to current rule in Algeria: "Everything? Mean-ing: culture, creation, protest, the pen that aspires toward the individual, that takes up a path by chance, that traces its thought in derisive, ironic, or angry fashion. This writing becomes the target of young men, peasants, desperate and indignant; these 'madmen for God' ['*fous de Dieu*'] who have been sufficiently drugged, manipulated, twisted, and disgusted to lash out against . . . intellectuals, among them the most modest, sometimes the most discreet, in every case the altruistic who write by con-viction and who vindicate the right to seek their own truth, their own errors as well" (*Ces voix* 244–45).

16. Assia Djebar deals frequently in her autobiographical works with the difficulty of writing in French, the language of violence and domination inextricably linked to the history of colonization in her country: "this stripping naked, when expressed in the language of the former conquerer [. . .], this stripping naked takes us back oddly enough to the plundering of the preceding century" (*Fantasia* 157); "because I write and I speak in the language of others [. . .] am I not compromising myself [. . .] in an objective alliance with the murderers of my first mother?" (*Ces voix* 148).

17. In *L'Amour, la fantasia*, the narrator elucidates her goal of reviving and resus-citating the lost voices of women in her homeland, from her cultural and religious tradition: "Writing does not silence the voice, but awakens it, above all to resurrect [*ressusciter*] so many vanished sisters" (*Fantasia* 204).

18. Part of what I call the "right to representation" here is the recognition of good stories, of effective drama. The Qur'an consists largely of commandments and warn-ings, with only a small part of the writing devoted to stories. Highlighting the inter-est and importance of these stories and their dramatic content may be part of Dje-bar's recurrent use of the theatrical metaphor: "I loved the simplicity of Isaac's song, in whose unhurried stanzas the dramatic quality [*la dramaturgie*] of the tale swelled to its climax" (*Fantasia* 171).

19. Djebar's account reveals that Oum Hakim has fought on both sides of the re-ligious divide: "She wanted to leave. Leave with him. Fight. Like in the past, at that

time against Islam, his Prophet and his faithful" (140); "Fight. Fight on horseback, on a camel, and for Islam from now on" (142).

20. The Muslim holy book, which dates back to the seventh century, remained available only in the original Arabic for hundreds of years; the first translation didn't appear until the mid-twelfth century. Jacques Derrida touches on the "sacred" nature of Arabic and its special relation to the Qur'an in his comments on translation: "every idiom to be translated is sacred, the letter is holiness itself. In the relationship between the literal nature of the Arabic tongue and the Qur'an, there is a specificity to this sacredness" ("Fidélité à plus d'un" 263).

21. One convert to Islam is a foreigner from Alexandria, a Christian who becomes a Muslim upon arrival in Medina. Despite the fact that she has left behind her roots, she occasionally speaks in her native language, but only in private. Caught in the act of singing in her mother tongue, Sirin must defend herself against the accusations of her husband: "'I thought you were Islamicized!' 'Is it contrary to Islam to speak the language of one's father and mother?'" (Loin 195). Islam is in this instance more than just a belief; it is a language as well.

22. "This day of revelation, this day when God sent his word down in Medina to protect women who come, even in flight, to Islam" (169).

23. "'Muhammad is dead, Islam is not dead!' proclaimed the first caliph a bit later. 'Which Islam is not dead?' the stubborn voice of Fatima seems to question" (75–76).

24. "[T]he first at the head of an interminable procession of girls whose de facto disinheritance, often enforced by brothers, uncles, the sons themselves, will try to install herself in order to contain bit by bit the insufferable feminist revolution in Islam during this Christian 7th century!" (79).

25. Denying women their inheritance is a clear divergence from Muhammad's teaching. The narrator exclaims in reaction to such "*écarts*" that all should not be in the hands of men: "As if everything belonged to men's domain. Everything, including women's right to inherit!" (86). In Algeria, a 1984 ruling made legal this exclusion and clearly worked against the rights of women: "In the height of 'socialist' Algeria, the family code (1984) makes the exclusion of women legal" (*Ces voix* 260). In *Vaste est la prison*, the narrator often evokes her maternal grandmother's experience; *this* Fatima took advantage of her right to hang onto her goods in the context of a divorce: "In the end she decided upon the separation of property that is provided for in Islamic law" (*Vast* 238).

26. "She claims her refusal, improvises her revolt, puts in verse her disdain over the cowardice of her companions: during a period of six months, she says no, she imposes this no on her husband, cousins, on all her family ['*gens de la famille*'] . . . and she dies. Of not having written it?" (*Ces voix* 259–60).

27. Assia Djebar gains inspiration from this early figure whose eloquent revolt serves as a model: "To make the voice vibrate: fourteen centuries after the first revolutionary woman in Islam, the 'girl,' I follow humbly in her footsteps: I make an effort in the shadow of the fire of her eloquence, she who was burned before me" (*Ces voix* 261).

28. If Djebar is opposed to anything, she is opposed to constraints. In a television documentary, Assia Djebar claims that she does not do work in Arabic precisely because this language has been imposed on the Algerian people following Independence from French rule in 1962: "[I]n '62, they Arabized. They expelled instructors from the university; that was the true drama. . . . I was 25 and I was teaching (but not in Arabic). . . . I like the Arabic language in every country except Algeria. . . . I did not allow myself to be Arabized because it was a constraint" (Kamel Dehane). This marks a departure from her early desire to study Arabic as a second language at the lycée in Algeria. She recalls that they declined her request because it was impractical to hire an instructor for only one student who wished to study this language. The difficulty of learning Arabic in Algeria in the years just prior to the Algerian War is explained in Derrida's *Le Monolinguisme de l'Autre* (see especially pp. 65–71).

29. It would not be going too far to note the parallels in Djebar's own "conjugal trajectory," as outlined in *Vaste est la prison*. After the disintegration of her passionate first marital union, the second was less exciting and, consequently, short-lived.

30. It is significant that Assia Djebar's given names are Fatima-Zohra. Possibly to avoid the obvious connection, the writer never refers to the Prophet's daughter Fatima by her *two* first names, identical to her own. The fact that Djebar does not make explicit such similarities between herself and her textual creations is a significant part of her humble and intricate autobiographical enterprise.

31. One of the most striking examples of Djebar's capacity to say no is found in the passage describing her divorce in *Vaste est la prison*. The specific Arabic word she pronounces is provided in the text, along with its normal contextual significance, that of the initial word in the formula of submission. Djebar obviously reappropriates the word and turns it to her advantage, demonstrating complete control of the situation and a refusal to submit to the expectations of the two men before her: "The judge asks me one last question, which he repeats. I merely say '*Lla!*' ('No!') because I have the ludicrous and in fact ill-timed notion that this is the beginning of the *chahadda*—according to them, the words of submission. So I will only say one word in their learned language: no, *non*, lla!" (*Vast* 315).

32. The speed of the Djebarian text is not uniform. Slowness also has its place in her writing as well, as Djebar reveals in the following comments on movement and language in her work: "Little by little, the slow rhythm takes over, I don't know if it is the others in me (mothers, sisters, ancestors) who carry us away—the language and me its rider—or if it is the language of writing" (*Ces voix* 150).

33. Dealing with doubt is an integral part of Djebar's exploration of religion in *Loin de Médine*, where we find the following embrace of speculation and interpretation with respect to the recorded sayings on the life of the Prophet: "A *hadith* is never entirely certain. But it opens and traces, in the space of our interrogative faith, the perfect path of a meteor perceived in the dark" (62). The "interrogative" aspect of faith as it is expressed here is crucial to Djebar's critical distance with respect to sacred texts in this re-reading.

34. In a television interview, Assia Djebar affirms the importance of Islam as a setting for her work: "I consider myself to be in the Islamic 'air' as a narrator and novelist" (*Lieux d'écrivains*). The word 'air' carries many possible meanings; since this was an oral interview, this homophone could be spelled a number of ways (*air, aire, ère*) to correspond to different ideas: air, music, period.

35. "A writing '*against*': the *against* of opposition, revolt—sometimes silenced—that shakes you up and runs through your entire being. Against, but also *right up against*, in other words, writing of *rapprochement*, of listening, the need to be close to, to discern human warmth, solidarity, a need that is undoubtedly utopian" ("Idiome" 10).

36. It is significant that Islam's roots are firmly planted in a loving relationship between husband and wife. Muhammad's voice in *Loin de Médine* praises the power of love for its ability to bring men out of silence by inspiring them to express their feelings: "Know that, for a woman, nothing is more important than to bring out and make visible the love that her husband has for her, even if he remains silent! Only a wife can have the power to push her husband out of his silence to show his love!" (69).

37. The conciliatory power of love between couples is most salient in *Les Nuits de Strasbourg*, where relationships between unlikely men and women transcend religious differences. Thelja, a Muslim Algerian, finds a companion in François, a Frenchman, just as Eve, an Algerian-born woman of Jewish origin, chooses to marry Hans, a German. If Djebar celebrates the potential of mixed-race unions in this text, it is in part because such potentially positive marriages were forbidden in her native land: "Unlike the Antilles and other societies, we did not have the possibility of natural *métissage* since there was an Islamic interdict" (*Ces voix* 184); "the only cross-breeding [*métissage*] that the ancestral beliefs do not condemn: that of language, not that of the blood" (*Fantasia* 142).

38. "In the transmission of Islam, an acid erosion has been at work: Tradition would seem to decree that entry through its straight gate is by submission, not by love. Love, which the most simple of settings might inflame, appears dangerous" (*Fantasia* 169).

39. A number of recent publications have addressed Islam, redressing its wrongs, explaining its intersections with other practices, or seeking to provide context for its beliefs and traditions: Miriam Cooke's *Women Claim Islam: Creating Islamic Feminism through Literature* (New York: Routledge, 2001), Abdelwahab Meddeb's *La Maladie de l'Islam* (Paris: Seuil, 2002); Fethi Benslama's *La Psychanalyse à l'épreuve de l'Islam* (Paris: Aubier, 2002), and Abdelkébir Khatibi's *Le Corps oriental* (Paris: Hazan, 2002).

40. Derrida explains the interconnections between the two phenomena (religion and *mondialatinisation*) in the following way: "The so-called return of the the religious attempts to come back to the literal nature of the idiom, to the proximity of home, nation, *jus soli*, blood lineage, filiation, etc. To put off the threat or to incorporate it in oneself, one appropriates technoscience, telecommunications, tele-mediatization, the effects of globalization, etc. Auto-immune processes" (*Papier machine* 342–43).

The nature of these two phenomena makes it difficult to apply any generic classification to their relation: "the co-extensiveness of the two questions (religion and worldwide Latinization) marks the dimensions of what henceforth cannot be reduced to a question of language, culture, semantics, nor even, without doubt, to one of anthropology or of history" ("Faith" 67).

41. One of many examples is in *La Femme sans sépulture*, where Ramadan is translated into other terms: "You see, it's Lent [*carême*] and I'm fasting" (147).

42. The words of this song come from a famous saying by Sheikh Ben Badis, a strong proponent of cultural nationalism in Algeria in the 1930s. Anne-Emmanuelle Berger has edited an excellent collection of essays that address the connections among history, religion, and language titled *Algeria in Others' Languages*.

43. *Loin de Médine* is a novel that works to debunk the myth of "unicité" in faith: "against those Muslims who only have one demand, the irreducible oneness of their faith" (43). It does so in many ways, notably by demonstrating how Islam has evolved over time, how what is taken as a "given" in behavior and belief was not always accorded this status. Djebar is careful to show the forgotten roots of certain practices: "Tabari noticed in his time that they carried out neither the prayer at dawn nor the prayer at dusk, but they forgot that it was to celebrate the strange wedding of the past!" (49).

44. "No, he buried me! According to the tradition. . . . He honored me, according to Islam!" (210).

45. Prior to its disappearance, the body of Zoulikha was exposed to the elements day and night, as well as to the gaze of men, women, and children. The question of suffering prior to death (as well as disrespect after) is crucial to this textual composition. Zoulikha is an unusual woman, for she found the strength to leave the expected roles for women in her society and fight among the men in the maquis. Her terrible death by torture recalls the narrative reflections on death and masculinity in Islam in *Vaste est la prison*: "Because there is no Isolde in Islam, because there is only sexual ecstasy in the instant, in the ephemeral present, because Muslim death, no matter what they say, is masculine" (*Vast* 108); "I really thought that every death in Islam is experienced as masculine; because our proudest women in the end die as men so that they only bow before the greatness and magnanimity of Allah" (349).

46. Assia Djebar has recourse in other texts to the image of Christ's suffering on the cross, partly because this religious event has entered into the French language in an almost imperceptible way, as in the following expression: "I heard you bring up this calvary [*ce calvaire*]" (*Oran, langue morte*, 283). References to Christ and Christianity are sometimes taken humorously, as in the following exchange between a married couple in *Les Nuits de Strasbourg*. Eve and Hans find laughter in a reference to Christ. "Eve slaps Hans" [. . .] "—You want to strike the other cheek, now? . . . I am not Christ, 'my love'!" [. . .] "He finished in English, at least a neutral terrain, a minuscule space, a small earth filled with hope, 'my love,' two eternal passwords, flying from the other shore . . ." [. . .] "She perceived the irony: 'I am not Christ!' . . . She understood: 'strike again, hit me then'! My love, my sweet love !'" (162–63).

47. "[M]y naked feet: he kissed them in silence, sometimes wetting them with his tears" (*La femme* 211).

48. The conception of "good" Christians in Algeria as really being Muslims without realizing it is a common one in Assia Djebar's writing, as in this passage from *Vaste est la prison*: "[A]lmost as a miraculous exception, they would acknowledge some kinship, sometimes just one person, a man or a woman, whose value they tacitly appreciated, and they would then grumble among themselves: 'This Christian, he's essentially a Muslim and doesn't know it!'" (340).

49. The mother of the main protagonist in Djebar's recent novel, *La disparition de la langue française*, expresses an opinion on the beliefs of her future daughter-in-law that resounds with the message and context of this passage on Félicie: "She may be from any country, of any faith, it matters little to me. God is for all Creatures. I'd rather take my leave knowing that my Berkane has a real wife at his side!" (58).

50. The growing tendency to relativize religions is a contemporary phenomenon accompanying globalization, according to Bruno Étienne: "The apparent relativism is one of the consequences of the mobility of persons, the globalization of information, and generalized channel surfing [*zapping*]. The whole of great religions have gone from the status of the only true religion to a religion among others. No one can ignore the religion of the Other any longer" (81).

51. The juxtaposition of the terms "*indigène*" and "*musulmane*" in this quotation alludes to the difficulty of finding appropriate words to describe the "native" inhabitants of Algeria during the period of French colonization. Often the religious designation "Muslim" was applied to refer to all "indigenous" peoples, but this word often seemed to be interchangeable with the adjective "Arab," with its ethnic connotations. Confusion of race and religion is something ethnologist Germaine Tillion observed first-hand in Algeria: "In practical terms, the notion of race is often confused with language, and with religion. Algeria is no exception to the rule, and the usual fashion of 'racially' situating an individual consists in defining him as 'Muslim' or 'non-Muslim'" (34).

52. Edward Said's *Orientalism* famously identified the relation of the Occident to the Orient: "the Orient has helped to define Europe (or the West) as its contrasting image, idea, personality, experience" (1–2).

53. "Was I being faithless? No, irreverent and thoughtless perhaps, but seeing here, on the contrary, a return to what is truest" (*Vast* 331).

54. "For my society—not only Berber society, but Muslim as well, Islamic culture in general—defines itself first of all by an interdict of the eye" (*Ces voix* 181).

55. "[T]he traditional cultural role of women in the Maghreb is to conserve a plural word [*parole*] that provides the rhythm for the daily family and religious life" (*Ces voix* 74). It is perhaps because women are in charge of conserving and providing religious memory for their families that Djebar reacts positively to the religious content of Paul Claudel's plays when she reads them as a high school student: "my pleasure in finding, in the absolute of Claudel's heroines, a reflection of what . . . my maternal culture, my penchant for religiosity?" (292).

56. "If the language thus brandished often appears as a real risk for the 'angry young men' of the pre- or post-decolonization, it is different for women" (*Ces voix* 70).

57. In the writer's words, "[W]hat am I? My relationship to myself as an Algerian, born to Muslim parents, of Muslim culture with its taboos, a sort of liberation thanks to school, but French school, the school of colonization" (*Lieux d'écriture*).

58. The definition of freedom is ultimately up to each woman. Djebar is not prescriptive in her vision for women in Islam, nor is she dismissive of more conservative responses to religious tradition. She provides examples of surprising behavior, as in the case of a protagonist named Isma in *Ombre sultane*, a strong, resourceful woman who has traveled the world and who opts to return home and don the veil despite years of rebellion against this practice.

59. Derrida insists that faithfulness in translation is not solely dependent on a "literal" closeness to the original. In his view, the countersignature effectively holds in the balance the "sacred" original and the transformed translation: "sometimes it is better to have a translation that is less faithful literally [. . .] and that is more productive, that brings about certain effects in the language of arrival. [. . .] It is a question of another faithfulness and a transaction between two fidelities. It seems nonetheless that translation should force itself to be the most faithful possible, not out of a concern for calculable exactitude, but because it reminds us of the law of the other text, of its injunction, its signature, of the other event that took place already before us, and that we must respond to as heirs" ("Fidélité" 262–63).

60. According to Ronnie Scharfman, Assia Djebar "gives herself away" when she uses this "name" in the text: "But Djebar betrays herself when she reveals to the francophone reader that Isma means 'the name' in Arabic, and functions thus in ambiguous fashion as a doubled 'I/not-I'" (129).

~

CHAPTER THREE

Histoires à Contretemps: Syncopated Histories: Writing on the Offbeat

There is no history without iterability, and this iterability is also what lets the traces continue to function in the absence of the general context or some elements of the context.

—Jacques Derrida, in Derek Attridge, "'This Stange Institution Called Literature': An Interview with Jacques Derrida" (1992)

But this condensation of history, of language, of the encyclopedia, remains here indissociable from an *absolutely* singular event, an *absolutely* singular signature, and therefore also of a date, of a language, of an autobiographical inscription. In a minimal autobiographical trait can be gathered the greatest potentiality of historical, theoretical, linguistic, philosophical culture

—Jacques Derrida, in Derek Attridge, "An Interview with Jacques Derrida" (1992)

This chapter follows the reflection on religion in Assia Djebar's writing to examine another recurring theme in her written compositions: History.[1] It is no secret that Djebar's educational background consists of a specialization in this discipline, and her works are often studied for what they reveal about the past, since much of her writing is based on detailed documentation and careful research. In this chapter, I concentrate on some of the overlooked aspects of Djebar's own "history," as a writer and as a subject *in* her writing. I contend that the chronology and content of her texts accompany changes in her personal life that are subtly revealed in the written work. I also explore the *form* that History takes in Djebar's writing, examining the *anecdote* as crucial to her project of self-representation within the larger context of the place and time of her life. I show that selecting anecdotes to represent specific revelatory moments from the past allows the writer to zoom in (as in her cinematic work) on aspects of the past (official and personal) that have not been brought out in the writings of other historians, often male and "foreign" to her native land, and provides her with a unique textual strategy that is in step with that of other "postcolonial" historians who treat the past with distanced respect, no longer dupe to the "myth of the story of history as a simple representation of the continuity of events" (Ashcroft et al., 355). Anecdotes are similar to the "soundbites" of discourse, to the "refrains" of musical pieces. They are at once singular and repeatable—like the signature—and therefore memorable. This chapter will build up to the "revelation" of the anecdote (the secret of the chapter that I have just given away for the sake of clarity) in a manner that resembles the anecdote itself, which moves toward a clinching phrase, a climax, often in the form of a "punchline." Djebar's use of anecdotes punctuates the past with discontinuity, paying attention to and even stressing the "off beat," placing the accent on stories that slip through the official account in order to bring out different rhythms and tease out other truths, whether personal or communal.

Djebar's early publications do not reveal her training as an historian, in her own analysis: "During the 1980s, I realized that I had long been a professor of history and that, up to that time, I had separated my relationship with history from my novelistic work" (Mortimer, "Entretien"). If her first novels do not contain a strong historical component, then her later autobiographical works such as *L'Amour, la fantasia* certainly make up for this absence. Djebar asserts that her more recent writings pay special attention to—and benefit from—what she calls "this historical dimension": "By reintegrating this historical dimension (thanks to my films, for both of them are related to history), [. . .] I gained a more ample vision of the future, as well as more appropriate questions about the present" (Mortimer, "Entretien" 200–1). It is significant that her experience behind the camera inspired the novelist to "reintegrate" History into her literary production,[2] and to discover that inserting the past into the text contributes to a more penetrating narrative gaze into the present and the future. This chapter focuses on *Vaste est la prison*, the most autobiographical of Djebar's books to date and the only one to elaborate on her filmmaking enterprises, to determine how Djebar works with her background in the academic discipline of "History" to ultimately open up representations of the past to new perspectives and varied interpretations.

While a number of critics have addressed the treatment of History in Assia Djebar's writing, few commentaries stand out as memorable in the way Anne Donadey's discussion of the "palimpsest" does. The figure of the palimpsest, drawn from *L'Amour, la fantasia*, is effective in describing the multiple layers of historical representation in Djebar's work:

> The transmission of the History (of the country) as it is tied to a (personal) story translates itself on structural and aesthetic levels through a system of superpositions that turn the movie and the novel into a palimpsest: the superposition of written European archives and the oral transmission of history, as well as the rewriting of history through the intermediary of fiction; the superposition of diverse voices and feminine figures; finally, the superpositions of different periods of Algerian history. ("'Elle a rallumé'" 103)[3]

Djebar disrupts any presupposed hierarchical divisions when she juxtaposes— or, rather *superposes*—written records and oral versions of the past. This superposition does away with a linear, progressive view of historical events by placing one perspective of the past atop another, allowing both to be observed simultaneously.[4] In musical terminology, Djebar can be said to be composing intermingling melodies, rather than providing a single homophonic line followed by a different one. This oft-recognized gesture in Djebar's recent work of according importance to the ongoing verbal histories as they are transmitted from one generation of women to the next, of "filling in" some of the resounding silences in the official historical accounts by putting these recounted stories into print, is the recurring refrain and central theme of *Vaste est la prison*. The very title of the novel echoes this transposition from oral to written form: the elusive phrase comes from a Berber song.

According to a brief note printed at the foot of *Vaste est la prison*'s "table of contents" in the original French version, this novel is not the first written work to publish the words of this Berber tune. Jean Amrouche placed the words of the song alongside those of other melodies as early as 1939 in *Chants berbères de Kabylie* (*Vaste* 350). But the printed words were obviously not enough to capture the impact of the piece; audio versions of the Berber melody quickly became available to the public as well, thanks to the inimitable voice of Amrouche's sister: "The song was often sung and recorded, in the Berber tongue, by Taos Amrouche" (350).[5] It is appropriate that mention is made of these Algerian-born precursors who attempted to protect the memory of this special song through two different means: writing *and* technological recording devices. This effort to capture the music of their land and people is reflected in Assia Djebar's double project of creating novels *and* films.

History and Autobiography

In a statement quoted above, Djebar attests to the influence filmmaking had on her writing. Not only did her cinematographic experiences of the 1970s (a decade of literary "inactivity") bring her to incorporate her educational expertise in her creative work, they also inspired her to look inward, to turn to *herself* as a subject of writing (and writing subject). While the connection between historical writing and autobiographical writing has not been fully explored in relation to her oeuvre, it would be difficult to exaggerate the importance of History to Djebar's autobiographical enterprise. Reflecting on the first volume of her unfinished "Algerian Quartet," *L'Amour, la fantasia*, the writer avows that it was History that provided the necessary foreground for her to speak in a personal, intimate manner. While much has been said about the role of the French tongue, of this "language of the other" in allowing an Algerian woman to speak in the first person, remarkably little emphasis has been placed on what Djebar herself identifies as *the* crucial cover for her move to autobiographical writing:

> With respect to the *mise en abyme* of history in this book, this technique allowed me to escape the interdict proper to women: even in oral conversations, one does not say 'I,' one does not speak of oneself [. . .] historical research did not put into question what I call interior violence. The violence of history emerges when one writes it as if it were staged and it's contradictory. [. . .] But from the moment you write it, you inscribe it in color and words, *it is therefore a violence in slow motion*, a violence anesthetized by the style and form that you provide. This is not the worst violence; the worst is connected to the struggle with oneself. Each author has to deal with it in individual fashion. Historical memory protected me. The historian in me made it possible for intimate writings to come forth. (Hornung and Ruhe 182–83; my emphasis)

Writing History is what allows Djebar to write her story. Under the protection of her academic specialization, she is able to deliver some of the most intimate aspects of *herself* in the text.

The importance Djebar accords to the violence of History is not surprising given the series of conquests that have wreaked havoc on her native Algerian land for centuries.[6] What is surprising is that this historical violence pales in comparison with the battle with oneself, in the writer's eyes.[7] For her, the inner wars are much more "terrible" than those waged outside. Beginning therefore with the lesser violence, that of History, provides her with a point of entry into the more vicious encounter with herself. It is crucial that the violence of both historical and personal writing is contained, even "anesthetized," by the writer's chosen *style* or *form*. The textual markings, in Djebar's analysis, are capable of slowing down violence, of bringing it to a calmer, more manageable speed. In musical terms, Djebar is trumpeting the composer's right to indicate the tempo of the written piece; in this case, she is calling for a "diminuendo," and an "augmentation" or lengthening of the original time values. However violent the subject matter, the ultimate emphasis is up to the writer. She provides the time signature, the accent marks, knowing that these indications convey crucial messages with respect to the written piece. In her search for the proper form in writing, Djebar returns to her first teachers of History, those whose method of instruction differs widely from the one with which she came into contact in school.

Djebar speaks of herself in the third person in the final sentence of the quotation above ("C'est l'historienne qui a permis que les écrits intimes puissent se livrer"), seeming thus to divide her activities as an historian from those of the autobiographical novelist, a division that could be interpreted to suggest a desire to separate formal training from private experience, or the "professional" from the "personal." Such an interpretation would not hold water in the case of this writer, however, since her propensity for historical reflection is closely linked to familial ties and actually predates her educational specialization by as much as fifteen years:

> I would add that this historical memory is connected for me to the memory of my maternal grandmother. [. . .] Fifteen years later, I studied history and met the other history, written history, but the other side. My grandmother had initiated me in the Arabic tongue, in her archaic style wrapped in poetry, to a history, certainly half-legendary, but interiorized. (*Le roman* 26)

At the tender, impressionable age of four or five, Djebar was regaled with stories. In her doctoral dissertation, she refers to one of them to illustrate the impact it had on her as a youngster. According to this brief written account of her maternal grandmother's tale, the elderly woman remembers that her husband's cousin was among the prisoners of war placed in cages at the port of Marseilles. The locals who came to gaze at the foreigners as though they were exotic animals found the features of the boy astonishing: "Why does he have blue eyes? Those people aren't all black then?" (*Le roman* 26). With a punchline like this, it is no wonder that Djebar remembers the story: "My grandmother told me that when I was four or five. And this story penetrated me."[8] Its content *and* its delivery were effective, and the story stuck. What she gained from her grandmother's recollections was more than a yearning for History; Djebar drew from the storytelling episodes an appreciation for and an understanding of the importance of *form* in communicating the past. She found that *what* was told was dependent on *how* it was told. Stories were memorable not simply because of the events they recounted, but because of the *way* these events were recounted.[9]

The autobiographical narrative from *L'Amour, la fantasia* delivers a similar message when it evokes the radio-transmitted messages that accompanied wintry mornings of the annual *fête du mouton* in the Algeria of Djebar's childhood. The story of Abraham and Isaac struck the young girl's heart, not simply because of its various twists and turns of plot, but mostly because of its *form*, a *mélopée* (192). The deep and lasting impression of this annual concert seems to defy logic, and while she quotes from the biblical drama to convey its general content, the narrator ultimately gives up her quest for retrospective explanation and yields to the power of this auditory recollection: "Palpitation de cette musique." (193). I return to this pivotal early moment (explored in greater detail in the previous chapter on religion) because the emphasis on music's ability to influence sensibilities and establish durable memories carries over into the domain of History.[10] In contrast to the official accounts of the History of her homeland, the voices of her forebears sing an unforgettable tune, and provide Djebar with a model that she employs in both of her films and then carries over, in a unique transposition, into her writing.

Foreground Music: De L'Histoire aux histories

When speaking of her conception of cinematographic production, Assia Djebar uses a composite word of her own invention: "*image-son.*" These two constitutive elements of movies combine to produce a powerful effect on the viewer,[11] one that has the potential in Djebar's work to rectify some of the wrongful stereotypical portraits dating from the colonial period. I will return to the importance of the first part of the term "image-sound" later; the audio portion of Djebar's two feature-length films is what I would like to focus on for the moment. In her own analysis, this aspect provided the initial overriding impetus for filmmaking: "[W]hy did I go into audiovisual work? For the sound and the word, the feminine word that I wanted to seek at its source, if possible. When I say the word, I mean to a great extent the music, the noise of language" (*Ces voix* 182). In *La Nouba des femmes du Mont Chenoua*, an unusual scene is constructed around a meaningful image at a standstill: a grandmother is seated before her granddaughter on a large bed. Since movement is at a minimum, sound takes center stage.[12] The music that emerges in the film seems to echo a deep inner quest for the original language, for the elusive mother tongue that is ever out of reach for the writer: "I, an Arab woman, writing classical Arabic poorly, loving and suffering in my mother's dialect, knowing that I have to recapture the deep song strangled in the throat of my people, finding it again with images, with the murmur beneath images" (*Vast* 206).

In an unexpected twist, Djebar hints that film may be just the place to re-discover the song of her people. Contrary to popular understandings of the medium, this moviemaker believes that the visual is not the predominant sense: "'Filming': that is, first closing the eyes to hear better in the dark, and then opening them again only for the flickering instant of birth" (*Vast* 205).[13] Advancing "in the dark" toward the appropriate cinematic sequence is part of Djebar's unique approach; but while she seeks out "the new" in this manner, she finds herself nonetheless inspired by "the old." The painful ex-periences of her ancestors, the moments of mourning that moved those who came before her, propel the filmmaker onward in her quest for threnodies, for lost songs of lamentation.[14]

The figure of the grandmother in the film is not solitary; this remarkable woman who holds within her the memory of all (*"la détentrice de la mémoire de tous"*) is joined by a chorus of contributing voices as the camera zooms back to take in the larger picture.[15] Allowing a number of women to whisper various histories in what Djebar refers to as the *"scène de la Transmission"* opens up her personal family history to similar histories of other members of the "tribe." The young girl's grandmother is not a soloist, but rather a chorus member, and her own special timbre is complemented by the vocal perform-ances of others around her. The music they collectively make in the film is accentuated by a musical accompaniment by a modern composer: "It is a se-lection from a quartet by Bela Bartok that magnifies the sequence shot [*plan-séquence*] of the whole" (*Le roman* 27). Opting for the music of this particu-lar composer is significant, for Béla Bartók's collections of peasant folksongs from his native Hungary are reminiscent of Djebar's own research in rural Al-geria. While some might consider Bartók's investigation of the "humble" tra-ditions of his homeland to be unpropitious for an international career as a celebrated artist, his findings certainly didn't stand in the way of his creativ-ity. To the contrary, they undoubtedly *contributed* to his innovative composi-tions, as traditional music from his native land inspired him to insert similar intervals and rhythms into his pieces.[16]

Another level of sound is added to the whispering voices and musical quartet in this scene from the film *La Nouba*. As Djebar explains it, a voiceover gradually crescendos to "cover" the voices of the *"diseuses de l'His-toire."* This additional stratum in the multilayered soundtrack thus slowly "takes over" to comment on the scene unfolding before the spectator's eyes: "And recounted history repeats itself / [. . .] / And history repeats itself next to the coals / With broken words / And voices that seek each other / And old scorned women / Because they don't speak French." The pronunciation of these contentious words puts a different spin on the touching sight of grandmothers communicating with their grandchildren. What seems at the outset to be a harmless, tender scene of storytelling becomes a politically charged moment: the poem alerts the spectator to the heretofore unspoken criticisms leveled at these voices of History.

The subtle ironic twist of the poem's message hinges precisely on the subject of its verses' criticism: language. The poem was originally written in French by Djebar for a collection titled *Poèmes pour l'Algérie heureuse*. In the film, the poem is read in Arabic translation, in fluid language that flows, as Djebar describes it (*Le roman* 27).[17] Calling attention *in Arabic* to the fact that these elderly women are viewed by some as "*vieilles méprisées*," that they are considered with disrespect—even scorn—because of a "lack" of competence in the French tongue is a smart linguistic move in the film. It is one thing to accuse these elders of not speaking French *in French*; it is quite another to make the same accusation *in Arabic*.[18] The charge that these Algerian women do not speak French seems entirely out of place when it is made in their dialect. It also seems inappropriate time-wise: the women learned to speak in a region (the Aurès) and a period (mid- to late-nineteenth century) that escaped the direct domination of the French colonizer. Blaming them for not mastering the tongue imposed by this colonizer is thus not only misplaced, it is ill-timed.

The three auditory layers of the scene are paralleled by three temporal levels contributing to its creation: the autobiographical event of the young girl listening attentively to her grandmother's tales dates back to around 1941, approximately thirty-five years before this filming; the poem found its way to print in 1968, about eight years prior to this scene; and the scene itself, at the heart of the movie, was staged before the camera in 1976, two years before the film came to fruition (*Le roman* 27–28). These different moments in time all point back to a memory that predates them, located in language: "Thus, the deepest memory is tied to Arabic" (*Le roman* 27). The Arabic tongue spoken by her ancestors, the language of the *diseuses de l'Histoire*, was denied Djebar when she entered the French school system as a child. While the poem's accusation could never be turned against its author, its inclusion in the film reveals a deeper longing on her part. Indeed, knowledge of French does not efface the pain of not knowing "her" language in the same way.[19] The greatest source of nostalgia for a writer naturally stems from the inability to *write* the "first" language: "For Algerians, [. . .] this unchosen franco-phonie is weighed down by a sort of nostalgia, a frustration to not be able to write in 'their' language" (29). When Djebar asserts that she could have been a *poetesse* in Arabic, she is mourning the loss of a written tongue that would have permitted her to express herself otherwise.[20] This personal lament is communicated through the voiceover in the film. The soundtrack works to change the way the spectator sees the images on screen;[21] the spoken words put into question the apparent tranquility of the storytelling seen and underscore the fact that things are not always what they seem.

In her second film, *La Zerda et les chants de l'oubli*, Assia Djebar applies her skills as an historian to the task of filmmaking, relying this time exclusively on archival footage shot by French colonizers in the Maghreb in the first half of the twentieth century. By rearranging these images, the moviemaker rein-terprets them, reworking "Maghrebian memory from the first half of this cen-tury" (*Ces voix* 151).[22] Remixing these recorded images is far from an inno-cent activity, and Djebar feels the explosive weight of the past as she works (153). What the filmmaker testifies to is an awareness that the past is still "present," that its wounds, even if hidden, are not yet healed. She also shows that the past is not set "once and for all," that it remains to be interpreted, and that points of view on former events evolve with time and vary accord-ing to perspective. She communicates these truths in *La Zerda* by taking the images from the hands of the dominant power and changing their import, "simply" by changing the sound effects that accompany them. Leaving the images intact, Djebar changes the way the spectator sees them by carefully choosing a new soundtrack.[23] Djebar thus transforms the typical arrangement of "background music," deciding instead to foreground music as the central element of the movie.

In *Ces voix qui m'assiègent*, Djebar revisits the work of editing *La Zerda*: "Silent images, whose noise I had cut in advance, the rumbling." After this initial silencing, she faces a dilemma that others would have solved differ-ently: "I know that others, would make their polished soundtrack out of a thunderous bombardment, of frightful cries after a plane dive, screams of panic, to the rhythm of the ocean, sonorous waves worthy of an opera: a spectacle!" (152). Djebar opts for something unusual, choosing not to sensa-tionalize the featured events in Hollywood fashion, but rather to let an anonymous woman's voice provide their rhythm, to the tune of the follow-ing words from the movie soundtrack: "Memory is the voice of a woman / stripped / night after night, we strangle it / under the bed of a deep sleep" (152). This song, composed by Djebar, contains a repeated word that casts a dark shadow on the otherwise joyful image it accompanies: "*makhdoucha* (flayed)" (152).[24] This plaintive song lasts three minutes and twenty seconds, according to the filmmaker, reminding us with precise detail that film is a medium that takes place in time, and that timing matters. Indeed, every second counts in an hour-long cinematic project: "I realize that I began this film, this stubborn research into my ancestors and myself, with verve: frivolity of these profuse images of hatred and suspicion that I will melt in measured [*chronométré*] time" (*Ces voix* 153).

Despite this awareness of the need to condense the hours of recorded material for the final cut of the film, Djebar makes no compromise when it comes to investing herself in the work of collecting voices and images. She is engaged in lived experiences in their duration, and demonstrates a patience that accompanies her understanding that it takes time to recognize the other, and the self, and that artistic work demands immersion "for the duration."[25] Such a respect is rare among contemporary artists, according to Paul Virilio, who asserts that the very concept of "duration" is currently in danger.[26] A sympathetic narrative voice explains in *Vaste est la prison* a need to relive the agony of a murdered friend, not in fast-forward, but in actual time: "Approaching, for just a fraction of a second if need be, the extent [*la durée*] of his martyrdom" (*Vast* 343). Taking her time is part of Assia Djebar's project, and this commitment to getting to know her subjects, even if it takes a while, contributes to the rigorous, lasting, indeed *durable* quality of her artistic creations.

From Snapshots to Moving Pictures: Finding the Right Timing

The first part of the title of Djebar's second film, *La Zerda*, refers to a *fête*, a festival filled with food, dancing, and celebration. It is this "exotic" occasion that attracts the cameras of foreigners eager to capitalize on their contact with this colonized land and its people, as Jeanne-Marie Clerc describes it:

> It is indeed the celebration that the invaders will photograph and film later, illustrating thus the apogee of the colonial empire through thousands of postcards and documentaries. The platitude of these images will find its equal in the euphoria of the legends and commentaries, destined to highlight the foreignness—and exoticism for tourists—of these routine spectacles, destined only for their displaced curiosity. (100)

These images of her Algerian compatriots in action, stills and video clips exported to the European continent to pique the curiosity of those unaccustomed to such sights, belittle not only the featured activities but also, especially, the people themselves. By focusing on selected "representative" images and allowing them to stand, out of context, for an entire society, postcards and brief documentary films do an injustice to the pictured subjects. Most often, they perpetuate a preconceived view of the colonized population; those holding the camera inject their prejudiced perspective into the finished product and project an incomplete, typified image of the culture and people captured by their recording apparatus. Djebar's cinematic response constitutes a corrective to some of the wrongs committed in these stereotyping procedures. In line with a number of books—from Malek Alloula's *Le harem colonial* to Leïla Sebbar and Jean-Michel Belorgey's *Femmes d'Afrique du Nord*—that call attention to the postcards from this period of Algerian History, Djebar denounces the "negatives" of this colonial impulse by providing her own commentary. Since there are no "counterimages" to complicate the picture, no photographs taken by the Algerians of their European invaders during the colonial period, the former have no choice but to respond with an alternative narrative to render more complex the seemingly straightforward visual representations.[27] Providing the cries and laments from the "other side" of the picture is part of the filmmaker's goal of *contextualizing* the images on screen. Revealing the feelings and reactions of the colonized fills in some of the gaping holes in the visual story. In the words of Jeanne-Marie Clerc, Djebar's movie soundtrack marks a departure from "simple historical illustrations" and reveals what until then is occluded from the pictures: the "*bande sonore*" (101). Clerc's affirmation that images are capable of dissimulation, that pictures can often hide the truth, is crucial to understanding Djebar's perspective on the representation of History.

In *La Chambre claire*, Roland Barthes intimates that the advent of the photographic image lends new credibility to the past. In this view, pictures might thus have the power to prove, and thereby convince us that events have taken place despite our hesitancy to believe them. In a series of filmed interviews with Bernard Stiegler, Jacques Derrida reflects aloud on what Barthes calls "l'*effet* photographique," the impression that a photo irrefutably represents a moment that was "present" in the past:

> In any case, it is structurally supposed to have captured this irreplaceable present: "that" was "there" once, and the singularity of this "once" will be unquestionable; it will testify, "that was there." It not only proves; it also testifies. Of course, we understand well this "effect" and the "poignant" emotion—to take up Barthes's word—that this produces rightly in us. (*Échographies* 110)

Despite this admitted emotional effect of photographs, their authenticity is always, immediately, put into question: "But this effect can be composed, it isn't natural, and it always runs the risk of being artificially constructed. There is construction even in the photo that is not manipulated; and one can always in addition overcharge it with technical inventions of every type" (110). Leaving aside the fact that technological advances have made all sorts of manipulations possible (to the point that photographs do not ever have the final word in a court of law), pictures are arguably subjective from the outset, inevitably reflecting a specific angle. The camera focuses in on particular objects in its viewfinder and neglects to include other aspects of the picture. Photos are therefore, by nature, selective; they are also incomplete to tell a story. Despite the adage that "a picture is worth a thousand words," images alone are often not enough to communicate the whole message. They require additional information that will provide context: place, time, and circumstance are among the essential factors that condition the taking of pictures.

The great danger of the contemporary profusion of images is the lack of appropriate commentary to explain them. Current critics of photographic representations in the media are quick to call for an astute reading of the images that bombard the public: "It is [. . .] essential to learn to read images. The hierarchy in news leads to [. . .] battles in the editing room. The result is images that we must read in specific ways. Juxtaposing two images, for example, is already to construct a discourse. Manipulation is always present" (Caujolle 55). In *La Zerda*, Djebar pulls together used images to give them a different spin, infusing them with new meaning and inspiring spectators to critically re-view/review their contents.

In contrast to a handful of book projects that examine postcards depicting Algerian society in the early 1900s, Djebar has chosen to respond to the problematic visual representations of the former French colony with another medium: film. There is a specific reason for this choice, for it adds a temporal dimension that is not present in the same way in the printed picture or the published word.[28] The running musical commentary that frames the selected images takes place *in time*. While it shares some characteristics with the photograph, since it too records something that existed once in the past, the musical phrase is distinctive because it cannot be limited to a single instant, to an infinitesimal sound bite.[29] Instead, it must be appreciated in its duration, as Bernard Stiegler explains—with the assistance of the phenomenological thought of Edmund Husserl—in his volume on "Le temps du cinéma":

If cinema can be sonorous, it is because film, as a technique of photographic recording capable of reconstituting movement, is itself a temporal object that emerges from phenomenological analyses proper to this type of object. A film, like a melody, is essentially a flow [*flux*]: it is constituted in a unit as a flowing. This temporal object, as flow, *coincides* with the flow of consciousness of which it is an object—the consciousness of the spectator. (33)

The "movement" of cinematic production is of critical importance to Djebar who continually returns to this idea in her written work, on a number of thematic and stylistic levels. The thrill that she derives from space and movement inspires her to literary works to the extent that she even likens writing to running, as we have already seen.[30] It is not an accident that the layouts of two volumes of the Algerian quartet, *L'Amour, la fantasia* and *Vaste est la prison* are characterized by the presence of *movements*, in the musical sense of the word. It is significant that these movements convey the most overtly autobiographical moments of the written text, suggesting that for this author, revealing the self is synonymous with music and bodily displacement, with dance. There is a certain symmetry to the composition of the novels, as the movements constitute alternating chapters located in the *troisième partie* of both books. In *Vaste est la prison*, seven movements revisiting moments in Djebar's personal and familial history are interspersed with chapters focusing on the filming of *La Nouba des femmes du Mont Chenoua*. In *L'Amour, la fantasia*, five movements contain within them different subdivisions, all titled "Voice," with the exception of the final three that are termed "A Widow's Voice." These voices speak from the recorded archives surrounding the filming of *La Nouba*.[31] Time constraints necessitated the exclusion of most of this vocal testimony from the final movie cut,[32] but these stories were not forever lost, even if the task of reviving them in the written text in French is not easy: "Can I, twenty years later, claim to revive these stifled voices? And speak for them? Shall I not at best find dried-up streams? What ghosts will be conjured up when in this absence of expressions of love (love received, 'love' imposed), I see the reflection of my own barrenness, my own aphasia" (*Fantasia* 202).[33] In step with the metaphor of the "blind leading the blind," Djebar describes the difficult project of the mute "speaking" not "for," but *near* the mute.

Photo-synthesis: Bringing Asphyxiated Voices to Light

Losing one's voice is a recurring theme in *Vaste est la prison*. A number of women, at different times and in varying circumstances, find themselves suddenly speechless. The first, and perhaps most strident example, is found in the person of the narrator's mother. Bahia is literally dumbstruck upon the death of her dear sister, Chérifa. The passing of this sibling, seven years her elder, is simply too much for the six-year-old child to bear. The scene is a dramatic one, set up with brief phrases that create the tone in cinematic style: "Lamentations of women. . . . The little girl crouched at the head of the young dead woman" (*Vast* 240). The image of the child is sober, silent in the midst of wailing mourners. The action begins when a cousin (who happens to be a poetess) rips her veil and then slowly slices her left cheek right in front of the open-mouthed Bahia. The bleeding woman then cries out in verse, improvising on the Berber song that provides the book's title: "So vast the prison crushing me / Release, where will you come from?" (243). These words enter so deeply into the young girl that they render her motionless and speechless. The brief scene ends with the carrying off of Chérifa and the next segment begins—after the pause of a double space in the text's script—with the following staccato rendition of the effect this event had on the younger sister: "In the days that followed and then the weeks, then the months and seasons, one after the other, Bahia did not speak. Did not smile. Did not sing" (243). When a year has passed without a single sound uttered by her daughter, Lla Fatima allowed a woman from the region to work her magic for one day, and the very next morning Bahia spoke softly, naturally, as if no time had elapsed between her last words and these comments on the weather.

It is interesting that the narrator does not imagine this period of speech-lessness to represent a deep inner torment, describing her future mother as "calm" and "cool," but "serene" (238). Another character in the novel whose very name evokes peace and serenity experiences a regular "laryngitis" every time she becomes pregnant, which is often (310). Hania, "the peaceful, or the pacified," is convinced that her voice goes ahead of her, arriving before her in the oasis of her upbringing where she customarily gives birth among her sisters, mother, and aunt; Hania doesn't worry unduly about the short-lived loss. When her mother-in-law pleads her case and her husband gives his consent, the fertile wife is allowed the freedom of movement she desires, and she heads to be with her loved ones. She systematically regains her ability to speak every time she returns home for birthing. Outside the confines of the restrictive marital environment, she finds her "voice," with every nuance this word communicates: expression, opinion, quality, and individuality. It is more than "anecdotal" that the place where Hania finds this liberty of ex-pression is an oasis. In the midst of an arid desert, the oasis is peaceful spot: a haven graced with greenery, with plants and trees, with *breathing room*. As

accomplished singers can attest, the secret to voice is breath. Shut in a sti-
fling domestic situation with children to care for and a husband to please,
Hania's voice was not free to explore the range of its capacities. Stuck in an
inflexible role, the only way to find temporary reprieve from her sentence
was, ironically, to lose her voice.

In the midst of these evocations of lost female voices, Djebar plays back a
scene from her own childhood in which she and the neighbor boy are climb-
ing a tree. Maurice offers his hand to help the younger girl come up to his
level, but she refuses his assistance, fearing the condemnation of her father.
The intriguing aspect of this scene is that it contains no audible accompaniment whatsoever. The narrator seems to describe the scene with retrospective incredulity: "The most incomprehensible thing about my memory is that
I remember this scene of the tree stripped of words, with nothing at all uttered by myself. It is accompanied by no sound: no laughter, no exclamation,
not the slightest word exchanged" (*Vast* 271).[34] It is significant that in this
scene devoid of *voices* ("the voices of our dialogue have vanished" 264), the
actors are also deprived of *motion*: "I stay on my branch, immobilized" (270);
"there is no doubt that this frozen state of voices is what gives the pictures of
the boy its clarity, its immutable presence" (271). This early memory predates
language acquisition in French,[35] and the narrative reveals that the longing
look toward the top of the tree, that the wistful gaze at the face of this beautiful boy, contains a desire that cannot yet be articulated. Djebar vividly remembers being without language, hence without voice.

This scene, recalled perfectly down to the last detail, is presented like a
photograph: the description is clear, but the movement is missing. The four-
year-old girl and the twelve-year-old boy are frozen in time, fixed at this particular moment in muted, motionless poses on the branches of the tree. The
unforgettable frustration she feels due to this inability to speak and move remains with her. In the years to come, its memory undoubtedly contributes to
Djebar's intermingling twofold mission: creating a unique narrative voice in
tune with the multiple voices of women from her native Algeria.[36] Restoring
lost voices in and through writing is the driving purpose behind her recording projects. In creating these compositions that bring together discrete songs
from diverse lips, she knows that voices must be given space, for movement
is crucial to their development, it is essential to their music. Voicing her own
experience simultaneously with that of others requires an understanding of
the technique of "voicing," according to the dictionary definition: "blending
in an ensemble."[37] In order to "blend" better with the other voices in the
group, Djebar's own voice is silenced every night: "Every night my voice
leaves me as I awaken the sickly sweet suffocations of aunts and girl cousins

that I, a little girl, glimpsed and did not understand. Wide-eyed, I contemplate them, and later was able to picture them again and finally understand"
(*Vast* 348). Out of the dark, Djebar brings these asphyxiated voices to light
. . . through writing.

Writing does not put out these voices; it *revives* them, giving them new
life and unexplored possibility: "Writing does not silence the voice, but
awakens it, above all to resurrect [*ressusciter*] so many vanished sisters" (*Fantasia* 204).[38] When her mother was silent for months as a child following
Chérifa's premature death, she was doubly silent because she didn't write:
"At the age of six, my mother turned her back on her dead sister. Annihilated her. Did not write about her. How can one write about her? [*Comment
l'écrire?*]" (*Vast* 348). Aware that "the dead woman [had been] dead too long
because never spoken or written about," Djebar adopts the gesture of writing
to make reparations for this oversight. Her *lamento*, this written cry denouncing "the blood of History and the oppression [*l'étouffement*] of women"
(347), highlights voices that have been overlooked for years. She is restoring
to History its lapses, *in writing*, with a recognition that History is *written*, and
that the way to reinsert the missing stories into the official score is to *write
them in*.[39] But the question remains: "*Comment* l'écrire?"

Musical Notation: Inheriting Invention and Improvisation

How to write music? This is the dilemma Assia Djebar's mother faced as a
teenager, wanting to put on paper the notes she sang with her mother, her
aunts, with the women from other families whose ancestors had fled their
homes in southern Spain for North Africa. Three centuries after this trans-
plantation of an entire community, little remained apart from some sewing
techniques, a slight accent, *and music*: "Above all, the music known as *an-
dalouse* that was called 'classical'" (*Vast* 174). At the age of fifteen, the
mother devised her own system of notation, and the journals containing
these musical transcriptions became the most precious possessions in her
mother's (re)collection. One summer during the Algerian War, the mother
was away when the French soldiers entered her home; the men slashed this
"mysterious writing" because they interpreted it as a secret language for "na-
tionalist" messages (175). The code of her own imagining, the solution she
had devised on her own, was suspect in the eyes of the colonizing force who
wanted to quell any possible plots against it. Language is dangerous, especially if it is indecipherable, and those who seek to put down any opposition
feel they must destroy all suspicious documents, wiping out the traces of centuries without a thought for their inestimable value.

In the context of the end of the Algerian War, the destruction of these papers would appear incidental. After all, other women were lamenting the loss of husbands and sons, and the disappearance of some written work is incomparable to the death of a family member. But this knowledge did not ease the mother's pain. Mourning the loss of this writing and of its music was not simply an expression of selfish regret for a few individual moments of creativity, for the journals contained within them centuries and generations of tradition and transmission from one generation of women to the next. The result of the mother's invention was intended to be a concrete heirloom for her offspring, an answer to her daughter's imploring question: "What was this legacy that she inherited and what did she transmit to me of this memory already covered in sand?" (*Vast* 174). Unable to write again, incapable of equaling her youthful erudition and resourcefulness, the mother knew this writing was gone forever, and that her musical heritage was irrevocably effaced.

The erasure of writing, the effacement of cultural heritage, is a theme that receives greatest attention in the *deuxième partie* of *Vaste est la prison*. This subsection, the shortest of the three major parts of the novel, is the densest in historical material. It recovers, in non-chronological sequence, different elements of the intriguing discovery of an indecipherable script carved in stone, on a stele from Dougga in northern Tunisia. The mysterious inscription, object of intense interest and scrutiny by different archeologists in different circumstances from the seventeenth to the nineteenth centuries, bore two languages, one identified without too much difficulty, but the other completely unrecognizable. Specialists were stumped, mystified by this writing that resembled nothing they had ever seen. They were of course aided in their study of this unidentified language by the companion text, which provided the context—even the translation—of the unknown symbols. Despite their derived knowledge of the signified, the signifier remained elusive, and the source of these signs escaped identification until the mid-nineteenth century, when the secret of this writing finally became clear.

The novel contains clues that part of the reason it took so long to "crack the code," to unearth the language behind the mysterious stone inscription, is that specialists made the mistake of looking only to the past for answers. Two men in particular, Temple and Falbe, are depicted as foreigners who came with this limited approach to the North African ruins: "the two foreigners, the Englishman and the Dane, have come only for the past" (*Vast* 141). Their attitude was similar to that of others who sought answers to this puzzle in the distant past; while the subject of study was fascinating, it was definitively *over* in their preconception. They thought they were in search of a long lost alphabet, of a forgotten language. The narrative voice doesn't trumpet the truth in absolute terms, it doesn't sing out solutions in a re-proachful tone; it instead poses questions, a series of suggestions that subtly mark the hitherto inarticulated point of intersection between the written and the oral in Berber history: "Then suppose this strange writing came alive, was a voice in the present, was spoken out loud, was sung"; "in short, what if Berber had always been a written language? Was still written? Since the dawn of time?" (147, 150). The trained specialists were looking in the wrong place. All along, the answer was right before them: the ancient language was Berber, a living tongue with resonance in the present: "And leaving scholars in their studies to seek and study and listen and suppose . . . always with the thought that they are on a quest for some lost meaning—underground echoes. And yet the writing was alive. Its sonority, its music, its rhythms still reeled on around them" (*Vast* 148).

The failure to see this fairly obvious connection is arguably related not only to a temporal, but also a *geographic* decontextualization. The narrator discloses the actions of an Englishman named Thomas Reade who in 1833 purchased the stele with the greedy goal of selling it to the British Museum in London. In 1842, he wrought irrevocable damage on the ancient site, hir-ing a group of workmen to demolish the façade of the monument of which the stele was a part, and cut the coveted object in two for easier shipping. Re-moving the written inscriptions from their context in this way[40] constituted a "crime" according to Reade's countryman Nathan Davis, who denounced this pillage and the avarice that inspired it. Even when French archeologists carefully rebuilt the mausoleum in 1910, it was not the same, for the stele was gone: "the mausoleum is once again standing, almost intact, but stripped of its double writing" (*Vast* 145). The theft of this writing results in more than a material loss, as in the case of the destroyed writing belonging to the mother. This form of expression constitutes an *inheritance*, left behind by the royal Tin Hinan, the ancestor of the noble Tuaregs of Hoggar. When a team of archeologists discovered this legendary woman's remains in 1925, this mythical figure evoked in dreamlike stories was transformed into a historical individual. Her skeleton solidified her existence, rendering unquestionable the dates and places she inhabited. But her bones are not all that this re-markable forebear left behind: "Tin Hinan of the sands, almost obliterated, leaves us an inheritance. [. . .] Our most secret writing, as ancient as Etruscan or the writing of the runes, but unlike these a writing still noisy with the sounds and breath of today, is indeed the legacy of a woman in the deepest desert" (*Vast* 167).[41]

The inheritance women like Tin Hinan and Bahia leave for those who come after them is not fixed or immovable, nor is it "pious" or "sacred." It is something that falls in line with Derrida's reflections in *Sur Parole*: "The experience of inheritance is fundamental, but the word often carries pious or edifying connotations of which I am also wary. Maybe we should find another word. There is a passing on [*passage*] from one generation to another, from one place to another, a relay [*relance*]: transfer and relay" (58). In a reflection titled "Taos, or the song of the Phoenix," Djebar explains in close detail the way such transmission from one generation to the next takes place in the specific case of song: when Taos Amrouche performs in public the ancient Berber tunes she learned from her mother in private, she is delving into her heritage (*Ces voix* 134–35). But while she sings the same songs her mother did, Taos Amrouche interprets them in a different voice, that of a "conqueror" (135).[42] By performing the private songs of pain in a triumphant tone, with a voice of victory, Amrouche builds upon the music of her heritage, transposing it to another key and subtly transforming its message.

Vaste est la prison is a book that continually questions the concept of inheritance, returning to this theme to explore social and communal artifacts and determine what ultimately has value, what lasts, what remains from the past, what we retain from the meanderings of History. In its pages, the idea of *"héritage"* represents a space in which to create, indeed to invent, as Derrida explains it: "the invented thing will be protected by a system of conventions that will ensure for it at the same time its recording in a common history, its belonging to a culture: to a heritage, a lineage, a pedagogical tradition, a discipline, a chain of generations. Invention begins by being susceptible to repetition, exploitation, reinscription" (*Acts of Literature* 316). The "new" therefore interacts with the "old," building upon inherited traditions to come up with unforeseen ways of life and expression. In a rapidly changing world depicted with the ambiguous term "globalization," invention is ever more a part of our daily lives. Since she is an avid user of the Internet for culling information and communicating worldwide, Djebar is constantly aware of the ways this particular medium is transforming "writing" as we know it. The concision and immediacy both of news briefs and e-mail messages have an impact on her creative processes. Indeed, her novels bear witness to this "technological heritage" of her age, just as they reveal the multiple inheritances that were her birthright.

Like another Algerian-born intellectual, Jacques Derrida, Assia Djebar cannot claim one single cultural tradition as her sole heritage. The examples of the double maternal inheritance (Andalusian and Berber) provided in the paragraphs above are only two strains of the numerous influences she can claim as her own. The many cultures and languages of the unique environment of colonial Algeria represent endless sources of creativity and ingenuity for her, as for Derrida.[43] In her work, Djebar incorporates her various "inheritances" in a manner that points toward something truly innovative, in concert with Françoise Lionnet's observation: "Women writing in postcolonial contexts [. . .] become quite adept at braiding all of the traditions at [their] disposal, using the fragments that constitute [them] in order to participate fully in a dynamic process of transformation" (*Postcolonial Representations* 5). Weaving together the various vocal patterns of the different languages she hears, Djebar composes a harmony that reflects original tunes without reproducing them down to the exact detail.[44] As Derrida indicates, an inheritance is seldom passed on in unchanged form. While they depend on knowledge and skills that have been transmitted and draw inspiration from their heritage, "authentic inheritors" go beyond a mere rehearsal to compose and *sign* something distinct: "Authentic heirs, the kind we can wish to be, are heirs who have broken enough with the origin, father, examiner, writer, and philosopher to go forward and sign or countersign their inheritance with their own movement. To counter-sign is to sign something else, the same thing and another thing in order to make something else come about. The countersignature presupposes, in theory, absolute freedom" (*Sur Parole* 60). In her inventive novels, Djebar finds her own movement to countersign her heritage. She "finds her voice," so to speak, as emerging from an origin that is characterized as much by her maternal lineage as it is by the "paternal" tongue.[45] She finds her voice, *so to speak* that heritage, so to write her inheritances in another tongue and thereby "pass on" something that bears the sound imprint of her oral tongues in the written text.[46] The mobility and freedom that the French language has given her in her personal and professional trajectories translate into movement in the text: "Autobiographical text or fictional text, [. . .] when I begin a text, what is essential is the movement, the mobility of the text" (*Ces voix* 115).

In a talk titled "Violence de l'autobiographie" delivered in Germany in June 1996, Djebar addresses the movement of her first overtly autobiographical work, treating of the personal quest it inspired: "My text became an urgent personal quest, both intimate and collective; it progressed into a demanding search for an obscure form, for a structure that, little by little, I had to *invent*" (*Ces voix* 107; my emphasis). It is my contention that Djebar illustrates the "obscure form" she sought so diligently and used so effectively in the first three volumes of her autobiographical quartet here, in this spoken discourse. She prefaces these words about inventing the novel's structure in this way: "allow me to dip into an anecdote regarding the publication of *L'Amour, la fantasia*, in March–April 1985" (107). After briefly situating this new book in relation to her earlier publication of short stories, *Femmes d'Al-*

ger, Djebar recounts the "*trouble violent*" that took hold of her when she realized that this private text was going to be read: a letter praising the novel rendered real its heretofore unimagined readers, and the author came down with a painful case of tendonitis in her shoulder on the spot! She finishes this segment of her speech in this way: "That's it for the anecdote" (108). It is no accident that Djebar evokes the challenge of finding the appropriate form for writing fiction and autobiography in the midst of an anecdotal passage. Novels like *L'Amour, la fantasia*, but also and especially *Vaste est la prison*, thrive on a structure dependent on anecdotes. This "invention" in Djebar's written work may be much closer to her heritage than one would think.

Finding Form: Anecdotal Evidence Past and Present

The web site for a publication by feminist literary critic Jane Gallop calls attention to a relatively new topic of theoretical discourse among academics: anecdotes. The write-up on the book's contents indicates that this work dismantles a number of binary oppositions to establish a connection between the two components of its title:

> "Anecdote" and "theory" have diametrically opposed connotations: humorous versus serious, specific versus general, trivial versus overarching, short versus grand. *Anecdotal Theory* cuts through these oppositions to produce theory with a sense of humor, theorizing that honors the uncanny detail of lived experience. Challenging academic business as usual, Gallop argues that all theory is bound up with stories and urges theorists to pay attention to the "trivial," quotidian narratives that theory all too often represses.[47]

The word "theory" in this blurb (which largely quotes from page 2 in Gallop's book) could easily have been replaced by "History" *in the past*, for History (especially "in the nineteenth century mould" Ashcroft et al., 355) was often assumed to be serious, general, overarching, and grand, granting little space to the "uncanny detail of lived experience." As an academic discipline, History was not supposed to pay attention to the trivial, but instead to focus on the essential. Fortunately, developments in the field have led to the recognition that excluding "trivial" narratives of the quotidian is arguably harmful, as such an approach misses out on crucial aspects of human life. Paul Carter addresses one of the common misunderstandings of History and the historian's task in the past by employing the metaphor of the theatre:

> It is not the historian who stages events, weaving them together to form a plot, but History itself. History is the playwright, coordinating facts into a coherent

sequence: the historian narrating what happened is merely a copyist or amanu-
ensis. He is a spectator like anybody else and, whatever he may think of the
performance, he does not question the stage conventions. [. . .] This kind of
history, which reduces space to a stage, that pays attention to events unfolding
in time alone, might be called imperial history. (*Post-Colonial* 375)

Carter underscores the preference of this "imperial history" for "fixed and detachable facts" that can be removed from their contexts: "Orphaned from
their unique spatial and temporal context, such objects, such historical facts,
can be fitted out with new paternities" (376). "Fitting out" historical facts
"with new paternities," as this post-colonial critic puts it, is an act of writing
that clearly goes against the assumed "spectator" status of the historian. An
historian is far from an objective spectator, despite the lofty, unbiased goals
of the discipline, as Jeanne-Marie Clerc points out with respect to the work
of Assia Djebar: "Therein lies a new recognition of History as writing first of
all, and the one who holds the pen cannot deny that which makes up his or
her specificity as a singular person" (107).[48] History is ultimately a human
operation, and is therefore, from the outset, destined to reflect human limitations.

As the title of Carter's essay shows, the critic is less interested in the typical temporal approach to history than he is in what he terms "spatial history."[49] For him, "spatial forms and fantasies" make up "a form of non-linear
writing" that mirrors human existence: "our life as it discloses itself spatially
is dynamic, material but invisible. It constantly transcends actual objects to
imagine others beyond the horizon" (376). Acknowledging the role of imagination is not a conventional gesture when it comes to understanding History, but Carter is far from the only theorist to open up the discipline to reflections of this kind. Dipesh Chakrabarty, in *Postcoloniality and the Artifice of
History*, argues in favor of "provincializing 'Europe,' the 'Europe' that modern
imperialism and (third-world) nationalism have, by their collaborative venture and violence, made universal" (385). In this view, the key to "provincializing Europe" lies in "writing over the given and privileged narratives of
citizenship other narratives of human connections that draw sustenance from
dreamed-up pasts and futures" where the nightmare of "tradition" created by
"modernity" no longer holds power (388). According to Clerc's analysis of
Djebar's written and film projects, imagination is one of the original aspects
of Djebar's approach to History (107). The central scene in the film *La
Nouba* begins with a grandmother and a granddaughter sitting on a bed: this
location acquires new significance in light of the attention of postcolonial
critics to dreaming and imagination in constructing History. It is the place

where the two female figures have liberty to revisit the past and to tell stories, thereby keeping their family histories alive, but it is also the place where they fall asleep, slipping out of consciousness and supplementing memory with invention. In the comments of Carter and Chakrabarty, the flexibility of these dreams and imaginings include the present and extend to the future, opening up the temporal dimension of History to possibilities—spatial and other—situated outside of linear time.

"History" is too often concerned with causes and consequences, with concrete events, and with developments over time. The presuppositions of these concerns are sometimes anathema to the experience of the "antihistorical, antimodern subject" that "cannot speak itself as 'theory' within the knowledge procedures of the university," according to Chakrabarty. This inability to speak oneself as a postcolonial subject is due to a "procedure that subordinates [. . .] narratives to the rules of evidence and to the secular, linear calendar that the writing of 'history' must follow" (384). The "secular, linear calendar" is imposed on postcolonial subjects without taking into account other possible relations to both time and History.[50] According to Tejaswini Niranjana's reading of *Time and the Other* by Johannes Fabian, "the process of secularizing, generalizing, and universalizing Judeo-Christian time is seen [. . .] as contemporaneous with the rise of colonialism" (*Siting Translation* 79). In this view, such categories as "primitive" or "traditional" become "in the discourse of ethnology, not objects of study but temporal categories of Western thought" (79). Assia Djebar, in her comments on the History of her homeland, completely destabilizes the idea of linear progress. Colonialism was a terrible setback to the educational system in Algeria, and women were the primary victims of this reversal of fortune:

> Certain cases in Algerian regions demonstrate how history jumps, advances, and then goes backward. I can provide an example from my mother-in-law's family, the mother of Malek Alloula. Like many women her age (she is now 70 or 75 years old), she doesn't read or write French and she doesn't find this abnormal. On the other hand, her mother (who would be 100 now) had been to French school and obtained a diploma. My mother-in-law said to me: "During the Algerian War when I was in Oran and my mother in Tlemcen, she would read the newspapers and as soon as she saw that there had been an incident in Oran, she would call me on the phone." The mother was therefore in the world of French writing, but the daughter was not. (Hornung and Ruhe 189–90)

Given the "backward" direction women's education took in the case of her stepmother's family, the temporal distinction ethnologists establish between "tradition" and "modernity" is less convincing. If "orality" is on the side of "tradition" and "literacy" is on the side of "modernity," then the fact that 90 percent of Algerians were illiterate in 1962, at the close of French colonial rule, is enough to give one pause.[51] Telling this story as she does here, in the setting of a colloquium on autobiography, Djebar once again has recourse to the ultimate resource of her written form: the voices of women come through in Djebar's tale.

Building on Michel Foucault's assertion that "effective history affirms knowledge as perspective" (156), Niranjana articulates the necessity for a narrative strategy that takes History into account without falling into the trap of a teleological historicism, "which Derrida has rightly categorized as a manifestation of Western metaphysics" (37). Niranjana uses the word *historicity* (rather than History) to "include the idea of change" that is missing from many "colonial discourses" that "present the colonial subject as unchanging and immutable"[52] in the hope that "the use of historicity / effective history may help us sidestep the metaphysics of linearity" (38). Djebar creates a narrative strategy that at once uses archival documents from the official records of History and "recuperates" the stories of her countrywomen.[53] The narrative strategy not only disrupts accounts of the past by inserting "lost voices" to fill in the gaps, but also, as the figure of the palimpsest suggests, places the present on a level with the past, writing *simultaneously*, in a sense, with the writers whose works pepper the text, as in the following phrases from *L'Amour, la fantasia*: "I, in my turn, write, using the language, but more than one hundred and fifty years later [. . .] I slip into the antechamber of this recent past, like an importunate visitor, removing my sandals according to the accustomed ritual, holding my breath in an attempt to overhear everything" (*Fantasia* 7–8). In *Vaste est la prison*, the narrator highlights the present of her writing, while insisting that this present coincides with her description of events from 138 B.C.: "But I, today's humble narrator, a woman, say that whereas Jugurtha at Dougga reads in the ancestral language for the last time, the writing of Polybe is nourished by all this simultaneous destruction" (*Vast* 161). The sentence continues in the original French, in a complicated maneuver that places her writing (with its oral quality, emphasized with the repetitive "*je dis*," or "I say") over the ancient text of the famous historian while suspending a young character's reading of an even earlier script, that found on the stele. Calling attention to the "here and now" of the writing of the novel while suspending an action from the past creates a complex temporality that blends pasts and present in such a way that the two are contemporaneous, as in this quotation from philosopher Françoise Proust: "the past is not posterior to the present; it is the present's contemporary. The past constitutes itself at the same time as the present, or rather, at the very moment when the present takes place, it fixes itself as past" (36).

The word "History" itself usually refers to the past, but it is also a term applied to the present, hence the complexity of the word and its connotations.[54] According to a number of theoreticians, History is a rather recent invention, and our perception of historical events—such as wars—as dated events is a fresh development. Despite this newfound awareness of History, it is difficult to remain abreast of contemporary occurrences. Djebar expresses a sense of urgency that overcame her when writing *Vaste est la prison*, precisely because of the speed of forgetting that characterizes our time:

> Apart from two or three chapters written earlier, the whole book was written in three months of anguish, following the death of Abdelkader Alloula on 15 March 1994. I physically felt the threat of an Algeria that was going to become like the former Yugoslavia, with an effacement of recent history [. . .] people spent their time discussing whether the state of Algeria was going to disappear. First of all, the important thing about Algeria was not its national status. Algeria is twenty centuries and more! (Hornung and Ruhe 186)

These spoken words turned text are important because they reveal a larger historical picture than is typically addressed in archival documents that only go as far back as the French invasion in 1830. Algeria, Djebar points out, existed long before it became a nation, and this complex history of peoples and languages is crucial to understanding the country's present makeup. But the long History of Algeria is not what pushed Djebar to complete her third volume so quickly: it was the concern that the recent History would be effaced. This fear of erasure provides the titles for the first two parts of the novel, and propels the narrative toward its bloody end: In "Le sang de l'écriture— Final—," even writing in blood effaces itself: "Blood does not dry, it simply evaporates" (*Vast* 358).

The rush of History that provokes Assia Djebar's writing is described in Françoise Proust's noteworthy study of historical time, *L'Histoire à contretemps*. As Proust observes, "Modern time does not unfold cumulatively and peacefully, it is made of strikes that hurt and arrive at an absolutely insane speed. The world is at war, each day is a day of war" (53). Given the speed with which time passes, Proust advocates a writings that would come "right in time [*juste à temps*]" (52), at the last minute, before it's too late, "before history puts itself back into movement" (53). Derrida, in a close reading of the Shakespearean *Romeo and Juliet*, also employs the word "*contretemps*" in his analysis of the way the proper name functions in the play. In an introduction by Derek Attridge, it becomes clear how "Derrida responds to, and connects [. . .] features of the play by means of a focus on contretemps, a word which in French can mean both 'mishap' and 'syncopation,' while the phrase 'à contretemps' suggests both 'inopportunely' and, in a musical sense, 'out of time' or 'in counter-time'" (*Acts* 414). Not limiting his analysis to the proper name, Derrida extends his study to examine the larger phenomenon of naming as a cultural practice responsible for "instituting and enforcing temporal and spatial homogeneity." The tragic events of Shakespeare's play reveal the shortcomings of naming and lead to an "understanding of the force of contretemps both in the play and in the institutional and intellectual context" (414). Failing to take into account the history that predates the naming impulse leads to its ultimate demise: "In their confounding of homogeneous time and place, therefore, countertime and mishap echo an absolute heterogeneity with is 'anterior' to times and happenings, and the various labels by which we try to order them" (415).

In English, the word "contretemps" is also used, often to refer to a quarrel or a disagreement, but also to evoke an inopportune occurrence, an unforeseen event that disrupts the normal course of things. Djebar's writing follows this model, intervening in a timely fashion, just at the pause, *on the offbeat*, before the rhythm swipes away the memory of the previous phrase. Her writing disrupts the normal course of things, denouncing wrongs past and present in unexpected manners that make it clear that no History is yet established, that History is an ongoing process of dialogue and discussion. What form does this "*écriture à contretemps*" assume then in Djebar's written work? For that, she looks to the women of her homeland.

During a decade of silence, Djebar published no written texts. But that did not mean she was inactive; to the contrary, this was a time of intense listening and learning. She recalls her experiences in the small mountain towns of her childhood in a television interview:

> When I went in search of women, peasants and mountain dwellers, in the mid-1970s, I thought that it was women who kept the memory of the war of resistance in their flesh and their daily lives. I spent days in small villages in the mountains, I went up to places where there were no roads and I found women everywhere, from my father's tribe, from my mother's tribe. These women evoked their memories of the ways they had suffered from the war and had acted during the war. They evoked them *in anecdotal form* [*sous forme de l'anecdote*]. I discovered that for me, as a writer whose work stems from orality, these women brought me much not only with respect to memory but also with respect to form. They told me the most awful things but in a sober, natural manner. (*Lieux d'écrivains*; my emphasis)

The women from her homeland recount stories in the form of anecdotes, and Djebar learns from their storytelling techniques. It is significant that she should mention *memory* in treating of anecdotes, for these short accounts of interesting or humorous incidents are often easy to recall. They remain in one's mind just as a musical phrase does because of their rhythm and their tone. As Djebar explains, the most terrible things are not dramatized or sentimentalized in the anecdotal mode: they are explained in a measured, matter-of-fact manner, as if the horrors of war were natural.[55] Anecdotes tend to go right to the point, avoiding too much description in order to focus on the essential aspects of the story. Djebar is aware that time is "of the essence," in our contemporary world; her background in filmmaking forced her to condense hours and hours of footage into mere minutes of final product. The anecdote is the form of storytelling that responds to the pressures of a "globalized" world and that speaks to readers who are a part of that world. But the anecdote is not simply a reaction to contemporary globalization, since it finds its origin in the techniques of other times and places, in the tales of Algerian women who are following in the tradition of their female ancestors before them.[56]

Anecdotes have become a mode of composition for Djebar's autobiographical texts. Instead of presenting a linear history of a single life, this writer chooses significant episodes from her past, pivotal moments in her existence, in order to give an idea of her personal trajectory. She inserts these instants into larger narratives that testify to the experience of others, from family members to friends to legendary characters like Tin Hinan and Jugurtha. She doesn't seek to be exhaustive. She realizes that truth may not lie in revealing every possible detail but rather in disclosing crucial events. She carefully elucidates dates and places, but these dates and places can arrive at different locations in the text. Chronological jumps like those found in the thwarted love story in the long opening *partie* of *Vaste est la prison* are paralleled in later sections that are marked by temporal discontinuity encouraged by cinematic techniques such as sudden flashbacks. Careful notation of date in the narrative itself provides the proper name of the event (of the past and of the moment of writing)[57] because it singularizes absolutely. The "singularity of the date" is put into play in great literary texts, according to Jacques Derrida: "to write so as to put into play or to keep the singularity of the date (what does not return, what is not repeated, promised experience of memory, a promise, experience of ruin or ashes)" (*Acts* 42). Marking singularity and preserving dates is what Djebar does in her anecdotal compositions.[58]

The moment captured by the anecdote risks death; it threatens to disappear forever. The anecdote preserves the moment from such a fate, but the proper of the anecdote is that it survives only if it is *repeated*, according to Françoise Proust, for the anecdote will die if it is not retold. Its survival is dependent upon "the necessity and urgency of its *transmission*" (272–73, my emphasis). The anecdote does not ask to be explained or deciphered; it is free from the burden of interpretation. Its meaning is solely tied up in its repeatability, for it is there that its truth emerges.[59] The notion of repeatability brings us back to the signature, which by nature is a repetition of *other* signatures, an act that is "always already repeatable."[60] According to Derrida, "the signature becomes effective—performed and performing—not at the moment it apparently takes place, but only later, when ears will have managed to receive the message" (*The Ear of the Other* 51). He underscores the importance of the *countersignature* that occurs when the text is read, or "heard" by another: "In some way the signature will take place on the addressee's side, that is, on the side of him or her whose ear will be keen enough to hear my name, for example, or to understand my signature, that with which I sign. . . . A text is signed only much later by the other" (51).

Anecdotal writing constitutes the method *par excellence* to assure that the text reaches "the ear of the other" and thus receives its countersignature. Short accounts of interesting or humorous incidents, anecdotes can also reveal aspects of history or biography that were previously unknown. By inserting meaningful anecdotal moments into the written text, Djebar defies the literal meaning of the original Greek word *anekdota*, "things unpublished," and thereby transforms the very concept of the anecdote, "translating" it for a contemporary audience. She reappropriates the oral nature of the anecdote from her native land and transforms it in print for a readership in French. This potentially transgressive act of putting down on paper and thus giving substantial, concrete form to what has been transmitted orally serves a much larger purpose than telling a personal life story.

The detached nature of the anecdote, marked not only by a relative emotional detachment in its telling but also by its detachment from the continuity of History, is a fundamental aspect of the anecdotal in Djebar's writing. She explains in an interview granted a German literary review on the occasion of the 2000 Friedenspreis des Deutschen Buchhandels that her way of conceiving of a short text—and by extension her way of coming up with a plan for a novel—consists of sketching out a series of fragmentary strains that she weaves together to a certain extent, but largely leaves in their natural fragmentary state.[61] Not only is reality fragmentary, as Djebar indicates in her comments, but so are memories, and this writer who describes herself more as an "historian of memory" than a straightforward historian (Schimmel 44). She knows that remembered moments often return to us in flashes, like anecdotes, or photographs. While their dates and places can remain crystal clear, they do not "play themselves back" in our minds in "real time" or according to "chronological continuity." Temporal jumps and discontinuity mark the first part of *Vaste est la prison*, as the narrative voice avows: "I do not know why I have drained these springs of self, with so many convolutions, in a disorder that is willfully not chronological" (*Vast* 118). This story from her own life recalls anecdotal moments from various occasions that are similar to the documented jumps in part two of the book, where the action skips from the seventeenth to the nineteenth century before making the (backward) leap to 138 B.C. This episodic writing escapes linear expectations to tell stories in unforgettable ways. Vivid scenes stand out in the reader's mind, not because of their logical inclusion in a chronological continuum, but because of their striking emergence and their *truth*: "The writing of truth—historical or otherwise—is not continuous: it does not establish connections of causality or even chronology between events, but, after each tableau, it pauses, it 'takes a break,' and for each event, it starts over again, as if the event were unique, the first and the last" (Proust 253).

Giving Up Photos: Historian of the Future

In the fourth movement of the third part of *Vaste est la prison*, the first-person narrator revisits her early childhood, evoking a series of key scenes that left an impression on her. This movement concludes with a lengthy description of a photograph that the narrator presumably has before her. She carefully examines her father, still in his twenties and dignified in appearance. The narrator explains that, having come across this photograph after all these years, it is only today that she has the opportunity to scrutinize the faces of the boys in the picture. She also has the chance to study her own appearance, in her own words: "They put me in the middle, on the front row: little girl with a rounded forehead, her black hair cut short, her gaze perhaps resolute, although I cannot really characterize it" (*Vast* 274). Perhaps because she was still so young at the time the shot was taken, she insists that she now has absolutely no recollection of the event. Despite this forgetting, she finds herself reminded of a flood of details surrounding this eventful click of the camera: "Thanks to this picture, I remember now those first days at school" (*Vast* 272).

Djebar relies on the visual trace of this autobiographical moment in a speculative reconstruction of the circumstances surrounding its occurrence.

How did it happen that she, the young daughter of the schoolteacher, found herself at the center of the second row of a class filled with boys at the village school in the Algerian Sahel? She is undeniably there, in the midst of this group of the opposite sex; the photo serves as proof of this precise instant in the past. To add to its credibility, the photo is dated: 1940. But nothing remains of the occasion in her memory, and she must therefore rely on her experience and imagination to "reconstruct" the moment it was taken (*Vast* 275). In order to explain her own incongruous presence in the all-boy assembly, she has recourse to questions and suppositions:

> And I? I would have waited there, docile and silence, at a slight distance, off to the side. It was the first time: no one had explained to me the etiquette of class photos. Suddenly . . . Suddenly, how did my father get so carried away? He looked at me, he saw me alone, waiting, intimidated as usual. What came over him? Some sudden affection? Some vague sense of injustice at seeing me alone, isolated from these children, as if excluded? For a second he forgot that I was a girl and thus, for his boy pupils, someone separate from them. . . . He came to get me, he took my hand; he made the boys in the front row back away and had me sit in the middle facing the photographer. (*Vast* 276)

In this passage, Djebar chooses a specific narrative path, even as she highlights the uncertainty of her choice. She slips from interrogation ("Et moi?") to assumption ("Je devais attendre") and finally to a straightforward assertion in the indicative: "Il m'a regardée." In the final analysis, she creates a harmonious picture of the situation, in line with other memories of her school days, memories that have since become "textual" memories as well. The image of the young girl heading hand-in-hand with her father to school in *L'Amour, la fantasia* resurges here: "hand in hand with my father, who was the only Arab teacher of French, and also the only one proudly wearing a dark red Turkish fez of felt" (*Vast* 272). In light of the importance of the father's hand—this hand that holds hers, leading her to French and to freedom—in other passages, it is not a mere detail that he takes her *by the hand* in this scene, to include her in the picture.

This intriguing photograph is not included in *Vaste est la prison*. It would be interesting for the reader to study the picture in conjunction with the narrative comments that concern it, but this is not a possibility. The object is described as real, as concrete, but nowhere does it figure in the novel. This autobiographical work thus marks a departure from a number of texts that, like *Roland Barthes par Roland Barthes*, include personal photographs as part of the publication. *Jacques Derrida*, by Geoffrey Bennington and Jacques Derrida, shows off a selection of pictures taken at various points in Derrida's trajectory, including a class picture from the academic year 1939–1940 (312), *the very year* of the picture described in Djebar's autobiographical novel. Hélène Cixous delivers no fewer than thirty-three photographs in "Albums et légendes," a special section in a book co-authored with Mireille Calle-Gruber. *Photos de racines* lives up to its provocative title: the pictures are of Cixous and her family members, of her children and ancestors, as well as of pivotal places in their genealogy, in their unique history so deeply affected by a larger History that determined their comings and goings, their exiles and imprisonments. Cixous includes among these photos other images—one of anti-Semitic propaganda from her mother's German town of Osnabrück, and another of a train deporting Jews from this same location—that could have led to a different family story and an altered family tree.[62] Her closing reflections center on an image for which there is no photo, however: "Image: I am three years old. I have followed in the streets of Oran the Pétain Youth parade. Dazzled, I go home singing 'Maréchal here we are.' My father takes my brother (two years old) and me solemnly on his knees. He solemnly tears the photo of Maréchal Pétain that I brought back, and he explains it to us" (204). Caught up by the music and mesmerized by the printed image, the young girl had not understood the danger of the political message behind these enticements. Tearing up the picture and explaining why she should not fall for its attraction, the father instills in his small daughter a sense of historical awareness that will accompany her for life. While the melody might be alluring, it should not be sung if the words aren't right.

In an issue of *World Literature Today* devoted to Assia Djebar, the first picture ever taken of the recipient of the 1996 Neustadt International Prize for Literature is featured (vol. 70, no. 4). The large photo, located beneath a brief text by Djebar, bears this caption: "Assia Djebar (*second row, center*), 1939, with her father (*far right*) and his charges at a village school in Africa's Sahel region. 'In *Vaste est la prison* I have written the story of this photograph,' notes the author" (786). For those familiar with the novel, the reproduction of the photo is practically an epiphanous sight. After having read the description of the still image, readers will be intrigued see "the real thing." But these readers may also ask why it was not published earlier. The fact that the photo is not a part of the book in which its "story" is told is important. The item was obviously available in the archives, it was not a figment of the writer's imagination, and could have at least been available in an appendix to the work. It would seem natural for an historian to want to provide such documentation, after all. But I would argue that even if providing evidence were the ultimate goal of the novel, it is quite possible that Djebar is of the opinion that photos are not the best way to prove her point.

In *La Mémoire saturée,* novelist and theoretician Régine Robin addresses the many ways in which our contemporary world is concerned with the past, to illustrate the argument that we risk "saturating" our memories with the plethora of unimportant or even inaccurate details that bombard us. The unfortunate result of the current obsession with History is the forgetting of some of its most important lessons. In this vast study, Robin accords a special place to photographic images and puts her finger on their shortcomings in representing the past:

> What is decisive is the work of interpolation, alteration, and modification of the imagination that only knows portions and fragments. The duplication through photography limits this work of interpolation. There is no longer any possible alteration. One can only interpolate through the work of palimpsest, there in the space of lack and forgetting, transformation, trace, and path. A faithful recording of data would block the work of this living memory, substituting for it an artificial memory incapable of supplementing these missing aspects: full memory. (393–94)

The work of the palimpsest, according to Robin's definition, relies on "interpolation," a term referring in its simplest sense to additions or changes. If it is important, as this critic asserts, to allow forgetfulness and missing elements to influence "working memory," then the fixed nature of the photograph makes this visual supplement an ineffective tool. Indeed, the "artificial memory" furnished by the photo is anathema to a palimpsestic reconstruction of the past. The possibility of telling stories is anachronistic in a society marked by "the shock and the instant photo": "[F]aced with their impact, it has become impossible to narrate, to recount. There is no more narrative" (393). Picking up on the "involuntary memory" of Proustian fame, Robin maintains that this special form of recall is unique to literature, and cannot be reconstituted through photography or film. It is plausible that, in order to tap into the memory Robin touts as characteristic of literature, Djebar has consciously refused to insert photographs into her autobiographical works.

The workings of memory are of far greater significance in *Vaste est la prison* than the reconstruction of a linear History. The narrator purposely jumps around in time, underscoring a desire to create something outside the bounds of chronological expectation. At the beginning of the fourth movement, the question of the exact date of a childhood memory arises from the very first line. The answer is not out of reach, for she knows the details of this period perfectly: "Bombing of North Africa by the German air force. Any textbook about this period would give me the precise date, of course—what month in

1940 or 1941, perhaps even later." (*Vast* 258). If she could easily pinpoint this date by consulting a history book, she could also find out a forgotten aspect of her mother's behavior by asking her. Despite the ease of correction and her historical training in precision, the narrator leaves unanswered the questions she evokes with respect to her early childhood: "I shall rely only on this child's memory" (258). Relying solely on memory allows the autobiographical writer to delve more deeply into her personal past and to restore her impressions and feelings on paper. What matters is not the exact date of the occurrence, but how it occurs in her recollection.[63]

Many of the photos in Cixous's *Photos de racines* are of grandparents and great-grandparents whom she never met in person. Because they passed away before her birth, the stills are the only images she knows them by. An overwhelming majority of the pictures feature someone she was very close to, however: her father, who died of tuberculosis in 1948, when Cixous was just a child. This terrible circumstance contributes to reflections on death and loss in her experience: "My life begins with graves. They go beyond the individual, the singularity. I see a sort of genealogy of graves" (*Rootprints* 189). A number of critics, from Barthes to Derrida, have identified photographs with spectral images; they have connected pictures to ghosts. This connection is clear in *Vaste est la prison*, for the narrator examines the faces of the boys around her in the school picture with their tragic ends in mind:

> Yes, I am staring at the pupils in my father's class. What have they become fifteen or twenty years later—that is, during the war for independence? The majority must have gone back up into the mountains, which, at the time of this photo, watched them, seemed to expect them. More than half died there: in the ditches, under a hail of gunfire, or in hand-to-hand combat. (*Vast* 275)

If the technique of photography has enabled these individuals to live on, beyond their mortal end, then this form of preservation can be seen as pointing forward to even more complicated technological developments, including film and telecommunication, that Derrida sees as capable of investing phantoms with unprecedented power (*Jacques Derrida* 321). If the future belongs to specters, then Djebar just may be an historian of the future.[64] In her words, "The dead (men) are returning onto Algerian soil" (*Vast* 349).

If Djebar is "giving up" photos by not inserting them directly into her autobiographical written work, she is not "giving up the ghost" in so doing. She exhibits an understanding that we need to be "haunted by history," in Homi Bhabha's terms. As Bhabha explained during an oral presentation titled "Literary Engagements," such a haunting does not mean an obsession with beginnings and ends, or with origins and outcomes, but rather a concern with the "in-between of acting and speaking." When the word "*fantômes*" finds its place in Djebar's work (*Vaste* 230, 293, 332), the words "writing" and "movement" are never far away. The specters of photographs (both real and missing) are not fixed images for Djebar; she keeps us guessing and keeps them moving, so that neither their meaning nor their date can be "pinned/penned down," demonstrating that they did not exist once and for all in the past, but that their memory continues in the present, that past and present are intertwined, and ultimately that History involves not just the past, but also the present, and that it even looks forward to the future as well.

In *Mal d'archive*, Jacques Derrida visits again, from another angle, the figure of the Marrano. He evokes the work of Yosef Hayim Yerushalmi to better illustrate the way in which archives—including photographs—should open up to the future. Drawing from Yerushalmi's writing, Derrida points to the possibility of an "historian of promise," a term that I would like to apply to Assia Djebar. In Derrida's words, "Good sense tells us there is no history or archive of the future to come. A historian as such never looks to the future, which in the end does not concern him. But meaning something else altogether, is there a historian of the promise, a historian of the first door?" (*Archive Fever* 70). In my reading, Djebar is open and attentive to the future. She constantly writes in the "wake of death," for her homeland is plagued by misfortune, by bloodshed, and by murder past and present. But she never allows herself to abandon hope. Continuing to write, allowing the ghosts of her ancestors to return alongside the memory of so many others, enables their voices to go on long after they have been forcefully silenced. In the very gesture of writing, of putting pen to paper, Djebar expresses optimism and belief in the future. She hangs on to History and allows it to haunt her work, not in order to repeat it in an endless round, but to move beyond this background to make new music that integrates the past without dwelling on/in it. In her compositions, Djebar feeds on imagination and improvisation to carve out innovative melodies for the future.

Notes

1. I have opted to write the word "History" with a capital "H" to refer to the "official" version of events that Assia Djebar inserts into her fictional work in various ways. I would argue that Djebar's treatment of this History disturbs the sacrosanct nature that the term seems to acquire when it is capitalized, but it is useful to retain this form of the word to distinguish it from the multiple "histories," the varying versions

of past events springing from individual stories, that Djebar includes in her writing. Critics of Djebar's work are not uniform in their treatment of this concept: it often is spelled "History" and just as often "history." The absence of a universal standard with respect to this term is revelatory; it begs the question of what H/history really is, and calls attention to the problematic nature of defining this (nonetheless indispensable) concept.

2. Assia Djebar reiterates and comments on the conditions that brought her to incorporate History in her work in *Ces voix qui m'assiègent*, where she gives the dates for this transformation in her approach to creative productivity: "[E]ven if the result of this moviemaking quest hadn't met with a violent, sometimes aggressive incomprehension in Algiers in 1978 or 1979, due to critical presuppositions from the universe of Algiers at this time [. . .], it was nonetheless in these circumstances that I had a desire to take up History again as a subject of writing. And 'my' history first of all" (*Ces voix* 103).

3. While this sentence doesn't mention the superposition of language (French and Arabic, or Berber), Donadey reflects on this linguistic aspect of the palimpsest later in her article, with respect to the novel *L'Amour, la fantasia* and the film *La Nouba des femmes du Mont Chenoua* (108–109). In a discussion ensuing from Donadey's comments, Assia Djebar explains that her limitations in written Arabic necessitated the palimpsestic structure: "if I had had the choice of a written Arabic of transmission, my work as an historian would have been simpler. I chose the palimpsest and I am like those who were short of parchment in the Middle Ages. I only have French, since when I went to school they didn't give me the choice to keep my language. For the last 25 or 30 years, writers in Algeria can be bilingual or trilingual, but I am bilingual, with an oral Arabic and a written French" (Hornung and Ruhe 180).

4. Hafid Gafaïti is another critic who detects the simultaneity of Assia Djebar's treatment of History, past and present: "through the angle of her autobiographical enterprise, characterized by a constant dialogue with the history of her country, the continuity of Assia Djebar's œuvre is made up of the simultaneous questioning of colonial discourse and the dominant political discourse in postcolonial Algeria" (159).

5. In *Ces voix qui m'assiègent*, Djebar refers to *Histoire de ma vie* by Fadhma Aït Mansour-Amrouche as a striking autobiography written in French by a woman born in Kabylia. This autobiographer was the mother of Jean Amrouche, "le poète," as well as Taos Amrouche, "la cantatrice inoubliable" who learned the songs that brought her success from her mother: "Fadhma suffered as she improvised Berber songs (her daughter Taos will collect them directly from her lips)" (89–90).

6. Hafid Gafaïti calls attention to the violence that is communicated in Djebar's writing, particularly in *L'Amour, la fantasia*: "In this perspective, writing reveals itself to be the space of violence that accompanies the violence of History. Writing is the instrument of usurpation or possession of the other, the colonization of signs that accompanies and follows the conquest and invasion of this homeland with which the narrator confuses herself" (154).

7. Djebar affirms that what she calls "the violence of autobiography" is different from, and more painful than, the violence of History: "what I call the 'violence of autobiography' [. . .] is not the violence of history. There is more pain in the autobiographical parts" (Horning and Ruhe 181).

8. In *La mémoire tatouée*, Abdelkébir Khatibi expresses a similar experience with History through storytelling, for it enters into his consciousness and occupies his thoughts to the point of "possession": "In this collective song, completely new for me, I felt happy, the guardian of a first freshness. Beyond disenchantment, this period still controlled even my smallest palpitations. Like a childhood never gone astray, the story has the scent of a euphorbia, mixed [*confuse*], and that possessed me" (114).

9. When she recalls the lengthy recording sessions that were a part of the filming of *La Nouba*, Djebar affirms that listening to these women from her homeland made her more attentive to their *manner* of speaking than to the content of their speech: "Little by little, it was no longer what she said that mattered to me. [. . .] It was much more the manner in which she relived her past. It was then that suddenly all that I had known up until the age of ten or twelve and that I had forgotten came back: the way women speak, their way of being with their memory" (Calle-Gruber, *Au Théâtre* 84).

10. The link between music and remembering is articulated often in Djebar's work, as in this striking phrase from *Vaste est la prison*: "Pauses in an inner music [*Points d'orgue d'une musique à porter en soi*], never to be forgotten" (*Vast* 113).

11. Djebar is of course not alone in her analysis of the crucial combination of image and sound in the cinematographic context. Bernard Stiegler is a theoretician who maintains that an effective use of these two essential elements gives credibility to the stories films tell: "The techniques of image and sound [. . .] inspire belief in the stories they tell with a singular power, never equaled" (*La technique et le temps* 30).

12. "This image of the oral transmission of tribal History by an elder woman to a very young girl, I portrayed it in sequence at the very center of my film. [The ancestor] recounts the former century, but little by little the story, in murmured words, becomes music" (*Le roman* 27).

13. Djebar goes so far as to insist in an interview that she must become (temporarily) blind in order to "really" make movies: "I believe that one cannot really make movies unless one closes one's eyes at times and feels what it is to be blind" (Calle-Gruber, *Au théâtre* 83). In her fiction, this procedure is touted as well: "I am really moving toward the work of image and sound. My eyes closed, I grope in the dark, seeking the lost echo of the lamentations that made tears of love flow, back at home" (*Vast* 205).

14. Another sense is added to those of sight and hearing in this recurring image: touch. "Feeling her way" in the dark adds an unprecedented aspect to filmmaking and opens up possibilities for seeing and hearing differently.

15. Djebar describes the scene as follows: "the transmission of all the women ancestors, tellers of the collective History, appears to be multipled: a long sequence scene unites numerous old speakers [. . .]; all of the stories unfold simultaneously, for I want to translate the multiple transmission as it comes, always from women" (*Le

roman 27). It is worthy of note that women are emphasized in Djebar's work, because the role of "transmitting tradition" in Arab societies has not typically been conferred upon women. It is a strictly determined task that dates back to the days of Muhammad; it depends upon one's name and ancestry, upon a proved identity and a promised continuity to ensure *authenticity*: "A chain of transmitters is composed of the names of those who carry a prophetic tradition: scholars worthy of faith with well-established identities and who have dates in their lives that prove that they were able to meet to effectively insure the transmission of the tradition. [. . .] A 'blank' in a chain of transmitters invalidates the chain and throws a doubt on the authenticity of the tradition in question; it breaks the rhythm of recitation or the reading aloud" (Sublet 34).

16. According to the *Grove Concise Dictionary of Music*, putting his aural observations into written form through transcriptions had a permanent effect on Bartók's music: see http://w3.rz-berlin.mpg.de/cmp/bartok.html. Bartók is also known for complex contrapuntal work in his compositions. The Hungarian-born composer is special to Djebar because, according to her account, he is the only one to have visited her native region in Algeria: "He's the only great musician who came to the source, in the Aurès mountains, in 1912–1913: he spent three months there and gathered many pieces of music" (Calle-Gruber, *Au théâtre* 93). This connection to Algeria is made explicit in the credits: the film is dedicated to Bartók, "come to a nearly mute Algeria in 1913 to study popular music." The choice of the "quatuor" in one of the most crucial scenes of the film could be interpreted as a reference to Djebar's projected autobiographical quartet.

17. Assia Djebar's two films have in common a unique characteristic: they each have two original versions, one in French and one in Arabic. The specificity of these cinematographic productions depends upon a "simultaneous translation" that, from the beginning, occupied the mind of their author who was fascinated by the distance between the two idioms: "My interest in the inner voice in *La Nouba* centers on the gap between the languages. One would have to compare the text of the inner voice in Arabic with that in French because the two movies I made have an original version in French and an original version in Arabic. I wrote the inner voice in French and then I had it translated into Arabic" (Calle-Gruber, *Au théâtre* 83). In my comments on language and translation here, I am obviously referring to the Arabic version of *La Nouba*.

18. The 115-minute film was originally made for RTA (Radio-télévision Algérienne), hence the motivation for translating Djebar's poem into Arabic for the purposes of the film's distribution.

19. Djebar puts it this way: "I would have loved to enter into this language, that I already knew, but with modern pedagogy; I really could have become bilingual then" (*Le roman* 29).

20. While much of her writing could be considered "poetic" in the large sense of the word, Djebar has composed relatively few poems. She interprets this "lack of poetry" to the fact that she writes in French, and not in the language of intimacy and

affect: "I possessed French as a language of thought, not as a language of interiority and affection. It seemed to me, on the contrary, that I could have been a poet in Arabic" (*Le roman* 29).

21. Anne Donadey employs the word "counterpoint" in her analysis of a particular moment in *La Nouba*: "The counterpoint, or disjunction between sound and image is noteworthy in the story of Zohra" ("Elle a rallumé" 110). This technique of contrasting image and sound is crucial to what Donadey identifies as the "*palimpseste oral*" in the film's narration.

22. It is important to note that Djebar does not "reappropriate" these images, that she is not involved in a game of possession that implies ownership and domination. She avoids falling into a vindictive cycle when she treats History in a different manner, as Mireille Rosello points out in another reference to the "palimpsest": "Djebar changes the whole matrix of stereotypical historical narratives. History remains a palimpsest, and it is not treated like a re-possessed object. Djebar allows layers of writings to accumulate rather than proposing an alternative genealogy that would be constructed on the same model as the one she wishes to contest" (*Declining the Stereotype* 159).

23. The film's two versions, Arabic and French, are not identical, partly because of a dispute with an Algerian "bureaucrat" who disagreed with a historical "detail" in the Arabic-language version: "I had to go to Algiers to answer the questions of a functionary. 'What do you mean five Arab centuries? Algeria has always been Arab and always will be.' I replied that I was an historian. Count: from the sixteenth century on, the dynasties are no longer Arab until the seventeenth century, when the Turks arrived. . . . In the end, we were able to negotiate one word in the Arabic version" (*Au théâtre* 88).

24. The repeated word in this song recalls its use in *L'Amour, la fantasia*, to refer to Djebar's paternal grandmother who remains even more "present" in the granddaughter's memory than the outspoken maternal grandmother because of her quiet touch. The celebrated saying about silence speaking louder than words proves true according to this account: "The memory of my father's mother remains as green, perhaps more so, thanks to her caressing hands. Only her former silence continues to hurt me [*m'écorcher*] today" (*Fantasia* 197).

25. The filmmaker explains that she dedicated two years to her first film, *La Nouba*. This devotion gives evidence to her recognition of the value of spending lengthy months to get the right shots. In an article on Algerian women writing, historian Benjamin Stora quotes Djebar on the importance of duration in her novels: "Thus, more than determining a time (a day, several years, even more), or if necessary a date, what is essential is duration, the interior time of each of the characters which is embraced in multiple years in a sentence but which can reconstitute a day, an hour in many pages. Then, above all that, there is the interior duration of the book" (83).

26. In *Ce qui arrive*, Virilio addresses the way contemporary conceptions of works of art have changed along with market and information systems: "If, according to the

sacred formula 'art is long and life is short,' the shattering entry of contemporary works in the all-powerful commerce of news—commerce in which we know that merchandise no longer has any worth after twenty-four hours (or even twenty-four seconds)—has destroyed the notion of DURATION that until now was attached to the estimation of the object, as well as this other tangible quality that was its RARITY, the fact that the work was considered unique from its conception, or that it became so over the course of centuries" (70).

27. Alloula stresses the unequal nature of photographs during this period, since there are essentially no images of the colonizers as seen through the lens of the colonized (11). Alloula specifies that the photographs in his study date from the "golden age" of the colonial postcard: 1900–1930. After 1930, colonial cinema and tourism took over the job of capturing and diffusing images from Algeria. He insists that there is no other example in History of such a plethora of pictures of women, intended to be delivered to public observation (11–12).

28. Despite the differences between the two media, Djebar's experience as a filmmaker influenced her writing techniques, and vice versa. The process of editing a film, choosing which aspects to include and in what order, is not unlike that of editing a book. In both cases, timing matters: "When editing, it was necessary to take up everything again, like a novelist who constructs a novel: know how, at one moment, the images should appear." (*Ces voix* 180).

29. Bernard Stiegler delineates the difference between photo and phonogram this way: "The phonogram, like the photograph, proceeds as an analogous technique of artificial memorization. This is why what is true in the picture is also, to a certain point, in every phonogram: listening to a concert recorded on a disk, I include in my listening the fact that the concert 'was,' that it took place. But the truth of the photo is only that of a phonogram up to a certain point because in the phonogram I am dealing with a fluid object, a flowing that modifies the terms of analysis: the musical object is a flow that cannot reduce to a momentary sound cut" (*La technique* 33).

30. Space and movement stand out in contrast to the "imprisoning" of Algerian women against which Assia Djebar's life and work rebel: "So, intoxicated with space and motion, I dreamed my life; I danced my little life of an odalisque who has left the frame for good" (*Vast* 321). Djebar goes so far as to insist that the most powerful driving force behind her work is *movement*: "the movement of my characters—they, the beings of my genealogy and their wives who, in a sense, watch me, defy me, expect that I allow them to enter, in spite of myself, in spite of them, in the house of this foreign language—this movement becomes my only master, that provides my élan" (*Ces voix* 150). Not only are the characters in movement, the text itself is dynamic (*Ces voix* 115).

31. In an interview with Mireille Calle-Gruber, Assia Djebar states that she did not initially plan for the third part of *L'Amour* to be related to the present. It was in the course of writing the book that this testimony became relevant to the novel's historical content. This later addition is, in the author's own words, a *counterpoint*: "When I began to write the volume, the third part was not supposed to have relevance for the

present. It was in the act of writing that I understood that I was reconstituting the war of the 19th century and it was necessary to address the war lived by women. The use of this material of sound locating [repérage sonore] only came after, as a counterpoint, as the memory of the women of my tribe" (Au théâtre 94).

32. Djebar indicates that hours of interviews were condensed to just minutes for the film: "Of these 25 hours, I only kept 15 minutes; I only interjected the live sound of five women, three minutes each" (Au théâtre 94).

33. L'Amour, la fantasia is a novel emerging from a specific aphasia in the French language. Djebar frequently explains that this autobiographical work hinges on a linguistic quest: "One day I discovered that, up to a certain age, I had never been able to say words of love in French" (Ces voix 107).

34. This scene recalls an earlier textual moment from Vaste est la prison that is also silent, this time under the author's direction: "A scene from a bad dream, frozen in a wan light. A scene from a melodrama whose sound I cut deliberately" (103). The music from the nightclub is muted, and the characters are immobilized, as though posing for a camera, not acting in a film: "One night scene from this period stands out, luminous and dreamlike, a still scene whose sound, for no reason, I had cut off—leaving wide-open mouths in the masks of protagonists, amplifying their passionate gestures, emphasizing the silent destiny of their angry gaze" (102). In L'Amour, la fantasia, the narrative voice describes a mute dream: "The sound in my dream however is switched off" (193). The expression "son coupé" in the original French quotation (217) echoes the title of Djebar's penetrating afterword to her collection of short stories, Femmes d'Alger dans leur appartement: "Forbidden Gaze, Severed Sound."

35. The narrative voice reflects on her inability to express herself: "So I did not yet speak French" (Vast 271). This observation, indicating the necessity of speaking in a particular language to make oneself heard, stands out in contrast to an inner, "languageless" voice evoked earlier in the text, later in the life of the young girl: "Inside me a colorless voice. [. . .] The voice spun out clear and hard; it did not speak in French or Arabic or Berber but in some language from the hereafter spoken by women who had vanished before me and into me" (105). This voice communicating in a "langue d'au-delà" may not be conventional, but it speaks nonetheless; its music and its tone carry meaning that transcends the bounds of any one specific tongue.

36. This is not an entirely harmonious project, for it involves uncovering wounds and treating pain in seeking vengeance for the silenced voices of the past: "I seek rather to avenge her former silence" (Fantasia 195).

37. "Voicing" is a musical term that, according to the American Heritage Dictionary, refers to the "tonal quality or blend of an instrument in an ensemble, especially a jazz ensemble, or of the ensemble as a whole" http://dictionary.reference.com/ search?q=voicing. The mention of its relevance to jazz will prove important later in this chapter, for this particular form of music is known for improvisation and syncopation, two important features in Djebar's creative work.

38. Writing these voices does not fix them, nor does it limit their meaning. To the contrary, it opens up their messages to multiple interpretations, to diverse and un-

foreseen readings. In her reflective comments, Djebar unearths the threat that writing will freeze a single version of a vast and varied oral tradition: "In short, so many stories [. . .] and so much movement is disorganized because they are incessantly seeking an exit. As soon as they are written in French, under my fingers, will these stories become fixed? Statufied? Will they be immobilized to take a pose for aesthetic effect, for the ears of others?" (*Ces voix* 147). This series of questions contain within them the answers, for Djebar's awareness of the possibility of fixing stories once and for all through writing spurs her to circumvent this possibility in the construction, and the content, of her texts.

39. History is traditionally written from the perspective of the victor, of the colonizer, of the occupier, Mireille Calle-Gruber reminds us: "For History is also a stolen gaze, always written by the other: the conqueror, the colonizer, the occupant" ("Pour une analytique" 215). In *Vaste est la prison*, we find an affirmation of this view of History in the specific instance of the siege of Constantine in October 1837; the documents are all one-sided: "Everything is told from the point of view of those laying siege, sometimes in vividly realistic detail" (139). The men who dominate have historically been the ones who have also, as a consequence, held the privileged pen. In rewriting History, Djebar demonstrates that the colonizer's point of view is not only narrow, it is often grossly inaccurate.

40. The description in *Vaste est la prison* reveals that the inexperienced and uninstructed workers carried out their task with complete disregard for the "palimpsestic" structure of the monument, which revealed a history of construction and layers of support and interconnection: "The local workers hired on the spot lack the technical means to detach this stele carefully. The other blocks of stone stacked on each other should have been pulled away to get to the block on which the inscription fit" (144).

41. While the menacing title of the *deuxième partie* of Djebar's novel, "L'effacement sur la pierre," sends the message that no inscription is "set in stone," that no writing is guaranteed to last, the encouraging rediscovery of the Berber script indicates that there is always hope. Writings that were thought extinct can resurface, just as ancient monuments can be found again.

42. Taos Amrouche at once remains faithful to her mother and diverges from her teaching, indicating that no inheritance remains entirely intact in its transmission: "between mother and daughter, between this mother and this young woman, a transfer has taken place: this means a faithfulness, a water that flows at the time of the passing between the two voices, between the two ages, maybe between the two destinies. This transfer has proved to be a change of values. [. . .] A change in tone has taken place, an amplification that is not only of a musical nature" (*Ces voix* 135–36).

43. Derrida's words reveal that filiations are always multiple in any location, but that they are particularly rich and complex in Algeria: "My problem, or my stroke of luck, that which pushes me ceaselessly to reflect on inheritance, is the fact that I belong to a great number of filiations. This is rather common, but I must say that from a cultural point of view, I am lucky to have been born in Algeria, in a Jewish community of French language that crossed all sorts of filiations through all sorts of wars

and tragedies. In the culture that is mine, I will never finish citing my fathers and mothers. This gives me much freedom, because when filiations are multiple, one can play one against the other and one without the other. To leave behind my modest case, I believe that a filiation is always multiple. A sole filiation is not a filiation. More or less multiple, more or less intertwined, but there is always more than one father and more than one mother" (*Sur Parole* 61).

44. The improvisation that characterizes Djebar's inventive work ("my rhythm of work, whose apparent improvisation astonished them" *Vast* 255) is reflective of her maternal/musical heritage. The improvisations of her mother's celebratory songs constitute joyous memories: "My mother enthusiastically brought us pastries and recited the verses with me. The celebration—with the *caïd*'s daughters all there, in our house this time—ended with musical improvisations" (*Vast* 296).

45. In an interview, Djebar refers to French as her paternal tongue: "French is also a paternal tongue for me" (Mortimer 201).

46. Djebar addresses the specificity of "her" French language, influenced by her spoken tongues: "the muzzled sound of oral tongues behind her, muted languages from offstage [. . .] I attempt to transfer [*transmettre*] some of their sound, their movement" (*Ces voix* 149).

47. Nancy K. Miller grapples with the separation of "anecdote" and "theory" in an essay on "Teaching Autobiography": "A while ago I read a call for papers for a volume of personal essays on 'the making of feminist scholarship.' The editors warn the potential contributors that there will be 'no room for untheorized narrative or the merely personal anecdote.' The stringency of their language haunts me as I write this piece. How can you tell the difference between the merely personal and the theoretically acute? What are the grounds for establishing the difference? Who decides?" (130). Miller goes on to argue in favor of an anecdote that will give her "a thematic transition" and allow her to "make the argument through narrative" (131). Both Gallop and Miller, along with Lynn R. Wilkinson and Toril Moi, participated in a panel on "Anecdotal Theory" at the 118th Annual Convention of the Modern Language Association on 28 December 2002.

48. Derek Walcott's reflections on the "muse of history" resonate with Clerc's contention that History is writing, and that the perspective of the writer is inevitably communicated in the written account: "In time every event becomes an exertion of memory and is thus subject to invention. The farther the facts, the more history petrifies into myth. Thus, as we grow older as a race, we grow aware that history is written, that it is a kind of literature without morality, that in its actuaries the ego of the race is indissoluble and that everything depends on whether we write this fiction through the memory of hero or of victim" (*Post-Colonial* 371).

49. This concept is particularly a propos of Djebar's work. She addresses space with respect to the experience of filming in her homeland: "I found my everyday space [. . .] this freedom. This space, in actual fact, is like me. So, I think, begin a film story, when the space that is right for it is really found. Go all around this space" (*Vast* 225).

50. In *La Mémoire tatouée*, Khatibi poetically juxtaposes two very different views of History: the first familial and religious, characterized by order and a predetermined destiny; the second "national" and secular, characterized by chaos and unpredictability: "Living for my mother is a way of remembering, our genealogical tree—through its flowering—distanced the crushing of history. The latter began with the Prophet and ended in paradise or in hell; I had a place assured in a predestined location since, as a child, I was covered; children who die land straight in paradise. At school, we discovered chaos. A page turned, a dynasty fell; the head of a king! The dynasties knocked each other about, the tribes stomped their feet in the dust and, from time to time, the eccentric head of an illuminary who, after producing grocer's miracles, raised up a troop of grasshoppers and crossed, irresistibly, a country that had been devasted thousands of times. Moved by this disorder, the colonial West decided to intervene for the good of everyone. Hallelujah colonization! Hallelujah gallant history!" (70–71). Debra Kelly's *Autobiography and Independence* contains analyses of colonialism and nationalism in the work of Assia Djebar and Abdelkébir Khatibi, alongside that of Mouloud Feraoun and Albert Memmi.

51. In *Langue et pouvoir en Algérie: Histoire d'un traumatisme linguistique*, Mohamed Benrabah gives a lucid account of the History of Algeria from a linguistic perspective. In his view, the History of this North African land is engraved in its linguistic variety. Benrabah provides the following statistic for the level of illiteracy at the end of French colonization: "In 1962, the rate of illiteracy is estimated at 90%" (70).

52. Tom Conley elegantly puts his finger on the frozen "cultural identities" that colonized individuals are subjected to, and argues that such individuals must escape from such a dangerously fixed identity, outside time and class: "When colonized subjects step into the identity traps put forward in literature, cinema, national expositions, or other cultural productions, they risk being assimilated 'into a cultural identity frozen by the ethnology. . . , isolated from society as a whole, withdrawn from history, and doomed to repeat itself in a quasi mechanical way.' To steer clear of the trap, the colonized population must shed the garments of a timeless and classless 'identity' before producing tactical means, local 'ways of doing things,' that cannot be co-opted either as commodifiable products or as oppositional units in a Western— and eminently tedious—narrative of conflict of race, class, and gender" (278–79). Aijaz Ahmad, in a response to Fredric Jameson, argues eloquently for the reinsertion of the Third World into History. He indicates that Jameson's analysis of the production systems of the First and Second Worlds leads to a division "between those who make history and those who are mere objects of it." Ahmad asserts that "this classification leaves the so-called third World in limbo; if only the First World is capitalist and the Second World is socialist, how does one understand the Third World? Is it pre-capitalist? Transitional? Transitional between what and what?" (78).

53. I use the word "recuperate" with the work of Gareth Griffiths in mind. Griffiths gives a helpful definition of the "strategies of recuperating" the past among postcolonial societies, according to the example of the Australian Aborigines: "Strategies of recuperation and texts which insist on the importance of re-installing the 'story'

of the indigenous cultures are, therefore, [. . .] crucial to their resistance. Such recu-
perations may be the literal recuperation of the texts of pre-colonial cultures, the narratives of the dreaming or the body of pre-colonial oratures, or [. . .] attempts to rein-
scribe the dominant culture of colonial society by re-telling the moment of encounter
and invasion through indigenous eyes and discourses" (239).

54. In his autobiographical novel, *L'écrivain public*, Moroccan writer Tahar Ben
Jelloun equates History with the surrounding political events, with the period he was
living in and its wars, factos that inevitably have an impact on the smaller "educational" world he inhabits: "The European students remained together; I found myself
in the Arab clan. It was during the period of the Algerian War. [. . .] Relations between us were often aggressive. I believed that I had been socially promoted by
changing high schools; I discovered instead racism and the brutality of history" (59).

55. When Djebar uses the word "sober" to describe the storytelling, this adjective
is not meant to contradict the (often) humorous nature of the anecdote. It refers instead to straightforwardness and concision. In *Vaste est la prison*, humor is introduced
in several instances, exemplified by the first-person narrator's ability to laugh at herself, while making literary allusions to illustrate, and punctuate, her story: "'I started
to act out the princess of Cleves with my husband! Well, everybody—and he first
among them—believed that I had chosen to play the part of the domesticated [tamed]
shrew! A simple mistake of repertory!' Then I laughed" (*Vast* 316).

56. Sara Suleri, in her article on feminism and the postcolonial condition, picks up
on the importance of anecdotes in women's writing, identifying them as crucial components of bell hooks' *Talking Back: Thinking Feminist, Thinking Black*: "hooks' study is
predicated on the anecdotes of lived experience and their capacity to provide an alternative to the discourse of what she terms patriarchal rationalism" (277–78). Suleri
takes a rather critical stance toward the inclusion of anecdotes in the text, arguing that
a connection between these accounts of lived experience and current history is needed.
Suleri's concern about an absence of history is indeed valid. But I would argue that history and theory are inherent in anecdotal testimony, that they cannot be dissociated
from stories of "lived experience," especially in the writing of Assia Djebar.

57. In a brief section introduced by the italicized name *Jugurtha*, Djebar histori-
cizes not only this legendary historical figure but also the moment of the writing:
"June 1993: I had planned a few days of peace in Copenhagen"; "I see—thanks to this
commemoration of that yesterday (the yesterday, that is, of 138 B.C.E.)" (342–43).

58. The complex status of writing as that which is singular and also repeatable
is explained by Derrida in connection with the condensation of History that we
find in the autobiographical inscription: "writing, in that a singular mark should
also be repeatable, iterable, as mark. It then begins to differ from itself sufficiently
to become exemplary and thus involve a certain generality. This economy of exemplary iterability is of itself formalizing. It also formalizes or condenses history"
(*Acts* 43).

59. "The meaning of the anecdote dies at the end of its recitation and it only lives
again when it is recited anew" (Proust 273).

60. This phrase is taken from Kevin Hart's analysis of the proper name and the signature in Derrida's work: "Moreover, no signature can refer to a pure presence, a unique moment of signing; for, as we have seen, a signature is always already repeatable" (13). In Derrida's *Shibboleth*, a direct connection is established between the signature and the date: "In its essence, a signature is always dated and has value only by virtue of this. It dates and it has a date. And prior to being mentioned, the inscription of a date (here, now, this day, etc.) always entails a kind of signature: whoever inscribes the year, the day, the place, in short the present of a 'here and now,' attests thereby to his or her own presence at the act of inscription" (*Acts* 391).

61. In Djebar's (translated) words, "When I write short texts, I work like a painter, I first make a study and sketches from a variety of perspectives. In the same fashion, I conceive of my novels as if I were an architect. And since in reality things are fragmentary, I seek to reproduce this fragmentation" (Schimmel 43).

62. The train in *Photos de racines* is overflowing with passengers, and the crowds are thick alongside the cars: all caught in a moment that precedes the tragedy to befall them. The figures are indistinguishable from one another, blending together in a mass of humanity that seems already to be composed of skeletons, of ghosts. While her immediate family escaped the brutality of this deportation, other relatives were not so fortunate: "The families of my mother, very large as Jewish families often are, had two fates: the concentration camps on the one hand; on the other, the scattering across the earth" (*Rootprints* 189).

63. Neglecting the precise date in these textual evocations of traumatic events may represent a desire to separate private pain from the documented domain of History. It may also reveal a consciousness that the devastating personal damage wrought by these events does not date uniquely to its occurrence, but can be felt most acutely in their aftermath, in time that cannot be "located," as Dominick LaCapra explains: "A prominent motivation for the conflation of structural and historical trauma is the elusiveness of the traumatic experience in both cases. In historical trauma, it is possible (at least theoretically) to locate traumatizing events. But it may not be possible to locate or localize the experience of trauma that is not dated or, in a sense, punctual. The belated temporality of trauma makes of it an elusive experience related to repetition involving a period of latency" (724–25).

64. The novelist/filmmaker is aware of the future, as she indicates in her comments on the young protagonist from *La Nouba* who does not attend school, and whose example does not bode well for the country's future: "Aichoucha, the illiterate shepherdess, eight years old, scandalous in today's Algeria—and this was only seventy kilometers from Algiers. In actual fact Aichoucha is the real outsider in these regions where I think I see the future dawning imperceptibly" (*Vast* 257).

PART TWO

HÉLÈNE CIXOUS

CHAPTER FOUR

~

Settling the Musical Score: Orality, Rhythm, and Repetition in Writing Wrongs

A single note of music can encapsulate a heart, a heartbeat, its voice, its dawn.

—Abdelkébir Khatibi, *Aimance* (2003)

To converse is to walk with time.

—Abdelkébir Khatibi, *Pèlerinage d'un artiste amoureux* (2003)

It is appropriate that a chapter on music should find itself at the midpoint of this study, since the topic is *central* to my analysis of autobiographical writing from the Maghreb. Music is present as a more or less implicit theme running throughout this study, but it is here, in the middle of a section devoted to the writings of Hélène Cixous, that I will explicitly examine music and its workings in the text. The purpose of this chapter is to reveal the critical importance of music in writing, to expose its highly charged nature, and to demonstrate that far from constituting a "neutral" medium, music is capable of effecting change, of writing—and righting—wrongs.

This chapter necessarily includes a certain amount of description, and engages in several close readings of Cixous's work in order to unearth the ways in which her texts can be called "musical." While a number of recent articles on her writing have employed musical terms and touched on the implications of writing musically, few have done more than mention a need to appreciate the musical attributes of Cixous's writing.[1] This chapter seeks to fill

187

in some of the gaps in this scholarship, looking not only at the way music is notated in Cixous's corpus—from some of the earliest publications to the latest fictional and theoretical works—but also at the way music can be seen as a corrective to injustice.

Three main themes interweave in this chapter: orality, rhythm, and repetition. These three motifs provide points of entry into Cixous's carefully composed texts. First, the "oral" component of Cixous's written work stems from its inclusion of dialogue, its polyphonic mingling of different voices, and, most radically, from its neologisms that play on similar sounds and diverse meanings. Second, the "rhythmic" can be identified as the unusual style of this author who composes with differing time signatures, often affecting the visual aspect of the printed page with blank spaces, unusual punctuation, poetic phrases, and long, sinuous sentences. Rhythm is a question of "voice" and "breath" in Cixous's work, two facets of spoken interaction that find their place in the written text. The final theme, "repetition," plays itself out in various ways. Rewriting of known stories from the mythology of Greek literature to the tales of biblical fame exists alongside another rewriting on a very different scale: that of Cixous's own personal and familial history. Constantly reworked and revised, stories are repeated in a form that is always already different, resonating with the first version and yet setting itself apart with a new tune, however slight in its variation. In this vast corpus, discrete compositional pieces can be considered to contribute to an ongoing musical line; in this interpretation, each publication can be appreciated for its singular qualities, as a single bit of creativity. But each text can—and should be—valued for its place in and resonance with a series of publications that bear the same signature. In this view, the whole is strengthened by each of its parts.

The strong political bent of Cixous's largely personal writings is not anathema to the "musical" style of her writing. I argue throughout this chapter that, rather than distracting from serious issues, inscribing music in her work allows this sensitive, informed activist to treat of them in the written text, but perhaps not in predictable ways. Putting forth the "poetic" even in works that boast a "theoretical" label is a sly, subtle solution to dry, formulaic writing that communicates "coldly" and fails to touch its reader. I contend that Cixous "does things with words,"[2] that she accomplishes goals in the "real" world by creatively articulating ideas on paper. Her writing reveals her conviction that language carries considerable power; for this reason, no word or term can be taken for granted; each must be examined, deconstructed, and exposed for the etymological amalgam that it is. She knows that even the most banal terms are loaded, carrying histories and colors and therefore requiring nuanced use. She responds irreverently to rules of grammar, pronunciation, and spelling by doing things *to* words, disconcerting the "official" tongue by delineating its "faults" in playful ways. The word "faults" here can be taken as "imperfections" or "errors," as Cixous often points out inconsistencies and contradictions in language. But the word "faults" can also be understood as dangerous points of friction, as in the intersections of a geological fault with another plane of reference, and by extension, "boundaries between incompatible or irreconcilable beliefs, cultures, etc." Challenging boundaries by calling into question their fixed locations—whether linguistic or metaphorical—is something Cixous does with her own musical voice, in her own musical time.

It is significant that her major language of composition is French, that this particular idiom fits her purpose so effectively.[3] French is a tongue that lends itself well to music, and Cixous rhapsodizes with the plethora of homonyms and homophones at her disposal. Of course, her relationship to this language is not a smooth one, as the autobiographical narrative reveals in *Benjamin à Montaigne*: "I have fought my whole life, you have to say it. I am a colonized woman. By whom? By France. There are words that don't come and that I find in German. What chagrins me is that I am dressed from head to foot in French and German overtakes me" (213). France has colonized her German mother, whose voice is expressed in this quotation, and Cixous is a child of (that) colonization. The hazards of history have "given" her (to) this particular tongue, and she has made the most of it as a "French" writer. The colorful variations she creates in her texts are not limited to language: they work *through language* and its unexplored potential to change the way we conceive of serious questions in our contemporary world, from the situation of women to that of refugees.

One of the obvious advantages to Cixous's moving, lively, "musical" creations is that her words are memorable. They replay themselves in the reader's ear, much like a refrain from a familiar song. This repeatability means that Cixous's writing should be read aloud, for the aural games she engages in can easily be overlooked on the page. She introduces the oral into the written, particularly in the context of her German mother's inventions in her "*français languétrangère*" (*Benjamin* 209), to make a statement. Blurring the boundaries between what is written and what is said, Cixous disrupts the sacrosanct border between written and oral French. While her knowledge of French spelling and grammar is impeccable, she doesn't reproduce it dutifully in her texts. This gesture of disobedience at once asserts her individuality and opens to other possibilities for meaning making and mutual understanding. She unquestionably *writes well* in her work, but she questioningly *does not write "too" well*, introducing elements that would alert the "spell check" and overwhelm the "grammar corrections" on any computer. For this scribe who works by hand, no automatic function overrides her inventiveness, and she gives her imagination free rein when it comes to manipulating language in order to find musical notations to leave a written record. Despite the obvious value placed on the spontaneity of oral interactions, Cixous ultimately privileges written transcriptions in her life and work because spoken statements do not suffice. One must *write* in order to truly make an impact, to leave a trace, and to create the words that will continue to resonate long after they are "heard" in reading. The challenge she faces in this project is to properly give place to music so that the vibrations continue long after the notes fade away.

Reading by Ear

In his open letter to Jacques Derrida in *La Langue de l'Autre*, Abdelkébir Khatibi proves himself to be a reader of Hélène Cixous's recent writing. He refers to *OR* as a *"boîte de merveilles,"* indicating his admiration for this unusual text. Khatibi's evocation of Cixous's recent work follows a discussion of the specific status of the Jewish community in his native country. In contrast to the situation of Derrida and Cixous in Algeria, Jews in the Moroccan Protectorate did not lose their citizenship,[4] but their access to languages was nonetheless remarkably restricted: "During the Protectorate, education took place with a whole mosaic of interdicts that worked to maintain the separation between communities: distinctive ethnic-religious signs and, necessarily, those related to language" (26). Khatibi explains that this separation of communities meant that access to written Arabic was formally off-limits to the schools of the Jewish Alliance, as well as to Franco-Berber schools. In like manner, students in Franco-Muslim schools were forbidden to study Berber: this was Khatibi's own case. Addressing his bilingualism, or even plurilingualism, necessarily entails mention of these educational conditions during his formative years, for Khatibi found that the Protectorate, in order to "protect" languages, put them into conflict with each other: "That was the Protectorate and its 'protection' of languages, placing them in a position of war" (27).

Cixous's name appears in this reflection because her texts illustrate what Khatibi terms *"la folie de la langue;"* they play with the French language that accompanied colonization and assumed a position of privilege throughout the North African countries of Morocco, Algeria, and Tunisia: "*Folir*, she says. It's a beautiful word. [. . .] In *OR*, an élan, an excessive, sweeping movement makes the book roll along. [. . .] Uprooting language to make it en-chanting, to make it fairylike" (*La Langue* 27). These laudatory comments on the inventiveness of Cixous's prose come on the heels of a reminder of the linguistic restrictions that reigned during the time of the colonial presence in the Maghreb. For Khatibi, *OR*—along with other texts by Cixous—stems from this historical and geographical background and goes beyond it, creat-ing compositions that transcend tradition and defy expectations (generic, or-thographic, grammatical, and other). He insists on the speed of the writing, a speed that can send the reader's head into a spin: "The rapidity of the syn-tax, flow, unrolling, then the changes in perspective and airborne spatializa-tion (wings, angels, leaves of words), the figures, the dates, and the letters all boiling" (27). Reading this unusual prose, understanding its rhythm and its fragmented form requires an appropriate slant, an adapted method. Indeed, the unprecedented style found in Cixous's texts can only be appreciated if one reads a certain way, in the view of this critical analysis: "*It seems to me impossible not to read by ear this voice and its brilliance*" (27). Khatibi puts these words in italics for emphasis. He insists not only that one *should* read the text by ear, but that it would be *impossible not to*.

Reading *by ear* is perhaps not the kind of reading we are accustomed to, especially when it comes to prose texts. While poetry is often recited aloud and the critical eye is trained to spot rhythm and meter, cadence and mea-sure when it comes to this coded form of composition, prose often escapes this careful attention. In reading fictional and theoretical texts alike, there is a natural inclination to search for a message, and in the rush to "get to the point," it is easy to overlook the text's unique language, its music. In his first autobiographical novel, Khatibi calls for a new form of writing that would necessitate a new form of critical reading: "Counterpoint of an (unreason-able) passion, it would be the workings of a palimpsest, of a perpetual double palimpsest, close to music. Critics would have to change their perspective and consider the ideal bilingual text from the point of view of music" (*La Mé-moire tatouée* 205). It is not an accident that the writer and theorist who finds Cixous's work worthy of "reading by ear" should advocate a writing, and a reading, that take a *musical approach* to the text.

Criticizing the work of a Maghrebian-born writer like Cixous on the ba-sis of its message alone would mean disregarding a fundamental aspect of that message: its form. Certain critics may be reluctant to embrace the effi-cacy of the Cixousian text, arguing that "word games" and "neologisms" are inadequate to change the world and positing instead the goal of a text artic-ulating in clear, unmistakable language a solely pragmatic message.[5] Such an attitude is entirely inappropriate to the powerful effects of the written word, however, and to its capacity—even in clever twists and turns that seem to belong only to the realm of "play"—to change the ways we perceive things.[6] This is true in a general sense, as a number of works have demonstrated from different perspectives, and it is true in a particular sense, as the corpus of works by Hélène Cixous have shown. If a body of criticism seems to be lacking from the angle Khatibi calls for, it is surely because approaching written work from "the point of view of music" is not a clear task. And one might be tempted to think that it is not a serious one. This chapter seeks to explore what a musical approach to Cixous's corpus would consist of. It examines Cixous's explicit thematic treatment of music in her books and articles; it makes careful note of the instances in which Cixous refers to music in interviews and self-reflexive statements; it strives to convey the musical qualities of Cixous's texts. This final goal of letting the music "sing" for itself is undoubtedly the most difficult part of this chapter, since articulating the musical is a challenge. But critics have been numerous to point out that the great strength of Cixous's canonical essays, particularly "Le Rire de la Méduse," is its performative nature: it at once trumpets *and* demonstrates a specific type of writing.[7]

Musical Voices: Notating Orality

It may seem at first glance inappropriate to consider "orality" in a study devoted to a highly educated woman like Cixous, who has long been versed in letters and who composed a doctoral dissertation on James Joyce at a comparatively young age. But it is my contention that her childhood and adolescence in Algeria during the time of French colonization exposed the writer to the important questions that surround the phenomenon of "orality" and sensitized her to alternative forms of expression. In this section, I will make a few broad statements about French colonization and postcolonial discussions of "orality" in general and "Creolization" in particular in order to draw some conclusions about the workings of the oral in Cixous's writing.

The so-called civilizing mission of French colonization carried with it in the eighteenth and nineteenth centuries the goal of teaching illiterate peoples to read and write. While these skills contained obvious merits, they also threatened the "oral" cultures that characterized much of the African continent and the islands colonized by the French. Writing tended to "fix" one version "once and for all" of a story that, in its tradition, was open to multiple versions in the improvisational moments of its telling. Also, the passage from spoken to written form was not evident in the case of many oral expressions that lacked equivalents in writing. The dialects and variants of

French in the Antilles prove particularly resistant to fixation in writing, and a proliferation of creative fictional and theoretical writings from the likes of Edouard Glissant and Maryse Condé are illustrative of the multiplicity and variability of these tongues.[8] Affirming Creole in writing is not solely an aesthetic question: it is political as well, for the ways in which written texts resist dominant culture while remaining largely within the rules of that dominant culture's language subtly but effectively contribute to awareness and thereby effect change.[9]

Cixous has devoted herself throughout her career to raising awareness of unacknowledged regions of the world and overlooked portions of the global population, highlighting with special care the situation of Third World women. In her reflections on her writing for the theatre, the author and playwright addresses the difficult task of bringing the plight of the illiterate woman to literate territory: "And another question: how can I, who am of the literate species, ever give speech to an illiterate peasant woman without taking it away from her, with a stroke of my language, without burying her with one of my fine phrases?" ("The Place of Crime" 151). Hoping to maintain the voice of she who has not had the opportunity for formal education, Cixous is skeptically aware of her own poetic proclivities. If she renders the peasant woman eloquent, the writer threatens to misrepresent the other. Cixous's concerns echo those of Assia Djebar, who has expressed on various occasions a hesitancy to claim herself as "spokesperson" for the Algerian women in her texts: "Don't claim to 'speak for' or, worse, to 'speak on,' barely speaking next to, and if possible *very close to*" (*Women* 2). It is no accident that these two women share a similar sensitivity to other women, seeking to come close to them and make their stories known without appropriating their words or misrepresenting them. These concerns are motivated in different regards by various factors, including a respect for others and a goal to improve the lives of women worldwide, but also by an appreciation for oral aspects of language that resist the transition to standardized, accepted written forms.

In a preface to an anthology of stories collected by African-American writer Zora Neale Hurston, John Edgar Wideman delineates the specific attributes of Creole speech. He points out that all spoken language "resists exact phonetic transcription. But Creole's stubborn survivalist orality, its self-preserving instinct to never stand still, to stay a step ahead, a step away, the political challenge inherent in its form and function, increases the difficulty of rendering it on the page" (xv). He maintains that putting this speech into writing brings to the forefront "extralinguistic tensions" in the literary work: "any written form of creolized language exposes the site, evidence and necessity of struggle" (xv).

In an article on "Deconstruction and the Postcolonial," Robert Young rehearses the conditions of domination in Algeria: "The French invaders destroyed the local administrative system and replaced it with a centralized administration, based on the production of *écriture*. Writing and imperialism, the violence of the letter" (194). Young italicizes the French word for writing in this quotation because of its importance for Jacques Derrida's work, which Young views as stemming directly from this early exposure to colonialism. Since, in salient ways, those who lived in the French colony of Algeria were subjected to linguistic dominance, it is no surprise that Derrida should exhibit a sensitivity to what he calls the "stakes of 'creolization'" in *Le Monolinguisme de l'autre*, recognizing the intertwined political and linguistic aspects of the term: "The phenomena which interest me are precisely those that blur the boundaries, cross them, and make their historical artifice appear, also their violence, meaning the relations of force. . . . Those who are sensitive to all the stakes of 'creolization' . . . assess this better than others" (9).

Derrida's interest in blurring—and crossing—boundaries to elucidate their artifice and violence echoes the concerns of critics from the French Antilles, namely Jean Bernabé, Patrick Chamoiseau, and Raphaël Confiant. Their collaborative work finds "Creoleness" to be a common characteristic uniting very different peoples who have the shared trait of having endured colonial rule: "Creoleness is the interactional or transactional aggregate of Caribbean, European, African, Asian, and Levantine cultural elements, united on the same soil by the yoke of history" (87).[10] The different uprootings and transplantations that are inherently part of "Creoleness" have led to a porous, flexible multilingualism: "Creoleness is not monolingual. Nor is its multilingualism divided into isolated compartments. Its field is language. Its appetite: all the languages of the world. The interaction of many languages (points where they meet and relate) is a polysonic vertigo" (108). The vertiginous sounds of "creoleness" are not only aural in their effect; they are also meaningful. They have the capacity to turn linguistic tradition on its head: "Living at once the poetics of all languages is not just enriching each of them, but also, and above all, breaking the customary order of these languages, reversing their established meanings" (109). It would be difficult to find a more convincing explanation or apology for Cixous's writing.

When Cixous composes a "polysonic vertigo" in her written work, she is not accomplishing an easy task. While it may seem effortless to put spoken words in print, the experience of "translating" oral expressions into written form proves that, to the contrary, it is a nearly impossible undertaking, as studies of creole reveal: "'Oral literature' is an oxymoron. *Creole speech is approximated*, at best, by any form of written transcription" (Wideman xvi, my emphasis). The approximation of spoken word in the written text necessarily entails loss: "Translation destroys and displaces as much as it restores and renders available. In the case of these oral narratives, some major missing dimensions are the immediacy and sensuousness of face-to-face encounter, the spontaneous improvisation of call and response, choral repetition and echo, the voice played as a musical instrument, the kinesics of the speaker" (xvi–xvii). Cixous's textual creations seek to restore some of the "immediacy"[11] and "sensuousness" of encounters that occur between people; they aim to render aspects of the "spontaneous improvisation" of interaction that takes place in voice and in body—in time; they hope to evoke the "choral repetition and echo" that are a part of the resounding music of life. Although she didn't grow up speaking the creoles of Guadeloupe or Martinique, she bathed in a "multilingual murmuring"[12] on a permanent basis in Algeria. Both in the streets and at home, a buzz of languages—real and invented— made up her soundtrack in the formative years.

Playing by Ear

In "Albums et Légendes," Cixous recalls her childhood, and the singular linguistic apprenticeship she experienced with her father. This polyglot dabbled in a number of languages on a regular basis, and demonstrated considerable respect for idioms. But his multilingual talents were not only used in serious settings; in the home, with his children, he used linguistic play, in and between languages, to let loose what Cixous calls his "second language": "the laugh. Humour was a second language for him. He played on everything, members of the family, situations, and above all signifiers. He was the enchanter. The universe was slightly translated" (*Rootprints* 197–99). Translating the universe in light, slight fashion was partly the result of the predominance of her mother's tongue in the household, where the maternal grandmother who spoke no French had also taken up residence. This familial language became the source of nimble play, of jokes: "So my father had forged, in a Joycian way, an entire system of jokes on the German language that became part of the family idiom. We all juggled" (198). This wordplay took place orally; it constituted everyday banter that the members of the family tossed back and forth aloud. But it proved to be a training ground for written acrobatics as well, as the mention of Joyce suggests in this passage. Cixous was predisposed to appreciating the antics of the Irish-born writer thanks to her father's sense of humor and love for languages in all their forms: "Perhaps the verbal virtuosity or versatility that there is in my writing comes to me from my father: as if he had made me a gift of keys or of linguistics" (198).

In her exchanges with Mireille Calle-Gruber in *Photos de racines*, Cixous emphasizes the marvelous preparation her father's instructive word games gave her for writing: "My father played pedagogically with us at word-and-seek. So it is tied to the wonderful beginning. When I was two years old, I was in the middle of the written: working on the signifier. It was indissociable from my very life" (95).[13] If Cixous underscores the similarity between oral and written play/work with words here, she is not establishing an equivalence between the two forms. For her, there is a decided difference between the oral and the written, as she reveals in "La Venue à l'écriture": "Speaking (crying out, yelling, tearing the air, rage drove me to this endlessly) doesn't leave traces: you can speak—it evaporates, ears are made for not hearing, voices get lost. But writing! Establishing a contract with time. Noting! Making yourself noticed!!! ("Coming" 15). The exclamatory tone of this passage reflects its eagerness to embrace writing as a form that preserves in ways that outlast the echo of the spoken. This early text observes that oral words don't leave a trace, even if they are shouted at the top of one's lungs; writing is the antidote to this fleeting nature of words, it would seem.[14] Even if her mother is her greatest confidant, the one to whom she can tell all, this textual figure does not hear, let alone retain, all that her daughter says, as the narrative voice of *Benjamin à Montaigne* reveals. The most effective place for expression seems to be the written text: "I tell her all that you can say and she breaks it up into little morsels without wasting a moment. The rest, I write. You cannot complain to anybody in the world with the voice" (224). Writing, by "establishing a contract with time," assures that words will ring again, that their resonance will not be lost on inattentive, unmindful ears.

The seemingly privileged status accorded to writing in these passages is located solely on the level of preservation and reverberation, for Cixous strives in her work to diminish the distinction between oral and written, translating oral qualities into her writing as often as possible, all while highlighting the difficulty of such a translation. *Benjamin à Montaigne* is a text that deals extensively with the challenge of transmitting her mother's voice in writing. The narrator evokes a series of recording sessions that attempt to copy on magnetic tape the inimitable language of her mother. If her father gave her the gift of linguistic play, her mother gave her the present of a foreign mother tongue, "her priceless idiom" (206–7) that is her French peppered with innovative phrases and pronunciations: "her practically rococo modalizations, her improvisations of hyphenated words, her frank, cruel statements, the summary executions devoid of pathos of nameless people described and impaled in two or three gestures, her genius is in her zcalpel her zooms" (208). The narrator, even after years of exposure to this manner of speaking, finds herself exhausted by its rhythm and content: "I am exhausted, I'm taking her intoxicating course of second-language French [français languétrangère]" (209). The disruption of our expectations for teacher and student in this phrase is revealing: perhaps the one who has less of a handle on the language is better apt to teach it. It is the canonized writer of French letters who takes lessons from her mother, lessons of French as a foreign tongue.

This refreshing language of Cixous's writing is in perpetual movement, always going toward something new and never sitting stagnantly in the complacency of "mastery."[15] The mother's tongue—idiosyncratic, always in motion—has inspired Cixous's œuvre: "She has always remained so arriving [arrivante] so schoolgirl she is still in the process of learning French from [depuis] Osnabrück, she pursues herself, perpetual improvisation of the self" (208). This truncated sentence appears contradictory in its juxtapositions of established and invented words stemming from the verbs "to stay" and "to arrive;" the reader is tempted to ask how the mother could at once "remain" and move "toward arrival." But the text indicates that it is not illogical to "stay arriving," to continue to arrive with/in a language, all while cultivating the paradox that is this enigmatic mother. The phrase itself sows uncertainty: the "depuis" could be interpreted temporally, and refer to the mother's departure from her native town; the "depuis" could also be interpreted geographically (in accordance with recent evolutions in the use of the term among French speakers), and thus refer to the mother's apprenticeship of the language as occurring from her native town, as point of departure. Cixous is given to coining words that end in the progressive "-ance," such as "arrivance" or "Algériance": there can be little doubt that the open-ended emphasis on movement that she valorizes in these neologisms is indebted to the example of her mother, whose "perpetual improvisation" of her "self" serves as a model for Cixous's proliferation of autobiographical texts, improvisations of self and language marked by movement rather than "arrival."[16]

The linguistic games that characterized her childhood are especially unique because they didn't take place within one language, or even between two distinct tongues. Rather, plays on words wandered from one idiom to another, along a gamut of expressions that belonged to a host of languages. This plurality was of inestimable significance to the young child: "My languages. We played at languages in our house, my parents passed with pleasure and deftness from one language to the other, the two of them, one from French and the other from German, jumping through Spanish and English, one with a bit of Arabic and the other with a bit of Hebrew" ("My Algeriance" 168). Unexpected bounds among a variety of languages enhanced Cixous's natural aural sensibility and sharpened her innate sense of pitch. The polyphonic nature of her early verbal interactions paved the way for a special conception of "writing by ear" as a mode of composition that focuses not on a single phonic element in its passing but on its resonance and interplay with other aspects of the textual structure. This is what Cixous refers to when she mentions music in *Photos de Racines*:

> When I refer to music, it's because music lets us hear directly that language is produced in an interplay with the body. One writes with one's ears. It is absolutely essential. The ear does not hear a single detached note: it hears musical compositions, rhythms, scansions. Writing is a music that goes by, that trails off in part because what remains is not notes of music, it is words. But what remains of music in writing, and which exists also in music properly speaking, is indeed the rhythm, it is indeed that scansion which *also* does its work on the body of the reader. The texts that touch me the most strongly, to the point of making me shiver or laugh, are those that have not repressed their musical structure; I am not talking here simply of phonic signification, nor of alliterations, but indeed of the architecture, of the contraction and the relaxation, the variations of breath. (*Rootprints* 64)

What is striking in this passage is the corporeal aspect of writing, and reading, by ear. Musical texts are *touching* in a very physical sense of the word, they draw their force from the breath of their creator and they carry that force in order to affect the reader's bodily rhythms—from shivers to laughter. The affectionate environment of Cixous's childhood home meant that the "sport" of leaping from one form of expression to another was not simply "translinguistic," it was "loving" as well ("My Algeriance" 169). The warmth of this background transforms the experience of writing by ear into a quest for the melodies of the heart: "I write by ear: the ear attuned to the musics of the heart" ("Le lieu du Crime" 262). This reflection comes from an essay on playwriting, a sort of composition that is specific in its touching of other ears, of the ear of the Other,[17] "*l'oreille du public*" (265).

One of Cixous's most successful pieces of theatrical writing is undoubtedly the 1999 *Tambours sur la digue*, which played at the Théâtre du Soleil under the direction of Ariane Mnouchkine. Recipient of the Molière award in 2000 for having composed the "*meilleure pièce de création*," Cixous has commented in a number of different venues on the special music she composed for the new voices of this play. The subtitle, "*sous forme de pièce ancienne pour marionnettes jouée par des acteurs*," reveals that the actors turn themselves into wooden dolls with rhythms and melodies all their own: "The language of marionettes is spoken differently from our own. I had to learn it, adjust to it.

Each language has the rhythm and the melody of the body that houses it" ("Coups de baguettes" 48). At the beginning, the playwright was tempted to give the characters humanlike phrases; but to make the play right, she had to make changes, shortening and lightening their discourse: "The first versions of *Tambours* committed errors of quantity, measure, and breath" (48). In search of this unheard idiom, this *"langue inouïe,"* Cixous explains that she had to make cuts for her out-of-breath creations: "I lightened up the text because in fact, a marionette can't speak much. The breath is short and staccato" (Noudelmann 119).

In a lively text springing from this theatrical event, "Le Théâtre surpris par les marionnettes," music takes center stage. The writer's comments to the actors instruct them on the "vocal music" that they must create: "Even the breath, you transpose it and place in the throat of the marionette a voice of music whose body, timbre, and volume are your creation." This musical writing is not uniform or predictable, but in the case of the marionette, it follows a regular meter: "The marionette writes with time, clear intervals, (invisible) spaces, separating and tying together in regular distances the phases, traits, bounds of passion, drawing out the space whence spring forth the cry, crisis, and access." This is a music that gives itself over to improvisation: "This music lends an ear, listens to the hesitations of the marionette, translates them in a polyphony, then, in a change of heart, alters the rhythm, obeying the spiritual breathings, receives and renders the variations of emotion." Variations of emotion govern this theatrical work, lending their rhythms and eruptions to the polyphonic composition. In an ironic twist, Cixous seems strangely at home in her search for the "foreign voice" of the marionette. Amidst her reflections on this creative production, one brief sentence stands apart in its own paragraph: *"Pour sol, la musique."* This is a transposition of frequent statements by writers who state that their territory, or their homeland, is located not in a national assignation, but rather in a *linguistic* entity. For Cixous, as for many writers, neither country of origin nor current place of residence determines her identity. But, in contrast to the affirming statements of a number of contemporary authors, Cixous does not claim to belong to a single language—and, by extension, literary tradition—either. In this brief poetic pronouncement (*"pour sol, la musique"*), the earth is a note on the musical scale, and the writer finds her ground, and her grounding, in music.

Note Taking and Giving

Auditory recordings are not the only form of copying the narrator of *Benjamin à Montaigne* engages in when she listens to her mother's voice. In metatextual twists (that comment—often obliquely—on the present of the writing), the narrative voice writes down words spoken by this creative parent to whom she listens attentively: "This morning's word: *miséraboliste*. 'I don't like these *miséraboliste* films.' I note. The word passes" (212). The word may go by, but not without its notation: "I note all, I say" (218). The proliferation of notepads and writing utensils contributes to the goal of taking down notes as quickly as possible, not to let any spoken pearl disappear. The recording apparatus is put into movement as well, even if their eventual usefulness is questionable. Keeping the mother's voice, along with that of the grandmother, is a gesture meant to make up for the effacement of another voice, that of her father: "The voice of my father is dead, and I can't mourn it [. . .] in my voice memory the paternal notes will spread over the memory of their sound" (*Benjamin* 219).

Taking notes is an activity that has been thematized with ever greater frequency by Cixous. In "Writing Blind," an essay published in *Stigmata: Escaping Texts*, she indicates that (her) writing depends on jotting down words as they strike her, lest the moment pass without a trace:

> If you do not grab them in the instant they pass, these pulsations are lost forever. In the moment where in passing they brush by us, they whisper in our ears, knocking at the doors of our senses, at our ears, at our nostrils, they wake in us thoughts never yet formed. [. . .] So, have on hand a notebook, a bit of paper, and capture the rapid traces of the instant. That the past which arrives at full speed will engulf in a few minutes. What has just happened will perish. Strange and exultant encounter of the quick and its end. One moves ahead while leaving behind. Human destiny: to be a flesh of forgetting [*chair à oubli*]. And to have no more vivacious desire than to wrest one's prey from forgetfulness, to keep the passing in the present. ("Writing Blind" 146)

Already an established writer at the time of these considerations of the writing process, Cixous at once gives advice and reflects on her own approach to the act of putting down words. For her, writing is a "tactile" experience; she writes by hand, finding her rhythm with the movement of pen on paper, far from the mediating elements of keyboard and screen. The time of writing is of special significance to her, for although note taking is a permanent, ongoing activity, she favors taking notes during the "in-between" moments, neither at night nor during the day, but in these indeterminate hours of dawn and dusk: "Very often I write at crepuscular hours. [. . .] I take notes which for me are seeds. Sometimes I do it late at night, when I am in bed. These are moments of collection, at these moments things gather themselves together. Notes, succinct. And the morning—before daylight. Between night and day" (*Rootprints* 105–6). Writing at the interstices of the defined timeslots of sleep and wakefulness, straddling the border that differentiates day from night, Cixous makes note of impressions and feelings that are often characterized as dreamlike.

It is important that Cixous's recent comments on note taking have recently focused on dreams. The urgency with which the narrator of *Benjamin à Montaigne* copies down every word her mother utters during waking hours is intensified in the moments of awakening in *Manhattan*, when the dream threatens to flee her memory forever. The narrator of the later text feels compelled to note her dream with fervor: "For my part I sit upright with a jump and I rush to note the dream that is receding [. . .] *note* I say, note the scene that wants to elude you [. . .] your duty as a living being is to disobey the foreign council instilled in your brain. Note or you will lose the memory of your being. I note" (*Manhattan* 227). Jacques Derrida has reflected at length on Cixous's capacity to "write (the) dream," to put into the literary text that which by definition seems to escape written expression:

> She writes to the dream, if I can put it that way, like in the expression navigate [. . .] to the wind, drawing energy as well as the figures of her writing from the phantasmoniric, the flow of which (that's the miracle and the magic) is not interrupted by waking, by the moment when the most impeccable vigilance watches over this writing that is the most surveyed, the most knowledgeable, the most composed, in its atomic core and in its great musical units that are also rhythmic, narrative, theatrical, and naturally tropical, semantic, and thematic. [. . .] I know no other exemple of such a miraculous alliance between night and day, between the wild turbulence of the dream and the calculating culture of a literal and literary staging of an œuvre. ("H.C. pour la vie" 72–73)

It is no accident that Derrida should mention the musical component of Cixous's written compositions. Cixous affirms music as essential to the act of writing: "To write is to note down the music of the world, the music of the body, the music of time" (*Rootprints* 46).

Derrida is of course not the first critic to underscore the importance of music in Cixous's œuvre. In *Photos de racines*, Mireille Calle-Gruber provides a clever musical scale (175–76) that she alters slightly in her more recent study of Cixous's œuvre *Du café à l'éternité* (90–91). Conceiving of the entire corpus of works published under the name "Hélène Cixous" as belonging to an elaborate musical ensemble is a well-founded idea. In the critic's words: "From book to book, Hélène Cixous has constructed for herself an entire collection of registers and keys. An entire scale: to play, to climb and to descend. Scale of what is possible, musical scale" (*Rootprints* 175). When she revisits this concept in *Du Café à l'éternité*, Calle-Gruber not only puts her finger on

202 ⌒ Chapter Four

the possibilities the musical scale provides, but she also reworks an important sentence in order to demonstrate that music *accomplishes something specific*: "Thus, from book to book, Hélène Cixous has constructed for herself an entire collection of registers and keys *to explore hurt worlds* [*sonder les terres accidentées*], where the undecidable extends to all extremities" (*Du café* 90, my emphasis). In this rewriting, Calle-Gruber takes into account the fact that the musical qualities of Cixous's work are more than aesthetically pleasing; they are effective tools for sounding out damaged places and people.

The musical scale that Calle-Gruber proposes is not a simple, predictable scale in a "major" key. It dips into "minor" and "diminished" keys and intervals, discontent to stay in a single, straightforward "mode."[18] Indeed the variations prove infinite: "The interval variations are endless: sharps, quartertones, blue notes, blue devils" (*Du café* 91). Picking up on such subtle changes of key is not an easy task for the reader, which is probably why Cixous provides clues in the text for reading properly: "Reading Hélène Cixous's books takes place in the between-tones, between-letters, between-words, between-time, between-songs, as if the text were covered with invisible diacritical signs sketching out the paths of interpretation" (*Du café* 91). These "paths of interpretation" are indicated by the author, but it is significant that they are only hinted at: the ultimate interpretation is not the property of the composer, but rather that of the interpreter.

Calle-Gruber's scale includes citations from various works by Cixous that contain the note in question; for example, "the nymphs speak in fa" is taken from the text that trumpets a musical title, *Beethoven à jamais* (*Rootprints* 175). For the first note of the scale, we find the following allusion in *Photos de racines* to another of several recurring composers in Cixous's work: "it is the note *do* in Schumann's ear (*On ne part pas, on ne revient pas*)." In the second variation of this musical scale, found in *Du Café à l'éternité*, the "*do*" is defined by a quotation from *Beethoven à jamais*, in which the note is likened to an eagle whose fall (rather than flight) is unending, and beautiful. Both of these references are rich, but I would like to suggest that an even more appropriate citation for this initial note—for the note that provides the tone for the rest of the scale—can be found in the recent *Portrait de Jacques Derrida en Jeune Saint Juif*: "He set the tone [*Il me donnait le do*]. All unawares, as a gift is given. I must have begun to make notes" (6). In this poetical reading of Derrida's work, Cixous engages in a reminiscent passage, in a fictional rendering of a specific memory: a conversation in Paris, at the café Balzar, in 1963. This pivotal moment was to mark the beginning of a friendship, affective and intellectual, between the two writers.[19] Cixous plays with words, and with their music, in this passage. She recalls that she saw Derrida from behind, that the view she had was of his back (*le dos*), and she transforms the spelling of this anatomical term by dropping the "s," turning *her back* on the body and referring, in this case, to music: Derrida provided Cixous with the note she needed to create her scale. He gave her the impetus to create, to invent, to compose her own music. And all this was unintentional. He provided her with the key to writing freely and unequivocally, as one gives a true gift. This encounter between two Jews from Algeria—whose similar itineraries brought them to the metropolitan capital—predated publishing for her; it proves to be a powerful memory because its occasion gave her inspiration. Once she had found the right key, Hélène Cixous began to note.

In music, "giving a note" is an expression that refers to the sounding of a specific key on the scale. A musician may ask for a certain pitch, and another musician with a tuned instrument or an exceptional ear will provide it. It could be said that Cixous has given notes in a number of senses. In many of her essays, particularly "Le Rire de la Méduse" and "La Venue à l'écriture," she provides the keys to writing, inspiring other women to take to this medium in order to voice their experiences.[20] In unique, indefinable works like *Photos de racines*, the writer gives of her own notes, where they are published in note-like form inside boxes, sketches of her notes for the readers to see, glimpses into the writing process at work.[21] These fragmentary notes are conceived as windows that give multiple perspectives and open-ended possibilities: "The windows in the text give onto Hélène Cixous's notebooks" (*Rootprints* 11).

The words Cixous notes down in her position as scribe are not inconsequential. She acknowledges their importance in clear terms that indicate we are all spoken, speaking beings: "We are chattered chatterers. Exhalers-breathers of sentences (= precipitations, elocutions of soul states). Words, sentences (1) express (2) shape our state and our fate. / I am a registrar, a gatherer of sentences" ("The Book" 412). The expressions we utter, as well as those we write, are capable of expressing our situation, but they are equally capable of *changing* our situation. The constative function of language is also performative; words are not only descriptors, they are actors. Taking account of their power means that employing words in the written text is never an innocent operation: denouncing a wrong means already to act on that wrong, for pointing it out means already to change it. Gathering sentences is a "playful" undertaking with "serious" consequences: it has the capacity to shape lives.

Rhythm for Remembrance:
Striking the Right Note for Memory

Hélène Cixous has recalled, on several occasions, an early scene from her childhood that she has retained with accuracy, a scene in which her father explained to her the danger of singing enthusiastically the name of Maréchal Pétain (*Photos* 206). As a precocious toddler, Cixous quickly joined in the collective chant without understanding entirely what the movement was all about.[22] Her recollection of this occasion is revelatory for a number of reasons, one of which is its emphasis on the musical aspect of the experience. When the words were given a particular rhythm, the young child was able to participate in their pronunciation, even if she didn't understand their import. Music, or chant, can have the effect of an incantation, drawing people under its spell without a conscious realization of what is happening to them. While in the case of her own experience, the words carried by the rhythm were problematic, such is fortunately not always the case. Cixous, by finding the appropriate cadences in her writing, is able to work against the political enchantment that caught her up in its cause before she was aware of the true message behind the attractive beat. Her early sensitivity to words *and* tempo helped shape her affinity for writing with a unique pace, and her father's instruction made her aware of the pitfalls of appreciating form at the expense of content. Following this event, such a disjunction was—and remains—no longer possible for Cixous.

Cixous's recent work of fiction, *Manhattan*, contains numerous reflections on voice, on music and its indispensable role in determining meaning. For the writer whose self-reflexive text demonstrates an auditory sensitivity to the voices of her characters, the greatest challenge is to properly translate them in the written work:

> [S]aid my brother in a slow and melodious voice without reproach or accusation, I listened enchanted thinking: *everything is in the intonation*, the same phrases pronounced with the accents of sandals would be directed against me these were not, how to do it I thought worried and enchanted how to render in writing the gentleness of a mournful spoken word, *it is always a question of voice and tone* I thought, what is missing on the page is the music that I should indicate here: 'Song of my brother to the Standing Cow, himself mooing in the bush, himself the Standing Cow at the edge of the field, himself caught up by the vision by the fable.' (216, my emphasis)

The intonation of the spoken voice changes everything,[23] in the narrator's analysis, and the same words can take on entirely different connotations depending on their music. *Son* and *sens* are never far apart; in fact, they are interconnected. This passage ends on a humorous note that returns to the content of the discourse emitted by the brother's voice: "[Y]ou cannot see a standing cow without making it into a literary cow" are the teasingly accusatory words he speaks in his slow, melodious manner. While the narrative voice indicates that she should call this the "Song of my brother, etc.," she has not actually applied this label as a subheading in this text. She *has* applied a similar label to portions of other texts, notably *Le jour où je n'étais pas là*, where two different choruses, that of the "Mongoloids" and that of the "Drummer Chickens," make their appearance under italicized headings.

The titles *Chœur des Mongoliens* (66) and *Chœur des Poules en Batterie* (103) may initially cause the reader to smile, even to laugh, not simply because of the sudden, unexpected interruption of the chorus (reminiscent of Greek tragedy) in the midst of the contemporary text of fiction, but also because of the apparently ironic tone of this music. A close look at the words of these choruses, however, changes their tune. The singers in these choirs are at once to be taken literally and metaphorically: Mongoloids and chickens are oppressed groups, and they are meant to represent the predicament of other oppressed groups. Their cries of lament are for themselves, but these notes can be immediately transposed to speak for and to the cause of others who have been singled out and put down for arbitrary reasons, such as race and sex. The second of these two examples focuses on the plight of chickens, winged animals denied flight and destined for the dinner table. This chorus is part of a larger, ongoing concern for animals in Cixous's œuvre, a topic of predilection that reveals her care for victims on all levels. At the close of the chorus, these startlingly sober words establish a clear connection between victims of the animal kingdom and those of recent human history: "My mother has better things to do than listen to my Choir: there's a fascinating show on the Concentration Camps" (105).

While many of the complaints of the Mongoloids in their chorus can be applied to Cixous's own son around whom the book revolves, they can also be relevant to Jews of Algeria. This is most striking on a linguistic level, for "Mongoloid" is a term that is no longer "politically correct" at the time of writing: "In our day we no longer say *mongolien*, Mongoloid isn't good. We say *trisomique* it's better [. . .] Down syndrome, advised medical term. There were no Mongoloids from that point on" (67). The Mongoloids whose voices make up the chorus have not been dissuaded, for they continue to call themselves Mongoloids despite linguistic proscriptions and prescriptions: "Mongoloid to Mongoloid we repeat ourselves" (67). Shortly after this part of the chorus, the narrator jumps in and makes the following parallel point on the use of appropriate terms in the Algeria of her childhood: "In Algeria during the world war in 1940 there was also a substitution of advised terms for precarious persons, instead of Jews from one day to the next they *advised Israelites*, instead of Arab the *advised term indigenous*, instead of 'I want' advise 'I would like'" (67). Inserting these details in the midst of the chorus is a well-placed gesture. It underscores the facility with which we get caught up in the "music" that surrounds us, allowing ourselves to be influenced by the general tune without paying attention to the words. Applying new terms to refer to groups of people often enacts violence against those people, even when such terms are meant to convey respect. Employing "politically correct" expressions such as "Israelites" and "Indigenous" to refer to "Jews" and "Arabs" in Algeria may not be the solution to eradicating the racial prejudices that accompany the original terms. Instead, these "euphemisms" are unjust and even insulting: they apply labels that are frequently incorrect to describe the people they are meant to name. Just as the Mongoloid "orphans" choose to *name themselves* in their chorus, opting to hang onto a term that others have judged outmoded, so the Jews and Arabs of Algeria should exercise the right to determine how they are called.

The musical form that Cixous chooses to convey her messages does not detract or distract from their content. To the contrary, rhythm carries (their) meaning, and makes messages memorable. The writer is convinced of the indissoluble connection between music and meaning: "The music and the meaning are absolutely indissociable. I have the impression that the truth sings true [*la vérite chante juste*]" (*Rootprints* 46). If truth hits the right note, if it is decidedly in tune, that doesn't mean that it has to be exactly on the mark. Absolute precision in writing is not possible because of the shortcomings of words to express experience, and because of the multiple possible sorts of music and meaning located in and stemming from the same terms. Cixous addresses her job as a "work of approximation," a meticulous, conscientious task that aims always toward the unattainable:

It is work by approximation: in the end one keeps 'the-closest-possible.' And that is what I do. [. . .] The implicit discourse is not: 'it's not quite that,' but rather: 'that's it, but that proposition, that sentence also says *more than that*.' And it's the 'more than that' which at times I want to make heard all the same. Let us speak now of this 'making heard': it recycles or I recycle, writing recycles when it hears itself: when the author has just written a sentence and I hear the prolongations. Prolongations of meaning. I hear it continue vibrating. For me everything is in the vibration; and I say to myself: will our ears hear the vibrations? That is to say: will the economy of the text, its woven construction, allow the vibrations to be heard? For us to hear the vibrations, there must be silence. (*Rootprints* 66)[24]

The rich reflections of these words, spoken aloud in a transcribed conversa-tion, resonate with multiple interpretations. Cixous comments repeatedly, in written and oral form, on "the book that she will never write," on the text that will never reach print, on the words that forever exceed and evade rep-resentation. What becomes clear in such comments is a wider message that even the books that have reached publication, even these works that bear her signature and figure as part of her œuvre, are not closed. Reading is a con-stant, ongoing process that entails multiple perusals of the same passages and that goes on even after the contact with the book. The vibrations that make themselves felt in the text continue to move outside the text, they reverber-ate long after the initial encounter. What Cixous terms the "more than that [*plus que ça*]," the extra, supplemental, additional music and meaning that may even have escaped the author's conscious application, will carry on, pro-longing the textual effects of the reading experience. The emphasis here on the ear is significant, for Cixous's texts are meant to be read *aloud*—they are intended to be *heard*—since the acoustic plays on words and homophonic in-ventions can easily slip by the eye. Paying attention to the aural threads of the woven construction of the text leads to a fuller appreciation of the writer's work as poetic *and* political, as musical *and* meaningful.

Familiar Voices: The Concerto of the Everyday

The unique voice of her mother intervenes in a number of Cixous's texts, but it resounds with particular force in *Benjamin à Montaigne*.[25] The narrator re-turns frequently in this work to the question of language, to the inimitable language of her writing, with its unusual twists and turns of phrase that mark it as originating in and emanating from the unparalleled tongue of the mother: "this language that is not hers but that came to me from her, because of her, in spite, against, with, through, come under her voice" (202). But the mother's voice is not the only one to come through in the text, as a section titled "CONCERTO" communicates the sounds of a family meal as heard from the floor above: "Voice. Loud voice of (my) mother. Loud voice of (my) brother. Wood. Bangs of doors: cupboards kitchen. Drawers kitchen. Plates. Stacks. Glasses. Voice of (my) niece: litany. Noise of white teapot. Noise of ladles" (107). The effect of these short, staccato sentences is cumulative. They seem to pile up, one after the other, building with increasing speed in an inescapable crescendo: "Noices of pan covers noise voice of (my) mother. Plates. Loud laugh of (my) brother. Cry of my mother. Rising voice of my brother. Lowered voice of my mother. *Tak-Schmakt*: onomatopoeia of my brother. Noises of bowls. Veiled voice of my sister-in-law. Cough. Yells of (my) niece" (108).

The dinner "concerto" is an ordinary scene, one that has taken place in the past, one that repeats itself in the narrative of the present, and one that will likely play itself out again in the future: "The same scene begins again 31 July 2000. Let's hope it will be replayed in July 2001" (109). The very ordinariness of the meal means that it is not obvious fodder for literature, but this is no "ordinary" literature. Cixous transmits the notes and rhythms of this scene with a truly clever composition. The laughter, comments, and miscellaneous noises build in volume and intensity until they come to an unexpected rest at the height of their activity; two phrases appear on two separate lines, in the fashion of poetry: "In the background slamming of the gate" is followed by the brief indication "*Silence soudain.*" The sudden silence is "echoed" in the layout of the text by the insertion of a blank space that seems to separate the scene in two. At the climax of noise and movement, everything comes to a standstill and this mute immobility is *visible*. When the text takes off again, it does so with a bang: "Sudden canon. First bark. Second bark. Rabbit voice. A short sharp cry. Bird voice. A short sharp cry. The beautiful bronze vibration of my brother's voice, climbs beating in the stairway, beating in my office 27 July 1998" (*Benjamin* 108). The vertiginous play on words and sounds that Cixous effects in this condensed portion of highly alliterative text is a tongue twister and a mind bender at the same time: "'*Elles glapissent, la cuisse, la cuisse, c'est l'Allemagne dans la cuisine' tonne le bronze de mon frère*" (109). This acrobatic phrase is filled with turns that revolve around the hum of the dinner scene: the German mother and her sister squeal over the chicken leg, the French word for "thigh," "cuisse," reflecting and resonating with "cuisine." Taken as a whole, this passage presents textual play at its best. But it is more than just fun and games.

Putting the anecdotal, the quotidian into written form—taking down the notes that make up the everyday—is anything but a meaningless enterprise. In a lengthy interview with Kathleen O'Grady in March 1996, Cixous expresses her disagreement with those who try to clearly divide the "personal" and the "political." She addresses the case of Derrida, whose "philosophical" writings are necessarily "political" as well: "his philosophical writing is a writing that is always political, that always has political effects—and it is the same thing for me" ("Guardian of Language"). While all of her writing is political, like Derrida's, it is often not political in the same ways, since she has chosen to privilege poetry in writing of family and self:

> Everything takes place as if a certain public only labeled "political" that which has as its unique goal or center a reference to historical-political events, events that could appear in newspapers and history books. But the political—it's so simple, I'm ashamed to have to say it—does not relate only to the political scene, to political events reported by the media; it obviously begins with the subject's discourse about the self, that is to say all that makes up the political scene: relations of power, oppression, enslavement, exploitation. All of that begins with the personal, within the family and inside myself [. . .] I was, in a certain way, born political, and it is even for political reasons that I began to write, and that I began to write *poetry* as a response to political drama. ("Guardian")

Insisting on the power of poetry to respond to political drama is a significant gesture in this oral encounter.[26] Some of Cixous's work may at first glance seem devoid of political substance, but a closer look at the recurring refrains— even in the most personal of texts—reveals multiple layers of meaning. As Cixous argues here, injustice begins with the self, and with one's interactions with one's most intimate companions. The music sung at the dinner table in the home reveals the power differentials that exist in the world at large. Bringing out the tunes of this seemingly innocent scene not only provokes laughter: it provokes thought as well.

The fast-moving dinner concerto reiterates near its end a crucial point in Cixous's understanding of voices: *they are many.* The mention of voices in all their varieties is so common in Cixous's theoretical and fictional work alike that we could consider it a "pedal point," a sustained note held throughout her corpus (even when harmonic changes take place in the score). Not only does each individual possess *a unique voice* with its own timbre, music, and expression(s), each individual has *a number of voices*, adopting different tones for diverse situations: "I have a high round voice underneath a moderate wing. There is a voice for celebrating, a voice for piercing, a voice for reproaching, a voice for hawking" (109). The fascinating personage who haunts a recent work of fiction, Gregor Samsa, is all the more intriguing because of his multiple voices: "Now [the letter] advances and plays. It's a *tone* of poetic musical regret, it sounds like the voice of G. over the phone, slow dense heavy supple enough and uneven to adapt to the discreet modulations of a deploration" (*Manhattan* 113). In the narrator's recollection of her interaction with this man, her memory lingers on questions of voice and tone: "Questions of *voice* and *tone* come back insistently in my memory [. . .]

I should develop a linguistics of *the voice of* G. I can say today that a *very capital* part of his messages was found in *his voice* and the way he knew how to play it" (113). It is significant that Gregor (G.) knows how to *play* with his voice, that he has the capacity to work his vocal cords and thereby affect his interlocutor. This depth and flexibility incite the narrator to liken G. to an actor in several passages. Not only does he adapt to situations by playing diverse roles, he changes character by adopting diverse voices as well. His chameleon-like voice is all the more striking because it does not "fit" his body: "This nonsensical gap between the heavy voice and the thin physical envelope gave this voice the strength of law" (113). This commanding instrument gives him power over others in spite of his unimposing physique.

If she appreciates Gregor's ability to manipulate his voice and influence others, it is because Cixous realizes the power of different intonations to *say* different things. In a passage from *OR*, the first-person narrator addresses her cat, emphasizing the importance not only of calling the animal *by name*, but of putting the right tone of voice into the calling:

> Between my cat and me the pact passes through pronunciation. Not only do I call her intensely, it is a question of a marriage proposal every time. In the timbre of my voice lying on her name a question unites us, "Do you want to?" she hears and the movement of her body is a yes I want to, yes, and every time it is for life. I am very conscious of this, I never throw out her name like a piece of fish. (*OR* 22)

Pronunciation assumes a capital role in this verbal pact; the choice of register and the slow, prolonged rhythm of the proposal count as much as, or more than, the words. The music determines the message, again and again. It is noteworthy that this pact is not concluded once and for all, that it is not dated and signed in the past with permanency; it is renewed daily, it is repeated regularly, constantly updated and revised for the moment. Here, repetition draws from the past, but adapts to the present and points to the future as well. Repetition is never an empty incantation of yesterday's words, but a continual questioning, an ever-new proposal, that respects the other, and the other's name, as ongoing affirmation of difference and evolution. The imploring song that the narrator uses to call her cat is familiar and repetitive, yet it is never the same.

Voice is not only audible; it is also tactile, in Cixous's understanding. One can literally *touch* another with one's words, as the narrative voice reveals in *Le Jour où je n'étais pas là*. This book can be considered a hymn, perhaps a requiem for a deceased son, and the mother seeks to speak, to touch the child with her voice prior to his passing: "'Georges, petitgeorges': I hold out the hands of my voice [. . .] I hold out my voice, take my voice, I press upon him [. . .] I pull him to my chest while singing I lick his ears and the nestling [*niais*] shivers" (90). It is her hope that her voice and its song will draw him out of his silence, will give him inspiration toward life and language, will save him.[27]

Speaking Silence: Writing in the Rest(s)

Cixous's sensitivity to the son's muteness in *Le Jour où je n'étais pas là* implicitly recognizes that silence is not a void, that it is actually pregnant with meaning, with possibility, that it is far from "the opposite" of speaking.[28] Indeed, keeping quiet is a way of communicating, as Cixous acknowledges elsewhere: "Our dialogues are often mute. / This doesn't prevent them from taking place" (*Rootprints* 46). If her work is largely inspired by loss, that loss is exemplified by silence. Lost loved ones have often provided Cixous with a literary voice, with inspiration: "There is a silence in my story. / That I cannot forget. The last silence of my father. / Night was falling. I was traversing the garden of childhood" (*Le Nom d'Œdipe* 17).[29] Seeking the sound of the final silence of her father has moved the writer to numerous creative texts that not only pay attention to silence, but also provide a place for silence in the written work.

It has often been remarked that Cixous's writing straddles multiple generic borders, confounding set categories and refuting classification. The two quotations in the previous paragraph come from two very different "works," but they both exhibit an affinity with poetry. The short lines and the pauses between them situate these citations outside normal definitions of prose. Since it is a question in these instances of "notes" published in a book of interviews (*Photos de racines*) and an opera libretto (*Le Nom d'Œdipe*), it is not surprising that these portions of text resemble poetic composition. Creating work that comes close to poetry is revelatory of Cixous's respect for this form: "Poetry works with silence: it writes a verse, followed by a silence, a stanza, surrounded by silence. In other words, there is time to hear all the vibrations. As for prose, one of the differences with respect to poetry is precisely that there are no silences" (*Rootprints* 66). Cixous's "poetic" composition is not limited to the two texts in question here. It arguably extends into much of her written production, creating space for silence in texts that would otherwise be called "prose" in works that exemplify the "ideal" writing she evokes in *Photos de racines*: "Most of the time, pages leave only a little room for silences, ruptures, spaces. Ideally, I would prefer to write my texts as I hear them: that is, as poetry" (66). Cixous inserts silence into her writing not only rhythmically, but visibly as well.

In the passage titled "Concerto" from *Benjamin à Montaigne* that I have examined above, the insertion of a concrete, visible space between the two halves of text that make up the family dinner is an example of a very literal "writing in" of a moment of rest amidst the commotion of the repast. Rather than skipping over this instance of quiet inactivity, the author has chosen to assert it as part of the written passage, in the way a composer includes rests in the musical score.[30] The absence of sound is as significant as the loudest chords in the piece. In fact, in Cixous's analysis, the most striking "songs" in her writing function like musical rests. In a recent article for *New Literary History*, Cixous refers to the two choruses from *Le Jour où je n'étais pas là* (without disclosing this text as their source) as interruptions, as irruptions: "Into the published volume, in the middle of the story, I let in, let pass, an irruption of forgettings: for example the mongoloid chorus. The percussion chorus of chickens" ("The Book" 411). These breaks are essential to the script: "It resembles a scene on stage animated solely by interruptions. Stops, fishbones, angles, tracing the agitation of the soul. It resembles the pauses in a Beethoven score" (411). The German composer's musical notation is motivation for similar movements—and pauses—in Cixous's writing.

In *Photos de racines*, Beethoven is again evoked in the context of stops. Cixous speaks of these pauses in laudatory terms, praising the emotional effect that such music has on her, and addressing the possibility of writing in a similar manner:

> What overwhelms me with emotion in the text of Beethoven, that is to say the stops, the very forceful stops in the course of a symphony. Suddenly, my own breath is bridled sharply by the reins. We are suspended up there, above ourselves in the soundless air. And. We restart, in a leap, a path or a heart higher up. Who writes like that—like emotion itself, like the thought (of the) body, the thinking body? I have a passion for stops. But for there to be a stop, there must be a current, a coursing of the text. Always the mystery of difference, of *différance*. Never the one without the other. (*Rootprints* 64)

The passion for silence is contingent upon the music that surrounds that silence, upon the notes that lead up to and follow the soundless moments. The rests in the writer's texts draw their power from *context*: they are dependent on what surrounds them for their impact. It is obviously in reference to Derrida's conception of *différance* that Cixous closes this reflection. The ideas of differentiation *and* deferment inherent in this renowned neologism are not without relation to music, as Cixous intimates when she addresses the subject: "difference constitutes music, yes. Sound is a difference, is it not? It is the rubbing of notes between two drops of water, the breath between the note and the silence, the sound of thought" (*Rootprints* 47). These differences in sound may be subtle, but that doesn't mean they aren't compelling.

It is important to note that silence does not exist separately from the written score. It is an integral part of the composition, just as in music. In reflecting on her work, Cixous refers to its musical, silent aspects as if these two adjectives were in harmony: "So this is part of my work. It is situated in the musical and silent environment of the text that produces effects in my writing. It is because I hear writing write" (*Rootprints* 67). Music contains silence, and silence contains music: the two are interrelated. The two are also complicitous in their textual function: unconventional forms of meaning making, they serve as particularly effective vehicles for transmitting emotion and experience. As Cixous relates, writing makes use of silence to communicate that which is not expressed through the written (or spoken) word: "It is the art of writing [. . .] to know how to make this appear, at sentence-corners, with silences, with mute words; all that will not have been pronounced but will have been expressed with means other than speech" (*Rootprints* 48). Silences can work (in paradoxical fashion) to "*faire entendre*," to "make heard" that which is not always said, and this is where the rhythm of the writing comes into play.[31]

Counting Measures: Musical Time

Silences in the musical phrase can be considered as periods of waiting, as moments of expectation: the double meaning of the French verb "attendre" is appropriate to describe what often takes place during the "rests" of a piece. When the sounds come to a stop, the listener is in a sort of "in-between" stage, still hearing the echoes of the notes that have just played and already anticipating the notes that will resound in the imminent future.[32] If the rest carries a fermata in the musical score, the indefinite nature of the waiting/expecting that makes up the listener's experience is intensified, since the length of the pause is up to the performer's discretion, independent of the tempo. This suspension is one of many possible ways in which music "plays" with textual time, making it seem to linger interminably at a "standstill" and then accelerate rapidly so that passages go by "in no time" at other points in the piece. Drawing on a comment by the Russian composer Igor Stravinsky, contemporary music critic Alex Ross addresses in simple terms the manner in which music changes our relationship to time: "Music has a way of putting to sleep those portions of the brain that count the minutes [. . .] in a live performance, you become attuned to the fantastic clocks of musical time, which race forward, rewind, stop dead, and otherwise interfere with the ticking of reality" (189). Cixous is acutely aware of the complex workings of textual music on the "ticking of reality." This awareness comes through in the various ways in which she represents and addresses time in her writing.

In *Photos de racines*, Cixous speaks directly to the question of time in her written production, explaining that the topic is of crucial importance to her work: "I have a different relationship to preservation, to loss, to the persistence of the past, etc., to all the affects, emotions, attitudes aroused by the mysteries of time, to forgetting, memory, anamnesis. These are the themes that occupy me (him also), and to which I respond with a music that is different from his" (*Rootprints* 88). The "him also" in parentheses here is a reference to Jacques Derrida, who shares Cixous's concerns but who treats them "with a different music," as she puts it.[33] Her focus on the "mysteries of time" in the form of memory and forgetting is exemplified textually in chronological jumps that defy notions of linear development and progress: "To write by shreds [. . .] in the present as in the archpast, in pre-vision, in the true chaos of verbal tenses, crossing over years and oceans at a god's pace, with the past on my right and the future on my left—this is forbidden in academies, it is permitted by apocalypses" ("Writing Blind" 143). The discontinuous nature of this writing is lifelike, in Cixous's analysis: "This is done in the way life happens to us, by gusts, by events, depositing discontinuous elements" (143). Since life *and language* are neither monotonous nor predictable, the written text does not seek to make them so. Cixous exploits the fragmentary nature of existence in her texts: "In language I like and I practice the leap and the short-cut, ellipsis, amphibology, speed and slowness, asyndeton" (144).

The coexistence of "speed" and "slowness" in this sentence resonates with another evocative passage from the same text on writing: "*One must play language quick and true like an honest musician, not leap over a single word-beat. Find the slowless inside the speed*" ("Writing Blind" 144). Cixous uses italics to emphasize here a point that appears counterintuitive: slowness would seem to be anathema to speed, but Cixous maintains that the former can be found *within* the latter. The two concepts are not in contradiction with each other, they are not "opposites": they are interrelated. What's more, they are subject to interpretation. What appears slow to one person may seem quick to another, and the same slowness may be reinterpreted as quickness by the same person in a different context. What Cixous has pointed to all along in her textual production is the *elasticity* of time, and the relativity of temporality, as this comment in parentheses from the early "La Venue à l'écriture" reveals: "But a year, I've learned, is too long and is nothing. I learned all the subtleties of time very early, its elasticity in inflexibility, its meanness in compassion, its ability to return" ("Coming" 23).[34] In a recent publication, *L'Amour du loup et autres remords*, Cixous revisits our unsteady relation to time in a reflection on letters as manifestations of the "disorders of our time. We are temporal disorderlies, we are prey to Time, to its essential discord" (152).[35] The discordance of time is not "unmusical"; rather, its cacophony creates a music of its own, an unusual combination of tones and notes that reveals the past and captures the present, making memories for the future.[36]

Holding fast to time often means writing it down quickly, as it passes, as Cixous attests: "I always work on the present passing" (*The Hélène Cixous Reader* xxii). But the urgency of her transcription does not detract from the reading experience in/of time: savoring it slowly, in written form. The resonance of the phrase depends on giving it the time it requires: "That's why it is good to write, to let the language try—like we try a caress—to take the time a sentence, or a thought needs to create love, to create resonance" (*Sorties* 171).[37] The process of writing, for Cixous, is inextricable from the webs of time, as she evocatively states in "Writing Blind": "I set myself to weaving time. A year without a book—this has not happened to me, a year without the fabric of life" (149). "Weaving time" is an apt description of Cixous's writing, for her texts incorporate time "immemorial" in the form of biblical references, and they draw on the works of "world literature" (from different ages) signed by Homer, Montaigne, Shakespeare, Thomas Bernhard, and Clarice Lispector—to name but a few of her literary inspirations—in a demonstration that *books transcend time*, that they not only permit travel in time, but they undo the regular rules of calendar and clock: "books were created as a world that forever destabilizes due dates, a blink of a telephone on the bookshelf and it's [. . .] 1804 and I pass five morning hours in a row with Stendhal" (*OR* 24).[38] The reader travels back to the beginning of the nineteenth century, and a different calendar year, along with the narrative, living several epochs simultaneously.

Resonances and Rewritings: Playing (with) Music

The temporality of writing and reading can differ from one text—and from one moment of the same text—to another. Like a composer, Cixous gives tempo indications at different moments in her work, often in explicit references to music, as in "La Venue à l'écriture": "*Requième Conférence sur l'Infinimité*" (45) is a playful title that overturns and resituates a sober musical mass. In *Manhattan*, time turns musical in a passage that is far from somber, despite the connotation of the musical form evoked in the two verses that read as lines of poetry on the printed page: "And all of that is a musical form:

a Dies Irae / Vroom Vroom Vroom Vroom says my mother" (207). This passage is taken from a section subtitled *DIES ILLA*, a heading that plays further with the thirteenth-century Latin hymn on the Day of Judgment referred to within. The "illa" refers to the feminine, of course; it also harks back to an earlier work of fiction by Cixous, a 1980 text that bears the title *Illa*. This intertextual reference to another of her works is one of innumerable resonances that characterize Cixous's œuvre. The parts can be appreciated separately, but their interaction with the ensemble to which they belong is the most striking note of this creative production. The recurring themes that appear again and again in different texts are always present in new ways, as Mireille Calle-Gruber observes: "And like the arms of a clock, passing again is not repetition but always passing *otherwise*" (*Photos* 165).

The mother's repetition of the onomatopoeic "Vroom" in the quotation above from *Manhattan* echoes a passage that comes just slightly earlier in the text: "I was charmed by the Vroom, Vroom, I was not Ulysses, I could not resist the choir of the dead Georges Georges Georges and Gregor I remained immobile pinned down" (199). In this relatively short phrase taken from a much longer sentence, Cixous includes two of her favorite repeating "myths," the first taken from the siren episode of Homeric fame, and the second from her own textual creations, in which the first name "Georges" refers to her deceased father and son.[39] The chorus chanting the names of these lost loved ones has put her in a trance; her ears open to these intoxicating sounds, the narrator is unable to resist. The story of Ulysses intertwines and intermingles here with the stories of her family members, in a textual web that constantly returns to the same subjects, that frequently repeats itself, but always anew.[40]

The novelty that characterizes Cixous's use of repetition in her texts is what frustrates readers who seek predictability and comfort, clamoring for self-sameness in written production. Neither her name nor her signature remains unchanged throughout her publishing career, for Cixous will be the first to valorize "play" as a means of expressing the difference that not only marks one person from another, but that characterizes the same person from one moment—and from one circumstance—to another: "Pure I, identical to I-self, does not exist. I is always in difference. I is the open set of the trances of an I by definition changing, mobile, because living-speaking-thinking-dreaming. [. . .] The difference is in us, in me, difference plays me (my play)" ("Preface" xviii). In this published version of a text originally composed in French, the play between the first person pronoun "je" and its homophone "jeu" doesn't translate into English. This is one of countless instances in which a serious, substantive message is transmitted in a playful, creative text that relies in the original on what Cixous admits is the "French ear": "In French the phrase 'who are I' (*qui sont-je*) also plays the music of the differance writing/voice; for our French ear hears, when I pronounce my question, the phrase 'who muses?' i.e. who dreams" (xvii). This explanation intended for an Anglophone readership states what normally goes unsaid in Cixous's texts: meaning is much more than words on paper, it is an affair of the ear. Mutual understanding depends on a particular French verb in its various states: "hearing" (*entendre*) resonates with "getting along" (*s'entendre*) on the musical scale, and indeed the two are close.[41]

Sight Reading: Always the First Time

Cixous has a "childlike" approach to writing, approaching language as something ever new and always surprising.[42] She plays games with words, pointing out their incongruencies at times and at others delighting in their resemblance to other terms and expressions. This textual perspective on what can easily become tried and trite has propelled her to point out aspects of language—and, by extension, prejudices and presuppositions that have become a part of our thought processes—that often escape our "adult" attention. Her refreshing, rejuvenating tactic of putting words to paper may remind her readers of their lost wonder at the magic of language, and this is certainly one of the qualities of Cixous's work. But her writing is not limited to a "naïve" approach, even though such an approach has its merits. She reinfuses words with new force due to an idiosyncratic manner of "seeing" and "hearing" for the first time,[43] but she also gives them renewed meaning because of a new reading of their histories. The delicate balance she strikes between youthful excitement and mature erudition in writing is precisely where I locate Cixous's genius. When she affirms in *Photos de racines* that we read languages by their roots (93), the writer is referring to a highly developed, knowledgeable practice that depends not only on a familiarity with etymology and linguistic evolution in a general sense but also on the origins and developments of literary, philosophical, and historical terms in their specific contexts.

Cixous regularly focuses on unusual topics, treating them as serious, worthy subjects of literary composition. She evokes *animals* of all sorts, domestic and wild, and incorporates them into the written work as if they were characters on the same level as humans.[44] The opening lines of her most recent publication affirm the importance of these beings in her life and work: "The characters gathered under the roof of this volume are animals (with which I have been allied and affiliated, body and soul, from the origin of my passionate life)" (*L'Amour du loup* 9). A second passion in Cixous's writing is *love* in all its forms, including the physical, corporeal meeting of two beings as exemplified in this passage from *Souffles*: "A same desire, harmonizes, the orchestra stirs, the wand rises, and the lightning strikes. Love! hits! The universe, roaring, strikes! Love! [. . .] The woman! Opened! The cry!" (56). This is just one of many passages that re-create the lovemaking scene, always with a fresh approach to the union of bodies and souls that such momentary passionate connections point toward. As in this quotation, music is the preferred means to communicate what by essence seems to defy description; the movements of sound best accompany the movements of the heart and its desires.

Dancing with Derrida

While recent articles and reviews comment on the remarkable affinity between Cixous and Derrida, none has yet pinpointed some of the ongoing textual references that have subtly marked their work from early in their careers. These important references to each other bear witness to a mutual longstanding influence that has given rise to two very different œuvres that nonetheless draw from many of the same personal, historical, geographical, and philosophical sources to sing similar words to different tunes.

In *Limonade tout était si infini*, the female protagonist composes a love letter that simultaneously denounces war and extends thanks to the missive's *destinataire*, Elli. The letter seeks to express gratitude by intertwining musical terms with a worn word marked by overuse: *merci*. Playing on the phonetic components of the two syllables that make up this term, Cixous evokes the "sea" and the "mother" in relation to "*mer*," the words "if," the emphatic "yes," and, importantly, the musical note in relation to "*ci*": "[W]rite me in the key of *si*" (*Limonade* 66). This 1982 text finds resonance—and keys to understanding—in the 2001 *Portrait de Jacques Derrida en Jeune Saint Juif.* The latter publication contains a close reading of "Circonfession," a semi-autobiographical reflection that reveals much about Derrida's early life and his relation to his mother. In this text, Derrida unveils his secret name, a name unknown to the public prior to the publication of this work in 1991, a name that immediately recalls the one to whom the letter of *Limonade* is destined: Élie. Cixous puts this name into play, highlighting the repetition of the syllables "el" and "li" in a passage from Derrida's text, taking off from this starting point to make statements about her friend and his work: "He reads this name of Elie, which links him to literature, to elect, to lie, to bed, childbed deathbed, and to all of the Elies, if one elides it makes zélie in French, zealous, this line of Elies, Elie author of delicts unmentioned or elided in the family" (*Portrait* 15). This play with the revealed appellation comes on the heels of an evocation of Cixous's first meeting with Derrida, a meeting first depicted in Derrida's "H.C. pour la vie, c'est à dire." Picking up on his cue, Cixous refers to his written memory and cites him in her text: "'it's *as if*—I quote him—'we had *practically* [*quasiment*] never been apart.' I quote him exactly. This *as if* [*comme si*], his signature" (6). This "si" of hypothesis, of possibility, of approximation, is what Cixous singles out as Derrida's *signature*. It is also the "si" of "merci"—the note that provides the intonation—in the letter from *Limonade*. These examples intimate that Derrida has always already been present in Cixous's œuvre, long before the explicit references that characterize her most recent publications. They also indicate that this literary dance with Derrida is truly an intertextual affair.

It is in "Circonfession" that Derrida reveals his legal first name, "Jackie," and the source of this appellation. In her *Portrait de Jacques Derrida en Jeune Saint Juif*, Cixous plays creatively with this given name by aligning it with that of the film star who is Derrida's namesake: "In these sketches we shall catch glimpses of the book's young hero rushing past from East to West, or from one shore to the other, in appearance both familiar and mythical: here he is for a start sporting the cap of Jacques Derrida Koogan, as *Kid*" (viii). While the identity of the "Kid" in this passage is transparent, it isn't quite so clear in an earlier allusion found in *Neutre*: "parchment covered in signs traced by the famous Kidd" (*Reader* 13). This crypted reference to Derrida's name appears alongside textual clues that reveal themes from his early publications, *De la grammatologie* and *L'Écriture et la différence*, works that coincided with his adoption of a "serious" name, Jacques.

In *Benjamin à Montaigne*, Cixous engages in a complicated, ongoing reflection on names, as the very title of this work suggests. Derrida is often present, but under the label "mon ami," as in this incomplete sentence rich with designations: "My friend is an œuvre sometimes clothed with his body" (128). Here we understand that the unnamed individual in question is at once a personal acquaintance, a writer, and a body. But his identity remains uncertain at this moment in the text. It is later, when the narrator is taking note of her mother's unusual French language, that the latter cracks the code: "Foreign words present themselves immediately, summarily repairing just at the right moment the D system says my mother, what is this D I say to her, D? It's D? says my mother, figure it out yourself, it's Derrida your friend the discoverer who invented this expression?" (212). Cixous puts Derrida's initials into play at different points in this inventive text[45] ("ce pêle-mêle de Jugement Dernier" 216), as in a string of others.[46]

This dizzying dance of names is accompanied by an equally head-spinning series of dates. In Cixous's reading of "Circonfession," she calls attention to the different temporalities of this multilayered text that includes lengthy quotations from an earlier notebook: "The writing surarrives and puts time out of joint [. . .] this whirligig of dates, pursued by anticipatory memory: I write in 1977 that which I shall rewrite in 1977–1989 that will rewrite itself in 2077 [. . .] there is no time, there are only dates" (*Portrait* 59). Cixous's corpus is marked more and more by dates, by specific months and years that mark the present of the writing: "I cross out April 1999, and I inscribe July 2000. I ask myself why I inscribe these dates, and I've always done it, it is a way of mirroring, I lean over a piece of paper so that it will tell me today yes you are here" (*Benjamin* 32). This apparent need for reassurance from the text may stem from a feeling of being "outside time," and thus without the important reference points that hours and dates provide.

Cixous's close connection to Derrida stems in part from his presence and encouragement at the outset of her career, at a time when she didn't feel she had a place. As she maintains in her account of her first meeting with him, Derrida gave her "le do" (*Portrait* 13), he provided her with the key to writing. In *Photos de racines*, Cixous avows that she felt "temporally" lost at this time: "A desert leading to an effect of atemporality. There was no time. The presence of J.D., whom I read, was inscribed in the timeless space where I was" (*Rootprints* 83). Her work was indeed in a "desert," far from that of her contemporaries: "That epoch was so much not my place!" (84). The continuous interaction between Cixous and Derrida, in person and in writing, is crucial to their mutual creative energies. And their special, indefinable position in French letters, while it has gained in reputation and respect, remains a lonely place, even in the last few years: "As time passes, I continue to say to myself: if there were not Derrida, I would feel very alone in the world—in the space of the French language" (*Rootprints* 84). Publications in tandem, such as *Voiles*, and books and articles dedicated to the work of the other have brought recent attention to the dance that has provided movement, rhythm, and music to both writers for years. For each of these thinkers, finding themselves in step and in tune with another has proved to be an invaluable source of inspiration.

Coda

For Cixous, writing is music. It touches us profoundly, to the cores of our corporal being: "It is the music that is not noted down musically but that is in language, that produces uprisings in us, humours, hungers, births" (*Rootprints*

47). It follows from this lofty statement that the great challenge of writing is to find a way to note—in language—that which is normally noted through another system of signs. If it manages to strike the *right* key, the music of writing will cross borders and touch all in its sonorous wake, regardless of linguistic and cultural origins: "we respond with all our body because it is true. Everyone. There is a sort of universality of music" (*Rootprints* 46). The irony of the writer's task is that a very idiosyncratic, personal voice is required to create a "universal" work that resonates within each reader. For Cixous, developing this voice depends on listening, to the past as well as the present: "So writing then? Yes, it is, from this chorus of songs of the whole of time, making a new song stream forth. Sometimes this is called a style. A new language? No. A virgin way of listening and making the always newold language speak" ("Preface" xxi).

In May 2003, at the Cartoucherie, a theatrical production on which Cixous collaborated did not boast her name as author. Like many of the plays she has helped bring to life at the Théâtre du Soleil, *Le dernier caravansérail (Odyssées)* was a collective creation, but this time Cixous did not figure on the program as a playwright. In a review for *La Quinzaine Littéraire*, Monique Le Roux draws these conclusions on the play's content: "In short, the text [. . .] only plays a limited role here, despite the name of Hélène Cixous as part of the ensemble. It resonates, not as a means of communication, but as a cluster of sounds that represent the obstacles to language that refugees know" (21). Unwittingly, this critic of the theatre has underscored the transforming power of Cixous's signature style as musical performance. In this recent piece for the stage, Cixous has opened her ears to the sounds of refugees. This aural opening to others finds its parallels in the opening of her heart and mind, as she has shown affectionate understanding in her rendering of the plight of those who have fled dictatorships and wars. Intelligent, comprehensible words are not the only means of communicating their predicament and sharing its intensity. If she has refrained from signing this work as sole author, it is because she has signed it within, in her own unique, inimitable voice, that of an engaged, participative listener, gathering the strains of experience to create new music that really speaks.

Notes

1. The colloquium at the Bibliothèque nationale de France held the 22nd through the 24th of May 2003 featured two papers that dealt with music in Hélène Cixous's œuvre. Béatrice Didier's reflections on "Cixous, Music, and Hoffman's Stories" highlighted the fleeting nature of music ("*sitôt notée, déjà dérobée*"), underscored

the difficulty of "speaking" music ("music speaks us, but we cannot speak it"), and made note of the need for attentive readers ("there must be readers capable of hearing the music of this prose with a trained ear [une écoute accrue]"). Abdelkébir Khatibi's comments on "Testamentary Writing" evoked music as a natural gift ("the gift of music, our other natural language besides silence") that is a source of "unheard of" pleasure ("jouissance d'un sens inouï, la musique même"). Marie-Louise Mallet addressed music in Cixous's *Beethoven à jamais ou l'existence de Dieu* in an earlier colloquium, this one held at Cerisy-la-Salle from the 22nd to the 30th of June 1998. Her "notes in the margin" of this musical text convincingly tie together Beethoven's compositions with the musical variations and themes of Cixous's composition. The same colloquium provided Jacques Derrida with an occasion to reflect on music in the context of Cixous's work. Derrida posed provocative questions such as what happens when music (and also, on a different level, *belief*) is transposed into literary form ("H. C. pour la vie" 16) and distinguished Cixous's literary production from that of other writers of the twentieth century precisely because of its *music*: "I don't know of another œuvre [. . .], I have never read anything in this century that comes from a more powerful calculation of writing, the polyphonic composition, the timbre of the voice amplified by songs, the formal work that seems punctuated with signs on the page, the rhythms of the textual body aligning themselves though the word, spoken before and beyond the verbal, in the place where watching and dreaming [. . .] succeed in going past their own borders to push the limits and provoke the reader" (22).

2. I am playing here of course with J. L. Austin's 1962 publication, *How To Do Things With Words*, a work that was important in calling attention to "speech acts," or the performative capacity of words.

3. Cixous is not content to play only *within* the French language, however, and jumps frequently from one idiom to another to make her points, as we shall see later. But French is so rich with similar sounds and spellings that she draws continually from this tongue to say things *differently*.

4. Khatibi refers to Derrida's revelation that his French citizenship was revoked, along with that of an entire community of Jews in Algeria, in 1940. He makes it clear that the Jewish community in Morocco was not subject to such a revocation: "In parentheses, that was not the case in Morocco: following the dahir in 1864 (a bit before the Crémieux decree), the Jewish community benefited from citizenship and a judicial stature that respected its beliefs. This is therefore another context" (*La Langue* 25).

5. Critics such as Sandra Gilbert and Toril Moi have described Cixous's work as existing in a very complicated relationship to theory, at least in the Anglo-American understanding of the latter's political pertinence and influence. In her introduction to the English translation of *La Jeune née*, Gilbert feels a need to explain that Cixous's writing comes from "another world": "For an American feminist—at least for this American feminist—reading *The Newly Born Woman* is like going to sleep in one world and waking in another—going to sleep in the realm of facts, which one must labor to theorize, and waking in a domain of theory, which one must strive to (f)ac-

tualize" (x). (It is significant that Gilbert chooses to title her introduction "A Tarantella of Theory," for the idea of a rapid dance in 6/8 time is in step with the musical thrust of this chapter.) In her treatment of Cixous in *Sexual/Textual Politics*, Toril Moi notes the difficulty of grasping the full impact of Cixous's writing, and she goes on to assert that the "intensely metaphorical" and "poetic" aspects of this writing accompany an "antitheoretical" stance: "Her style is often intensely metaphorical, poetic, and explicitly antitheoretical, and her central images create a dense web of signifiers that offers no obvious edge to seize hold of for the analytically minded critic" (102).

6. In *The Empire Writes Back*, the power of words to create worlds is expressed in unequivocal terms: "Language exists, therefore, neither before the fact nor after the fact but in the fact. Language constitutes reality in an obvious way: it provides some terms and not others with which to talk about the world. . . . Worlds exist by means of languages, their horizons extending as far as the processes of neologism, innovation, tropes, and imaginative usage generally will allow the horizons of the language itself to be extended." (44)

7. Although the term "écriture féminine" has come to characterize her contribution to feminist criticism in various anthologies, it can hardly be considered the sole defining aspect of Cixous's writing. It is significant that the English translation of Mireille Calle-Gruber's essay "Le Livre d'Heur(e) d'Hélène Cixous" (originally published in *Photos de racines*) contains a subtitled section that reads as follows: "Giving the feminine, giving the music." I would argue that the "feminine" in Cixous's theoretical writings can often be replaced by "music," and that this term more accurately describes the type of "in-between" nature of the texts and their messages, as elucidated by Calle-Gruber: "Hélène Cixous' books give precisely the feminine, the music (*donne le la*): other entries to meaning; the between at work which escapes classification; a between-two, which makes three and more; a between-time which exceeds time" (*The Hélène Cixous Reader* 213).

8. The large number of recent novels and essays that draw from and praise orality can be seen as a corrective to the assumption that written forms of expression are more "civilized" and "modern" than oral traditions. This corrective is in step with a similar move on the part of postcolonial critics, as Bill Ashcroft, Gareth Griffiths, and Helen Tiffin describe it: "Post-colonial cultural studies have led to a general re-evaluation of orality and oral cultures and a recognition that the dominance of the written in the construction of ideas of civilization is itself a partial view of more complex cultural practices" (*Key Concepts* 165–66). In *Éloge de la Créolité*, Jean Bernabé, Patrick Chamoiseau, and Raphaël Confiant refer glowingly to the advantage that a strong oral culture offers writers: "A real galaxy with the Creole language as its core, Creoleness, has, still today, its privileged mode: orality. Provider of tales, provers, 'titim,' nursery rhymes, songs, etc., orality is our intelligence; it is our reading of this world, the experiementation, still blind, of our complexity" (*In Praise* 95). Translating orality in(to) literature is not an impossibility; it is a challenge that requires ingenuity and promises fruitful results: "*we shall create a literature*, which will obey all

the demands of modern writing while taking roots in the traditional configurations of our orality" (97–98).

9. Jean-Paul Sartre's statements on naming in his essay on literature reveal that the very act of identifying things in language (no distinction is drawn between speaking and writing here) brings about change: "To speak is to act; anything which one names is already no longer quite the same; it has lost its innocence . . . by speaking, I reveal the situation by my very intention of changing it; I reveal it to myself and to others in order to change it. I strike it at its very heart, I transfix it, and I display it in full view; at present I dispose of it; with every word I utter, I involve myself a little more in the world, and by the same token I emerge from it a little more, since I go beyond it towards the future" (36–37). While I concur with Sartre on this point, I disagree with his assertion that "One does not paint meanings; one does not put them to music" (28). Meanings put to music are convincing and powerful, as Cixous's written production proves.

10. In her reading of Cixous's "Le Rire de la Méduse," Gayatri Spivak calls Cixous "a Creole," undoubtedly basing this assignation on the original definition of the Spanish term *criollo*: "like Derrida, Cixous is, in the strictest sense, a Creole, a Frenchwoman born and raised in early childhood in Oran in the days before the Revolution" (53).

11. The timing of her writing is frequently a subject of reflection; Cixous emphasizes that she writes *in the present* in a number of texts, referring most obviously to her use of the present tense. But in "Writing Blind," the writer addresses her writing project as the notation of the present *before* it has passed, settled, or had time to become fixed in memory or language: "I note, I want to write before, at the time still in fusion before the cooled off time of the narrative. When we feel and there is not yet a name for it. [. . .] The tempest before fixation" (*Stigmata* 141).

12. In *Ces voix qui m'assiègent*, Assia Djebar indicates that writing in the Maghreb is synonymous with multilingualism, whether the writer is of European descent or possesses roots in the North African region: "In short, writing in the Maghreb today would mean writing with a French ear and voice: for the so-called 'pieds-noirs' French, with echoes of Spanish, Italian, Maltese, etc.; for others, the 'natives,' inscribe in a slightly deviant French because heard with an Arab or Berber ear, write right up against a multilingual murmuring" (29).

13. The coexistence of the French words for "work" and "play" in this passage disrupts the binary division of these terms; in the writings of Cixous, the boundaries between these supposedly opposed words are effaced: work and play interact and interface on several levels. Play and work are essentially intermixed in Cixous's texts. She demonstrates in her writing and in her reflections on writing that *playing* with words and *working* (with) the signifier are closely associated enterprises: they are the stuff of writing, both pleasurable *and* painstaking. The enjoyment she finds in her textual undertakings does not undermine the serious nature of the work she realizes in writing.

14. Writing is also, importantly, a means of warding off forgetting, of preserving the past in memory. As the narrator of *Benjamin à Montaigne* reminds us, things that

are written are more suited to recall, at least for the first-person narrator: "I only remember what is written" (66).

15. Thanks to the presence of her mother's language in the home, and multiple languages in the street of her Algerian "homeland," Cixous is aware of the difficulty of calling a language one's own. She does not submit herself to the law of any one tongue, but opens up her writing to play among idioms, to games that transcend strict linguistic boundaries and allow different forms of expression to interact. Her written work is an "overture" in the musical sense and in a larger sense of opening up: "Languages pass into my tongue, understand one another, tenderly, timidly, sensually; blend their personal pronouns together, in the effervescence of differences. Prevent 'my language' from taking itself for my own; worry it and enchant it. Necessity, in the bosom of my language, for games and migrations of words, of letters, of sounds; my texts will never adequately tell its boons: the agitation that will not allow any law to impose itself; the opening that lets infinity pour out" ("Coming" 21).

16. In "My Algeriance, in other words: to depart not to arrive from Algeria," Cixous provides an explanation of this title by focusing on the grammatical form of the neologism that is distinctly hers: "I like the progressive form and the words that end in –ance. [. . .] To depart (so as) not to arrive from Algeria is also, incalculably, a way of not having broken with Algeria. I have always rejoiced at having been spared all 'arrival.' I want arrivance, movement, unfinishing in my life" (170).

17. The Ear of the Other: Otobiography, Transference, Translation is a work containing texts and discussions with Jacques Derrida on the subjects of autobiography and translation. I make allusion to this work here because of its emphasis on play and what it means with respect to proper names and the disciplines of psychoanalysis and philosophy. In his recorded and transcribed comments for this publication, Derrida returns to the biblical scene of the origin of multiple tongues, the scene featured in his essay on translation, "Des Tours de Babel."

18. In music, a mode is a musical scale that can be played over an octave using only the white notes of the piano keyboard. By metaphorical extension, sticking to the "white notes" could be meant to indicate writing that avoids dealing with peoples who are not Caucasian, or evades contentious topics altogether.

19. This friendship has been of great significance to Cixous, particularly when she has felt like an anachronism, not at all at home in her time. The "décalage" between her writing and that of her contemporaries, coupled with hostility on the part of French institutions, have contributed to a sense of solitude and "exile": "What I read had an exiling effect on me. I had no place in this era! I felt such a foreignness. If it hadn't been for Derrida, I would have thought I was crazy." (Rootprints 84, translation modified).

20. While much emphasis has been placed on the corporal aspects of her evocations of "coming to writing," it may be more appropriate to focus on the musical component of that infamous call to write the body: "In the language I speak, the mother tongue resonates, tongue of my mother, less language than music, less syntax than

song of words, beautiful Hochdeutsch, throaty warmth from the north in the cool speech of the south. Mother German is the body that swims in the current, between my tongue's borders, the maternal loversoul, the wild tongue that gives form to the oldest of the youngest of passions, that makes milky night in the French day. Isn't written: traverses me, makes love to me, makes me love, speak, laugh from feeling its air caressing my throat" ("Coming" 31).

21. This is the writing process to which she refers in various reflective essays that could be considered "metatextual": "How did I 'write' this? I took notes. I thought: I'm going to do the portrait of October which comes and which passes. It was in a notebook, on detachable sheets. This is not a diary that follows the course of the days. October presented itself in breaths, fragments, emotions, sorrows, and I think that that is how one writes: in discontinuous fashion" ("In October 1991" 89). An innovative publication, *The Writing Notebooks*, includes photographic extracts from Cixous's notebooks accompanied by English translations for readers to peruse in order to visualize Cixous's "discontinuous" work.

22. Abdelkébir Khatibi brings up similar memories of the power of collective chant with respect to the period when his native country had just gained independence from France: "Let's listen to sung youth [*la jeunesse chantée*] that provided the rhythm for our parades"; "In collective song, brand new to me, I felt happy" (*La Mémoire tatouée* 112; 114).

23. In *Le Monolinguisme de l'autre*, Derrida addresses the importance of tone—and intonation—in his writing, privileging it even over content, in a certain sense: "If I have always trembled before what I could say, it was fundamentally [au fond] because of the tone, and not the substance [non du fond]. And what, obscurely, I seek to impart as if in spite of myself, to give or lend to others as well as to myself, to myself as well as to the other, is perhaps a tone. Everything is summoned from an intonation" (*Monolingualism* 48).

24. Sartre's comments on silence and its relationship to words (and music) in "What is Literature?" resonate well with Cixous's assertions: "Silence itself is defined in relationship to words, as the pause in music receives its meaning from the group of notes around it. This silence is a moment of language; being silent is not being dumb, it is to refuse to speak, and therefore to keep on speaking" (38). In his preface to Léopold Sédar Senghor's 1948 *Anthologie de la nouvelle poésie nègre et malgache*, "Black Orpheus," Sartre goes one measure further to address the situation of the colonized subject who "makes silence with language": "since we cannot keep quiet, we must *make silence with language* . . . since the oppressor is present in the very language that they speak, they will speak this language in order to destroy it" (303).

25. In "La Venue à l'écriture," the voice of the mother is credited with the "music of elsewhere" that Cixous finds within herself: "I had this luck, to be the daughter of the voice. Blessing: my writing stems from two languages, at least. 'Foreign': the music in me from elsewhere [. . .] my German mother in my mouth, in my larynx, rhythms me" ("Coming" 21–22). In *Benjamin à Montaigne*, the narrative voice addresses the writing process with these words: "I listen to my interior music at will" (107).

26. In another interview, "Hélène Cixous in Conversation with Sophia Phoca," Cixous revisits her publishing history and highlights the important decision she made in opting to work with Antoinette Fouque and *Editions des Femmes* shortly after the publishing house's conception in 1975. In addressing the "political" aspects of this choice, the writer elucidates the subtlety of her "poetic" compositions: "At that time I had written fifteen books already. I was on my poetical way, which is by definition more subtle than what any type of political discourse allows. For strategical and pedagogical reasons political discourse has to communicate in simpler terms than poetry" (*Wasafiri* 11). The poetic does not exclude the political, in Cixous's view, but is located on a register that arguably allows for a more nuanced, complex vision of issues that cannot easily be reduced to the simplistic terms employed in many settings, whether they be "strategic," "pedagogical," or other.

27. The power of a mother's song to evoke change in children is the subject of a touching passage from *Osnabrück*: "In other homes, the other mothers kneel before their little girls who play at cooking and say: my treasure, my little pearl, my heart of gold, [. . .] the other mothers have the mysterious, perfumed charm whose name I don't know, I thought, hypnotized by the fabulous opera of other homes. [. . .] The modulated song of the mother caused the child to shine and swing, I saw these metamorphoses with my very eyes, in other homes" (170). If the narrator differentiates the songs of other homes from her own in a regretful tone here, such is not the case elsewhere. In "La Venue à l'écriture," the mother's song is a veritable opera, intensely inspiring both pleasure and pain: "In a certain way, an opera inhabits me. [. . .] A music floods through me, inculcates me with its staves. I am childhood, my mother sings, her alto voice. More! Encore! a lovely tongue licks at my heart, my flesh takes in the German that I can't make out. O *Lied*! *Leid*! Song and sorry, blood and song! *Leid*! *Leib*! Sorry and body. *Leib*! *Leich*! *Leis*! Lay, hymn, milk. *Lieb*! I am loved. Letters love me. *Leise*. Soft and low. I sense that I am loved by writing" ("Coming" 53).

28. In his elegant essay on translation, José Ortega y Gasset highlights the undeniable importance of silence to language, and indicates that it is this silence inherent to the message of language that renders translation particularly difficult: "The fact is that the stupendous reality, which is language, will not be understood at its root if one doesn't begin by noticing that speech is composed above all of silences. A person incapable of quieting many things would not be capable of talking. And each language is a different equation of statements and silences. All peoples silence some things in order to be able to say others. Otherwise, everything would be unsayable. From this we deduce the enormous difficulty of translation: in it one tries to say in a language precisely what that language tends to silence. But, at the same time, one glimpses a possible marvelous aspect of the enterprise of translating: the revelation of the mutual secrets that peoples and epochs keep to themselves and which contribute so much to their separation and hostility" (57).

29. These words are taken from an opera titled *Le Nom d'Œdipe: Chant du corps interdit*, for which Cixous composed the text. Published in 1978 by Editions des femmes, the words from this musical event focus considerably on time and (its relation to)

story, as this accumulation of short verses reveals: "Not even an hour. / Only time. / A time without duration, hardly a minute / without thickness, without time. / Except an instant. / Deep enough powerful enough, / Enough present and ancient / So that all our history can live again there. / In one time. / The last / Oh give me this moment! / This nothing" (15).

30. At another moment in the same text, Cixous plays again with pauses, cutting off a sentence quite early so that it is just a fragment and separating it from the brief sentence that follows by a significant blank space of two lines. The text enacts what it describes, cutting off a breath in a convoluted twist summarily explained by a telephone call: "A breath cut short my" / "The telephone rang" (*Benjamin* 87).

31. The truth that meaning exceeds the strict denotation of words is particularly clear in Cixous's inventive compositions. When she asks, "Why do we love music that is without words?" (*Photos* 46), the writer is ruminating over the importance of sound in daily experience. Her rhetorical question serves as a springboard for an exploration of her idiosyncratic texts that seek to incorporate the unspoken, elusive noises of lives, the pauses and clamors that often escape description but make up soundtracks inseparable from words and actions. The knowledge that the *way* something is said acquires as much importance as *what* is actually said motivates Cixous's aforementioned description of her oral interaction with her cat.

32. Cixous has spoken of her own "variable" relationship to time, specifically to "stalled" time and the challenges it presents: "One can think of years as extremely variable units: little ones, big ones, empty ones, years full of years. [. . .] But I also know the time that is neither living nor dead. The time that no longer passes at all. The halt of time that fills the expectancy of the heart with an eternal immobility" (*Rootprints* 96–97).

33. Derrida addressed what I would term the "music" of his writing in a televised interview turned text. *Échographies* contains the following phrases uttered by the philosopher whose attention to "breath" and "rhythm" risks to be lost in a hasty reading. An awareness of this "other speed" of reading influences his reworking of the text: "When I write, I often say to myself: 'So. . . . You pay attention to this sentence, you work on its breath and its syntax, you pay attention to its rhythm, etc.' And then, given the places of reading [*les lieux de lecture*]—and this is even truer when I rework the copy of an interview that will be printed in the press, which does happen, even if it's rare—I know that the text will be read at breakneck speed; I try therefore to integrate into my calculations the fact that the text will be read at a different pace" (101).

34. For Cixous, writing the changes in tempo that characterize our lives is the ultimate, unattainable goal: "That is the text, I believe, that will never manage to be written: a text which takes into consideration the dilation and contraction of time. All things we know perfectly well. The fact that all of a sudden, a day has the duration of a year; or that all of a sudden, a terrible thing, time stops. How to write that? I don't know. I've had the experience, but I still don't know how it would be expressed. . . . For writing goes at the speed of the hand. Life, and death, flash by. A fire

takes us, by surprise. Writing is way behind. How to seize the burning moments?" ("In October 1991" 81)

35. *Le Jour où je n'étais pas là* contains what may be the most evocative textual lamentation of the unequal passing of time, of its elusiveness and its ineffability, in reference to the short life of her deceased son: "There was always this time lag on our time; things in my son's life took much more time to materialize than the time of our lives beside him. Maturing, dying, everything took time. On the one hand, he never stopped making us wait for him, as if held back by the mystery of slowness. On the other hand, underneath the slowness lay an extreme speed but a speed of a different nature than our speeds. [. . .] Youth, adolescence, maturity, ages, all his seasons completely other than ours" (88). These comments on the specificity of her son's irregular, unregulated relationship to time resemble her comments in other texts on the general disorder of human relationships to time: "We are divided, pushed, displaced in our place, passed up by the present moment" (*L'Amour du loup* 152).

36. In her preface to an English reader containing a selection of her published texts, Cixous addresses the literary memory that contributes to her work, and touches on the way in which her work adds to that memory: "I inscribe an additional memory in language—a memory in progress—of what I have read personally, noticed, retained from a text or a language to the other" (*Reader* xxi).

37. The presence of the verb "aimer" in this quotation is not accidental: other texts liken the experience of "savoring the moment" to loving, of opening oneself to slow time to opening oneself to another, such as this passage from *Vivre l'orange*: "To all of my amies for whom loving the moment is a necessity, saving the moment is such a difficult thing, and we never have the necessary time, the slow, sanguineous time, that is the condition of this love, the pensive, tranquil time that has the courage to let last" (*Reader* 88).

38. Calle-Gruber finds inspiration in Cixous's œuvre for the following eloquent insight into the way in which the writer uses (musical) movement to transform the passing of time: "The movement of Hélène Cixous's writing escapes the fatality of the human condition: writing it always *Rediviva*. Against the time of Chronos, a contretemps, the writer plays the movement, orchestrating, following, preceding, accompanying the movement and thus managing to *pass time [passer le temps]*" (*Du Café* 156).

39. In *Angst*, we find a passage that also refers to these names, but that refrains from naming: "When you were slipping on your dress he told you his name. He had his back to you. His three names hurt your ears. They were your son's names. Chance was on his side. Or a will more impressive than chance" (*Reader* 73).

40. Cixous's corpus is so vast that many of the repetitions it contains have escaped detection, or have simply not yet made their appearance in published studies, with the exception of Claudine Fisher's recent "Cixous and the Un/forgettable Child." This essay juxtaposes two texts that deal with the trisomatic son: the 1972 *Neutre* and the 2000 *Le Jour où je n'étais pas là*.

41. In *Photos de racines*, Cixous explicitly draws a connection between these terms when she addresses language and roots: "Talking is a marvelous act that escapes us: it

is to hear Language speaking its languages in language. To hear oneself, to overhear oneself, to catch one's own hints [*S'entendre, se surentendre, se sous entendre*]" (*Rootprints* 84).

42. In her preface to an English-language anthology of her work, she describes writing as an initial encounter with words: "Writing consists first of all in hearing language speak itself to our ears, as if it were the first time" ("Preface" xix).

43. The simultaneity of seeing and hearing in Cixous's writing project is made clear in "La Venue à l'écriture": "And while I gaze, I listen. What happens takes place simultaneously in song. [. . .] What flows from my hand onto the paper is what I see-hear, my eyes listen, my flesh scans" ("Coming" 53).

44. The book (or the *récit*) also occupies a place of critical importance in Cixous's corpus. In a complex metatexual twist, Cixous highlights the importance of the book as an autonomous force in a number of writings, most recently in *L'Amour du loup*. This text contains an entire section devoted to this topic, beginning with this bold declaration: "The book is the character of the book" (109).

45. A set of initials belonging to a popular supermarket, Leader Price, transforms itself under her eyes into a secret reference to her friend: "I write LP until the day when I fell this LP tremble very lightly at the end of my fingers. It is because I've written it so much that I find myself saying: Le Poète. [. . .] These letters were telling me something in secret. Elle P El Poète El Point El ephant acronym of my friend" (*Benjamin* 33–34).

46. Cixous is not the only critic to interrogate, reflect on, and play with Derrida's name in print. "Borborygmes" is a creative text by Jean-Luc Nancy that spins Derrida's name in different senses in order to reflect on this "bizarre barbarous fore-noise [*arrière-bruit*]" and its relationship to language, autobiography, and music: "Music fundamentally lost, that of art and general articulation, of discourse, of form and meaning, offering of the unnameable, arche-trace of the sonorous tearing upon which air closes while vibrating: the spirit of philosophy beginning with the matter of music." For Nancy, the name is indispensable to the idiosyncratic language and melody of the writer: "A proper name, thus, as rhythmic and melodic idiom of origin itself, its only poem" (178).

CHAPTER FIVE

~

Prelude to a Fugue, Out of North Africa: Uprooting and Rerouting in Autobiographical Fiction

I have shame [*une honte*] in Algeria that bears fruit.

—Hélène Cixous, "Obstétriques cruelles" (2000)

I cling to each of the places I fled and every hated hateable moment is for me a vital transfigure that I would not exchange for one gentle, moderate moment in the world

—Hélène Cixous, *Les Rêveries de la femme sauvage* (2000)

This chapter could have been placed first in these reflections centering on the writings of Hélène Cixous, but its presence here, as a "final" note, is appropriate because of its "timing." Cixous is a familiar name to scholars in literature departments in the United States and elsewhere, but she has long been associated outside of France almost exclusively with "feminist" studies. This compartmentalization of the writer and her work, based on a select few "theoretical" texts—including "Le Rire de la Méduse" and "La Venue à l'écriture"—that are hardly representative of her widespread and varied œuvre, has led to many misunderstandings. Biographical notes and critical reviews alike have overlooked her birthplace, assuming that she is a "French" woman from "France,"[1] and failing to address the specificity of her life's trajectory and its importance for her literary production.[2] It is only rather recently that critics have begun to consider Cixous's work in connection to her native land, partly because her writings of late have openly addressed

231

Algeria, and partly because of current attention to Algeria in general, and to the situation of Jews from Algeria in particular.

In her 1998 article titled "Remembering the Jews of Algeria," Nancy Wood identifies a fresh trend of outspoken personal and political expression among Algerian Jews, and she wonders why it has emerged at this particular moment: "why are claims of Jewish-Algerian specificity surfacing now—whether in historiography or popular memory—more than three decades after an exodus to the metropole when such distinctions were neither recognized nor sought?" (179). In response to her own query, Wood draws a significant connection between the present climate in Algeria and this seemingly sudden (re)turn to the native land among intellectuals: "As Algeria's civil war intensifies [. . .] former Algerian Jews have been prominent among those expressing solidarity with Algeria's beleaguered democratic forces (Derrida, Cixous, Jean Daniel to name but a few)" (179).[3] It seems that the urgency of current events has inspired a certain "coming out" and taking of a stand on questions concerning Algeria. But while their recent writings may explicitly speak to the country's past and present, it would be wrong to assume that their native land has been missing from these writers' earlier textual production. This chapter will demonstrate that in the case of Cixous, Algeria has sparked and shaped her literary work from the very beginning.[4] Contextualizing the writer and her writing necessarily entails an examination of the place and time of her birth, of the ways in which her early experience led into and set the tone for her life's work.

Faltering Beginnings: Loss and Bereavement

In her recent article, Wood makes reference to an unforgettable event that forever marked the Jews of Algeria: Vichy's 1940 *Statut des juifs* deprived them of their French citizenship. In *Le Monolinguisme de l'autre*, Derrida details this loss, evoking the October 1870 Crémieux decree that had granted French citizenship to Jews in Algeria seventy years earlier. He insists that the artificial nature of citizenship is highlighted when one sees it offered and retracted within a relatively short period of time: "inscribed in memory as a recent acquisition: for example, the French citizenship granted to the Jews of Algeria. [. . .] Or, better French citizenship, less than a century later, for the same Jews of Algeria" (16).[5] Wood points out that this loss placed Algerian Jews in a precarious position: "Neither French, metropolitan, or Catholic on the one hand, nor Arab or Berber on the other, the place of Jews within colonial Algeria was inherently unstable, vulnerable to the forces of deracination and enculturation" (171).[6] In Derrida's recollection, there was no possible "identification" for the *"Juifs indigènes,"* as they were called at the time. Not only was *identifying with* others an impossibility, but *identifying oneself* was also a hopeless undertaking (*Monolinguisme* 87).[7] Given this traumatic early childhood experience (Cixous was only three when her citizenship was revoked), it is hardly surprising that when it comes to identification, Cixous is at a loss.

In her autobiographical textual moments, Cixous returns frequently to the age that coincided with the revocation of her citizenship. She was young, but she was wise enough to realize that she would make a definite, definitive break with the land of her childhood when the opportunity presented itself:

> When I was three, the age of decisive experiences and analysis, I knew that I was destined to leave. Of course it would be later on, but it would be as soon as possible. That destination, destinality, decision, was so strong that I have been able to say: when I was three I left. It was pure departure. I had no aim or vision of arrival, no goal, no desired country, I was in deferment and flight. In quasi-original detachment. Where to land? ("My Algeriance" 167)

These strong statements support my assertion, visible in the title of this chapter, that Algeria can be considered a "prelude" to the fugue to come. Describing herself as "in deferment and flight" even prior to her actual departure, *in anticipation* of fleeing, the time spent in the land of her birth is indeed a "preliminary part, movement, strain" (in every sense of these words), separate from but introductory to future flights.[8] I am playing in a "bilingual" sense on the double meaning of *fugue* in French, referring to the musical composition but also to the act of fleeing, and the noun "flight" in English, which conveys the ideas of fleeing *and* flying. This association of words stemming from the Latin *fuga* in my analysis here resembles the writing of Cixous, who makes use of various languages in the "single-language" text, as well as the writing of Khatibi, who has coined the term *"traduction simultanée"* to describe the particular process of translation that he carries out in his work.

The musical connotations of the French word "fugue" make this term particularly apt to describe Cixous's writing, not only when her corpus is examined on its own, but especially when her work is placed in dialogue with the work of others. In the previous chapter of this book, a section titled "Dancing with Derrida" explored some of the interactions (textual and otherwise) between Cixous and Derrida. In response to the question of Algeria in recent works, the two writers have responded to each other in a round of reflections that combine to make up a polyphonic composition in a sense, in accordance with the Webster's Revised Unabridged Dictionary: "the theme first given out by one voice or part, and then, while that pursues its way, it is repeated by another at the interval of a fifth or fourth, until all the parts have answered one by one, continuing their several melodies and interweaving them." An example of different voices taking up the same theme at a different interval is found in *Portrait de Jacques Derrida en Jeune Saint Juif*, with the following single phrase intricately woven by Cixous, echoing and responding to Derrida's unveiling of the unstable situation and identity dilemmas of Algerian Jews:

> At last *Le Monolinguisme de l'autre* came along to say everything one was not supposed to say, a splendor of an apocalyptic testimony in a language that is merciless that owes nothing to anyone, about the plots against the soul, outrages, interlingual persecuations, the whole war beneath the surface of the Algerian wars, our daily lot, a history rich in tormentdreams, in battles between regiments of identificatory phantasms, my grandfather Samuel Cixous as a Zouave, we always were a strange bunch of Zouaves, the great book of our terrors tells it all, interrogations, torture, drawn and quartered by hyphens what does it mean to be a Franco-North African Jew is that something you add on or subtract or maybe you take it away from any attempt at collective action? Still we ask it and to have to answer, in a language that is Hebrew in French for us, for a belonging constituted of exclusion and non-belonging, what does it mean to be from Algeria not Algerian, Jew by the other, French by decree, disenFrenched by decree, to be constantly decreeicized, futhermore forever not-like, not like the other not like me, subdivided, circumceded, circumdecided, improbable, what is this verb to be, the great persecutor. (*Portrait* 117–18)

It is crucial that Cixous is able to employ here the plural possessive "*notre*," referring to the trials experienced in Algeria as "our continual lot," and sharing in retrospect the pain of these traumatic exclusions with another, even if these experiences were suffered alone in Algeria at the time.[9] Her position as always (excluded) "other" in a land in which she was taken for French by those of Arab and Berber descent, and for not-French (Jewish) by those of European lineage, has shaped Cixous's writing.[10] It also hints at a possible extension of the "we" in the passage above to refer also to other intellectuals whose connections to Algeria have influenced their thought. Couze Venn finds similarities not only between Derrida and Cixous, but also between their work and that of Camus, for example, because of Algeria: "the writings of those with a foot in the soil of Algeria [. . .] wrestle with a 'hauntology' of modernity, questioning the traces, peering into the invisibilities, all the while aware of the 'forgettings' which the out-of-jointness of contemporary times temps us into" ("Algeria and Occidentalism" 87). This provocative assertion merits a great deal of commentary, and this chapter will pick up on and develop the questions of traces and forgetting that naturally accompany inquiries into Algeria in a post-colonial context. For the moment, let us transform the Derridian neologism "hauntology" (from *Spectres de Marx*)[11] into "hauntings," to refer to the losses that come back to people Cixous's œuvre.

While the loss of her "French" identity wasn't easy, it was overshadowed by the difficult later bereavement of two members of her family in Algeria. Cixous's father passed away in 1948 when she was only ten years old, and her son died suddenly thirteen years later in her absence. In *Le Jour où je n'étais pas là*, these two deaths are evoked in relation to each other, and to the narrator, who acknowledges that the place of passing is significant: "The Place can only be the City of Algiers, says the Book. [. . .] If my son Georges is dead and gone in Algiers it is not an accident [*un hasard*]" (160–61). Her French citizenship was eventually restored[12] and Cixous is now a representative of France throughout the world, but two irrevocable losses at once tie her to Algeria and condition her flight from it: "Nothing could separate me any longer from Algeria, except for our two deaths Georges my father Georges my son keep lost reunited displaced in the desert scene of Saint-Eugène. Nothing can attach me to the country any longer except these two deaths" (161). If the specters of these deceased family members often figure as characters in her work, they are not alone.

If Cixous often evokes the pivotal age of three in her writing, it is not only because of the "official" events that shook up her life during that year; it is also because of the very personal event that disrupted everything about her connection to herself and her world. In *Osnabrück*, the very first line of the prologue brings up this monumental loss: "At the age of three-and-a-half I lost my mother" (9). The date, the street, and the city of this loss are provided in the second sentence, but this contextualization of time and place seems insignificant in comparison to the overwhelming loss of the mother: "Thus, my first memory associates my mother's imagined death and school. And since then, I have never stopped crying, going to school, learning, crying exchanging. Shedding of tears and absorption. Forgetting, overcoming the loss of my mother's body" ("In October 1991" 88). The voice of reason explains that the mother is not lost, that it is instead the father who has passed away: "Curiously, I know that it's not my mother I lost; it's my father who died and for whom I didn't cry" (88). But the mother is the one who haunts her: "I was haunted. I had in the heart a giant, inhabited domain of which I was a slave and to which attached a furor called maman" (*Osnabrück* 12). This haunting is not altogether negative, for its continual presence (configured as an absence) inspires invention through writing: "Or on the contrary: not overcoming it. Inventing. Representing to myself the horror of this loss" ("In October 1991" 88). Even as a very young child, she found solace in the written word, finding that the secret to living with loss is representing it in letters: "I learned to write right away with jubilation. I remember my taste for the form of every letter. I hurried. On paper among the legs of letters I was happy, exalted" (*Osnabrück* 12).

In an essay for which she gives (herself) the title "La Fugitive," Cixous reveals the paradoxical truth that loss can turn into gain, especially for a writer. She addresses the *loss* of Algeria even as she praises what Algeria *gave* her: "the programmed fatality of loss. Algeria already lost, not even lost, already spectral, already out of reach, without a past to become memory, without a future. She gave me subtly precious goods" (75). Algeria as a lost entity, already spectral even while she inhabited it, is something Cixous has not ceased to mourn. This mourning is not the disillusioned sense of having lost something that was once in her possession, for Algeria was admittedly always beyond her reach. She inhabited this place without ever having *a place* within it; she therefore suffered it not as *her* loss, but as lost: "I did not lose Algeria, because I never had it, and I never was it. I suffered that it was lost for itself, separated from itself by colonialization. If ever I identified it was with its rage at being wounded, amputated, humiliated" ("My Algeriance" 168). The personified traits of the country, marked by wounding and humiliation, resemble her own experience there, and seem to tie her to it lastingly in a bond of *distanced* solidarity. Indeed, fleeing did not truly mean leaving behind this place that has ever haunted her writing. If she is bereft, if she is *cleft*, these characteristics are not without value. To the contrary, they have provided her with the *clef* for composition: "I do not want to lose my loss, I hold onto my loss like the apple of my eye" ("Obstétriques cruelles" 112). Cixous wants to preserve loss, since it is what motivates her literary creation.[13] Algeria, the place of loss, is the key to writing:

> My writing was born in Algeria. No. I should say out of Algeria; out of a lost country, out of a lost father and of a foreign mother. All of these little traits which might appear as unsatisfactory were very fertile for me. I've had that luck to know first foreignness, exile, war, the phantom memory of peace, mourning [. . .] I knew that uprooting existed and that human moods know no borders, no nationality. ("The Two Countries of Writing" 193)

Algeria as *birthplace* turns into a *place of birth* for the writer. The source of pain is also the source of productivity, providing the motivation for labor, and for delivery, and this is a stroke of luck for the writer who translates loss in(to) literature.

Guarding Traces, Marking Scars: The Stuff of Literature

When she evokes her personal experience in Algeria, Cixous frequently has recourse to medical terminology to describe the emotional pain she suffered. Examples of this abound, but one striking instance is the following passage from *Portrait de Jacques Derrida en Jeune Saint Juif*. It seems that the inclusion of another who has shared the hurts of specific dates gives her free rein to address the *physical* ailments that injustice caused Jews in Algeria:

> If we don't have circumcision in common (here I shall cease to call it by other names)—at least that of the penis, for the other that of the heart, I too have known—the Circumcision to which Jacques Derrida has given its letters patent of noblewound, we do mirror a number of precise stigmata, dated Algiers 1867, 1870, Oran 1940, 1942, 1954, 1956, all those dates of Passovers, transfers, expulsions, naturalizations, de-citizenships, exinclusions, blacklistings, doors slammed in your face, dates of war, of colonization, incorporation, assimilation, assimulation, indigene/ni/zations that constitute the archives of what he calls "my nostalgeria" and that I call my "algeriance," dates and plaques, my doctor father's nameplate yanked off the wall by Vichy, the psychic rash of plaques at the evocation of nationalist-racist outbreaks, tremors and symptoms at the portals of Schools. (*Portrait* 5)

This sentence touches on a considerable amount of injustices committed in Algeria, detailing the devastating effect of Vichy's law on her father's medical practice, and allowing the metaphor to spill over into other parts of the sentence, where official plaques removed from the office door slip into another meaning, that of blotches serving as symptoms of illness. Cixous's language demonstrates that the ills carried out against those of Jewish heritage in her native land were not harmless, that they were as damaging, and as lasting, as dangerously infectious diseases.[14] Indeed, an "incurable malady" is the metaphor of choice for Algeria in *Les Rêveries de la femme sauvage* (41). If the land is without cure, so are its inhabitants, according to the first-person narrator of *Le Jour où je n'étais pas là* who studies herself and marvels at her ever-present smile in photographs taken years earlier in Algeria: "having no reason to smile without suspicion while I lived in Algeria. With my open mouth and all my teeth displayed shining I was like a wound that I never stopped committing even while I would have so liked to heal" (28). Likening herself to a wound in this autobiographical passage, the writer employs an unusual verb to refer to her own role in creating this lesion: "to commit." Usually used for "errors" or "crimes," this verb seems to indicate that the girl is responsible for her own injury, in spite of herself.

In *Les Rêveries de la femme sauvage*, the narrator reveals herself to be affected by an illness caught in/from Algeria:

I have Algeria in my lung in my throat I don't find it strange that she gives me fevers and annihilates my mental canvas with poisoned slatherings. I attribute the scars of my punctuated body to the bad-Algerian strength [*force malgérienne*] of my imagination, but it isn't that I think I see what I don't see, it's that I think what I see and I see what the French don't want to see. (110–11)

This ailment and its traces are a source of suffering both physical and mental, but they carry benefits for the afflicted. The intense discomfort due to Algeria is a gift to Cixous, for it furnishes her with a perceptive viewpoint that sees what "the French" do not.[15] Distancing herself her from those whose nationality she now shares (following the *peripeteia* of her earlier life), Algeria is the defining element that distinguishes her from her compatriots, removing the illusions that sometimes cloud their vision.

The coining of the word "noblessures" (translated as "noblewound") is crucial to understanding the passage from *Portrait de Jacques Derrida en Jeune Saint Juif* quoted above, for this neologism contains within it two very separate notions, "nobility" and "sores," and their unification in a single term indicates that a certain nobility emerges from, or is bound up with, painful experiences. Cixous's enumeration of the stigmata she has in common with Derrida appear almost to constitute a source of pride in this passage, and the reader is even tempted to interpret Cixous's comment on circumcision as a sort of lamentation that she does not have a similar physical trace of difference (communal *and* individual, not to mention sexual). This seemingly conflicting coupling of "*noblesse*" and "*blessures*" begins to make sense in light of other comments by the writer: "Nostalgia for the worst, that is what makes you write. [. . .] The fear of former madmen or prisoners or the deported or the humiliated it's Time that dulls the gleam or heals the wound. Pain is not in the torture, it is in losing torture's awful riches" ("Obstétriques" 112). In this view, painful experiences are a source of riches; they make up a mine that inspires written production with endless raw material. The only risk is that one will lose them through forgetfulness, and that is why wounds must be constantly stirred up, renewed in writing: "Because 'literature' is the very long scratching of the residue of wounds" (112). If Cixous continually revisits Algeria in her work, it is because this is fertile land for creativity, a place whose loss yields fruit unceasingly: "I want to keep the fruit the trace of the blinding light of the Apocalypse [. . .] a pomegranate [*grenade*] that explodes in your eye, but nonetheless a fruit" (112). It seems that any pain is worth the price for literary good.

One of the most touching specters that comes back to haunt Cixous's work is "Fips the dog." Cixous has put this childhood companion in print in fictional book-length publications like *Les Rêveries de la femme sauvage*, and she has revived him in shorter essays like "Stigmata, or Job the dog" as well: "you are the most living of the departed. The manifestation of Fips is the proof that there is no universal or absolute law of effacement" ("Stigmata" 184). This unforgettable pet attacked her one fateful day, and the marks are still visible: "Indelible are the traces of his cruel stay in my flesh and my soul. It is to him that I owe my scars. He is the innocent author of the signatures that inaugurated my book on my feet and my hands" (185). The unspoken sufferings of the animal and the girl led to the writing of the grown woman, her pain and her tears giving place, in time, to love: "And even so I loved Fips but not then, not there in the garden of war, not yet, but later" (193). This physical contact with another stands out in contrast to the distanced relationships that marked Cixous's early experiences in a land whose inhabitants treated her like an outcast. While her interactions—or lack thereof—with others in Algeria were painful on an emotional, and therefore invisible, level, this altercation with the dog marked her for life: it provided her with the visible wounds to match her hidden hurts. Recognizing the benefits of these scars, Cixous begins this essay with literary precedents, the most recent of which is Jean Genet: "For Genet the wound is the founding secret of all major creation" ("Stigmata" 181). Betraying her secret in this text, Cixous gives away her signature as well.

Strokes of Luck: The Chances of Birth

In a short story composed for a collection of childhood remembrances from Algeria, *Une enfance algérienne*, Cixous names Oran, the city of her birth: "Oran was always *La Ville*, the Absolute City, holy [. . .] the site of Signs where Alea the God of the hazards of my history had placed me to be born" ("Pieds nus" 57). The "hazards of her history"—the expression Cixous employs here that I have allowed to reverberate as a sort of catch phrase elsewhere in my analysis—were in many considerations strokes of *luck*, given the timing of her arrival and the fate of many Jews who were unable to flee a horrific, unimaginable fate in Europe.[16] Members of Cixous's own extended family was not as fortunate as she: "The families of my mother, very large as Jewish families often are, had two fates: the concentration camps on the one hand; on the other, the scattering across the earth. This gives me a sort of worldwide resonance. I have always felt it because the echoes always come from the whole earth" (*Rootprints* 189). The branch that survived the Nazi regime owed their existence to the flights of diaspora, to movements that predated the immediate need to escape persecution and death: "The Jews were the travellers of Europe. Not because they were expelled, but because they were searching" (184). As for her father's side of the family, these ancestors were also accustomed to movement, having fled Spain for Morocco following "the classic trajectory of Jews chased" at the end of the fifteenth century; her paternal great-grandparents later traveled to Oran in Western Algeria, where her grandfather became a businessman among whose holdings figured a boutique called "The Two Worlds" (182). This birthplace was a lively, diverse, multicultural, and multilingual seaside city seemingly located on the border between two worlds.

Flight is not only a characteristic of her direct ancestors; it is also a trait Cixous finds integral to Jewish tradition. Cixous makes the following thematic leap when she refers to her occasional trips to the cinema:

> I surrender myself to the Cinema. In flight, backwards, compulsively and without hope, in the tradition of Jonah [Jonas], the ancestor of my family, the derisory prophet, the incarnation of useless insubordination, he who knows for nothing, the first of Jews in general, the first of Jews from Osnabrück in particular, he who surrenders himself. But going in the opposite sense, like all Jonahs [tous les Jonas]. (Le Jour 37)

Jonas is the maiden name of her maternal grandmother Omi, who makes numerous appearances in Cixous's autobiographical work: "Omi traversed my whole life. She is a bit m,o,i. Omi is the eighth child, the youngest of her mother Hélène Meyer (there's my name)" (Rootprints 183). In accordance with the married name of her namesake, Cixous often flees. In this playful passage, her flight consists of a fleeting cinematic escapade, but at other times the act of fleeing takes on greater proportions, symbolic and geographic. What is interesting here is the connection established between her Jewish relatives and the biblical homonym who also fled, but who ironically ended up in the very town he had attempted to escape: Ninevah. This theme repeatedly surfaces in Cixous's writing, hinting that attempts at flight do not necessarily succeed, as in this phrase from Manhattan in which flight is thwarted: "once again I do what I did not want to do [. . .] I put myself in flight [en fuite], I do exactly that which I did not want to do" (11).

Fleeing does not always carry a negative connation, despite the fact that it often denotes an act that entails leaving behind responsibilities and commitments. Obviously, when it is a question of religious or political persecution, fleeing is the key to survival, and these were the conditions for the flight of Cixous's ancestors and relatives on both sides of the proverbial fam-

ily tree outlined in *Photos de racines*. In *Le Jour où je n'étais pas là*, the narrative grapples with difficult questions of her own past. The first-person narrator reveals that her child passed away in Algeria while she was across the sea
in France, and the circumstances surrounding this unexpected death remain
unclear. The voice of the narrator's mother indicates that the boy's fate was
left to chance: "I believe in chance [*hasard*]. Everything is chance, says my
mother. You can only count on chance—on that which you cannot count.
This child, when did he take his leave? The only day I go out" (94).

If the flights Cixous describes as belonging to her family history took place
in a collective manner, the departure of the young mother in *Le Jour où je
n'étais pas là* seems to be a solitary venture that, instead of preserving family
unity and promoting life, served to separate family members and resulted in
death. But it remains unclear whether or not she fled. The brother addresses
the possibility, and points to its difficulty: "Flee, says my brother. Where?
How? You can flee everything: family, child. Sister brother mother Omi me.
That takes courage. The courage to let go I have never had it says my
brother" (107). For him, it appears that letting go takes courage, and that is
why he is not able to flee. But a correction follows this assertion, for the narrator's thoughts affirm that true courage is not found in flight: "Courage, I
thought, is not found in the courage to flee" (107). Flight as "leaving behind"
can hardly be considered a courageous act, but another definition of this
movement is not precluded by this conclusion: these comments on flight
point to a text to come.

In the opening passages of *Portrait de Jacques Derrida en Jeune Saint Juif*,
Cixous recalls her first encounter with Derrida, a meeting that she describes
in a lively hyphenated expression as a coming together of "former children of
said-to-be-Jews-born-in-Algeria" (4). She lists their numerous points in common in general terms, evoking negative experiences exemplified by wounds
and bites, exclusionary measures and laws, and by a movement she links to
Jewish tradition: "struck with wonder as well at the same immense unique su-
perJew figures, having followed, from a great distance, this or that Abraham's
way [*la fuite en avant*] of keeping one giant step ahead of disaster, many occasions, all of them cruel, unfolded between us their fragile silk impression of
comprehension" (12).[17]

Tracing what she calls a "flight forward" back to Abraham (or another),[18]
Cixous shows the lines of flight that she and Derrida have taken to be part
of a longstanding tradition. But here, the focus of the flight is not on what
has been left behind, but instead on the forward motion that this movement
carries. Once again, the idea of *chance* emerges in this treatment of the first
conversation between the fugitives: "So, in the Café Balzar, to rhyme with

hazard, what did Gross and Klein find to talk of? Of exile and Joyce of phantasmic and literary Judaism, of the Jewflight of passages and of such very tame follies as being a foreigner-in-my-own-country, of circumconniving in the languages of translinguistic sport, of philosophical transports" (5).[19] If they have both fled the land of their birth, this flight has indeed given place to language and thought marked by movement in a positive sense.

Free Floating: Place and Displacement

When introducing herself and her work to the Anglophone reader, Cixous goes straight to the beginning of her life story: "I was born at/from the intersection of migrations and memories from the Occident and Orient, from the North and South. I was born a foreigner in 'France' in a said-to-be 'French' Algeria. I was born in not-France calling itself 'France'" ("Preface" xv). Cixous knows that her unusual initial situation at the crossroads, between movements and histories, between colonizer and colonized, is crucial to understanding her writing. Her unique start in a place officially deemed "France," but geographically and ideologically dislocated from France, prepared her for an idiosyncratic œuvre that unearths and explores injustice, to the beat of a different drum. The apposition of languages and philosophical movement in describing her interaction with Derrida, "les langues de sport translinguistique, de transports philosophiques," is not accidental, even if she characterizes their meeting as fortuitous. In different ways, the two writers blur the generic boundaries between poetry and philosophy, playing with language in serious manner. Growing up in what Cixous terms "Babelgérie," Algerian Jews could hardly be insensitive to words and languages, and to the defining roles they play in History: "In my home, in my family mixed with multiple, ancient exiles, I have known everything about human destiny and its connection to language use" ("La Fugitive" 77).

The use of languages, in Cixous's understanding, extends in several directions. There is the noticeable presence of multiple languages in Algeria, particularly in the city she inhabited as a child: "When I was little I lived in a city full of neighborhoods, of peoples, of languages" (Rootpoints 182). Many have commented on the particular mix of languages that make up Algeria; Assia Djebar enumerates four tongues that are crucial to culture in her native land: "the multiplicity of languages (Latin, Arab, Berber, and French) at the very root of Algerian culture" (Ces voix 213). Gilbert Grandguillaume also cites plurilingualism not only as revelatory of Algerian society, but as constitutive of it: "The plurality of languages in Algeria expresses the real plurality of the society, it is its determining component" (19). Cixous was sensitive and open to the sounds that surrounded her during her formative years, but she did not have access to these tongues since the homes of other children her age were off-limits and school did not offer classes in "indigenous" languages.[20] Her sense of being born a "foreigner" in Algeria was intensified by the fact that she did not speak Arabic: "To grow up in a country where you don't speak the language!" ("La Fugitive" 77).[21]

Another sense of the "usage of languages" is found in the process of naming and re-naming that often accompanies domination of people and territory. Cixous recalls the foreign sounds that constituted the map of her first city: "All of these boulevards in Oran that rang out above our ears the victories of the Empire: Magenta, Arzew, Austerlitz" ("La Fugitive" 79). This nominative re-appropriation was intricately tied up with the larger act of claiming possession over the conquered land: "For in Algeria the streets and boulevards were subjected to colonization, a highly insidious extension of the empire of the proper" (*Portrait* 98).[22] The irony of the matter was that French names were not uniform, since there were a number of designations in Arabic for different parts of town, but they often labeled the most inappropriate areas, such as the neighborhood in which Cixous's family took up residence in Algiers: "Where France had painted so many locations and quarters with French names, imagine a small Algerian town called Michelet of my neighborhood, 99% Arab, called Clos-Salembier, but all of this in an arbitrary mixture" ("La Fugitive" 79). As a child, these strange names bore onomatopoeic resemblance to other words that designated things from afar, unseen and bizarre: "I heard these names like strange examples of onomatopoeia taking place among the names of a vegetable or fruit essence, caroube, jujube" (79). But the linguistic operation was not content to stop there, for the "tyranny of de-nomination" included applying insulting, racist labels to everyone: "Never take lightly the impact of the name the impact of word-names, this was my instinct and my law from the moment I experienced the tyranny of de-nomination in Algeria, the way in which hurtful racist names flew, where every word that designated was an insult Arab Jew French everything" (79). It is important to note that Cixous indicates that no racial or ethnic group was exempt from this name-calling, that all designations were harmful, for it explains many of the writer's expressions of reticence with respect to self-designation and description. Language is not only insufficient to represent the person, it is by nature derogatory: as soon as a label is applied, it sticks, precluding the elaboration and nuance necessary to and inherent in the process(es) of identification.[23]

Growing up in Algeria was not incidental to the writings of Cixous, for it made her highly attentive to the traps of identity and the impossibility of

"self-sameness." Witnessing the revocation and restoration of her French citizenship made her wary of national forms of self-identification: "How could I
have been able to believe that we were 'French,' or want to be when we were
recitizenized after 1943, puppets of the whims of a State that established its
authority on a colonial Empire the jewel of which was North Africa" ("Letter" 190). As for her complex identifications as an established writer in
French, the adjective "French" is at once present and absent from her discourse; she is left to play with words, to play *on* words, in order to describe an
inherently problematic relationship to the nationality that is now *hers*, seemingly for good:

> I don't say I'm not French. I say: I'm un-French, which includes French and
> un-French. Or as I punned: Free-ench. My inner feeling has always been a feel-
> ing of foreignness. I have never felt, never, that I wasn't foreign. And I even
> felt guilty since I admitted I was integrated in society with my French passport
> and my status as a civil servant. Sometimes I even felt as if I was a liar. By and
> by I was pacified when I realised that in the so-called French 'nation' 75% of
> the French are not 'pure' French. (Phoca 13)

Pointing out the truth that most inhabitants of France are not "Français de
souche," or "pure" French, simultaneously provides a critique of nationality
in a specific context and puts into question all assumptions of "purity," thus
recalling Derrida's work of "deconstruction," according to his own description: "the first impulse of what is called 'deconstruction' carries with it toward this 'critique' of phantasm of the axiom of purity, or toward the analytical decomposition of a purification that would lead back to the
indecomposable simplicity of origin" (*Monolingualism* 45). Cixous's work returns to origins frequently, but only to depart again, in another direction:
"The orange is a beginning. Starting out from the orange all voyages are possible" ("To Live the Orange" 88).

The place of the sea in Cixous's work is undeniable, for while the "voyages" she mentions can refer to travel in general, they carry special significance with respect to this word in its English connotation. In the 1940s and
1950s, moving from North Africa to France meant crossing the sea, as Derrida recalls in his written reflections.[24] Returning to her namesake from
Greek mythology, Cixous refers to "Marlowe's beautiful verse, as he looks on
the face of the beautiful Helen: 'Was this the face that launched a thousand
ships?'" ("Preface" xxi). Connecting her name with departure is a valorizing
gesture, in harmony with a number of textual affirmations of movement out
of, and away from, places of origin: "I believe in Odysseus without Ithaca.

You leave. I believe in the power of the edge of departure. I come from, I want to come from. I come from Algeria. It gave me departures and I took them" ("La Fugitive" 76). The allusion to Homer's epic poem here is also a reference to Joyce's work, texts that precede Cixous's œuvre and arguably provide her with points of departure for creative productivity. But these two literary precursors are not the only ones to encourage Cixous to venture out to sea: her life experience, especially the coming—and going—of her first-born child, pushed her into the vagaries of the unknown, according to her retrospective comments. In *L'Amour du loup*, the writer explains that all certainty and stability were uprooted with her son: "The inexact child was an irruption of the unpredictable, of the incalculable in the presumption of calculations. I was twenty-two years old, a totally calm unknowing. I was anchored [*à l'ancre*]" (117–18). As always, Cixous is playing with words in these sentences, saying many things with loaded words, and alluding to much that will remain *unsaid*, at least in explicit terms. The final word of this quotation, "*ancre*," immediately evokes its homophone, "*encre*," indicating that her son is connected to writing, that his passing set her loose from her firmly anchored position, and that the disconcerting un-grounding that accompanied his short life and tragic passing meant that she too would always be passing, never sure-footed again: "You write with a foreign body, with a torn-off-child's-hand from your childhood. You don't recognize anything" (126–27).

For a world afloat, Cixous has to find the appropriate music in her writing: "For a floating world, flowing music" ("Le Théâtre surpris par les Marionnettes"). Creating this music means rendering an unrecognizable world on the page, a world characterized by new ways of seeing and hearing, and therefore by new ways of conceiving what surrounds us: "You have to imagine, the musician says, relationships that have not yet existed, words to say nearly impossible figures: listen to an image, look at a sound" ("Le Théâtre"). This music is in flux, batted about by the currents around it: "Music is also moved and uplifted from one bank to another of the continents, having no other law than the fluctuations of drama." This understanding of music and its relation to movement is what Cixous valiantly *translates* in writing, according to her own reflections:

I write texts that are very much in movement. *Mouvementés*. Eventful. That is what I imagine, at least. There ought then to be a metaphorical grouping, or collection that stems at once from the registers of transport, but also that always goes through [*en repasse*] the first of the means of transport which is our own body. What we are able to do as an exercise in translation with our body or as a translation of our affects in terms of the body is unlimited. (*Photos* 28)

The verb "repasser," at the center of this quotation, points to the operation at the heart of Cixous's writing enterprise. Coming back to the same themes, she is never content to let one text—and its particular voice—have the last word. Her composite collection of works is indeed a group of "passings," in which she treats again, in moving manner, topics that have been touched already, but in different ways. This is how the fugue works, as an imitative composition in which themes are stated successively in all of the voices of the contrapuntal structure. If Toril Moi is correct to critique the "contradictions of Cixous's discourse" (120), then I would assert that these contradictions are part of the contrapuntal workings of the text, where contrasting but parallel lines coexist in a harmonic relationship while retaining their individuality.

It would be difficult to overestimate the importance of "movement" in Cixous's conception of the term. In her published notes from *Photos de racines*, she evokes a predecessor whose influence on her work is clear: "Archimedes [. . .] thought the world—actively, transitively, the world in evolution. The world is not something to contemplate, to think the world is to make it. It is a movement without end. [. . .] To believe in the Truth as tension, as movement" (85). Cixous understands the world, and the self, to be in movement, and this is what she attempts to communicate in writing. Derrida's assertions in *L'écriture et la différence* underscore the importance of movement in language: "This overpowerfulness as the life of the signifier is produced within the anxiety and the wandering of the language always richer than knowledge, the language always capable of movement which takes it further than peaceful and sedentary certitude" (73). The movements that make up Cixous's life and work are always already distancing her from "sedentary certitude."

Composing texts in movement would seem to come naturally to someone who characterizes herself as a fugitive, defined by flight from the "accident" of her birth: "The fugitive. It was I [. . .] the fugitive was she that flees me / I fled [*c'était elle la fuie moi*] [. . .] Algeria is my thrown luck [*mon sort jeté*]" ("La Fugitive" 75). Despite her flight, the place of origin is always present: "I don't stop coming from Algeria" (79). One of the reasons for which there is this constant deferral to her origin is that she never "arrived" anywhere else, least of all in France: "Algeria had given me the departure. But France could not give me the arrival" ("Letter" 190). As a result, she is forever passing, describing herself as a "passerby" ("My Algeriance" 169), and indicating her contentment to "*stay passing*" (170). Her attitude toward her native land differs from that of Derrida, and others, who express nostalgic sentiments with respect to Algeria: "I cannot manage to arrive. . . . But no nostalgia. I had not been at home behind the fences of my native cradle" ("Letter" 189). Unlike other writers in French from North Africa who are considered by readers and critics to be "representatives" of their native land, Cixous has not been placed in this context, certainly—and rightly—because she can hardly be considered "representative" of Algeria. But this dilemma of not "belonging" to the land of her birth is certainly not unique to Cixous, and is precisely something she shares with a number of Maghrebian-born writers, no matter what their family history.

While other writers and intellectuals have followed similar paths, moving from the native land to France to pursue their careers, Cixous's itinerary is different because of its very early inclusion of the United States. Her familiarity with English and her doctoral thesis on James Joyce gave her occasion to apply for a Fulbright to conduct research in the U.S. when she was still quite young. This stay abroad, which figures prominently in *Manhattan*, was but an introduction to a country that was to have a great deal of influence in her life. American universities have welcomed her regularly, offering her opportunities to give lectures and teach courses to a diverse audience with very different expectations from those in France. Just as universities in the U.S. have given Assia Djebar an institutional home (while the exacting French system would not be welcoming because of degree requirements and bureaucratic necessities), so they have integrated Cixous's texts into course curricula, whereas the French educational system has not.

Nearly countless trips to the United States, and numerous journeys to destinations ranging from Eastern Europe to India now add to Cixous's list of travels.[25] Cixous's major displacement, from Algeria to France, was a revelatory move, according to her own account: "I left Algeria in 1955. Without grief. With no idea of returning. I removed my bandages. Enough silenced. Enough swallowed. I removed my gag. I began. At last I stopped being the one I wasn't. And I was the foreigner that I was. Unknown. Alleviated of my double the anger that had accompanied me until then. I no longer had to carry the sins of France I who as a child had been chased out and execrated by France" ("Letter" 193). She was able in many senses to start afresh in France, as a "foreigner" in a place where she didn't bear the burden of being "representative." The ironic twist of her personal itinerary rests on the fact that it was outside the borders of metropolitan France that she had to carry the responsibility of this country. Even though the nation had officially "disinherited" her, she was viewed as French by those around her, and expected to answer for the misdeeds of a country in which she had never set foot. In a touching final note in her essay, "My Algeriance," Cixous reveals a second irony: the friends she had sought so fervently throughout her childhood and adolescence on Algerian soil came to find her later, *in France*: "Algeria returns . . ." is the heading that points to the fact that Cixous's once-and-for-all departure from this land did not preclude its return to her, though removed and unexpected, in the form of Algerian "sisters" who remember the past and dream of the future *with* Cixous.

Orders from Algeria: A Literary Calling

In "My Algeriance," Cixous explains that her flight began in mind long before she physically left Algeria: "I only thought of leaving. Escaping. In the meantime I escaped without moving, in books" (171). This statement echoes the title of the collection in which it appears: *Stigmata: Escaping Texts*. The juxtaposition of these terms could be interpreted in various ways. First, we could consider them synonymous, taking "stigmata" to be another name for the "escaping texts" printed on these pages. Second, it would be possible to see these terms as chronologically progressive, the first term referring to the traces, or the scars from Cixous's early life, and the second designating the frenetic publishing activity to follow, of which this collection of texts is just a small portion. The term "escaping" is of course ambiguous by nature, either describing the texts as "escaping"—and this leaves unknown the thing(s) or person(s) one is escaping from—or referring back to the stigmata as eluding textual representation. All of these possibilities, and more, are translated in this multifaceted title. I would like to emphasize its resonance with another title of an earlier set of reflections from *La Jeune née*, "Sorties," a text whose subtitles translated into English yield the following: "Out and Out: Attacks/ Ways Out/Forays" (61). The literary movements that serve as thematic headings for her theoretical and fictional work did not emerge out of nowhere: Cixous reveals that her conversion to literature is directly due to Algeria.

In her most recent collection of creative critical texts, *L'Amour du loup*, Cixous again returns to Algeria, this time to reveal the order she obeys as a writer: "*I surrender myself to that which orders me to Algeria* beginning with these primitive scenes. Since these primitive scenes I am ordered—and this order is the order to write. I gave myself over to this order as to the letters of *Rêveries*, I went to arrive toward Algeria as toward the shore where everything arrives, I surrendered myself to live the non-event of arrival" (158). This order from Algeria is precisely what distinguishes her from the milieu to which she belongs, that of the "Parisian scene," as Cixous aptly puts it. She does not completely "fit in" even though she has made a name for herself in the "University" and in "Parisian culture," through her varied activities as professor and poet, in the large sense of these words:

This order into which I entered/returned [Cet ordre dans lequel je suis rentrée]—the order to write, *come from Algeria* to write from Algeria and that finally brought me back to her, it's also that which makes me *insep-Arab/inseparable [inséparabe]* from Algeria and Arabs and separates me from all that I belong to that is the Parisian scene, University, Parisian culture. Separation is a *part* of me. I am insep-Arab from Aïcha, Zohra, Hamida, Samia, Oran, Algiers, or, Al, El, g. (*Rêveries* 158)

Obeying this call to writing is not easy, for Cixous's natural instinct is to flee the past, to run from, not toward, the place of origin(s): "I learned to shatter my flights. When I say to myself: this morning, I won't write, not that, this thing is without interest, I certainly have other things to do, only serious tasks await me, [. . .] immediately the Dream says to me: [. . .] do, note me down . . . I know that you scheme and you flee. Do before thinking" (*Rêve* 11–12). In this work on dreams, the dream has the last word, and the writer gives in to the writing, rather than fleeing. She yields to the call.

The calling to write (almost like a call to a religious order in Cixous's creative rendering) is not limited to the place of birth; it is also occasioned by and destined toward the person who brought her into the world. In *L'Amour du loup*, Cixous makes a crucial connection between land and mother: "My own native town, foreign. Like my mother, foreign" (140). Cixous's writing is influenced by her foreign land *and* her foreign mother,[26] and in this context we can read the following words as indicative of her writing project: "What living being can say mama without making the call resonate more or less clearly? Whoever says 'mama' calls for help" (*Stigmata* 101). Her reading of a Brazilian writer whom she admires deeply gives Cixous an opportunity to unveil the crucial place of the mother in literature, from the work of Joyce to that of Marcel Proust: "Clarice Lispector knows that it is the mother one calls, or that there is calling of the mother, she knows it with a poetic knowledge, and she knows it also because she knows Joyce very well" (118). Cixous's "Obstétriques cruelles" and her "*Fremdworte sind Glücksache*" are in harmony with a textual enterprise that constantly refers to the mother (especially in recent publications), as a response to the loneliness of abandonment that Cixous experienced at the tender age of three, when her mother separated from her at the gate of the school in Algeria: "being alone is no solution, and what makes itself felt stronger than everything at the very last minute, is the need at least to name mama. To avow. To recognize that the *one* needs the *zero*. . . . Originally zero is not a number, but a marker of space. I transpose my zero in the omnibus and in life" (*Stigmata* 125). Her mother's chosen career in Algeria was that of a midwife; when Cixous was young, she was sensitive to the challenges of a single mother exercising a challenging but rewarding profession designed to help women. She was also attentive to the floods of women who came to the clinic to give birth.

It is no mistake that Cixous's efforts in the educational system in France include the founding of the *Centre de Recherches en Études Féminines* in the mid-1970s at the University of Paris 8 Vincennes, now located in Saint-Denis. This center for the study of gender and sexual differences is the only one of its kind in the country, and its continued existence depends on the dedicated mission of Cixous and her colleagues. It is certain that part of her desire to establish this doctoral program was tied to what she sees as a mistreatment of women in France. Cixous regularly denounces the prevalence of misogyny around the world, and explains in an interview that her early experience with "sexual hostility" in Algeria opened her eyes to its existence: "I had met sexual hostility before, it was a daily event in Algeria, it was open. I couldn't take a bus without being harassed. I thought Algeria primitive. . . . Algeria was a colony. As in all colonies violence is rampant and of course it takes sexual shapes and it will attack the weak first, women, etc." (Phoca 11). What was surprising to Cixous upon leaving Algeria was that this hostility was not unique to the colony, that is was just as present in France in "less aggressive" form, as "phallocracy": "In France misogyny is veiled and it is much more insidious and perfidious than anywhere else in Europe. It's awful because it doesn't say its name" (11). Cixous has decided to call its bluff, and to "say the name" of injustice—sexual, racial, and other—in writing. She has answered the call, coming from her childhood, to fight against oppression in all forms, open and occluded.

Spreading Wings: The Gift of Writing (as) Flight

If there is one single word for which Cixous is known, it is "*voler,*" this verb with more than one meaning in French that has provided a challenge to her translators in such texts as *La Jeune née*:

> To fly/steal is woman's gesture, to steal into language to make it fly. [. . .] It's not just luck if the word "voler" volleys between the "vol" of theft and the "vol" of flight, pleasuring in each and routing the sense police. It is not just luck: woman partakes of bird and burglar, just as the burglar partakes of woman and bird: hesheits pass, hesheits fly by, hesheits pleasure in scrambling spatial order, disorienting it, moving furniture, things, and values around, breaking in, emptying structures, turning the selfsame, the proper upside down. (96)

The linking of flight to language in this oft-quoted passage reveals in this translation that, contrary to her assertion, a particular language may offer a bit of luck: if "*voler*" volleys between theft and flight, it is in French that it does so. This particular tongue lends itself well to the disruption Cixous effectuates within it, as we shall see in a moment. For the time being, what matters is the pleasure and imagination involved in the routes that disorient the "sense police," those who govern and order meaning. Likening wordplay to travel is an important gesture, because it underscores the potential of language to change perspective. As a writer, Cixous is by definition also a traveler, according to her comments in "La Venue à l'écriture": "I travel: where people suffer, where they fight, where they escape, where they enjoy, my body is suddenly there. Worldwide my unconscious, worldwide my body. What happens outside happens inside. I myself am the earth, everything that happens, the lives that live me in my different forms, the voyage, the voyager [*la voyageuse*], the body of travel and the spirit of travel" (47).[27] Since travel is linked to language, it is possible to move in mind: "I was the mother of my mother then, of my brother, of my whold family, I took them in my arms, I carried them over the hills, I saved them from the Nazis. Since then I've invented all different kinds of transportation, known and unknown [. . .] I've been all the birds" ("Coming" 48).[28] The inclusion of the second unexpected word in a list of four verbs in this text reveals that this movement is designed, as in Cixous's dream of flight, *to protect*: "Flee, protect, escape, fly" (48).

For Cixous's flights in writing, French is the chosen tongue of composition. The writer explains her relationship to this language in "La Fugitive," a text whose title can be read in a straightforward sense (as "The Fugitive" in English), but that can also be heard musically, as the note "La" on the diatonic scale "Do-Re-Mi-Fa-Sol-La-Ti," followed by the adjective for "fleeting." Fleeing, as a lifestyle, has made Cixous sensitive as a writer to the fleeting nature of thought, taking down creative notes in their passing to preserve and protect those who speak.[29] French is the vehicle, considered separately from its national attachments:

> I liked "having French" in school, and just like my friend Jacques Derrida I had an amorous and conquering attitude toward this language. Not being that which I wanted to have, to take with me, *to straddle for my flights, to rub between my other tongues, to liberate as well from its classical colonizers*, its talentless users, pseudo-legitimate pseudo-owners who reduced it yesterday like today. I would have liked it intact, stolen away from the State, from National Education, from the political institutional prime, and I quickly found allies among the literary freed. I have never confused the language and the nation-state. I had French. But we didn't have Arabic. ("La Fugitive" 77, my emphasis)

Freed from its ties to the state and all of the national—political and educational, and especially colonial—implications this loaded term carries, French is free to flee, to float, and to fly.

Cixous could be called a "gifted" writer not only because she has talent, but also because she *offers* this talent to others. In "Fourmis," Derrida reads a dream turned text by Cixous in *Jours de l'an*, focusing on the gift found within: "if there is giving, it must give itself as a dream, as in a dream" (*Photos* 120).[30] She has given him this present just as he gave her the *do* in the episode she recounts from a mythic past (that carries a concrete date, 1963), in *Portrait de Jacques Derrida*; she gives as he did, *unknowingly*: "Hélène furnished me unknowingly with the word fourmi, giving it to me thus. Her dream gave it to me without knowing what it was doing, without knowing what I would do with it, without knowing period, because one can only give without knowing" (124). Giving him this word anew, as he has never seen or heard it before, Cixous grants Derrida room for innovative play, and she presents him with unsuspected, unexpected wings: "Her dream gave me the word not only as a term that I would play on today without playing, but as a word, and no doubt a thing, a living winged being, that I had never before seen in my life. It is an epiphany in my language and in the world that is tuned to it" (124–25). The harmony of word and world in Cixous's gift are in step with her largesse as a writer: "she gives in writing, she gives to write, she advances to the dream" (125). Going toward the ineffable, presenting language in refreshing ways, Cixous opens up worlds of interpretation to her readers. This is her genius and her generosity; the two characteristics are inextricably intertwined in her work: "Hélène has a genius for making the language speak, down to the most familiar idiom, the place where it seems to be crawling with secrets which give way to thought" (123). As we have already seen in the chapter on musicality and orality in Cixous's writing, she gives us resonance in language that often passes by unattuned ears: "She knows how to make it say what it keeps in reserve, which in the process also comes out of its reserve" (123). Cixous makes language speak, drawing it out from silence and secrecy and giving us fodder for different thoughts, for diverse discourse. Cutting back the restraints, Cixous sets language loose to let it fly its course.

Notes

1. One such example can be found in the website for "Women Writers Initiative France," which lists Hélène Cixous's "birthplace" as "France," without any indication that she was born outside the hexagonal space of metropolitan France: http://www .endicott.edu/newprod/iwli/france.html.

2. Recent efforts to correct these oversights include an article on the place of Algeria in Cixous's corpus in the first issue of a new review of literature from the Maghreb, *Expressions maghrébines* (Christa Stevens addresses "algérianité" in Cixous's œuvre in Vol. 1, no. 1, Summer 2002) and a later issue of the same review was devoted to Cixous in its entirety (Vol. 2, no. 2, Winter 2003).

3. Wood makes this observation in a special issue of the journal *parallax*, titled "Translating 'Algeria,'" containing contributions by Cixous and Derrida. Cixous confirms elsewhere, in an interview with Sophia Phoca, that the present climate in the place of her birth has stimulated her to respond: "Now it is again present because of the new and cruel circumstances storming Algeria, which bring Algeria back inside my field of vision, writing, etc." (13).

4. Cixous insists in her interview for *Wasafiri* that Algeria has always been an important part of her writing project: "But when I started writing I was still very near Algeria; I used to go back to Algeria regularly and it was with me all the time" (Phoca 13). In another interview, Cixous explicitly addresses the place of Algeria in texts that have not always been read as engaged in political and ethical ways: "my first narrative which was called *Dedans* reads in fact as an oblique ethico-political treatise on the conscious and unconscious situation in Algeria between the '40s and the '60s—one is not obliged to read it in that way, but that is what it is. There is always a political reflection and engagement running through it" ("Guardian of Language"). Other early texts have not been recognized for their political punch or their relationship to Algeria; the introduction to selected portions of *Vivre l'orange* in *The Hélène Cixous Reader* (a text that otherwise pays careful attention to multiple meanings in the French original, pointing them out and explaining their significance) makes no mention to the Anglophone reader that the city of Oran is present in the title, and that this title can be read in several ways, such as *Oran-je*, to illustrate the personal connection to the land; it seems that the following phrases may even elude the translators, whose task of rendering the French text in English is admittedly difficult: "Three looks around an orange, from here to Brazil go to the sources in Lalgeria" (88); "*the love of the orange is political too*" (90).

5. Derrida makes it clear that Algeria was never under German occupation, and that the decision to revoke French citizenship was entirely up to the French: "The withdrawal of French citizenship from the Jews of Algeria, with everything that followed, was the deed of the French alone" (*Monolingualism* 16).

6. Wood goes on to address the term "patrimonial memory," taken from Pierre Nora's *Les Lieux de mémoire*, and its insufficiency to describe the experience of the *pied noir* community from Algeria (177–78). Since this form of memory depends on a "localized heritage," the lack of "palpable attachments" in the form of "material or symbolic 'sites'" leaves those who have departed with a lasting melancholy over "the traumatic loss of an idealized love object" (178). While both may know nostalgia for Algeria, Jews and *pieds-noirs* experience it differently: "The circumstances of their departure may consign the former Jews of Algeria to this modality

of memory to some extent; however, the specificity of their history and their location within the colonial context also differentiates their *mémoire patrimoine* from that of their *pied noir* compatriots" (178).

7. Derrida indicates that identification was a problem for Jews in Algeria because all points of comparison were "foreign": "They couldn't identify themselves in the terms of models, norms, or values whose development was to them alien because French, metropolitan, Christian, and Catholic. In the milieu where I lived, we used to say 'the Catholics'; we called all the non-Jewish French people 'Catholics,' even if they were sometimes Protestants, or perhaps even Orthodox: 'Catholic' meant anyone who was neither a Jew, a Berber, nor an Arab" (*Monolingualism* 52). The deep irony of this "identification crisis" is that not only were Jews unable to identify with the French, the Berber, or the Arab population, they were also unable to identify with their own culture: "strangers to Jewish culture, a strangely bottomless alienation of the soul [. . .] the radical lack of culture [*inculture*] from which I undoubtedly never completely emerged" (53).

8. In a brief, suggestive article titled "Hélène Cixous: Initiatory Readings, Centrifugal Readings," Lynn Kettler Penrod places Cixous's writing alongside a text by Michel Tournier that treats of initiatory rites and centrifugal movement in primitive societies. The critic picks up on Tournier's negatively connoted phrase "permanent flight" to point out its revalorized significance in Cixous's œuvre and to connect it to music: "If 'permanent flight' has a special sense in Hélène Cixous's work, it is because it stems from the musical—a fugue defined as a textual voice, its successive imitations forming several parts which follow each other" (63).

9. In fictional works like *Les Rêveries de la femme sauvage*, the narrative voice laments the impossibility of employing this word, "nous": "I note: I am outside my house, I am nostalgic for that which will never exist, there is no judgment, I am outside all we's [*tous les nous*]" (112).

10. Poignant passages from a recent piece reveal the deep pain of being misunderstood by the "Algerians" with whom Cixous wanted to identify as a fellow "exile" in the land of her birth: "And know that the misfortune of my childhood lies in the fact that the Algerians—whom I loved and in whom I recognized our destiny as exiles there where we were [*exilés sur place*], of those who were condemned to deportation without going anywhere—did not recognize me as similar and they confused my brother and me with the common enemy. This confusion, this tragic disdain, programmed by historical facts that were excessively complicated and intertwined made me crazy, that is to say without place, *atopique*, impossible. I was neither this nor that, neither from here nor from there" ("La Fugitive" 79). Rejected by both sides of the conflict, Cixous suffered doubly, and her suffering was not even worthy of acknowledgment: "the incredible *atopicité* to which France and the French had condemned Algerian un-citizens, France the cross and its sword, we were its exorcised, and I was on both sides. I reflected, but I was not reflected upon" (80). The creation of the word "*atopicité*" is highly appropriate to designate the "placenessness" to which the young Cixous was condemned in her native land.

11. Derrida explains this neologism as follows: "Repetition *and* first time: this is perhaps the question of the event as question of the ghost. [. . .] Each time it is the event itself, a first and last time. Altogether other. Staging for the end of history. Let us call it a *hauntology*" (*Specters* 10).

12. In a lively essay composed as a letter never sent, Cixous refers to becoming a citizen again, and expresses her resistance to this renewed status that was not necessarily coveted: "How could I have been able to believe that we were 'French,' or want to be when we were recitizenized after 1943" ("Letter to Zohra Drif" 190).

13. In self-reflective comments on her œuvre, Cixous oscillates between the first-person and the third-person designation to affirm that loss is essential to the writing process, to the "saving" gesture of putting to paper that which risks oblivion: "Through the different readings that had been proposed from what I have been able to write—from what *Cixous*, as they say, has been able to write—it appeared that I am—well, *she is*—often preoccupied, perhaps principally, with loss and its paradoxes. This one, for example: I can only save from perdition that which I have already lost" ("In October 1991" 77).

14. In *Le Monolinguisme de l'autre*, Derrida also employs words such as "lesions" and "wounds," referring to the "franco-maghrébin" experience in terms of visible, physical suffering: "*what it is to be* Franco-Maghrebian. [. . .] The silence of that hyphen does not pacify or appease anything, not a single torment, not a single torture. It will never silence their memory. It could even worsen the terror, the lesions, and the wounds" (*Monolingualism* 11).

15. Cixous addresses the uniqueness of the French expression for "viewpoint," underscoring the importance of its untranslatable double meaning in this tongue: "About the expression 'point of view.' An expression that I wouldn't be able to exploit as I would like in a language other than French. For thanks to our language—language gives us gifts—, 'point de vue' in English is *viewpoint*, but also the point of nonview. There where there is no view. Point of view always goes with: no view" ("In October 1991" 79). A point of view must be plural in order for it to be effective: "it takes two for viewpoint to function" (80). Of all subjects, time is most affected by viewpoint: "The point of view on time is always the most subjective point of view" (81).

16. When Cixous refers to the coincidences that led to her birth on Algerian soil, she places the word "luck" in quotation marks, indicating thus that she is perhaps not as fortunate as she would have hoped, given the negative colonial environment that reigned in her native land: "I come, biographically, from a rebellion, from a violent and anguished direct refusal to accept what is happening on the stage on whose edge I find I am placed, as a result of the combined accidents of History. I had this strange 'luck': a couple of rolls of the dice, a meeting between two trajectories of the diaspora, and, at the end of these routes of expulsion and dispersion that mark the functioning of western History through the displacements of Jews, I fall.—I am born—right in the middle of a scene that is the perfect example, the naked model, the raw idea of this very process" ("Sorties" 70).

17. Cixous's metaphorical choice of "silk" in this passage harks back to Derrida's "Un ver à soie: Points de vue piqués sur l'autre voile," a response to her "Savoir," in *Voiles*.

18. Cixous is giving a nod here to Derrida's reflections titled "Abraham, l'autre," from an international colloquium titled "Judéités: questions pour Jacques Derrida" held in Paris in December 2000.

19. The name game Cixous engages in here, referring to herself as "Klein" (meaning "little" in German) and Derrida as "Gross" (and its connotation "big"), does not "come out of nowhere," so to speak. It constitutes another example of the intricately woven web of intertextuality between the two writers, responding to a footnote found on page 36 of the text they co-authored, *Voiles*. This footnote draws from the expression "contact lens" (in English in the original French text), to refer to a work by poet Paul Celan, *Gespräch im Gebirg*, and the name "Lenz": "Then because of the name Klein, another proper name immediately renamed by Celan and which was also that of Hélène Cixous's mother or grandfather. As if the name of Paul Celan had met the name of Hélène Cixous, following the poetic necessity of a time I do not believe to be in contestable: 'To meet him [i.e., Lenz] came his cousin . . . to meet the other, Gross came with Klein, and Klein, the Jew, made his stick silent before the stick of the Jew Gross" (*Veils* 97).

20. Cixous recalls that her father, a polyglot who dabbled in a number of tongues including Arabic and Hebrew, encouraged her to formally study these languages when she was quite young. After his passing, her study of languages moved to different climes, as she received degrees in English and pursued an interest in German.

21. Cixous explains in *Les Rêveries de la femme sauvage* that her education took place in a single language that communicated a single *Weltanschauung*: "In Algiers I fell into FrenchAlgeria [*Algériefrançaise*], and it was the school [*Lycée*] against which I could do nothing" (142). Other Algerian-born writers in French have illustrated that one of the most obvious and insidious aspects of the one-sided French educational system in Algeria was language. As Leïla Sebbar indicates in *Je ne parle pas la langue de mon père*, Arabic was the forbidden tongue in the school of her childhood: "At the whistle, the forbidden language is shut up, from murmur to murmur until there is silence, the boys enter the other world" (43). Jacques Derrida provides a thorough analysis of the various linguistic interdicts in the French school system in Algeria in *Le Monolinguisme de l'autre*. He points out the problematic nature of imposing a "mother tongue" on subjects who are nonetheless miles from the "motherland": "for all these groups, French was a language supposed to be maternal, but one whose source, norms, rules, and law were situated elsewhere" (41). The problems of speaking (only) a language "located" in this "elsewhere" that was France were multiple; the denied "entry" into the country of their origin, into their place of birth, was in large part related to linguistic separation (Derrida highlights the "interdict" on Arabic and Berber on page 37) to an inability to communicate in the tongue(s) of their native land, in the case of a number of Algerian-born writers whose education took place in French.

22. The volume *Key Concepts in Post-Colonial Studies*, by Bill Ashcroft, Gareth Griffiths, and Helen Tiffin, contains a sizeable entry on "cartography," indicating that maps and mapping are "dominant practices of colonial and post-colonial cultures," and that the act of drawing up maps during colonial conquest almost inevitably entails "renaming spaces in a symbolic and literal act of mastery and control." Colonized lands are thus "literally reinscribed, written over, as the names and the languages of the indigenes are replaced by new names" (31–32). In "Decolonizing the Map," Graham Huggan calls attention to the ways postcolonial writers highlight the instability of the renamed places and redrawn boundaries by considering colonized "spaces as shifting grounds which are themselves subject to transformational patterns of de- and reterritorialization" (120).

23. Derrida makes a distinction between identification and identity in a comment on autobiography: "In its common concept, autobiographical anamnesis presupposes identification. And precisely not identity. No, an identity is never given, received, or attained; only the interminable and indefinitely phantasmatic process of identification endures" (*Monolingualism* 28).

24. Derrida describes the sea as an "infinite space" separating him and his fellow students from the metropolis that was France, a space that he covered in a vessel called *Ville d'Alger*: "[T]he sea was there: symbolically an infinite space for all the students of the French school in Algeria, a chasm, an abyss. I did not cross it, body and soul, or body without soul [. . .] until, for the first time, sailing across on a boat, on the *Ville d'Alger*, at the age of nineteen" (*Monolingualism* 44). For him, as for Cixous, the first trip was to lead to many more; their professions and confessions have taken them to a plethora of places in the wake of that initial voyage.

25. Cixous treats lengthily of travel in *Benjamin à Montaigne*, a text predicated on a trip to Osnabrück by a mother and aunt who are two of the very few remaining Jews from this German town. Among the many insightful and provocative comments about the impossibility of return (temporal and geographic), we find this reflection in the first-person narrative voice on a personal distaste for travel: "Only I hate to travel. I don't stop traveling around the world as if what we call travel traveled me whereas every trip knocks me off route. Why did I prefer to travel by plane, to far-off countries I say to myself every time I obey my ticket. [. . .] Everyone runs according to their thrown luck [*le sort jeté*] at birth" (126–27).

26. It is worth noting that Cixous left *terre* and *mère*, land and mother, when she departed from Algeria in 1955, for her mother remained in the country during the war. The inability to help or to be helped accompanied and accelerated her flight (on the very day before the war began): "The day before, I had left, I had fled this earth in pain that I could neither caress nor help nor call my mother without offending it" ("Letter" 189).

27. The travel that she refers to here is associated with the night, and therefore with dreams, picking up on another definition of the word "fugue" in English as a dreamlike state of altered consciousness. The privilege Cixous accords to dreaming

in her writing is not unlike that given to reading (and writing), for both activities promote travel in spirit, outside the constrictions of "place" and "time."

28. Birds are an important theme in Cixous's work, most recently occupying central stage in two chapters from *L'Amour du loup*: "Aube partagée" and "Le réfugié."

29. Catching things as they pass, in the fleeting moment, requires speed: "In this moment I try to capture the mysteries of passing in order to give them to you; this is an attempt to note that which goes much faster than my conscience or my hand. But, the passing, by luck, leaves traces. I must react quickly" (*L'Amour du loup* 88).

30. In his reading of *Jours de l'an*, Derrida locates a passage containing the italicized words, *Histoire de Contretemps*. He points out that this expression resonates with his own study of contretemps in yet another reference to the coincidental intertextuality and often unspoken mutual influence present throughout their work: "the expression Story of Contretemps is in italics as for a title to be read; without our having passed the word between us, I had previously used contretemps in the title of an aphoristic text concerning an aphoristic couple that Hélène knows well, Romeo and Juliet" (*Photos* 122).

PART THREE

ABDELKÉBIR KHATIBI

French Transcriptions, French Transpositions: Transportation, Transnation, and Transliteration

Translation is poetic transposition

—Jacques Derrida, "Des Tours de Babel" (1985)

Poetry by definition is untranslatable. Only creative transposition is possible: either intralingual transposition—from one poetic shape into another, or interlingual transposition—from one language into another, or finally intersemiotic transposition—from one system of signs into another, e.g. from verbal art into music, dance, cinema, or painting.

—Roman Jakobson, "On Linguistic Aspects of Translation" (1959)

My goal to develop the intersemiotic stopped short: I realized that it was aspiring to the same thing as poetics [le poétique]

—Abdelkébir Khatibi, La Mémoire tatouée (1971)

The final chapter devoted to Hélène Cixous examined the writer's birthplace as a launching pad for the flight—figurative and literal—to come. In this chapter, I focus on the writings of the two other writers from the Maghreb who head this study: Abdelkébir Khatibi and Assia Djebar. My concentration on physical displacement as a theme in the life (and) writing of these Francophone writers is in step with the meaning of the French word "translation," a term that is not the exact equivalent of its English homonym. Different from traduction, the word that in today's parlance designates the foremost sense of what we call "translation" in English, *translation* refers most often to movement in space. In French-English bilingual dictionaries the term most often yields the single word "transfer," and in the Littré *Dictionnaire de la langue française*, it is first defined as "Action by which one moves [*fait passer*] something from one place to another" (1233). Its obvious affinity with *traduction*, however, indicates that movement from one place to another is not unrelated to movement in language, whether from one language to another or within a single language.[1] This chapter links movement in the form of travel to movement in text, focusing on the way their multiple journeys lead Khatibi and Djebar to theorize travel as a fruitful method of opening up one's eyes to others and to differences that lead to lively, dynamic textual creations. Transportation, not simply within the confines of a single country, but across nations, leads to literary innovation.

Traveling Times: Globalization as Life on the "Go"

One of the oft-cited characteristics of the phenomenon we have come to call "globalization" is freedom of movement. High-speed methods of transportation, from bullet trains to Concorde planes, have transformed the ways we view the world. What formerly seemed to be distant lands are now accessible to us. Trips that would have taken days, weeks, even months in the past can presently be completed in a number of hours. To accommodate even more people, tickets are affordable; not only do people save time when they embark on a journey, they save money too. As a result, travel—an activity once restricted to those with financial means, time, and adventurous spirits—has become a way of life for many.

The emphasis on ease of travel, on the efficiency of transportation systems and the affordability *and* availability of means of transport, has permeated recent discourse on displacement and nomadism. But movement is not always effortless. Both Khatibi and Djebar are avid travelers whose lives and works reflect a wanderlust, a constant desire to move, to see, to witness, and to be exposed to new places and cultures. But the journeys these writers and their characters undertake are sometimes painstaking and arduous, much like traversing mountains on foot. The current stress placed on facility of travel may overlook the complexity of trips; changing land and language in the space of a few hours may not be "easy" for those who choose to move about using contemporary means of movement. These transitions can be tough and draining, as Cixous's comments on travel suggest, but the results are often worthwhile. While trips may sap strength, they can also provide it. Freedom of movement brings with it liberation from confining spaces and limited ways of thinking;

exposure to new sites/sights and sounds can be an inexhaustible source of inspiration. Their prolific literary output may in many ways be connected to the fact that Djebar and Khatibi are so often "on the go."

In their chapter on "la nomadologie" in *Mille plateaux*, Gilles Deleuze and Félix Guattari set up against each other two different games to explore what makes each distinctive: "*échecs*" and "*go*."[2] While they characterize chess as a "semiology," Deleuze and Guattari judge "go" to be "pure strategy" and they underscore the diverging relationships these games have with space: "In go, it is a question of distributing oneself in an open space, of holding space, of keeping open the possibility of emerging at any point: the movement does not go from one point to another, but becomes perpetual, without a goal or a destination, without a departure or an arrival" (436). This description of space and possibility is pertinent to the itinerant travels of Djebar and Khatibi. It is true that their trips are often organized; as established writers and university professors, various duties require them to take a specific path to reach their destination for a conference or a lecture. But, in spite of their official engagements, these writers view these journeys more as jaunts than serious trips: Djebar and Khatibi love to travel for the sake of travel. Their autobiographical novels and theoretical texts prove that embarking on journeys involves much more than *departing* from a specific place and *arriving* in another. Taking a trip entails emerging from the confines of familiar buildings and spaces to get out and about; "taking off" means "perpetually moving," not in order to get anywhere in particular, but simply in order to "go."

Training (on the) Ground: The Lesson of the Labyrinth

Why is the Maghrebian subject drawn to movement in this way? What magnetic attraction pulls Djebar and Khatibi to explore other continents and languages? Is there a particularity that marks the experience of those born on Algerian and Moroccan soil, a specificity that propels them into the world? In an essay translated into English as "A Colonial Labyrinth," Khatibi addresses the colonial city and employs the metaphor of the "labyrinth" to explore the ways the colonized subject negotiates the spaces available to him or her:

> What I mean is that this so-called labyrinth is also a cultural way of treating space, of learning, how shall I put it, a psychology and strategy of walking, of meeting, of avoiding, of fighting, of fleeing, of all the displacements of the body when it is caught in a social network such as this one. One learns in these variously shaped neighborhoods a movement of nimbleness of the mind, if not

a certain malice. . . . I always have liked this movement of deambulation that allows one to find the rhythm of space and to look well at what is happening at one and the same time. A slow rhythm is necessary, a step that one can suspend in order to exchange a few words, some ritual sentences, but in fact also to neutralize the narrowness of the space, its promiscuity, the too closely intertwined situations that are suffocating at times. I have internalized, as have all the Jews of the mellah and each inhabitant of the medina, this psychology of detour. (8–9)

Khatibi's comment on the way he has "internalized" the space of the medina is particularly striking, for it demonstrates the importance of the spaces we occupy. We not only inhabit spaces; spaces come to *inhabit us*. Exposure to the "narrowness" of the space of the "medina," or the oldest part of the city, shapes Khatibi's movements and trains him according to its curves and shapes. Interaction with others is determined by the lay-out of the labyrinth: his psychology, indeed his "strategy" (this word echoes Deleuze and Guattari's analysis of the game of "go") of "walking," "meeting," and even "fighting," are influenced by the width and angles of the streets and the buildings that line them. Absence of interaction is equally determined by the architecture of the city, since "avoiding" and "fleeing" fall into the list of strategic activities learned in the labyrinth. Culture is inscribed in the city; learning to maneuver is much more than learning to go from one place to another: *how* you get around takes precedence over actually reaching a destination.

In an age when speed is of prime significance, when innovations in transportation efficiency include a new TGV (the reputed French high-speed train—*train à grande vitesse*)[3] that will depart Paris and arrive in Marseilles in a mere three hours and a Eurostar that will shoot you underneath the English Channel from Paris to London even more quickly, it seems incongruous to read Khatibi's comments on walking, and especially on finding "the rhythm of space." This "rhythm of space" is a far cry from a space ship rocketing into outer space; it is instead a "slow rhythm" that allows for suspension if necessary, in order to exchange a few words. It is an important rhythm, however, if the pedestrian hopes to observe, to truly see, more than one thing. Slowing one's step means emerging from tunnel vision to capture a larger, panoramic view. This measured pace does not seem to be the exact equivalent of that adopted by the "flâneur" of Benjaminian fame; but it could not be further from the hurried gate of the harried businessman in a large capital city. The Maghrebian writer, familiar with the labyrinth, finds a balance in movement; walking involves careful observance and acquaintance with one's surroundings. It involves a connection between mind and body, which seem perfectly at one, perhaps paradoxically so, in this ambulatory dislocation. Even within the confines of a tight, narrow medieval city like the medina, movement means freedom.

Franchir le Seuil: Contesting the Confines, A Woman's Experience

The ability to move about freely in public spaces is not something Algerian women take for granted. Djebar makes it clear in her autobiographical fiction that she considers herself lucky to have escaped the normal cloistering experienced by young Arab girls when they reach puberty in her native country. In *L'Amour, la fantasia*, the narrator explains her good fortune: "At the age when I should be veiled already, I can still move about freely thanks to the French school" (*Fantasia* 179). This was not a privilege afforded very many young adolescents, including Djebar's cousins who were forced to stay indoors throughout their teenage years and adult lives. Such confinement is at the heart of Djebar's *Ombre sultane*, translated as *A Sister to Scheherazade*. In this novel, a young woman rebels against enclosure and dares to venture out of doors in spite of the forbidden nature of such an act. Wandering the streets of Algiers brings great joy and a deep, exhilarating sense of freedom to Hajila, the second wife of "the man" whose children she must raise as if they were her own.

Hajila's journey out of the apartment, the crossing of this threshold, is as significant a trip as the steps she takes once she has made it past the concierge and onto the streets. The narrator addresses Hajila in the second person, underscoring the monumental move of "'going out' for the first time" (19), employing the adverb "secretly" to describe the "slipping out" (17), and addressing the "escape" more than once (18, 26). Once she is outside, Hajila begins to walk; she meanders these unknown streets of the city she inhabits. In accordance with Khatibi's description of navigating the colonial city, Hajila learns the rules of the road quietly and cautiously in the alternating chapters devoted to her discoveries. Hajila has been on some of these streets before, but always enclosed within an automobile, speeding along at a motorized pace; now, on her own, her rhythms are different and her own two feet carry her: "Once you are outside, all alone, you will walk" (*Sister* 19); "On you walk, Hajila, borne along by the light that enfolds you, models you" (19); "You walk, you skip" (30); "Once out of the house, you never tire of walking" (41). *Walking* is the privileged mode of viewing the city, the best method of becoming intimately acquainted with a place. Carried along in various vehicles, travelers often are kept apart from what they see. Enclosed in trains, planes, and automobiles, those who travel cannot get a *feel* for the places they see through hermetically sealed windows.[4] Physical contact with streets, buildings, and people is noticeably missing.

The repetition of the word "walk" in the citations referring to Hajila's outdoor adventures seems to mirror the act of walking itself, with the repetitive motion of placing one foot in front of the other. Repetition can be viewed as a return, and the act of walking outdoors plunges Hajila back into her childhood, when she was free to roam unveiled: "'To go out naked!' you think. This is a return to childhood!" (32). This revisiting of the past is a pleasant experience for Hajila, who does not feel as if she is retreating into a former self, but instead changes into a different person: "you the new woman, you who have just been transformed into another woman" (31). In Djebar's text, the ideas of repetition and return possess the positive potential to recuperate aspects of the past, such as the freedom of movement Hajila knew as a child, without regressing into a prior state.[5] They yield a renewed, transformed individual. Rather than provoking boredom, repetition opens itself up into *infinity* in a double sense: innumerable possibilities and eternity. The narrator addresses Hajila and evokes the positive conceptions of time that emerge from these daily promenades: "When you return in the evening you are filled with the sensation of the infinity of time. As if each day were a repetition of the last; as if intimations of mortality which had previously lain coiled up inside you were beginning to ooze away" (43).

When Hajila leaves the domicile to emerge in open space, she crosses a seemingly insurmountable threshold. She goes against deeply embedded traditional taboos and defies her husband's authority in doing so.[6] Compared with this "rebellious" border crossing, the crossing of borders by international travelers seems tame. But the questions of identity that accompany Hajila's departure from the enclosed space of the home find a resemblance in the crossing of borders between countries. Jacques Derrida highlights these identity inquiries in *Apories*: "The crossing of borders always announces itself according to the movement of a certain step [*pas*]—and of the step that crosses a line. [. . .] There is a *problem* as soon as this intrinsic division divides the relation to itself of the border and therefore divides the being-one-self of anything" (*Aporias* 11). Just as Hajila's identity is put into question after her "journey" outside, so travelers find themselves put to the test when going from one country to another. While Europe's borders may be little more than symbolic after the formation of the European Union, control at other nations' borders is currently tighter than ever.[7] The production of documents verifying identity and assuring right of passage is required; but all these papers and stamps presuppose what Derrida calls an "indivisibility" of identity (*Apories* 29). The bearer of a passport and a visa is also the bearer of the name printed thereon; this bearer is also therefore supposed to be the same person he or she was yesterday and the day before. But, as Hajila's case so aptly illustrates, *travel can provoke change*. Hajila is a new woman following her escapades in the sunlight; transnational trekkers cannot circle the globe without being affected by the things they see and do, touch and feel.

In a variety of interviews, Assia Djebar has confirmed the value of space to her personal development as a writer. In her view, crossing the threshold as a girl of ten or eleven coincided with her birth as a writer: "I believe that the first experience of consciousness the young girl at puberty—at the age of ten or eleven—takes place at the moment when she is going to go out, when she is going to cross the threshold. . . . I believe that for me, that was my birth to writing" (*Lieux d'écriture*). Writing therefore goes hand in hand with leaving the intimate space of the harem and heading out of doors. Djebar's writing style is intricately intertwined with *mobility*, and she owes her "larger geographical space" to the French language that permitted her to leave the home: "The French language gave me a larger geographical space. In my life as a woman I move a great deal. I write in cafés. I am in the street as much as I am inside and I owe that to my education in French. I received this mobility as something acquired" (*Terres francophones*).

Like Djebar, the characters in her novels become enamored with travel. The woman's voice that addresses Hajila in *Ombre sultane* knows what she is talking about when she evokes Hajila's wanderings. Isma is accustomed to such wanderings herself, and on a much grander scale. This first wife of "the man" became so enthralled with freely moving about the streets that she found Hajila, unbeknownst to the latter, and set her up as her successor in the home. Isma then departed alone to pursue her personal desires for adventure, we learn through the course of the narrative.[8] Her walks in the city where she lived spurred her on to travel the world and explore numerous other urban settings.[9] Isma's individual life "journey" makes the important point that women can escape subjection, recover "subjectivity" and gain status as subjects through travel. Isma's nomadic lifestyle also circles back to the question of the Francophone writer from the Maghreb—man or woman—and the desire to travel.

Transnationality: Urban Attractions

In his essay "A Colonial Labyrinth," Khatibi makes the following definitional statement about the nation: "In principle, each nation is a plurality, a mosaic of cultures, if not a plurality of languages and genealogies" (10). While this proclamation undoubtedly holds true for many nations, the North African countries known under the heading of the "Maghreb" are saliently marked by "plurality." The native countries of Djebar and Khatibi have storied pasts that have yielded distinctively "plural" societies rich in varying peoples, customs, traditions, religions, and languages.[10] The title of a collection of essays by Khatibi underscores the plural constitution of this region of the world: *Maghreb pluriel* (1983). This exposure to many differences concentrated in a relatively small geographical space may provide the impetus to travel. Maghrebian-born writers, aware of differences from early childhood, may be inclined to search for *more* differences, to continue their personal trajectories to new places, to take in fresh sights and sounds. The intense sensory stimulation in the medina accustoms Maghrebians to the new and unusual; strolling the labyrinthine streets appears to drive Djebar and Khatibi to seek unexplored urban spaces, elsewhere, beyond the borders of their native lands.[11]

The many cities Djebar and Khatibi visit make their way into their books in various ways. The importance of international urban centers as loci of people and cultures, as intense and concentrated places where different languages and customs come together, is undeniable in the writings of these intercontinental travelers. Cities not only provide a location and setting for the book; they often become characters themselves. They adopt individual traits and distinguishing features that make them come alive as if they were "living beings." The titles of some of Djebar's more recent works highlight the place of the "city": *Femmes d'Alger dans leur appartement, Loin de Médine, Oran, langue morte* and *Nuits de Strasbourg* immediately situate the text geographically.[12] Mapping the city—through descriptions of the streets and turns, through evocative passages containing parks, buildings, and cafés, and through mention of specific names of monuments and squares—is an essential part of Djebar's itinerant writing. Her "signature" markings at the end of each book reveal not only the dates of the book's creation; they are careful to underscore the *city* (and sometimes the *cities*) in which the book was conceived. But, while travel and cities are explicit themes in Djebar's writing, they assume crucial importance in Khatibi's numerous references to travel.

In *La Mémoire tatouée*, Khatibi outlines his journeys in a vertiginous tour of the globe. In the space of only twenty pages, Khatibi retraces his steps through a multitude of metropolises. He takes the reader on a whirlwind world tour: "London spread out its balance, its precision, its mask; I walked with conviction" (163); "It was Sofia under the snow" (168); "in India . . . I moved about the city" (169); "I had the keys to the city, ancestral Cordoba!" (170); "No plans on that day, walking through the Luxembourg Gardens" (173); "In Stockholm . . ." (175); "I was fleeing . . . to catch up with Havana" (177); "To flee New Delhi for Delhi, itself an indefatigable dispersion" (181); "Berlin to the left or the write, no matter!" (182). The breathless pace of these travels that seem to follow no logical path, the exhausting rhythm of these global city wanderings that have no apparent rhyme or reason, did have a *beginning*: there was a time of the first trip, the departure for Paris. Khatibi's recollection of that momentous occasion indicates that he knew this was the first of many voyages, that he was aware of his wanderlust and predicted he would soon become a nomad: "Before the departure for Paris, no promise to my mother to return intact: to depart forever. . . . She accepted my nomadic temptations, and she cried" (127). Taken together, Khatibi's texts can be seen as an endlessly moving world tour, continuing in the 2005 publication of *Féerie d'un mutant*. In this text, a central character named Med meets other characters in cities that include Berlin, Kyoto, New York, and Paris, in a disconnected narrative that seems to move to the rhythms of the jazz backdrop. This book itself has no end, if we trust the narrative voice ("The end of the Book? Rather its metamorphosis, a new transposition" 68), but constitutes another phrase in the "*Musique errante*" that is Khatibi's corpus.

The initial, significant moment of leaving the African continent for Europe is a crucial border crossing for any Maghrebian subject.[13] Traversing the sea, heading north, marks much more than a simple geographical displacement; it constitutes a transition to a different frame of mind. The Mediterranean can be seen to divide the Orient and the Occident, splitting the East and West neatly into two neatly separated categories. Taking the boat to France disconnects the Maghrebian subject not just from his or her native country, but also from his or her cultural background. After this crossing, the subject's intellectual and emotional outlook is forever changed; in Khatibi's analysis, there is no going back:

> Other-thought [*Pensée-autre*], that of non-return to the inertia of the foundations of our being. The Maghreb, here, designates the name of this separation, of this non-return to the model of its religion and its theology (no matter how well disguised under revolutionary ideologies), non-return that can shake up, in theory and in practice, the bases of Maghrebian societies in the element of their as-yet-unformulated constitution by the critique that should overturn it. This "other-thought" is posed in response to the great questions that shake the world today, due to the planetary deployment of sciences, techniques, and strategies. (*Maghreb pluriel* 12–13)

Despite the seemingly insurmountable differences involved in ways of thinking on the European and African continents, Maghrebian writers who experienced the period of decolonization can find useful theoretical frameworks among philosophers of the "West." I would argue that it is not an accident that an influential contemporary philosophical thinker originates from the Maghreb as well. Derrida's reflection on *différance* may be due, in part, to his unusual upbringing in plural Algerian society. Khatibi has drawn particular inspiration from "deconstruction" and established a direct commonality between it and decolonization.[14] The Moroccan highlights the usefulness of western thoughts on difference to the writings of Maghrebians exposed to this philosophy:

> That's why when we dialogue with western thoughts on difference (those of Nietzsche, Heidegger, and among our close contemporaries, Maurice Blanchot and Jacques Derrida), we take into account not only their way of thinking, but also their strategy and their war machinery, to put them to use in our struggle which is, necessarily, another conjuration of the mind, demanding an effective decolonization, a concrete thought on difference. (*Maghreb pluriel* 20)

Khatibi thus favors a reappropriation of western philosophy for use among Maghrebian thinkers. This method of using tools acquired through the former colonizer to further the former colonized subject's own ends is an effective way of overturning the negative results of prior misuse of power in the colony.

Khatibi's use of the term "machinerie de guerre" to refer to western philosophical thought as a possible "strategy" recalls Deleuze and Guattari's study of nomadic lifestyles.[15] The recurrence of this term "strategy" in these writings could easily be misunderstood to mean a calculated action undertaken to realize a specific predetermined goal. I would like to suggest that the nomadic lifestyles of Maghrebian subjects entail an entirely different sort of "strategy," one that falls in line with Deleuze and Guattari's understanding of the nomad "territory": "The nomad has a territory, he follows customary routes, he goes from one point to another; he is not unaware of the points. . . . A trajectory is always between two points, but the *in-between* has taken on all the weight, and enjoys autonomy as if it were a proper direction. The life of the nomad is *intermezzo*" (471, my emphasis). The word "intermezzo," with its musical connotations, is appropriate to describe the jaunts of Khatibi and Djebar who frequently "flit" from one place to another, finding themselves en route, in the position of "*l'entre-deux*." This "in-between" is not static, nor is it marked by lack of creativity: it is a "place" for gathering motifs, and momentum, for making music with words.

As we saw in the last chapter, Hélène Cixous's approach to what she calls her "Algerian accidence" results in taking pleasure in passing, and giving up the illusion of "arriving": "it was by 'arriving' in France without finding my way or my self that I discovered: the chance of my genealogy and history arranged things in such a way that I would *stay passing*" ("My Algeriance" 169–70). Cixous's view of her life's trajectory resonates with Deleuze and Guattari's description of the nomad, for whom the earth becomes simply soil or support:

> For the nomad, on the contrary, it is deterritorialization that constitutes the relationship to the earth, so that he reterritorializes himself according to deterritorialization itself. It is the earth that deterritorializes itself, in such a way that the nomad finds a territory there. The earth ceases to be earth and tends to become simply soil or support. The earth does not deterritorialize itself in its global and relative movement, but in its precise places, there where the forest recedes, and where the steppe and the desert take over. (473)

When Cixous asserts that she does not seek to take "root" in life, that she doesn't feel a "need to belong," and that she never desired a "localized country" but instead found that "the world sufficed" (167–68), she is embracing the sort of "deterritorialization" theorized by Deleuze and Guattari. Though she took off *in the direction of* France, she never *arrived* there. In fact, France never was a destination; nor will it ever be: "I went toward France, without having had the idea of arriving there. Once in France I was not there. I saw that I would never arrive in France" (169). For contemporary Maghrebian-born globetrotters, travel is not the same as aimless wandering, yet many are not going *anywhere* in particular. In these nomadic trips, what matters is most frequently not a destination but movement itself.

As Deleuze and Guattari's reflections show, the wanderer is not *lacking* a territory; it is not *for want of* a place to settle down that the Maghrebian writers evoked here choose to travel the world. It is instead a desire to leave possession and security behind and venture out into the unknown; an intense interest in open, undefined spaces compels writers like Djebar and Khatibi to explore: "The nomadic trajectory [. . .] distributes men (or beasts) in an open space, indefinite, *non communiquant*" (*Mille plateaux* 472). The words "*non communiquant*" carry the meaning of "unconnected" in English; the open spaces traversed by the nomad can be understood to be not directly "in contact" with other spaces. This idea is applicable to contemporary means of travel; underground transportation systems like the "Métro" and the "Chunnel" move people from one location to another effectively, but travelers cannot "see" where they are going. This lack of visibility means that those who employ these means of transportation suddenly emerge at their destination; they step out of the vehicle often feeling disoriented, transported as they are from one spot to another, from one distinct environment to a vastly different one without any continuity. Modern travel can be experienced in these ways as inherently *disconnected*. But the French verb "*communiquer*" also refers to communication, notably through speech. Verbal expression is sometimes shut off, or even "shut up," in the open space of the outdoors. The importance of language and translation—as well as silence and *untranslatability*—becomes strident when Maghrebian-born writers take to the road.

Plurality Within, and Without (Borders)

The plurality of Maghrebian society, already addressed in the comments of Khatibi in works such as *Maghreb pluriel*, takes obvious form in the multiplicity of languages concentrated in North Africa. The coexistence of many languages in Morocco and Algeria opens the door to a plurality of possibilities for Maghrebian subjects. In an interview for a television show aired in France, *Droit d'auteurs*, Assia Djebar insisted on the multilingual situation in her native land: "All that is living in Algeria (not only women) is always in a constant bilingualism, trilingualism with dialectical Arabic. I insist on this. In other words: a living Arabic, with an Arabic and a Berber, a Berber and a French (tongue)." Djebar goes on to give her opinion on what she considers to be one of the leading causes of the current contentious situation in Algeria: the imposition of literary Arabic on the Algerian people. This imposition of a culture and a language in opposition to the living culture and popular language has created chaos. Languages and cultures evolve over time; they cannot be controlled by external powers. When governmental authorities engage in such efforts, the results can only be harmful to the people. Maghrebian subjects need space to move, to change, to absorb novelty, and to *translate* into ever-new forms of expression.[16]

Transportation, or traveling from one place to another, necessarily involves translation, as Khatibi has pointed out in *Maghreb pluriel*. In Khatibi's analysis, passing from one language to another requires a translation that parallels transportation. In other words, a linguistic displacement *should* accompany a geographic one. He addresses this linkage with respect to metaphysical duality (western versus Islamic worldviews): "don't we risk passing from one to the other without shedding light on the translation and the transportation that are in operation there, imperceptibly, from one archeology to the other and from one language to the other?" (57). Khatibi's insistence on bringing to light the process of translation is pertinent to all texts composed by nomadic Maghrebian writers. Moving about, changing continents and cultures, requires changing sign systems and languages. Translation is inherent in travel, and those born in the Maghreb are predisposed to understanding this because of the plural languages spoken in their native lands.

While the Magrebian society at large is multilingual, as we have seen, Algerian-born Cixous was first exposed to multiple tongues within the microcosm of the home, in lighthearted fun: "We played at languages in our house." (168). The good-humored, jovial nature of these linguistic games enacted by her multilingual parents spared the young Cixous from any rigid sense of belonging to one specific mother (or father) tongue: "That translinguistic and loving sport sheltered me from all obligation or vague desire of obedience (I did not think that French was my mother tongue, it was a language in which my father taught me) to *one* mother-father tongue" (169). I would like to highlight Cixous's use of the word "translinguistic" in this childhood reminiscence. This introduction to languages beyond borders prepared Cixous for numerous travels and a lack of "adherence" to one country or nation, or even one continent: "My languages slid into each other's ear from one continent to another" (169). Her early "translinguistic" exposure enticed her to become a writer, a novelist, and a theorist who plays with multiple languages in the text. This "translinguistic" potential is visible in Khatibi's written work as well, where he uses his knowledge of many tongues to form a truly "multilingual text," with words and phrases from Swedish, Spanish, Arabic, German, Italian, and English interspersed throughout and intertwined with the French text. As Philippe Barbé argues in an essay on Djebar's *Les Nuits de Strasbourg*, this sort of "translinguistic" writing carries with it possibilities for changed identities, beyond national borders: "More than a monolangue expressing her lost Algerian roots, Djebar is trying to explore and map out, in the Alsatian context, a translinguistic territory that would allow her characters to recompose a new transnational identity supported by a linguistic interpenetration between French, German, Arabic, Alsatian, and English" ("Transnational" 130). Creating what Barbé calls "a translinguistic territory" in the written text, multilingual Maghrebian subjects can carve out a place for a "transnational identity" that is not limited to any one, or any two, language(s) or land(s).

As we have seen, "bilingualism" is not an appropriate word to designate the situation of Maghrebian subjects. Duality, or a clear contrast between two opposing categories—whether linguistic, cultural, religious, or other—is not a characteristic of Maghrebian society. As a result, the Maghrebian subject's worldview is complex from the get-go. Djebar and Khatibi cannot divide the world simply in two, they cannot define things in opposition to facile categorical "others." Instead, they must take into account the continuum of differences on a global scale. Moving beyond duality, beyond the borders that might separate "French" and "Arabic" cultures and languages, these Maghrebian subjects confirm through intercontinental trips what they have always known: defining the world is not easy.

Trailblazing, Trekking, and Trotting (the Globe)

There are difficulties involved in travel; there are inconveniences—for body and mind—that could be avoided if the subject chose to remain at "home," but these writers know from the outset that the very concept of "home" is problematic. Their plural societies make them realize that the ideas of "*patrie*" and "*chez-soi*" are relative and therefore fraught with difficulty. These Maghrebian "nomads" have responded to this realization by making their home in the world. They are not tied to national assignation; they are unconcerned with "belonging" to a "community" that is rooted in a specific place and tongue. They are instead, to use a word coined by Khatibi in the literary review *L'Intertextuel*, "internationalists": subjects who don't fit anywhere in particular, but who are, paradoxically, always at home.[17]

The question of travel, of physical displacement and corporeal movement, immediately evokes the question of bodies. People travel as embodied beings. While it is possible to be "transported" by words and ideas, by fiction and philosophy, the travel undertaken and addressed by Khatibi, as well as Djebar, consists of real, concrete, physical movement through space. Their trips resemble treks, in the sense that they require continuous, strenuous effort. These world travelers are often subject to stereotypical categorization because of their racial background. But I would argue that these idiosyncratic Moroccan and Algerian "natives" who serve as trailblazers, carving out very idiosyncratic paths, cannot be taken as truly "representative" of the regions where they were born. To the contrary, they must be seen as distinctly different, having opted for personal trajectories that meander and wander throughout the world. These individual paths have shaped and formed unique, singular characters (both inside and outside their written work) who defy logical categorical definitions and who escape any fixed labels because of their constant movement. They cannot be pinned down.

Unlike members of various nomadic tribes, Khatibi does not stick with his own in his travels. His itineraries are of his own choosing, often whimsical and self-indulgent, but always his own. In his fiction, the writer provides numerous examples of frequent, extensive excursions to the places that suit his fancy: "He had been assailed by all the colors. He took on their brilliance and, changing shape many times, went forward, lived endlessly, fell, was born again. Men accompanied him every step of the way: he borrowed their footsteps, the track of their tracks, traveling from country to country. He was seen to appear in different places, to run with unbelievable joy" (*Love* 45). While the joys and stimulations of these trips are manifold, and he finds himself enamored with travel in and of itself, "What he loved about the sea was the ancient idea of wandering. . . . Euphoric balancing: to be this flow, to be nothing but this flow" (44), Khatibi also alludes to the inherent *difficulty* of constant displacement: "He set off to explore the world, follow the track of his fictions. [. . .] No word belonged to him, not even his own name; but henceforth no one could speak for him. [. . .] His body was shaken with a nervous tremor, with a staggering density" (37). Extensive travel makes *everything* foreign; no words—not even one's own name—seem natural when one is constantly moving from one to another, with no place to set down roots and no place in particular to call home.

It is worthy of note that both Khatibi and Djebar engage in a writing rife with references to silence and shouts. These two extremes mark the limits of expression, the borders frequented by these wandering subjects in their many crossings. The aphasia Khatibi's narrator experiences when he travels finds its reverberation in the silence Djebar's characters experience when they step out of doors to view the open world. Hajila is utterly speechless when she removes her veil and takes to her feet in *Ombre sultane*. An inability to speak also accompanies the fugitive mother of the narrator in *Vaste est la prison*. In contrast, the autobiographical voice of *L'Amour, la fantasia*, relates an occasion in which she emits a terrifying cry as she walks alone on Rue Richelieu, in Paris: "Stop when I reach the end; simultaneously switch off this outlandish voice, this *lamento* which I involuntarily sing" (116). This cry not only startles a witness in the streets, it startles the narrator who is unaware of her high-pitched squeal.[18] The cry *and* the stifled cry are elements over which the urban wanderer may have little or no control. But crying out against certain things through writing is something over which intellectuals from the Maghreb have ultimate command.

Maghrebian-born writers drawn to travel may be equally drawn to crying out against injustices experienced along the journey, or screaming against the difficulty of accurately rendering the myriad peoples and experiences with which he or she comes into contact. A multitude of trips can only complicate an individual's view of an already complex global system. Visiting other countries and cultures firsthand, experiencing new foods, games, and ways of life in person may help facilitate understanding, but they also make any attempt at generalization difficult. Khatibi knows, with intimate certainty, that there are no easy answers to the truly difficult questions encapsulated in identity and language. This expert of "ambulatory sciences," to borrow a term from Deleuze and Guattari, allows space in his writing for the unknown, for the unusual and the inexplicable. Deleuze and Guattari provide this explanation of nomadic lifestyles and the "conclusions" that can be drawn from them:

> [A]mbulatory or nomadic sciences are not destined to take autonomous power or development. They don't have the means, because they subordinate all their operations to intuition and to construction, *following* the flow of matter, *tracing* and *joining* smooth space. (462–63)

This reflection recalls the poetic passage (cited above) from Khatibi's *Love in Two Languages*, in which the Moroccan writer tells of his love for the sea and his desire to be in this body of water's flow. Khatibi does not seek mastery or dominion; power is the last thing to enter his mind. Instead, travel represents an opening to multiplicity and *difference*.

Roughing It / Toughing It Out: Far from the Mainstream

Writers today can lend themselves to nomadic existences and still produce literary work with relatively little effort. New technology in the form of portable computers, fax machines, Internet operations, and so forth allow for writing in many forms in almost any geographical location. Physical displacement can no longer be seen as an impediment to creative literary production. This flexibility encourages more and more travel as stimulus for new ideas and innovative writing. But Khatibi, while he may make use of them, is not enamored only with international cybercafés. The type of travel he undertakes—walking streets and swimming in the ocean, sleeping and eating with the people of the cities they visit—is not that of the dispassionate tourist in a bus. His trips entail a corporeal "investment" in the new place and space. Smells and sounds are enhanced when travelers take the time, establishing a special rhythm, to absorb them in tandem with tangible, "hands-on," "total immersion" activities. He is fully engrossed in the subtle differences that make each person, and each city, distinct from the next.

The figure of the labyrinth, theorized by Khatibi in relation to the colonial city, is important to understanding the writer's seemingly insatiable wanderlust. The labyrinthine design of the colonial city not only educates them in the "strategy" of urban navigation, it also imparts to them a fearless desire to go forward, further, beyond the borders of the city, the country and the continent. In this, it is important to insist on the unique layout of the labyrinth. Unlike a maze, the labyrinth traditionally contains no dead ends. It may take a lot of wandering to find one's way to the center of the twists and curves, but one is assured either of reaching the innermost part or of winding one's way back to the beginning, to the point of departure. When advancing in a labyrinth, the task is to steadily continue forward; there is no preoccupation with false leads or sudden traps. Unlike the bold explorers of old, Maghrebian travelers today are certainly aware of the "global" nature of our planet; they don't fear falling off any sudden precipices that might mark "the edge of the earth." Their freedom of movement and desire to travel is ultimately due to the fact that those from Algeria and Morocco are not scared of getting lost. They are not petrified about finding their way home. They are assured that they can always find their way back to the point of origin if they so desire; but they don't hold to their home that tightly, having found a larger homeland in the world, and notably in the world of literature. They are not very concerned about where they started from—in large part because of a troublesome recent history of French colonization in North Africa—and they are even less concerned with where they will ultimately end up. What matters is not the first nation or the last in life's journey, therefore, but the trip across countries in the meantime, what I call "the transnational trek."

Constantly crossing borders, Khatibi is forever at the margins, as are the other writers in this study. It is appropriate that "margin" is an anagram for the adjectival designation "Maghrebian," for even as children in the mixed societies of Morocco, Algeria, and Tunisia, Maghrebians are frequently "on the border," both geographically and figuratively. The very word "Maghreb," used to designate this region of North Africa, is a relative term: meaning "sunset" in Arabic, the Maghreb is thus a synonym for "west," the direction where the sun goes down. This designation reveals a particular point of view, a singular perspective that could easily be manipulated through a change in location. One can chase sunsets, but one can never "reach" them, no matter how hard one tries. Just as Cixous admits that she has never arrived in France despite years of living in the country, so other Maghrebian-born writers like Djebar and Khatibi seem to demonstrate a firm awareness of the impossibility of ever really "capturing" a location, be it their homeland or an adopted country of residence. In response, they just keep going, they are continually "on the go," absorbing new experiences and taking in new spaces. They know that place doesn't matter as much as language, and they explore, through multilingual awareness and practice, the translinguistic potential to create new transnational identities.

For Khatibi, traveling is made up of much more than a passing fancy or a fashionable vacation trip. For this Maghrebian-born writer, trekking through countries and across continents is a way of life, opening up to true explorations and significant encounters that inspire new writing. The perpetual "in-between" state of this writer is the most provocative place to inhabit, and yields the most active literary production. Most importantly, it paves the way for multilingual translation in the written work. The presence of two "K"s in Khatibi's full name is significant, for it is meant to highlight the foreign nature of this appellation to the French language, where this letter is uncommon. In Abdelkébir Khatibi's very name, therefore, translation is already obviously at play. When he incorporates Swedish, Spanish, Arabic, and other languages into the French text, the reader begins to reap the true benefits of "transnational trekking."

Translittérations: "Labor on the Letter"

In "Incipits," an essay in a collection titled *Du bilinguisme*, Khatibi addresses Arabic appellations at length, focusing specifically on the French transliteration of the first and last names of fellow Maghrebian writer, Abdelwahab Meddeb. Khatibi maintains that the transliterated author's name on the cover of the novel *Talismano* represents, from the very first letter, "already a translation, or rather a complete transformation" (173). The implications of this transformation of the name are significant for the reading—or the "deciphering"—of the literary text, beginning with its cover: "The immense importance of the name, [. . .] I will only highlight here the literary effect of bilingualism and the operation of translation that present themselves here, from the beginning, as the double introduction to a text still closed, and that is waiting to be deciphered" (172). Khatibi's reading of several key passages from Meddeb's autobiographical work uncovers the two stages the author's surname has undergone in its "translation" from the original. In Khatibi's analysis, this particular case illustrates a "double transformation" in its passage from Arabic to French: "The transformation of a name: from the sacral and literary *koïné* to the Tunisian dialectical Arabic (diglossia), then from diglossia to the French (colonial) graphic" (178). Meddeb's own analysis of the harm done to his last name hones in on the derogatory change in meaning that accompanies the first alteration, from "*Mu-'addib*," meaning "master," to "*Middib*," referring to a simple "teacher" of children. The complete removal of sense is the worst blow, however, for the "stigmata of colonial intervention" reach their climax in the hasty copy errors of French officials who defy phonic resemblance *and* what the writer calls "*la logique translit-*

térale." The "Frenchification" of the surname—in accordance with the "*devoir municipal*"—may be well intended, but this action "transliterally" butchers the appellation, turning it finally into Meddeb (*Talismano* 218).

It is important to note that transliteration from one alphabet to another is by definition an "inexact" operation. The same name in Arabic can render a variety of equivalents in languages that use the Latin alphabet, as evidenced in different versions such as "Fatima" and "Fatma," "Malika" and "Maleka," "Isma" and "Esma" from the writings of Assia Djebar, or even "Khatibi" and "Kateb." The resemblance between the surnames of Kateb Yacine, the Algerian writer best known for his 1956 French-language novel *Nedjma*, and Abdelkébir Khatibi points to a similar origin in Arabic.[19] But this name—and the occupation it points to—isn't all the two writers have in common, of course. It is no surprise that Khatibi turns to Kateb in "Incipits," to examine the effect of the name on the written work in French: "this author does not write his own language, he transcribes his transformed proper name, he cannot possess anything (if it can be said that one appropriates a language), he possesses neither his maternal tongue that is not written, nor the written Arabic tongue that is alienated and given as substitution, nor this other learned tongue that tells him to disappropriate himself and efface himself in it" (189). Khatibi is addressing his own case as much as he is Kateb's in this passage. Between a lost mother tongue and a learned language that remains forever out of reach, the writer from the Maghreb can claim nothing as his "own," not even his name.

If Khatibi cannot address the name without placing it in linguistic context in the quotation above, it is because of the specific, meticulous work focusing on the "letter" in translating from Arabic to French. Khatibi carefully delineates the functioning of Meddeb's text, "I now attach myself to his work studio" (184), paying attention to the lexical use of dialectical Arabic in *Talismano* and the translation that accompanies this use.[20] The demanding task of the translator from the Maghreb is reminiscent of Antoine Berman's analysis of literal translation: "Here 'literal' means: attached to the letter (of works). Labor on the letter in translation is more *originary* than restitution of meaning. It is through this labor that translation, on the one hand, restores the particular signifying processes of works (which is more than their meaning) and, on the other hand, *transforms the translating language*" (297, my emphasis). Khatibi's evocation of the many new words invented and commented in Meddeb's text exhibits the transforming potential of these works. His treatment of this particular novel also reveals that paying close attention to the letter and its meaning is a practice that stems from the transliteration of the first letter, (that) of the name.[21]

In his treatment of the proper name in the context of translation in "Des Tours de Babel," Derrida provides a concrete example of the difference between rendering a common noun and a proper name in another tongue. Using the French word *"pierre,"* meaning "rock," and the proper name that is its homonym, Derrida asserts that the first term must be translated in order to communicate its meaning: "The noun *pierre* belongs to the French language, and its translation into a foreign language should in principle transport its meaning" (*Acts* 110). The first name "Pierre," however, does not belong to the language in the same way and is therefore not "translated" into a foreign language in identical fashion: "This is not the case with *Pierre*, whose inclusion in the French language is not assured and in any case is not of the same type. 'Peter' in this sense is not a *translation* of *Pierre*" (110). It is my contention that the "untranslatability" of the proper name is magnified in the case of Khatibi, as well as that of Assia Djebar, whose appellations in Arabic must be "doubly transformed," to pick up on Khatibi's terminology, in the process of transliteration.[22] This double transformation echoes the process of translation in the text, as I understand it, for "transcription" and "transposition" are complementary concepts necessary to understanding the unique writing of these wordsmiths.

Transcribing, Transposing: The Musical

The Francophone works of Khatibi are not "translations" in the normal sense of the word. They are composed directly in French, and no "original" exists in another language, whether the Arabic dialect of his native land, the Berber tongues spoken by his mother, or the other languages with which he has become familiar as a result of his travels and studies. This is why I have opted to apply two musical expressions, "transcriptions" and "transpositions" to the operations he undertakes in French. His texts are "transcriptions" in a double sense, the first of which refers to copying, or taking down spoken words, and this action is also appropriate to describe the work of other Maghrebian-born writers. This is the challenge Cixous accepts when she attempts to find the appropriate textual notations to render her mother's unique accent and expressions in French; this task is perhaps even more difficult for Djebar, who struggles to render in French voices that recount stories in their native Arabic and Berber tongues in Algeria. She affirms her project by insisting that her transcriptions do not stifle these voices, but give them room to breathe and space to live (on). Their writings, and those by Khatibi, can be called "transcriptions" in a musical sense because their rendering of the sounds and scents of their surroundings in North Africa in the

French text is equivalent to composing an arrangement for another instrument. They remain true to the original context, but they transcribe the strains and their refrains for a different medium. This understanding of "transcriptions" resonates with the concept of "transpositions." The change in instrument is accompanied by a similar change in key, a modification in tonality. Just as trained musicians become adept at transposing notes written for a C instrument to a B flat instrument, so these practiced writers become skillful at composing in another key.

The ideas of "transposition" and "transcription" are not mine; they are leitmotifs in Khatibi's work, subtly reappearing throughout his first publication in French, *La Mémoire tatouée*. In an aptly titled section, *"Fugue sur la Différence,"* the writer takes us on a transcontinental trip that includes a stopover in Sweden, and this is where "transposition" slips into the text: "Fashionable principle of paradise and transposition on a lovers' bench, whose word, they tell us, was caught by an invisible microphone" (176).[23] As for "transcription," this idea permeates the opening passages, in which the autobiographical text is likened to this form of copying: "To make a childhood, nothing will close off the idea of a transcription" (26). This conception of the writing project is reiterated in the preface penned on the occasion of the publication of a new edition of the book: "How to transcribe, without trembling, in a singular autobiography, the narrative of one's life and death?" (10). In his use of these terms with their rich musical connotations, Khatibi points to the depth and variety of his compositions. Going beyond the "interlingual" and the "intralingual" types of translation identified by Roman Jakobson, Khatibi incorporates music into the written text in ways that echo and reverberate beyond what Jakobson terms the "intersemiotic" (151): "The intersemiotic transports one to the others and all together: the text, music, and the visual" (*La Mémoire* 208). Translation as movement opens up language to the multiple forces that influence it, as we will see in the chapter to come. The textual compositions in French by Maghrebian-born writers Djebar and Khatibi are riddled with waves that belong to other tongues, linguistic and other, in all their forms of expression.

Notes

1. Roman Jakobson distinguishes "three ways of interpreting a verbal sign: it may be translated into other signs of the same language, into another language, or into another, nonverbal system of symbols" (145). He labels the first of these kinds of translation "intralingual" and the second "interlingual," or "translation proper."

2. A recent article by Sarah Smith provides this succinct description of the board game of go: "Essentially a territorial contest (its Chinese name, Wei Qi, means 'surrounding game') with roots in both Chinese and Japanese history."

3. In his autobiographical *La Mémoire tatouée*, Khatibi gives us these initials in a whirlwind review of the historical events that have marked his life: "*Le jour de la Très Grande Violence, bien sûr!*" (107). This day of the Very Great Violence points to the end of the colonial presence in Morocco, and signals the coming of independence.

4. In an interview for France Culture regarding *Benjamin à Montaigne*, Hélène Cixous talks about the trip around which this work of fiction is oriented. This journey (supposed to be a "return") gives the writer occasion to speak to modern modes of travel, and to point out precisely the lack of contact with the ground during her mother and aunt's privileged welcome in native town: "Their adventure is this: after fifty-five years they are invited to return (and each word becomes difficult to say, what does it mean 'to return'?) to their native town, Osnabrück, a small German town where they have never again set foot. And where besides, after having given in to the invitation [. . .], what happens to them—which is a metaphor or a paradox—is that they are not allowed to put their feet on the ground. They are royal guests in their role as Jewish survivors, as remainders, they are constantly carried, transported in luxurious modes of transportation, and their feet never make contact with the earth."

5. Repetition is arguably never exactly the same, especially in the situation of Hajila whose emergence into the daylight takes place in an entirely different context after her marriage. Derek Attridge, in an introduction to an anthology of Derrida's work in English translation, explains the conception of "iterability" in the following manner: "the necessary repeatability of any item experienced as meaningful, which at the same time can never be repeated exactly since it has no essence that could remain unaffected by the potentially infinite contexts (which are always contexts within contexts . . .) into which it could be grafted" (18).

6. In an interview for the television program *Lieux d'écriture*, Assia Djebar maintains that she has transported her inner taboos with her, despite her geographical and temporal distance from Algeria. Her comments demonstrate that perhaps no amount of travel can fully annihilate ingrained ways of thinking: "I think I transported within me my own taboos due to my Arab education and what ties me to my mother, my grandmother, and other women. And my concern in my novels is to make [readers] feel these interiorized taboos. It would be necessary for me to at once deliver myself from them and shed light on them."

7. Following the ignominious terrorist attacks of September 2001, the United States placed tighter security on all travelers, especially those entering the nation from abroad. Even well-established professors from elsewhere with regular appointments, like Derrida and Cixous, had difficulty obtaining visas for trips to the U.S.

8. The narrator, Isma, admits to her earlier deeds and explains the reasons for her actions midway through the novel: "I needed to reflect, and for that I needed to be out of doors! To walk, to look strangers in the face. I needed to be out of doors, but

to be forgotten! In a manner of speaking, to be annihilated! . . . Yes, I did run away. . . . I wrecked everything!" (80–81).

9. In a study of the pedestrian "mapping" carried out in Isma and Hajila's different trajectories, Adrian Fielder sheds light on the positive potential of outdoor movement for Algerian women beyond borders. He highlights the noticeable differences between Isma's and Hajila's "navigations" in the following comment: "Isma moves freely about a transnational space through creative and exuberant navigations of different cities, whereas Hajila must overcome her initial immobility to learn how to map out her own environment" (109). Isma's initial wanderings in the colonial city may have prepared her—even "trained" her—for longer, more involved globetrotting. Fielder's conclusions about the "possibilities for dialogue" among Algerian women seem to depend on the intersection of the local and the global, a conclusion that would resonate with Sara Ahmed's reflection on "feminism and globality" in *Strange Encounters: Embodied Others in Post-Coloniality*. In Ahmed's view, the local and the global must be articulated as a site of *differentiation* (178).

10. In her preface to *An Algerian Childhood*, Anne Donadey explains that North Africa's strategic position between the Mediterranean sea and the Saharan desert have made it a place of "multiple commercial, cultural, and violent encounters. . . . As a consequence, North African people have diverse origins: Arab, Black, Berber, and mixed blood" (vii).

11. I would argue that it is no accident that Djebar and Khatibi are magnetically drawn to cities. In "DissemiNation," critic Homi Bhabha calls attention to the place of the city as a postcolonial "gathering" space: "it is to the city that the migrants, the minorities, the diasporic come to change the history of the nation" (319–20). This is a phenomenon that marks our contemporary existence: "in the west, and increasingly elsewhere, it is the city which provides the space in which emergent identifications and new social movements of the people are played out. It is there that, in our time, the perplexity of the living is most acutely experienced" (320). Finally, and I contend that this is especially true in the "border" cities of the Maghreb, the city is the location where history and language place inhabitants in a position of *translation*: "For it is by living on the borderline of history and language, on the limits of race and gender, that we are in a position to translate the differences between them into a kind of solidarity" (320).

12. Cities also make up the titles of some of Cixous's recent books, such as *Osnabrück* and *Manhattan*, but these locations are less straightforward than they might seem; the "action" of *Osnabrück* takes place in the Algeria of Cixous's childhood, for instance, while the city of the title is only an imagined location.

13. For most, this departure is definitive; they will not return to their native land for more than a brief stay after this rupture. This is the case of Djebar and Cixous, for example. Khatibi is an exception to this rule.

14. In *Maghreb pluriel*, Khatibi establishes a temporal and philosophical link between "deconstruction" and "decolonization"; the critical thought attributed to

Jacques Derrida that shakes up western metaphysics accompanied decolonization in its historical event (47–48).

15. Deleuze and Guattari refer to "machines de guerre" with respect to families in nomad units. They rely on the renowned Algerian historian Ibn Khaldoun, whom Assia Djebar quotes frequently, for their information and analysis of the ways "war machines" in nomadic societies function differently from those in the nation-state (453).

16. The next chapter will focus on this multilingual situation found in the Maghreb, a situation that is often overlooked in critical reviews that focus on "bilingualism." Morocco and Algeria cannot be contained within the Arabic/French duel that so often pervades contemporary criticism of written works emerging from the pens of Maghrebian-born writers. Berber is a crucial third tongue influencing these writers. Spanish is particularly present in Morocco, but it can also be heard in Algeria, and other tongues such as Hebrew are often spoken in mixed Maghrebian societies. This consideration of multiple tongues opens up even greater opportunities for linguistic play and innovation in speaking and writing.

17. In Khatibi's words, "Insofar as I am a writer and an intellectual, I want to present myself as an interanationalist. I write in French, a language I did not inherit, but in which I am a professional foreigner" (L'Intertextuel 12). In Cixous's Les Rêveries de la femme sauvage, the mother presents herself as an "internationalist" of this sort, as a German Jew in a foreign land working as a midwife: "I have always been international. . . . As a midwife, I have always been international on my side. The baby is an international newborn" (107).

18. The "cries" of Djebar's tradition are important means of communication, as she reveals in this childhood memory of her mother's celebratory shouts: "My mother and our village nanny, who was a second mother to us, then let out that semi-barbaric 'you-you.' That prolonged, irregular, spasmodic cooing, which in our building reserved for teachers' families—all European except for ours—must have appeared incongruous, a truly primitive cry" (Fantasia 182). While the European-born inhabitants of her country might have misunderstood these yells, the young girl in whose honor they were let loose finds them agreeable: "there was more glory in this ostentatious clamour" (182). These "cries" are obviously a language of their own, subtle and varied, and outside the realm of easy translation. An article by Fatima Makherbeche titled "Youyous from here and youyous from there" provides a glimpse of the multiple capacities of this particular cry to communicate a whole range of emotions: "The youyou is the sound that comes from a vibration of the tongue and the rapid movement of the hand over the mouth; it is a guttural sound emitted by the vibration of vocal cords. It is above all collective because it is contagious, it is the sharing of an emotion with others. It is omnipresent, in all events of one's life, personal and familial, political. . . . It can also be the expression of joy, pain, or suffering" (45). The connection between such cries and music, and ultimately literary creation, is convincingly established in the work of Linda Lê: "The yells that escape from the black and gaping hole transform themselves into song. A song that raises up against the law, against the very authority of language" (335). "Cries" are ubiquitous in Khatibi's œuvre. In Le Livre du sang, a cry

is characteristic of "the music of Islam," marking the moment of the sacrifice that gave the narrator his name: "The music of Islam beats this way, for ears turned toward Mecca, capturing [. . .] a formidable cry, sustained from century to century, from millennium to millennium. The letting out of this cry, vrilling the orifice of the ear, pours over the latter with the dance of the mind" (64). *La Mémoire tatouée*, we discover that outcries are often associated with sexuality and pleasure ("strident cry of thousands of bordels at the edge of my nightmares" 35; "a woman quickly spreads her thighs to infinity, an opening fixes me, who cried?" 45); yells and screams seem to constantly accompany the narrator's travels: "A solo cry" (167); "Scream!" (181); "A solo cry" (181); etc.

19. Nafa Kamal breaks down the name "Khatibi" in the following manner: "First, the lexeme 'khat' that designates 'the trace of the written' in Arabic can 'semanticize' the 'K' and function as a signifying differential apt to express 'the written.' This meaning also contaminates the names '*KhaTiBi*' and '*KhaTBi*,' for they benefit from a relationship of *paronymie* with '*KhaT*.' These phonological and semantic slippings open up onto the verb 'to write' (*KaTaBa*) following a phonic analogy dependent on the phonemes /*KTB*/" (86).

20. It is no accident that Khatibi mentions first the verb "*médiner*" (184) and later connects this suggestive movement to the text's own topography: "time, the path of errancy (*médiner*, *médiner*) retains the topography of the text, its movement that jumps from one place to another, from one reference to another, from one language to another" ("Incipits" 185).

21. Khatibi devotes an early portion of his text to the very first letter of Abdel-wahab Meddeb's name: "I will say then that *Talismano* (the book's title, the book's cover) is inaugurated by the phoneme 'A', which opens the first name of the author" (173). His analysis of this letter continues for several pages, to illustrate that this text is profoundly affected by the inadequate rendering of this phoneme in French: "this text is hallucinated by this letter and its transformation" (175).

22. In contrast to Hélène Cixous, whose first name remains untouched in the passage to English, for example (even if "Helen" could serve as a "translation" of this "French" name), "Abdelkébir" and "Assia" are names that have already undergone considerable change when they appear on the cover of a work in French. Translation from one alphabet to another is arguably a necessity, whereas it is not obligatory in translations from one language to another within the same writing system.

23. The idea of "transposition" recurs in a recent text by Khatibi, *Vœu de silence*, in which the writer speaks of his vocation as a "poet" (in a large sense of the word) in its historical connection to music in different places, whether in southern France or Spain. He intimates that "transpositions" of contemporary literature reveal this heritage, that they serve as traces of this joyful past: "Singing in lyrical poetry was, from the time of the Andalusian *ghazal* and the troubadours, accompanied by music and dance, sometimes even by clowns and joyful satire. [. . .] Between the poet's word and silence, there exist transpositions of imprints, against a background of the abyss" (26).

CHAPTER SEVEN

~

Silence and Schizophrenia:
Subtle Slips of the Tongue

For each work is itself a border, a passageway and an obstacle between languages. It is a place of reincarnation for the writer, be he metropolitan or from outside the walls [extra-muros], to introduce (from French into French) idiomatic arrangements. It is a place to graft points of rupture, knots of dissidence and resistance in such a way that this language that we write—if we write—will be open to an infinite translation

—Abdelkébir Khatibi, *La Langue de l'Autre* (1999)

Maybe, in order to learn silence in the fold of each word, the poet is seeking to invent the very language of the unsayable [*l'indicible*].

—Abdelkébir Khatibi, *Vœu de silence* (2000)

The previous chapter centered on international travel and the importance of physical movement to the writings of Abdelkébir Khatibi and Assia Djebar. This chapter is a continuation and an elaboration of the particular types of translation at work in the compositions of these writers, focusing first on an ongoing textual dialogue between Jacques Derrida and Khatibi, and then examining the plurilingual aspects of "French" texts written by Khatibi and Djebar. In line with the Greek etymology of the "schizophrenia" portion of the title, then, this chapter is *split*: it comprises two parts that combine to provide a larger picture of the textual translation enacted by the writing subject who is manifestly "split," not simply *between two* cultures and languages, but *among a variety* of cultures and languages that make all forms of identifi-cation complicated for the writer of the self "in translation."

In an autobiographical piece that traces his idiosyncratic linguistic itin-erary, "Bilinguisme, dialogisme et schizophrénie," Bulgarian-born intellec-tual Tzvetan Todorov refers to the importance of appropriate *context* in the bilingual individual's experience. If each tongue is kept in its place, it isn't difficult to maintain one's sanity. Problems arise, however, when more than one language meet, especially when at least one is out of context, in a "polyphony" that threatens order and defies all semblance of "normalcy": "'Unrestrained polyphony' leads thus to schizophrenia, if we want to hang onto the common meaning of this term: personality splitting, mental inco-herence, and increased distress" (16). This particular form of madness threatens the hierarchy of established discourses and is therefore a menace of particular weight in totalitarian countries such as the one Todorov fled as a young dissident. The disconcerting experience of discovering that a speech prepared in French could not simply and harmlessly translate into his native tongue; everything changed when his location changed, and his instinctive reaction was to hush his words, to take shelter in silence: "If I lose my place of enunciation, I can no longer speak. I do not speak, there-fore I am not" (24).

The negative connection between silence and madness is disrupted in Khatibi's writing, as illustrated by this playful quotation: "Silence of the mad, nothing, absence of nothing, nothing! What island, West, have you found for your savages? And your buttocks in the tricolored flag, said the friend, *héhé*! *Héhé*!" (*La Mémoire* 186). While he gives place to silence in the writ-ten text,[1] much as Hélène Cixous does, Khatibi does not succumb to the "to-talitarian" forces that seek to make quiet the things that are not deemed wor-thy of speech, whether for the sake of "politics" or "literature." Losing a place of enunciation, in the case of Khatibi, does not mean shutting oneself up. In-stead, it entails a "dis-placed" sort of writing that emerges from a variety of places and speaks to different situations. Critic Réda Bensmaïa explains read-ing Khatibi's *Amour bilingue* in this way: "Something is moving, constantly shifting, thereby scrambling our reading of the text so that we cannot assign it (or bring it back to) a (geographical or rhetorical) place. 'Un mouvement de déport' (Barthes)—a 'trans-lation' interferes with our reading, making our access to the text even more difficult" (*Experimental Nations* 106). Bensmaïa goes on to describe how this textual movement works on the level of lan-guage: "Khatibi has switched languages, but he has done so in a breathtaking move that does not consist either in a reterritorializing return to Arabic or an Arabicization of French, but instead allows language to see double, making it 'loucher' in the active sense of that French word," in part by inserting "spacing" into the text (107). This "spacing" is foreign to writing in French, Bensmaïa contends, and it is for that very reason that it is effective to "translate the untranslatable" in writing.

Bensmaïa is right to identify the French verb "loucher" as important to Khatibi's writing project. But I would go further to suggest that the unusual act of "seeing double" in the literary text is in harmony with the *musical* nature of his compositions. When Khatibi himself mentions the "double" gaze through which he views himself, it is in connection to song: "In the vague terrain of French culture, we threw out songs with our belly buttons in the air, we scratched with fervor, the song declared itself, often a melodramatic number, myself a dog, ears erect, [. . .] while slipping into the void, I meet myself in the squinting look [*regard louche*] of a double" (*La Mémoire* 69). Torn between two conflicting strains in the "melody" (69) of his childhood soundtrack, the "selected pieces" from the books of his French school standing out stridently from the "mechanic muezzin" (69) and the "cry of the cock [that] didn't resolve [my] desire" that marks the night, "this night is for a people that is splitting" (72). Like his people, the future writer is torn,[2] but this rupture takes place on a plane that is critical to his creations. He describes a desire that is not diminished, even when the cock's crow points to the break of day. Caught between "Occident" and "Orient," he is left with desire of a specific bent, "*Là mon désir musical*" (207), a "musical desire" that drives the writer to self-expression in new, unexplored directions.[3]

Khatibi does not shy away from relating madness in personal ways in his written work, nor does he cringe when it comes to conveying silence through the text.[4] In *La Mémoire tatouée*, the writer puts his "mad identity" on paper (27), all while questioning the possibility of such an undertaking: "For the past that I choose now as motif for the tension between my being and its manifestations [*évanescences*] takes form according to my incantatory celebration" (26). The hints of madness in this sentence on the "chosen" past portrayed in the written text point to an opening up of this composition to all forms of memory, rational and illogical alike. Slips of the tongue, rather than being shunned and censored, are welcomed and highlighted. They not only demonstrate the madness of language, they also reveal much about the inner workings of the private mind, including its obsessions and preconceptions, but also its contradictions and inconsistencies. Two celebrated slips prove to be noteworthy: "A slip of the tongue comes back to me: mother instead of memory, double absence within a double chance" 26; "Sea, mother, memory [*Mer, mère, mémoire*], slips that escaped from this chilly nostalgia" 30. These slips of the tongue provide him with the initial chord for his composition: "Predestined arrangement, they'll tell me, since the sea [la mer] is the motif for the first melody" (30). Mother and mother tongue provide the key to Khatibi's œuvre.

Part I. Conversing and Converting Beyond the "Monolingual": Abdelkébir Khatibi and Jacques Derrida

> If I had to risk, God spare me, a single definition of deconstruction, brief, elliptical, economical like a slogan, I would say in less than a sentence: *more than one language.*
>
> —Jacques Derrida, *Mémoires pour Paul de Man* (1988)

> The language of the other returns word to word and obliges one to keep one's word. In this sense, there is "language of the other" at every word event. That's what I call the trace.
>
> —Jacques Derrida, *Parages* (1986)

In a little-known dialogue revolving around a prominent text, Jacques Derrida and Abdelkébir Khatibi bring to the forefront a topic of tremendous importance to Francophone writers: language. It is no accident that these long-standing friends whose interaction is characterized by mutual respect should focus on *languages* (in the plural) in a series of textual exchanges in a post-colonial, Francophone context. This first half of the bipartite chapter explores the plurilingual environment of Derrida and Khatibi's native regions, and then examines their writing as "conversing" and "converting" in/to French in a move that ultimately changes the terms of this language from an (impossible) effort to "master" it to an appreciation of its flexible hospitality.

Multilingualism

In *Le Monolinguisme de l'autre, ou la prothèse de l'origine*, Jacques Derrida engages with the work of fellow "Franco-Maghrebian" Abdelkébir Khatibi. He draws from a collection of critical reflections, *Du bilinguisme*, and a novel composition, *Amour bilingue*, to contrast the multilingual writing of Moroccan-born Khatibi with his own monolingualism: "I have only one language; it is not mine" (1). In an open letter to Derrida that responds directly to this text, Khatibi demonstrates that this oft-quoted assertion goes beyond a mere statement of linguistic limitation to point to the inappropriability of any language.[5] The conversation between Derrida in *Le Monolinguisme de l'autre* and Khatibi in *La Langue de l'Autre* constitutes a reflection on the tight connection between language and postcolonialism. Derrida's assertions and Khatibi's reactions reveal how the two of them are postcolonial subjects in different ways; each has a specific relationship to the French language because of his particular background. The lack of ownership evoked in the opening sentences of Derrida's *Monolinguisme* applies to any person with respect to any tongue; but it is particularly salient in the case of postcolonial Francophone writers and thinkers who—no matter how profound their knowledge of French—are constantly, keenly aware that they are speaking in the language of the other.

It is not surprising that language should figure in the very title of Derrida's contribution to an international conference on the topic of francophonie outside France; language has long been at the center of the concerns of French-speaking postcolonial theorists. The very act of writing in French for those originating in regions once dominated by the French is problematic, for this language of composition is inextricably tied to a history of conquest and subjugation in the worst sense. The fact that thinkers emerging from these regions must have recourse to the dominator's language in order to protest against their domination is troublesome in theory and wrought with difficulty in practice, as Djebar reminds readers in the afterword to *Femmes d'Alger dans leur appartement*: "The French language, for me, is the language of those people coming onto my land with the colonial conquest" (*Women* 184).

Linguistic domination is not specific to French history, of course. Other nations that took to colonization in the nineteenth century transported their language with them, and the very concept of "nation" very often accompanies the imposition of a single language. In harmony with this line of thinking, Derrida is careful to detail the universal "colonial" nature of any society: "Every culture institutes itself through the unilateral imposition of some 'politics' of language. Mastery begins, as we know, through the power of naming, of imposing and legitimating appellations" (*Monolingualism* 39).[6] But France's approach to language —including a strong desire for uniformity and ubiquity—differs from its near neighbors in Europe (such as Switzerland and Belgium) and manifests itself most clearly in its colonizing policies abroad. While there is an undeniable history of what Derrida calls the "'politics' of language" within the hexagonal borders of contemporary France, it is undeniable that the "colonial cruelty" experienced in Algeria (and, to a lesser degree, in Morocco) was quite different, and infinitely more intense than that experienced in the "homeland." Despite the geographical and ideological distance separating them from the country they were taught to call "the Metropole,"[7] "Algerian Jew" Jacques Derrida and "Moroccan Arab"

Abdelkébir Khatibi were compelled to speak the tongue of their "ancestors, the Gauls;" they were both colonized by the French language.[8]

When it comes to the question of the French language in the colonial territory, Frantz Fanon serves as an important "predecessor" to contemporary postcolonial discussion. In his seminal study of the psychology of racism and colonial domination, Peau noire, masques blancs, Fanon dedicates the opening chapter to "Le Noir et le langage," emphasizing the way colonized subjects seek above all to speak like the colonizer. This desire to refine their expression in the language of the other is an important result of the active approach the French took to colonization.[9] The intensive educational programs installed as part of the "mission civilisatrice" yielded well-versed intellectuals—from a variety of places around the globe—who "possess(ed)" flawless French.[10]

Both Derrida and Khatibi were inflicted with this passion for perfecting the French language during their apprenticeship. For those familiar with his oeuvre, it may seem contradictory that Derrida should place such importance on losing his "'French Algerian' accent"; but he was deeply marked by the preconceptions accompanying la belle langue: "any accent [. . .] seems incompatible to me with the intellectual dignity of public speech" (Monolingualism 45–46). An exploration of his past in "French schools where [he has] spent [his] life" (49) explains how Derrida "contracted a shameful but intractable intolerance" (46). In his words, linguistic impurity is unbearable: "at least in French, insofar as the language is concerned, I cannot bear or admire anything other than pure French" (46). This obsession with purity is not unique to Derrida. As he reveals in his autobiographical La Mémoire tatouée, Khatibi went so far as to "efface" his childhood and his culture in order to perform well in school. His efforts were not in vain, for his command of French was soon superior to that of native speakers in his class: "I taught the others to write their own language" (124).

This emphasis on the French language in the colonial Maghreb carried with it a heavy price. Writers reveal that excelling in the colonizer's tongue came at the expense of other means of expression. Rather than being taught alongside other tongues in this plurilingual region of North Africa, French was largely taught to the exclusion of other languages. For Khatibi, moving to French school meant giving up his study of written Arabic. For Derrida, it meant complying with "colonial censorships" and obeying the "interdict" against Arabic and Berber (Monolingualism 37). Granted, the study of Arabic was allowed (but certainly not encouraged), and Derrida underscores the humor of this situation: "Arabic, an optional foreign language in Algeria!" (38). But Berber was never even an option, and its suppression—along with the unspoken restraint on Arabic—attests to "the growing uselessness, the organized marginalization," indeed, the "weakening" of these languages, "calculated by a colonial policy" that promoted its own tongue above all others (38). For the pupils of the French school in Algeria, this imposed language could never be considered their own: "French was a language supposed to be maternal, but one whose source, norms, rules, and law were situated elsewhere" (41). The immense, incalculable distance between the metropolitan "elsewhere" that made the rules and the French colony where they were enforced forever alienated Derrida from the only language in which he feels comfortable: "For never was I able to call French, this language I am speaking to you, 'my mother tongue'" (34).

Conversing

The launching point for Derrida's personal reflection on monolingualism is a text by Khatibi titled *Amour bilingue*. This work—evolving around bilingual, even plurilingual, love[11]—strikes Derrida as remarkable not only because of its style but especially because of its content, for Khatibi is able to speak therein of his *mother tongue*: "He had only one mother and, no doubt, more than one mother, but he indeed had his mother tongue, a mother tongue, a single mother tongue *plus* another language" (*Monolinguism* 36). In part because he speaks more than one language, Khatibi is able to refer to his first language—his native language, the language spoken *by his mother*—as his "mother tongue." Since French is a learned idiom for him, it does not (nor will it ever) constitute his mother tongue, even if he claims he has sacrificed his entire being to it.[12] The term "sacrifice" in Khatibi's writing is significant; it not only bears relevance to his first name in Islamic tradition,[13] but it carries the connotation of "loss" that figures in the quotation Derrida selects from *Amour bilingue*: "Yes, my mother tongue lost me" (*Love* 66). In Derrida's analysis, this mother tongue is not lost from Khatibi's work: "he evokes a language of origin which has perhaps 'lost' him, but which he himself has not lost" (*Monolingualism* 36). For, if Khatibi has chosen French as his language of writing, he nonetheless infuses this written French with something other, with words and phrases and concepts (as well as syntax and even imperceptible rhythmic elements) from the "other" tongue(s) that subtly effect change on the written language from within, altering French in small but significant ways.[14]

In *La Langue de l'Autre*, Khatibi's overt correspondence aims to answer the questions and ruminations found in *Le Monolinguisme de l'autre*. Khatibi's published letter to Derrida thus serves as the first explicit instance of exchange between the two thinkers, even if we find their reciprocal influence—indeed their "intertextual friendship"[15]—present in other writings as well. The two literary, political, and philosophical currents with which they are associated have been compared in several texts: according to Khatibi, and recently according to Derrida, *deconstruction* and *decolonization* are similar, complementary movements. As early as 1983 in *Maghreb pluriel*, Khatibi proposed Derridian deconstruction as an equivalent of decolonization. He reiterates this alliance between the terms in *La Langue de L'autre*: "I have always believed that what carries the name 'deconstruction' is a radical form of 'decolonization' in what is called 'Western' thought. I wrote this and signed it long ago" (24).

If it is true that Derrida's thought may owe as much to his experience in Algeria as it owes to the Parisian intellectual milieu of his later educational training,[16] then it should be of little surprise to us that Derrida weds deconstruction and decolonization in his comments on teaching philosophy: "If decolonization is interminable like philosophy and philosophical deconstruction, it is because decolonization can be effective neither according to the simple mode of reappropriation nor that of opposition and reversal" (*Du droit à la philosophie* 161). Recognizing the difficulties deconstruction and decolonization have in common is an important movement in Derrida's thought that shows why two thinkers and writers from different geographical and historical experiences[17] can nonetheless engage in a fruitful and productive conversation in their works.

Derrida and Khatibi are contemporaries, appearing on the publishing scene at a specific moment in the "Franco-Maghrebian" experience (at the conclusion of the 1960s and beginning of the 1970s).[18] They witnessed the closing of an era, the end of French presence on North African soil and the start of something new in this territory. This turning point in History coincided with a turning point in their personal histories, and their approach to and position in "French letters" bears the (im)print of the end of colonization in their native lands. What they do in their writing is innovative, it is new, it plays with the traditional classifications of works in French, disrupts "genre" and traverses disciplinary boundaries. Indeed, in their compositions, philosophical and literary reflections cross, they intertwine, they *converse*. The precision, the exactitude of their work reveals a deep respect for, even a servitude to, the French language, yet it is *different* from the work of earlier writers from various French colonies who (paradoxically) sought subserviently to master French, but *only* in accordance with accepted, *taught* rules.[19] It is important to note that the *place* Derrida and Khatibi occupy in "French letters" was not always assured: they have been misunderstood and even derided for their lack of conventionality, for their unusual subject matter and their original approach. It is significant that they have been accepted and celebrated abroad before establishing credibility "at home"—critics in the United States and the United Kingdom welcomed the work of Derrida while he was encountering considerable skepticism in France. And Khatibi remains little known on the continent, while his *Maghreb Pluriel* has met with critical acclaim in American and British circles, as has *Amour bilingue* under the title *Love in Two Languages*, thanks to a brilliant translation by Richard Howard.

Converting

Translation plays a crucial part not only in the reception of his work abroad, but in the very writing project of Abdelkébir Khatibi. In *Maghreb pluriel*, Khatibi addresses the role of language in colonization and decolonization, and he addresses the way translation operates in the literary creations of many postcolonial Maghrebian subjects. In his analysis, their familiarity with several languages enables these writers to produce particularly rich "multilingual" texts in French: "I will advance the following: the so-called foreign tongue does not come to add itself to the other, nor does it operate with it in a pure juxtaposition: each language *signals [fait signe]* the other" (186). We find an even more explicit passage on the influence of the several languages he speaks and their translation in the written text composed primarily in French in an article called "Un étranger professionnel":

> I practice five languages more or less: Arabic, French, English, Spanish, Swedish, and several bits of an idiom communally called Berber. These phrases, foreign to French, thus arrive by quick, flexible association. I translate them, capturing them rapidly, avoiding facile neologisms and "telescopings" of dialectical words. Sometimes I translate them as they are, but rarely. I have a tendency, in this game of weaving, to disseminate the foreign lexicon in a syntactical movement. The syntax is my essential target. (140)[20]

Khatibi goes on to describe his personal writing process as a "simultaneous translation" of what he calls a "double multiple language," an enterprise that is "risky" precisely because the "meeting of languages"—or the "practice of several languages"—is ultimately an "infernal place" that is threatened by "confusion" but that can nonetheless open up to something else, a different rhythm marking the beat of (indeed, keeping time with) a different type of writing.

If the task of translating this "already translated" French writing into *another* idiom (such as English) *seems* daunting, that is because *it is*, and yet the difficulty of this activity does not discourage its accomplishment. In Khatibi's case, the translation of *Amour bilingue* has brought his work to the attention of critics who are not necessarily francophone. In Derrida's case, it is also *in translation*—through translated works—that he has gained much of his renown worldwide. And yet, as with the writing of Khatibi, Derrida's work is inextricably tied to the French tongue and is notoriously difficult to read and comprehend even in this original language of composition. Most translators would shudder at the thought of rendering such dense, meaning-filled poetic texts in another language. But Derrida, in a typical paradox, argues that it is precisely the *untranslatability* of his unique writing in French that *calls for* translation:

> The singularity may reside in this fact: while what I write and teach is tied body and soul to the French idiom and to the least translatable idiom, while writing in an idiomatic style that renders translation difficult is even a sort of rule that I give myself, foreign readings [of my work], far from being discouraged, are on the contrary increased. It is with the translators of all countries that I get along and work the best. This is something that is singular and difficult for everyone to conceive of: how is it that the most untranslatable is the most translated and crosses borders the most? (*Sur Parole* 56)

What Derrida is ultimately addressing in his comments on the translations of his texts into other tongues is the necessity of translation *within* the language of composition. The French of Derrida, like the French of Khatibi, is a special idiom that embodies their shared understanding of all great writing in French as that which must render the everyday, quotidian language "other" to itself.

In his reflections on language and writing in *La Langue de l'Autre*, Khatibi hones in on the importance of creating a sort of "foreign tongue" in French, evoking the importance of translating French *into* French: "Writing inside languages, translating French into French, is a difficult proposition to make understood. But Mallarmé, Rimbaud, Proust, and many others explicitly affirmed the necessity for the writer to invent idioms 'inside' French" (28). This affirmation of translation within the work composed in French is found in many places in Derrida's work, notably in his reading of Hélène Cixous. When addressing language in Cixous's inimitable novels and essays, Derrida is compelled to reflect on the translation at work within the "untranslatable writing" of these multilingual French compositions: "the trial of translation does not only take place between the French language (the dominant language of this œuvre) and other languages. The trial takes place inside, if there is one, the said French language, and it is more perfidious and unrecognizable, more decisive, there, for it comes into contact with the body of the writing" (123). When colonization imposes a language, the most effective way for the colonized writing subject to appropriate the inappropriable (that is all language) consists of turning that language on its head. Whether mono-lingual or plurilingual, the language of the other,[21] language itself as other, comes into play in the work of Khatibi and Derrida, disrupting rigid codes of acceptable writing and introducing other tongues, and along with these tongues other ways of seeing, of perceiving the world, and other ways of in-terpreting signs on a variety of levels.

Whether Derrida admits to it or not, his extensive study of other tongues and his close attention to etymology makes his texts those of a polyglot as well, even if their "multilingual" nature diverges slightly from those by Kha-tibi. The linguistic trajectories of their literary, philosophical works reveal the reality of our contemporary world as a place where subjects move from one place to another, often coming into contact with several idioms in a sin-gle locale, as in Algeria or Morocco, or with a single official language that changes with the crossing of national borders. Infusing their works with words, phrases, and syntax from other tongues effectively unveils not only the plural *linguistic* constitutions of "Franco-Maghrebian" subjects like Der-rida and Khatibi, it reveals their plural *ethnic* and *historical* backgrounds as well. By composing works that translate several tongues into French, and go even further to translate several *French* languages into French, Derrida and Khatibi effect a significant change on the conception of "Francophonie" as a defining feature of identity. According to Khatibi, working with several lan-guages in the French text can lead to a *"désidentification"* that brings with it benefits for the Francophone writer and the text (*La Langue* 141). Derrida delineates the play and the pleasure that take place in the text once it opens its space to "internal translation": "This translation translates itself in an in-ternal (Franco-French) translation by playing with the non-identity with it-self of all language. By playing and taking pleasure" (*Monolingualism* 65). This play and pleasure put any fixed idea of personal identity into question. They also put into question textual identity. Given the plurality at work (and play), how are we to define a "Francophone" text? Is it French *and*? It is French *but*? It is French, but *not only*?

From Mastery to Hospitality
Derrida chooses a citation by Caribbean writer Édouard Glissant as the first of two epigraphs heading *Le Monolinguisme the l'autre*, and he revisits this quota-tion in the midst of his reflection on language in the context of colonization. In examining Glissant's treatment of the "'colonial' alienation" of those who are unable to perfectly comprehend and reproduce the "appropriated lan-guage," Derrida focuses on an important term: *"non-maîtrise"* (44). If the colo-nial (and postcolonial) subject does not "master" the language of the colonizer,

298 ⌒ Chapter Seven

then neither does the colonizer, Derrida is quick to point out: "this experience of monolingual solipsism is never one of belonging, property, power of mastery, pure 'ipseity' (hospitality or hostility) of whichever kind" (*Monolingualism* 22–23). This move from the impossibility of "mastery" of any tongue[22]—whether it be one's mother tongue or not—to the possibility of finding "hospitality" within oral and textual speech, within the spoken and written word, is of crucial importance to Derrida's understanding of language.

Derrida draws from the work of another philosopher, Emmanuel Lévinas, to connect language to hospitality: "As Levinas says from another point of view, language *is* hospitality" (*Of Hospitality* 135).[23] Seeing language as a place of welcome, of acceptance, and of freedom are all implied within this generous statement of equivalence. But despite its positive connotations, "hospitality" is a concept fraught with ambiguity. As Derrida reminds us in a text emerging from one of his annual seminars, "hospitality" bears a double meaning: the Latin *hospes* gives rise to our words for *host* and *hostile*. Critic Mireille Rosello taps into this double meaning in her exploration of the pros and cons of translation in *Postcolonial Hospitality: The Immigrant as Guest*. In Rosello's view, translation is negative when it serves to promote the "dominant (linguistic or cultural) idiom" and thereby prolong a situation in which a host "shows no intention of learning the other's language" (92).[24]

Khatibi picks up on the Derridian notion of hospitality in *La Langue de l'Autre* and uses it to refer to the space the writer inhabits in his or her own text: "If I praise syntax, it is because it enlarges the space of hospitality where the writer is received as a guest in his own text, in the shadow of the reader" (38). This space of textual hospitality is the space of conversation, the idyllic space in which writer and reader interact, where they exchange thoughts and ideas in a variety of idioms, employing words that vehicle thoughts from various backgrounds and divergent experiences. This place of writer-reader interaction is the space opened up by Derrida in the *Le Monolinguisme de l'autre* when he embarks on a close reading of Khatibi's *Amour bilingue*, a space Khatibi enters into when he responds to Derrida and engages *Le Monolinguisme de l'autre* in *La Langue de l'Autre*. This utopian space of dialogue and interaction, where several histories and several tongues come together in sincere conversation is the enactment of hospitality in its finest sense.

Postcolonial hospitality in language, as embodied in Khatibi and Derrida, demonstrates an opening to other languages, to what Khatibi calls the *plurilangue*, in a gesture that continually recognizes the other as other, without seeking to reduce the other to the same.[25] Khatibi and Derrida are no longer holding to illusions of singularity of language, but instead to the singularity of a specific work. Each work is *singular* because it constitutes not only an acceptance of the other—and the other tongue—but because it encourages verbal exchange, it prods others to take up the *parole*—even, and especially, in the other tongue—because of the realization that "my" tongue is always the other's, and that it is never single, but filled with plurality, and therefore with possibility. Khatibi alerts us to the performative possibilities of linguistic hospitality: "When I write, I do so in the language of the other. This language is not a property; it is rather the empty place of an identity that is reincarnated" (41). As his geographical and literary itineraries demonstrate, the status of "Francophone" postcolonial subject is not limited or limiting; it is only a starting point from which to cross numerous borders and explore multiple horizons.

Part II. Translating Plurality:
Abdelkébir Khatibi and Assia Djebar

Thanks to this simultaneous translation, to this process of the graft, I record without reserve that which comes back to my memory

—Abdelkébir Khatibi, *La Langue de l'Autre* (1999)

Un été à Stockholm is a work of fiction in which Abdelkébir Khatibi depicts a "professional traveler" whose numerous trips are warranted by his vocation as an interpreter. The protagonist's services are needed at an international colloquium in Sweden, as the title indicates, and one of the most remarkable passages of the novel evokes the sport of "translating simultaneously" on the job.

The colloquium began in a great clarity of thought. My task became limpid. I who translate simultaneously, who listen then speak with a slight deferral, I adapted myself quickly to the position of sensor. [. . .] Yes yes, it so happens that I improvise. Improvisation under control, my voice sliding between the variations of the exposés. Keep up the tone, the rhythm, the vocal invention, that's my golden rule. Sometimes, the orator makes a slip. I correct, I rectify the shot. Always bring the orator back to the reason of language by diminishing the frequency of errors. [. . .] I am successively myself, the other, and again myself, between speed and the word, speed and silence. [. . .] I am there behind the glass to detect, anticipate, understand all the meanings of a word, a phrase, or a pun. All the meanings: clear or not, reasonable, more or less complex, or fuzzy; meanings filled with luminous thoughts, with gossip, with silliness, with unbearable pretention, so many unstable positions in the balance between languages. The faster the time of interpretation, the faster I read, I under-read the bodies of orators as if this polyform body were a recorded book on shiny tape.

[. . .] During the course of the session, I connect the succession of words, like a musical instrument. (48–50)

If Khatibi is prone to refer to his own writing as a "traduction simultanée," it is because he conceives of writing in many of the terms illuminated in this citation. The speed of the task of the interpreter is impressive, as are the variations in tempo. In this very text, Khatibi experiments with temporality, "playing" with speed in the passage above, but occasionally slowing the pace with longer, more languorous sentences. The time of the narrative varies in similar fashion; metatextual comments alert the reader to the presence of flashbacks and even "flash forwards," as in the following: "Said this way, this hurried sentence on the attraction of Lena is, truly, a flight forward [une fuite en avant]. It is later, on the way toward the Great Stockholm, that her beauty, shining or dark, will become closer, more intimate for me" (85). Anticipating and reacting immediately to the spoken words and body language of the speakers, the interpreter's activity is much like the writer's (even if the latter does not aim to cover up slips of the tongue and defer to the "reason" of language). Both are attentive to all the shades of meaning in a single expression, both are concerned to communicate with accuracy, and both have musical affinities. Most importantly for the purposes of this section of the chapter is the emphasis on taking in a *plurality* of languages and rendering them "harmoniously" legible to a listening audience or a reading public.

Plurality in the Maghreb

On the occasion of a colloquium on deconstruction and translation held in Morocco, Jacques Derrida emphasized the importance of *plurality* in the translation process.[26] The choice of this word was particularly apt given the North African region in which he spoke: the Maghreb is characterized by a plurality of peoples and cultures, as well as a plurality of languages. While no country is simple or uniform, postcolonial Morocco, Algeria, and Tunisia are especially complex and their linguistic situation reveals this complexity, as Abdelkébir Khatibi reveals in the very title of his collection of essays, *Maghreb pluriel.*

While postcolonial studies have been quick to recognize language as "the most potent instrument of colonial control," and therefore as "a fundamental site of struggle" for postcolonial discourse (Ashcroft et al., 283), most reflections on the topic have focused solely on the phenomenon of *bilingualism.*[27] This is understandable, for the postcolonial subject is in many cases a bilingual individual, proficient in both a mother tongue tied to the native land and a second language imposed by the colonizer. Many fruitful critiques

treat therefore of the "translation" inherent in the writing process of francophone subjects who communicate a "different sensibility" from their native tongue in the French text.[28] These analyses are helpful to comprehend
the ways in which the "silent" language of the native tongue informs the
written text in the adopted idiom,[29] but they tend to overlook the important
phenomenon of the *multilingual* writer from regions like the postcolonial
Maghreb. The binary models of "mother" versus "other" tongue, of "first"
versus "second" language, do not apply to works by the three writers at the
center of this study.

The specificity of the Maghrebian linguistic situation is the focus of Khatibi's comments on translation in his contribution to a collective work titled
Du Bilinguisme: "As long as the theory of translation, of the bi-lingual and the
pluri-lingual has not made progress, certain Maghrebian texts will remain
impregnable to a formal and functional approach" (171). The consideration
of the "plurilingual" subject in a publication devoted to bilingualism is significant. According to Khatibi's analysis, one cannot address literature from
the Maghreb without taking into account the *languages* at stake: "this
Maghrebian literature of so-called French expression is a narrative of translation. I am not saying that is is only translation, I specify that it is a question of narrative that *speaks in tongues*" (177). In order to demonstrate how
multiple languages present themselves in the French text composed by
Maghrebian writers, Khatibi engages in a close reading of a novel whose title itself bears witness to the multiplicity of tongues spoken by its author: *Talismano*. When Tunisian writer Abdelwahab Meddeb peppers his French text
not only with terms from his native Arabic but also with words and expressions from Italian, this third tongue playfully comes to disrupt the usual strict
division of the bilingual text in two. Here the language of the colonizer and
that of the colonized are no longer engaged in a strict face-off, and the resulting text is ludic and exuberant.[30]

Finding New Terms for Translation
When Maghrebian writers compose in French, as Khatibi shows in his treatment of Meddeb's novel, many of the preconceptions of traditional translation theory are ineffective to describe the complicated linguistic translation
at work. Customary distinctions between "source language" and "target language" no longer suffice to explain the operation of writing in a "foreign"
tongue. Not only are they unable to capture the complexities of the finished
product, they are rendered *inaccurate*, according to Khatibi, who insists that
there is an "inversion" in these terms. Khatibi takes his conclusion one step
further, and asserts that in the Francophone text from the Maghreb, the

"source language" itself becomes the "target language."[31] Indeed, the very distinction between "source" and "target" becomes blurred in the multilingual texts of Khatibi such as *La Mémoire tatouée* and *Amour bilingue*. As Djebar indicates on the opening page of *Femmes d'Alger dans leur appartement*, the predicament of the Maghrebian writer is that there is no single language from which to translate: "I could say: 'stories translated from . . . ,' but from which language?" (*Women* 1).

The multiplicity of languages in the Maghreb is due not only to the relatively recent presence of the French in Morocco, Tunisia, and Algeria, but also to a long history of invasions. In his detailed study of the interrelation of language and power in the largest of these three countries, Mohamed Benrabah calls attention to the steady stream of conquerors in Algerian territory, a list that includes the Phoenicians, the Romans, the Vandals, the Byzantines, the Portuguese, the Spanish, and the Turks (*Langue et pouvoir* 27–76). By the time the French launched an expedition against Algiers in 1830, Algeria was a land in which an interesting mixture of languages was spoken: Spanish in the west; Italian in the East; a *lingua franca* that combined a principally Spanish vocabulary with Turkish elements and a number of words from Greek and Latin (and that continued to exist long after the arrival of the French); Berber; and a local version of Arabic that bore the imprint of Algeria's unique history of domination (both linguistic and cultural) by these different invaders. As a result of her country's storied past,[32] the task of Algerian writer Assia Djebar is not easy.

Djebar's translation project, like that of Khatibi, plays itself out on the border of several languages. In these writers' native countries, Arabic itself is not a unified tongue; it can be divided into the literary, written version found in the Muslim holy book known as the Qu'ran, and the spoken, oral variety found in the local dialect. This "diglossic" situation serves to separate the educated from the uneducated members of society; while everybody has access to the Arabic spoken in the streets, only a few colonial subjects were fortunate enough to learn classical Arabic during French rule.[33] Those inhabitants who escaped the wave of Arabic domination in the seventh century speak Berber, a tongue that exists only in spoken form today. Berber is the language of Djebar's maternal lineage, the language still spoken by her relatives in the mountainous region of Kabylia. Among European tongues, Spanish still has significant hold in Morocco and Italian has clout in Algeria and Tunisia, but it is obviously French that dominates North Africa.

It is into French that Djebar translates the words of her countrywomen, spoken in different languages: "The multiple voices that besiege me—those of my characters in my texts of fiction—I hear them, for the most part, in

Arabic, in dialectical Arabic, or even in Berber which I understand poorly, but whose husky breathing and respiration inhabit me in immemorial fashion" (*Ces voix* 29). Djebar's work intends not only to translate dialectical Arabic and Berber for a French-speaking readership; it aims also to translate the *spoken* word into *written* form. The "double translation" inherent in novels, short stories, theatrical works, and essays emerging from her pen has a noble end: to speak "next to" and thereby relate the stories of many Algerian women without voice, to communicate for those whose experiences would otherwise remain silent and risk oblivion. But, for all of its nobility of purpose, this task is not without its challenges.

One of the greatest difficulties Djebar must face is the lack of precedent for her undertaking. She is eager to acknowledge the few who have written before her, in similar postcolonial contexts, but she admits that she is largely on her own.[34] This feeling of isolation is intensified by the bloodshed she has witnessed among her contemporaries; a number of personal friends and acquaintances from her native land have lost their lives because of the political views expressed in their written works. In a book dedicated to her Algerian comrades who met with death prematurely, Djebar puts forth the idea that Algeria, as a country *without writing*, remains *untranslated*: "The white of writing in a non-translated Algeria? For the moment, the Algeria of sorrow without writing; for the moment, an Algeria of writing-in-blood, alas! (*Algerian White* 229).[35] In another text, she explains why this Algeria has gone untranslated in present times, why words have not yet been found to render this country legible. In her analysis, the troublesome history of conquest and domination have entailed constant linguistic change and cohabitation of various means of expression, but current cultural subjugation has repressively sought to eliminate this plurality:

> That's [the case], alas, in my country, panting Algeria: due to fear of the second language, of the third, due to denial of a multilingualism inscribed in our culture since Antiquity (popular culture and educated culture), due to fear thus of the multiple in its infinite forms, my country, underneath a veritable cultural dictatorship, has been harassed by a pseudo-identitary monolingualism: a sole language vindicated like an armor, a carapace, a wall!" (*Ces voix* 33)

In such a hotly charged political climate as the one found in Algeria since the country gained independence from French rule in 1962, translation is not something Djebar can take lightly. She writes in French with knowledge of the danger others have faced for the choice of this contentious language as a vehicle for their thoughts and reflections. She therefore writes in French with an awareness of the present risk this language poses in her country. She also writes in French with an awareness of the troublesome past of this language in her country; the language of the colonizer accompanied the latter's brutal methods of subjugation. During the colonial period, French was the tongue of torture and torment. So when she seeks to render distinctly "non-French" voices in French, Djebar simply cannot engage in "hasty translation": "Obscurely constrained, I had to find an equivalence, without deforming [the voices], but without hastily translating them" (*Ces voix* 29). The careful search for equivalence that Djebar embarks upon in her texts is one that works in the interstices of a number of languages, occupying a liminal, third space that, while composed primarily in French, is not entirely "French."

Interlanguages

In her reflections on language(s) and writing, Djebar frequently has recourse to the term *"entre-deux-langues"* to describe her situation as a postcolonial subject.[36] In her analysis, the writer *between languages* is seldom complacent. For, as she sees it, "ex-colonial" wordsmiths inevitably encounter the uncomfortable inefficacy of any language to fully represent experience.[37] Djebar's coinage of the doubly hyphenated *"entre-deux-langues"* is reminiscent of the place of writing as described by Homi Bhabha. His term, "Third Space of enunciation," is crucial to comprehending texts composed by multilingual individuals, as it takes into account the *location* (in language) of cultural statements.[38] But both Djebar's *"entre-deux-langues"* and Bhabha's "Third Space" are concepts that must be enlarged and extended in order to adapt to the situation of the polyglot from the Maghreb. To find a suitable term for written texts in the interstices of *more than two* languages, we must look again to a complementary region of postcolonial linguistic diversity: the Caribbean islands. Jean Bernabé, Patrick Chamoiseau, and Raphaël Confiant put their voices together in praise of linguistic variation in *Éloge de la créolité*, a work that embraces textual and cultural complexity: "Being completely open to the whole linguistic spectrum offered by society, such is the state of mind with which we approached the issue of interlanguage, pedantically called 'interlect' . . . we believe that creative use of interlect might lead to an order of reality capable of preserving for our Creoleness its fundamental complexity, its diffracted referential space" (110). The notion of the "interlect" as a space not just *between two* languages but *among numerous* tongues is particularly pertinent in the Maghreb, where the coexistence of several languages has led Khatibi to refer to his native land as a "mosaic of interlangues" capable of creating a "concrete internationalism" (*Figures de l'étranger* 210).[39]

The celebration of plurality in Khatibi's writing constitutes a "mosaic" of sorts, bringing together fragments from a number of tongues, including but not limited to those that characterized his Maghrebian childhood. It is in the autobiographical *La Mémoire tatouée* that Khatibi exposes the multiple tongues and accompanying worldviews to which he was exposed as a youngster: "My father sent me to the French-Muslim school in 1945. . . . At school, a secular instruction, imposed on my religion; I became trilingual, reading French without speaking it, playing with several portions of written Arabic, and speaking the dialect on a daily basis" (64).[40] In her autobiographical *L'Amour, la fantasia*, Djebar presents her reader with a similar cross-cultural image of herself as a child attending a French primary school.[41] As a result of this early exposure to several languages, as well as continuous linguistic apprenticeship into adulthood, both writers infuse the written text with "multilingualism."

The Textual Practice of Multilingualism
The most obvious example of multilingual practice is the presence of italicized words and phrases from a foreign language in the French text. This is found in Khatibi's work, notably in *Amour bilingue*, a text that betrays its title by giving rise to numerous languages, not just two. The reader is initially tempted to believe that the "bilingual" love relation between a man and a woman is one in which the native speaker of Arabic communicates his affection in the textual tongue, French. But such is not the case: the object of the narrator's affection is not from the Hexagon, but rather is of Scandinavian origin, as the third/first-person narrative voice reveals: "The women who met him except for her should have lost their name or disfigured him and I should say to her in Swedish, 'Jag har inte glömt'" (*Love* 57). The insertion of this phrase in what the narrator calls the "adoptive language" serves to disconcert *and* dazzle the reader whose preconceptions are proved wrong in this plural text.

In theory, one of Khatibi's most interesting concepts is that of the "simultaneous translation" that takes place when the multilingual Maghrebian takes up the pen to compose a "Francophone" text: "The 'mother' tongue is at work in the foreign tongue. A permanent translation and removed discussion take place between the two, extremely difficult to unveil" ("Incipits" 171). In *Amour bilingue*, the novelist puts this reflection into practice, referring to the *simultaneity* that characterizes his work: "If I happened to substitute one word for another (I knew it was on my own behalf) I didn't have the impression that I was making a mistake or breaking a law but rather that I was speaking two words simultaneously" (*Love* 28). Khatibi's

application of "simultaneous translation" occurs most frequently in the narrator's expressed thoughts, such as when he evokes words that possess two
meanings in one language and only one signification in another: "Thus, he
said to himself, curiously, the word 'flower' doesn't refer us to the rhetoric of
any old language but rather indicates in my native speech both flower and
syphilis (nouar)" (55). Another exemplary case is found in the coincidence
of a word that exists in two separate languages and carries two separate
meanings: "I woke up completely, struck by this coincidence: *sin* stands for
the figure "two" in Berber and in Arabic, for a holy letter of the Koran" (43).
A similar attention to different meanings (for an identical word) in different tongues can be found in the title of Djebar's *L'Amour, la fantasia*, where
the "fantasia" carries completely diverse connotations in Arabic and in Italian.[42] Playing on the multilingual double meaning of various words is part of
the textual practice of Maghrebian writers who have a wealth of vocabular-
ies at their disposition.[43]

Musical Murmurs

It could be argued that the reader of Maghrebian Francophone texts must be
competent in a number of languages in order to appreciate the plurality at
work in these writers' creative compositions, but this is not the case. While
it is helpful to possess some knowledge of several tongues in order to fully understand the intricate language games in their *oeuvre*, vast linguistic competence is not a prerequisite to reading their work. Khatibi and Djebar both assert that what carries their text is not a strict translation from one (or
several) language(s) to another, but rather a transcription of experience that
can best be explained as a sort of "music" that communicates much more
than a simple paraphrasing of Maghrebian voices.[44] In Khatibi's words, the
ideal bilingual text would be what he terms a "perpetual double palimpsest—
close to music" ("Incipits" 205). This rapprochement between writing and
music is underscored in another passage which calls attention to the
"rhythm" inherent in the syntax of the written text: "A certain homology between music and writing: it's scansion, the rhythm of the body that speaks
and dictates itself" ("Incipits" 173).

The word "rhythm" emerges in conjunction with Djebar's work as well.
Djebar proclaims her "respect for the rhythm" of the French language and
her *"aspiration à la musique"* in bringing the stories of Algerian women to this
"paternal" tongue (*Ces voix* 150). When she describes her treatment of these
female voices in her text, it is the *rhythm* of their speech that takes precedence in the narrative style: "Yes, to bring back the non-francophone voices
[. . .] to the French text that finally becomes mine. These voices that have

transported in me their turbulence, their stirrings, all the more so in the rhythm of my writing" (Ces voix 29). This textual rhythm resembles a musical composition, one that brings together a number of different voices in an "interactive" text that Bernabé, Chamoiseau, and Confiant describe as a "polysonic vertigo" (108).

Creating a "musical" written work in which numerous languages intermingle has benefits, both on linguistic and political levels. In fact, multifaceted, multilingual texts reveal how tightly intertwined the linguistic and the political actually are. The closely related analyses of political pundits, trained historians, cultural critics, and literary reviewers alike reflect on the mutual influence of language reform and political policy. In Bruno Étienne's analysis, pluralism in society protects from monopoly and thereby guards against the establishment of rigid, exclusive categories.[45] On a linguistic level, the coexistence of a number of languages prevents totalitarian, prejudicial measures. This is the solution Mohamed Benrabah proposes to counter the current Arabization project in Algeria. Rather than give way to the imposition of a single tongue and a single Weltanschauung, Benrabah favors fostering the plurality of languages still spoken in Algeria today.[46] In his recent book on Islam, Abdelwahab Meddeb shows himself to be in favor of plurality, even when the "plural word" among various Islamic societies proves to be conflicted and unharmonious.[47] What matters is not uniformity and unanimity, but rather the polyphonic multiplicity of expression. Giving place to a variety of voices contributes most to Maghrebian composition, both social and textual.

When Khatibi calls for a new theory of translation for the postcolonial Maghreb, he is ultimately seeking a form of critique that embraces linguistic and cultural plurality. He is beseeching literary scholars to take into account the multiple factors constituting Francophone texts from his region of North Africa. He is asking for a recognition of the complicated translation that Djebar undergoes when she resuscitates stifled voices and revitalizes squelched cultures: "Yes, to bring back to the surface the traditional cultures that have been banished, mistreated, long despised, and inscribe them in a new text, in a writing that becomes 'my' French" (Ces voix 29). Khatibi calls for a new theory of translation because the operation present in his work, an operation he calls "simultaneous translation," is unusual: "I feel it like a simultaneous translation, through a rapid association of signs and images. [. . .] Sometimes I translate literally fragments from Arabic, but with concern. I'd rather let the mother tongue arrive, transformed" (La Langue 38). Khatibi admits that he occasionally translates from one language to another, but with hesitancy. He frequently just lets the "source language" come through. According to this description, the "translation" at work in Khatibi's text is more of a "transcription." Djebar engages in a similar textual feat, taking care to avoid didacticism and explanation in her "translated" work; it is noteworthy that no footnotes or special definitions can be found in the original version of *L'Amour, la fantasia*, whereas the English translation contains a glossary explaining the meanings and uses of no fewer than seventy-one words. Djebar does not adopt pedagogical tones when transmitting the voices and their contextually specific vocabulary in this or in other texts; her purpose is less to *instruct* and *inform* her reader than to *incite* the latter to discover stories—and languages—through *immersion*.

In Djebar's analysis, writing (in/of) the Maghreb today means something specific for postcolonial subjects. It is an enterprise dedicated to what she calls a *"marmonnement multilingue,"* as we saw in the fourth chapter, "Settling the Musical Score," devoted to Cixous. Djebar's texts, like those of Khatibi, inscribe this "murmur" in the form of a musical hum, translating a distinctive multicultural, multilingual heritage into another tongue. The resulting work in French is undeniably *multiple*: revealing not only its multiple sources but also what Derrida identifies as the "multiplicity of languages in any language."[48] By respecting cultural and linguistic differences and inserting elements that resist translation into their work, Cixous, Djebar, and Khatibi infuse the French text with *plurality*.

Notes

1. Khatibi highlights the fact that Arabic is a language that contains silence *within* it: "As Moncef Chelli reminds us, classical Arabic grammar itself uses concepts such as *as-sawamit* for consonants (the silences, the mutes) and *al-harakat* for vowels and diacritical accents (movements). This linguistic conception of movement, of stasis and silence, that belongs to our logic, to another metaphysics of the sign, demands to be treated in its element of theorization and classification" (*Maghreb pluriel* 182).

2. "Indeed, Occident, I split myself, but my identity is an infinity of games, of roses of sand" (*La Mémoire* 187).

3. Addressing desire in the autobiographical text recalls *L'Anti-Œdipe: Capitalisme et schizophrénie* by Gilles Deleuze and Félix Guattari, a work that explores the schizophrenic and/in his or her relation to desire: "schizophrenia is the process of the production of desire and desiring machines" (31–32).

4. Silence is referred to frequently in *La Mémoire tatouée*, as in the following rhetorical question: "Who will write their silence, memory of the slightest deletion?" (26). In a text dedicated to Jacques Derrida, *Vœu de silence*, Khatibi makes it clear that he conceives of silence in a musical sense: "The poet sees all these characters

without speaking himself now in the musical mode of silence. [. . .] This simultaneity allows the poet to construct beautiful metaphors on a melodious movement" (22).

5. Derrida is also attentive to the fact that language does not constitute property: "Because there is no natural property of language, language gives rise only to appropriative madness, to jealousy without appropriation" (*Monolingualism* 24).

6. For a careful study of the crucial relation between politics and language in the history of the French nation, see Michel de Certeau, Dominique Julia, and Jacques Revel's *Une politique de la langue*, especially pages 169–80. For a thorough and thoughtful examination of the interconnection between language and power in Algeria, see *Langue et pouvoir en Algérie: Histoire d'un traumatisme linguistique* by Mohamed Benrabah. Benrabah places French colonization within a larger history of invasions and dominations in North Africa, and indicates that Algerian subjects during the time of French occupation adjusted to the new language as they had in the past: "In fact, the colonial educational system and the French language were imposed on the oppressed society as a necessary evil for survival" (56).

7. As we have already seen, the French language came from a "Metropole" that was located "elsewhere," but intended nonetheless to be considered "homeland": "Elsewhere, that means the Metropole. In the Capital-City-Mother-Fatherland" (*Monolingualism* 41).

8. Derrida engages in numerous reflections on the language to which he was historically destined in a variety of texts, including his autobiographical "Circonfession": "for I give myself death, one only says this in a language that the colonization of Algeria in 1830, one century before me, gave me as a present, I don't take my life, but I give myself death" ("Circonfession" 263). In his own comments on the term that defines him, "francophone" Khatibi ardently maintains that the term "francophonie" is not uniquely tied to the significant occurrence of French colonization, but that it refers to something separate, to the emergence of the French language as a mixture of Latin lexicon and local syntax yielding a linguistic history that is not *only* tied to an instance of domination: "what one calls francophonie or francographie dates and does not date from the colonial and postcolonial period" (139). My ironic use of the term "nos ancêtres, les Gaulois" is an intentional nod to these words often evoked in Francophone texts by writers from colonized regions whose apprenticeship of the French tongue is accompanied by the inculcation (or indoctrination) of French *ideals* as well as French *history*—the first leading to a *prise de conscience* which often led to rebellion (in the name of *liberté, égalité, fraternité*), and the second proving laughable (as in this example of ancestors from Gaul) given its inapplicability to the case of those whose genealogical roots did/do not tie them to French soil. Hélène Cixous indicates that she was subjected to this term during her childhood in Algeria, as we have already seen: "Me too. The routine 'our ancestors, the Gauls' was pulled on me" ("Sorties" 71).

9. Fanon underscores the fact that acquiring a knowledge of the colonizer's tongue entails much more than simple linguistic competence; learning a new language means taking on a culture, an entire civilization: "To speak means above all to use a

certain syntax, to grasp the morphology of this or that language, but it means above all to assume a culture, to support the weight of a civilization" (17–18).

10. My use of the verb " to possess" in this instance is not innocent, as it resonates with the term "to master" a language, concepts that are refuted by both Derrida and Khatibi's comments on the inappropriability of the "foreign" (or the "native") tongue.

11. "The story of the bi-langue and the pluri-langue exorcized his obsessions" (*Love* 46).

12. "And I will have jealously vindicated my being sacrificed to the French language" (*La Mémoire tatouée*, vii).

13. "We will say it again, the day of my birth (1938) is the very day of Aïd el Kébir, the festival commemorating Abraham's sacrifice" (*La Mémoire tatouée* 10). In her close reading of Khatibi's autobiographical text, Lucy Stone McNeece picks up on the term of "sacrifice" and integrates it into her analysis: "Khatibi's novel invites the reader to become fully aware of what it means to write in a postcolonial context, and how close indeed writing is to one's sense of self and one's desire. He demonstrates that writing in the language of another culture involves no less than the sacrifice and the recreation of the self" (13).

14. Khatibi thus belongs to the generation of writers who "master" French and publish brilliant, new, innovative compositions in this foreign language according to Benrabah's description: "From 1945 on, Algerian writers began to change their tone and progressively assume political consciousness. In contrast to the silence of the preceding generation, this one experiences success because of its engagement, the quality of its literature, its perfect mastery of French, and the fact that it publishes in France. Just like their ancestors, these Algerian authors adopt the language of the invader and use it with brio. Often possessing great aesthetic and literary value, these new publications transform the French language, in content as in form" (60).

15. In "Encre blanche et Afrique originelle," Chantal Zabus examines the "intertextual affinities" between French thinkers like Roland Barthes and Jacques Derrida and "Maghrebian" writers such as Abdelwahab Meddeb and Abdelkébir Khatibi (262–63).

16. Critics Bill Ashcroft, Gareth Griffiths, and Helen Tiffin make the following assertion in *Key Concepts in Post-Colonial Studies*: "post-structuralist theories (such as that of Derrida) might be reread as less the products of the Parisian intellectual climate than inspired or significantly inflected by colonial experience" (193).

17. While their native territories belong to the same general region known as the Maghreb, these countries have histories that are markedly diverse in crucial ways that Khatibi underscores in his response to Derrida. For instance, the Jewish community in Algeria lost its citizenship while such was never the case in Morocco: "[T]hat was not the case in Morocco: beginning with the *dahir* of 1864 (shortly before the Crémieux decree), the Jewish community has benefited from a citizenship and a juridical status that respects its beliefs. It is therefore another context that formed my sensitivity and my particular interest in the Israeli-Arab conflict and its tragic destiny" (25).

18. This moment is addressed by Khatibi in *Maghreb pluriel*: "When we speak of this Maghrebian generation of the 1960s and we fix our attention on the political preoccupations of that period, we see ourselves retrospectively as torn between third-world nationalism and dogmatic Marxism in French fashion [. . .] we never accepted the fact that the French communist party, with which we sympathized at the time, was so slow to understand the Algerian liberation movement; and through this event, the emergence of a politics whose ideological base escaped it" (14).

19. Derrida admits that his desire to speak perfect French is motivated by a deeper desire to challenge everything tied to this language: "speak in good French, in pure French, even at the moment of challenging in a million ways everything that is allied to it, and sometimes everything that inhabits it" (*Monolingualism* 49).

20. In this passage, Khatibi employs a common tactic of his writing style that consists of infusing his texts with specific words recalling Derridian conceptions of textual analysis. The verbe "disséminer" resonates with one of Jacques Derrida's earliest publications, *La Dissémination* (Seuil, 1972).

21. Derrida reminds us that language always has a status of "other": "We only ever speak one language—and, since it returns to the other, it exists asymmetrically, always for the other, from the other, kept by the other. Coming from the other, remaining with the other, and returning to the other" (*Monolingualism* 40).

22. Derrida's attention to the idea of "mastery" with respect to language is related to the idea of a "master" who imposes his language on the colonized people. The ludicrous aspect of such imposition is clear with respect to the master's own lack of mastery over his "own" language: "For contrary to what one if often most tempted to believe, the master is nothing. And he does not have exclusive possession of anything. Because the master does not possess exclusively, and *naturally*, what he calls his language, because, whatever he wants or does, he cannot maintain any relations of property or identity that are natural, national, congenital, or ontological, with it, because he can give substance to and articulate [*dire*] this appropriation only in the course of an unnatural process of politico-phantasmatic constructions, because language is not his natural possession, he can, thanks to that very fact, pretend historically, through the rape of a cultural usurpation, which means always essentially colonial, to appropriate it in order to impose it as 'his own'" (*Monolingualism* 23).

23. This equivalence becomes especially clear in the case of a foreigner: "[T]he foreigner is first of all foreign to the legal language in which the duty of hospitality is formulated, the right to asylum, its limits, norms, policing, etc. He has to ask for hospitality in a language which by definition is not his own, the one imposed on him by the master of the house, the host, the king, the lord, the authorities, the nation, the State, the father, etc. This personage imposes on him translation into their own language, that's the first act of violence" (*Of Hospitality* 15–17).

24. Rosello mentions Khatibi's *Amour bilingue* and Derrida's *Le Monolinguisme de l'autre* in her reading of various postcolonial Francophone "texts" (novels and films) in her exploration of the "translatability of hospitality" (21). She concludes that both guest and host must be willing to take a risk (reminiscent of the risk Khatibi evokes

with respect to writing) of "being challenged, shaken, changed by the encounter." Without this risk, there is no hospitality: "The very precondition of hospitality may require that, in some ways, both the host and the guest accept, in different ways, the uncomfortable and sometimes painful possibility of being changed by the other, of his or her different values or points of view, will undoubtedly constitute the by-product and the visible evidence of hospitable gestures" (175–76).

25. Derrida accords great significance to the linguistic innovation of multilingual texts, deeming it capable of dismantling the colonizing power inherent in every language: "It is in *treating otherwise* each language, in *adding* languages to each other, in playing with the multiplicity of codes within every linguistic corpus that we can fight both against colonization in general—against the colonizing principle (and this principle is present far beyond the zones considered submissive to colonization)—and against the domination of language or through language" (*Du droit à la philosophie* 163–64).

26. See "Fidélité à plus d'un," especially pages 252 and 253.

27. A notable exception to this trend is the thorough and insightful article by Anne Donadey those title bears witness to "The Multilingual Strategies of Postcolonial Literature." Donadey alerts her reader to the multilingual context of Francophone texts from North Africa before giving a detailed analysis of the way Arabic and French interact in Djebar's corpus.

28. I borrow the words "different sensibility" from Françoise Lionnet in *Postcolonial Representations*. Lionnet addresses the way Francophone writers appropriate the colonizer's language: "the use of French is a means of translating into the colonizer's language a different sensibility, a different vision of the world, a means therefore of transforming the dominant conceptions circulated by the more standard idiom" (13). Some critics are reluctant to use the term "translation" in the absence of an "original" text; for a discussion of another term used to describe the "sort of translation" that takes place when a writer approximates his or her native tongue in a Europhone text, Chantal Zabus proposes the linguistic term "relexification" (314).

29. This reflection from Khatibi's *Amour bilingue* makes explicit reference to the "silent" mother tongue that emerges in the French text: "When I speak to you in your language, what happens to mine? Does my language continue to speak, but in silence? Because it's never eliminated from those moments. When I speak to you, I feel the flow of the mother tongue divide into two streams: one is gutturally silent, the other, running on empty, unmakes itself with an implosion into the disorder of bilingualism" (41).

30. Khatibi discusses the use of Italian in the following terms: "Italian, here, language of pure pleasure, paradisiacal language of the hedonic game, far from the violent contradiction of French and Arabic" ("Incipits" 179). In a similar way, though perhaps less pleasurable in the end, the third tongue of her Algerian upbringing comes to disrupt the rivalry between Arabic and French in Djebar's written work: "these two languages (for me, Arabic, the maternal tongue with its milk, its tenderness, its luxuriance, but also its diglossia, and French, stepmother tongue I have

called it, or adversarial tongue to explain the adversity), these two languages intertwine and rival with each other, face off or form a couple, but against the background of this third language of eternal Berber memory, an uncivilized and unmastered language" (*Ces voix* 34).

31. In Khatibi's analysis, "From that moment, the writing in French that restructures all of *Talismano*—by marking the game of the palimpsest—inverses by that gesture the relationship of the 'target language' to the 'source language,' or more exactly the 'source language' which is a diglossia between the phoneme and the grapheme, finds itself to be the 'target language'" ("Incipits" 192). Djebar seems to support this circular "return to the source" with her comments on writing in the foreign tongue, as translation which brings her back to the cries that initially inspired her: "Writing in a foreign language [. . .] has brought me to the cries of the women silently rebelling in my youth, to my own true origins" (*Fantasia* 204).

32. Djebar recognizes that diversity of languages is at the root of Algerian culture: "Such breadth in the understanding of Algerian texts allows for the inscription of the multiplicity of languages (Latin, Arabic, Berber, and French) at the very root of Algerian culture" (*Ces voix* 213).

33. These few owe their familiarity with this erudite tongue to years of study at the "*école coranique*." Djebar makes mention of her experience at this special school in *L'Amour, la fantasia*. Unfortunately, she did not spend enough time at the school to become proficient in written Arabic, and to this day her knowledge of the language remains primarily oral. In a poem recently published in *Research in African Literatures*, Djebar revisits this period of her childhood: "The *galam* in hand / my pen from Qur'an school / when, a girl, close to the orange trees / and the streams whose water sang / I learned to write / the first verse / the last" ("RAÏS, BENTALHA . . . Un an après").

34. In *L'Amour, la fantasia*, Djebar mentions Ibn Khaldun and Saint Augustine as precursors who have told their stories in another tongue following invasions and occupations in the Maghreb: "As with Augustine, it matters little to him that he writes in a language introduced into the land of his fathers by conquest and accompanied by bloodshed!" (*Fantasia* 216).

35. John Erickson translates this passage slightly differently in an article on the role of translation in Djebar's homage to her countrymen; in his version, Algeria itself is written in blood: "an Algeria written in blood, alas!" ("Translating the Untranslated: Djebar's *Le Blanc de l'Algérie*").

36. Khatibi bears witness to his location as a writing body between languages as well, as in the following statement from an article on bilingualism: "Rereading myself, I discover that my most completed (French) sentence is a reminder. The reminder of an unpronounceable body, neither Arab(ic) nor French, neither dead nor alive, neither man nor woman: generation of the text" ("Incipits" 207).

37. "Between-two-languages, for a writer unable to be other than a writer, means to place oneself in the nervous, unnerved, dis-nerved, painful, and mysterious air of all language: a situation often frequent for ex-colonial writers, from the lands of the French, English, Spanish, Dutch, or Portuguese Empire of yesterday" (*Ces voix* 30).

38. This "Third Space of enunciation" in Bhabha's critique can be conceived as closely related to his conception of "hybridity" (a horticultural term referring to a third species created by the cross-breeding of two species by grafting or cross-pollination to form a third, "hybrid" species). For more on the "Third Space of enunciation," please see *Location of Culture*, especially pp. 37–38.

39. Khatibi's use of the word "internationalism" recalls Bhabha's employment of the term in his discourse on cultural difference: "It is significant that the productive capacities of this Third Space have a colonial or postcolonial provenance. For a willingness to descend into that alien territory . . . may open the way to conceptualizing an *inter*national culture, based not on the exoticism of multiculturalism or the *diversity* of cultures, but on the inscription and articulation of culture's *hybridity*" (38).

40. The emphasis on religion in this passage is significant, for the Arabic tongue of Khatibi's illiterate mother is replete with expressions tied to Islamic culture, as evidenced in the following two quotations from *Amour bilingue*: "Living without belief: perhaps, but what became of the spirits, the phantoms and the angels of his mother tongue? He thought of the superstitious talk of his childhood and of his illiterate mother." (43); "In my country, there's a ceremony of the answer without a question: proverbial speech, empty maxims, unpronounceable ritornello. Spell this: there is no God but Allah" (81).

41. In both cases, it is clear that Frantz Fanon's comments on language and culture in *Peau noire, masques blancs* are well founded. Acquiring knowledge of the colonizer's tongue entails much more than simple linguistic competence; learning a new language means taking on a culture, an entire civilization. Both Khatibi and Djebar are acquainted with languages endowed with cultural baggage, as their numerous metalinguistic commentaries reveal in their critical essays and fictional works.

42. In the introduction to her English translation of *L'Amour, la fantasia*, Dorothy Blair makes careful note of the two meanings of "Fantasia" in the title: "The *Fantasia* (derived from the Arabic *fantaziya* [meaning ostentation]), is in North Africa a set of virtuoso movements on horseback executed at a gallop, accompanied by loud cries and culminating in rifle shots; the *Fantasia*, associated with ceremonial occasions and military triumphs, forms the *leitmotif* of the novel as well as providing its title. But a *Fantasia* (Italian for 'fantasy' or 'fancy') is also a musical composition in which, according to the definition given in Kennedy's *Concise Oxford Dictionary of Music*, 'form is of secondary importance . . . in the sixteenth and seventeenth centuries such compositions were usually contrapuntal and in several sections, thus being an early form of variations . . . compositions, in which the character of the music suggested an improvisational character or the play of free fancy'" (*Fantasia* iii).

43. It is precisely the existence of "double meaning" (and associated word play) that renders literary texts unique and *untranslatable*. Khatibi, arguably engaged in a textual conversation with Derrida, asserts that the great French writers of the twentieth century enact a translation of French within French: "Yes, who doesn't remember Marcel Proust's limpid phrase: 'Beautiful books are written in a sort of foreign language.' Yes, yes, that's the ideal, a dream, perhaps, of every inventive writer. . . . To

write inside of languages, to translate French within French, is a difficult proposition to make clear. But Mallarmé, Rimbaud, Proust, and many others, explicitly affirmed the necessity, for the writer, to invent idioms 'within' French" (*La Langue* 28). In speaking of his own work, Derrida affirms that finding a singularity that resists translation is, ironically enough, his goal *and* the secret to his success *in translation*, as we saw in the previous section.

44. The "translation" found in the texts of Djebar and Khatibi strictly confounds the conception of translation as "*métaphrasis*," or a rephrasing, as defined by Derrida: "*Métaphrasis* is the Greek word for translation, what happens from one language or from one sentence to another by the transfer of a 'that is to say.' *Metaphrasô*: I transport from one sentence or one language into another, I paraphrase, I *périphrase*, I translate, I pass by the metaphrastic copula of 'that is,' by the operation of a 'that is to say.'" ("H. C." 127).

45. As Étienne explains, "Pluralism presupposes a competitive situation and the end of monopoly, thus a situation of freedom of choice. The emergence of the question of the Other in pluralism does not allow for the construction of unmovable, exclusive categories. . . ." ("Le statut de l'islam dans l'Europe plurielle" 81).

46. In Benrabah's words, "This is our proposal for a solution to the question of the Arabic language in Algeria where Berber, Algerian Arabic and French will be able to exist side by side in a situation of equality and conviviality" (*Langue et pouvoir* 327).

47. In a book review of *La Maladie de l'Islam*, Mustapha Harzoune emphasizes the following phrase by Meddeb: "the freedom of a plural, conflicted word installs itself, maintaining discord in civility" (148).

48. "For there is always more than one language in a language, in what one calls a language. When one translates, one reduces the plural to the one. What is always difficult to translate . . . is the multiplicity of languages in a language" ("Fidélité" 252).

CADENZA

~

Nothing to Declare:
Crossing the Border from
Confession to Testimony

I have never breathed a word about music.

> —Jacques Derrida, Unpublished comments, 1 February 2003
> "Débat autour d'un livre: Marie-Louise Mallet, *La musique en respect*"

I couldn't live without testifying.

> —Abdelkébir Khatibi, *La Langue de l'Autre* (1999)

If the Greeks invented tragedy, the Romans the epistle and the Renaissance the sonnet, our generation invented a new literature, that of testimony.

> —Elie Wiesel, "The Holocaust as a Literary Inspiration" (1977)

I began these reflections with an overture addressing questions of language and identifications in the work of three writers from the Maghreb. In that opening chapter, I discussed "Francophonie" and its implications for contemporary writers from outside France whose literary compositions elude classifications dependent on "national" assignations. I argued for a revalorization of the term "Francophonie" in an inclusive sense consistent with its etymology, favoring broader considerations of work written in French. The subsequent chapters have evoked the specificities of the life trajectories and written works of Assia Djebar, Hélène Cixous, and Abdelkébir Khatibi, in light of the similar, yet different contexts in which they were born and grew up. Placing these voices alongside each other in unprecedented manner, I have attempted throughout this study to bring out the affinities among these three writers in their various texts of differing genres. I have also emphasized the "dissonant passages," the divergent notes that demarcate each from the others and set apart individual "signatures" that render any generalizing label inadequate to describe the person—and the œuvre. The proper name has occupied a primary place in this book, especially in the first two chapters where it became evident that the autobiographical writers in my study dedicate considerable reflection to names in their work. The subtle, careful inclusion—or omission—of an appellation shapes the literary text in monumental ways that are at once legal, social, and personal. The strains of naming are in harmony with the overtones of language that run the length of these chapters.

It goes without saying that writers such as Cixous, Djebar, and Khatibi do not take language lightly. While they often "make light" of language in the text, they always do so with serious intensity and heightened awareness of the many meanings inherent in every word, of the history present in each expression. They draw from a solid training in literary basics to create improvisational texts that have resonance beyond a single tongue, beyond the borders of a single nation and its culture. Concentrating on music as a thematic refrain and formal structure in these texts, I have sought to demonstrate that "language" is not limited to national idioms, and that it extends to include other modes of communication from silence to outcries. The emphasis I have placed on "translation," in a broad sense of the word, is intended to underscore the movement that occurs when writers from North Africa compose in French: texts by the three writers in my study are arguably "multilingual" and "multicultural," translating "foreign" experiences and concepts into the written work. These translations are never definitive, but instead point to the possibilities for new creativity, for variations to come. Aware of past and present history, these writers draw productively from it, paving the way for future compositions.

A cadenza is a technically brilliant, often improvised, solo passage toward the end of a concerto. I have chosen this title for these final remarks because rather than "conclude," I wish to point toward one of many possible further motifs to be developed with respect to the writings of Assia Djebar, Hélène Cixous, and Abdelkébir Khatibi. It would be inappropriate to propose a conclusion to this study of writers whose own works do not provide a predictable sense of closure, but instead constitute openings toward other writings. Like the solo performers of a cadenza, the writers in this study work alone, and they occasionally express the solitude that characterizes—and is necessitated by—their literary gestures. But, like the musician, the notes they create during solitary moments are meant to complement the notes produced by others in the orchestra, those that have already been heard and those that are yet to come. Much more than a parenthetical moment in the piece, a cadenza is the highlight, the exclamation point, the climax, and it marks an opportunity for the trained musician to showcase talent by improvising. Taking the strains of the original composer's work, the soloist may work and rework them, and play a composition that bears an inimitable signature.

The signatures of the writers in my study are often, and rightly, considered "autobiographical," even if none of their works can be labeled "autobiography" in the traditional sense of the word. Autobiographical literature in French always immediately recalls the seminal text by Jean-Jacques Rousseau: his *Confessions* remain the definitive point of reference when it comes to writing one's life story. But this work harks back to an earlier text of the same title, of course, and Saint Augustine's writings also occupy a central place in the work of Cixous and Derrida.[1] Indeed, the latter's autobiographical "Circonfession" is a creative (and personal) close reading of the Latin text. Augustine is also of significance to Djebar, who articulates affinities between her own case and his, pointing out that he was also from North Africa, and that his language of composition was not his "mother tongue." But, despite their familiarity with and appreciation for confessional narrative, it is my contention that these writers are not content to compose works that follow in this tradition. Instead of falling into the category of "confession," the autobiographical works of these contemporary writers from the Maghreb constitute "testimony," exhibiting a different conception of writing the self.

I am arguing here for a shift in terminology, moving away from the idea of "confession" because it entails two problematic ideas. The first is in the person of the "confessor" to whom one admits wrongdoing. In the hierarchical confessional scene, the confessor is the one with the power. This binary relation places the confessor in the superior position, able to judge the guilt of the confessant. The second troublesome concept in the term "confession" is that of implied guilt. It is assumed that one is confessing one's sins, and that one has been naughty and must be punished before he or she is exonerated. In the autobiographical works in my study, the writers do not seek forgiveness. In fact, they seldom admit to any crime. One notable exception is found in the case of the shocking avowals of Cixous; but even in these textual moments, she proudly claims her act and even defends it; she does not want to be absolved, asserting that great literature results from theft. In a number of texts, notably *Three Steps on the Ladder of Writing*, Cixous indicates that expiation is not the goal of her writing project, and warns that atonement is something to be avoided, not sought: "the moment we avow we fall into the snare of atonement: confession—and forgetfulness. Confession is the worst thing: it disavows what it avows" (45).

When Derrida asks if there has ever been an autobiography unmarked by confession, he just may be pointing to this "crossing of borders" toward a new term, "testimony," that occupies much of his work on the law, on hospitality, and on the law(s) of hospitality. Derrida locates confession geographically and chronologically, indicating its emergence—and persistence—as a distinctively Christian phenomenon.[2] While he seems to be searching here for a confessional form situated outside the confines of religion and its history, Derrida does not seem to be pushing for a simple "secularization" of confession.[3] Rather, he is gesturing toward a horizon with different premises, distanced from "notre culture de la subjectivité" (271), on the other side of the "border" between self and other, in line with this movement described in *Sauf le nom*: "Augustine does not respond only to the question: 'why confess myself to you, God, who know everything in advance?' He speaks of 'making truth' (*veritatem facere*), which does not mean revealing, unveiling, or informing in line with cognitive reason. Maybe it means testifying [*témoigner*]" (24).[4] The transition from confession to testimony is therefore present in the very work of Saint Augustine, in Derrida's analysis: "He answers the question of public testimony, the written. A written testimony appears more public and thus, as some will be tempted to believe, more appropriate to the essence of testimony, to the afterlife through the trial of testamentary statement" (*Sauf* 24).[5]

In their collaborative publication *Testimony: Crises of Witnessing in Literature, Psychoanalysis, and History*, Shoshana Felman and Dori Laub identify the power of testimony to accomplish things, to bring about change and exert an influence not only on events, but attitudes as well: "Testimony is, in other words, a discursive *practice*, as opposed to a pure *theory*. To testify—to *vow to tell*, to *promise* and *produce* one's own speech as material evidence for truth—is to accomplish a *speech act*, rather than to simply formulate a statement" (5). In this critical work, as in others that deal with "testimonial" writing, events are not remembered in a logical, coherent manner; this is a form that allows for representation of reality in step with the unreasonable, discontinuous nature of its experience, and its memory.[6] It is significant that Felman places emphasis on the address to the other that is inherent in the act of testifying:

> To testify—before a court of law or before the court of history and of the future; to testify, likewise, before an audience of readers or spectators—is more

than simply to report a fact or an event or to relate what has been lived, recorded and remembered. Memory is conjured here essentially in order to *address* another, to impress upon a listener, to *appeal* to a community. To testify is always, metaphorically, to take the witness stand, or to take the position of the witness insofar as the narrative account of the witness is at once engaged in an appeal and bound by an oath. To testify is thus not merely to narrate but to commit oneself, and to commit the narrative, to others: to *take responsibility*— in speech—for history or for the truth of an occurrence, for something which, by definition, goes beyond the personal, in having general (nonpersonal) validity and consequences.

Rather than being bound up uniquely with the self, the "testimony" of the autobiographical works in this study signals a commitment, a dedication, and an acceptance of profound responsibility toward a community, toward an entity that extends beyond the self.

The contemporary writers in this study are producing works in the wake of unjust acts committed against people in their country of origin. The personal emphasis of traditional autobiography (which is meant to be "universal," but in an arguably selfish manner) has turned outward to encompass families, clans, indeed to embrace entire groups of people who have been wronged. Such writing does not seek to expose sin and have it forgiven—and forgotten. It seeks instead to testify, to bear witness, to give testimony.[7] Its goal may be *only* to expose the wrong, with the understanding that in exposing it, the wrong is already changed. Writing is the act by which things are transformed, by which borders are crossed, by which new music is played, and heard.

The place of music in these contemporary autobiographical works should not be underestimated. While the strains may not always be harmonious, they do not fall into the trap of cacophony, I argue. Instead, they make productive use of *dissonance*, in accordance with Felman's understanding of its possibilities: "Testimonial teaching fosters the capacity to witness something that may be surprising, cognitively dissonant. The surprise implies the crisis. Testimony cannot be authentic without that crisis, which has to break and to transvaluate previous categories and previous frames of reference" (53–54).[8] Even though some innovative musical pieces may sound discordant, that does not mean their composers are not well trained in the art of "classical" music. In all art forms, the new often makes considerable breaks with the old, but it can still benefit from established methods *even as* it establishes a distance from them. Conceiving of autobiographical writing in musical terms that bear witness—or give testimony—to lived experience, marking a specific moment in time, is reminiscent of the improvising artist of the cadenza: heading in new directions during solo passages takes place within certain parameters, dependent on a composer's notes. In like manner, the *Confessions* constitute a musical keynote from which subsequent autobiographical texts can take off, as evidenced in these words by Derrida:

> But can a postscript ever interpret itself, in the sense of a hermeneutic reading as well as a musical performance, for example, without composing at least indirectly with the scansion of the Augustinian score? An analogous question could be posed for all that we call autobiography in the West, no matter what the singularity of its "here and now."

> Do you mean to say that every "here and now" of a western autobiography is already in memory of the "here and now" of the *Confessions*?

> Yes, but they themselves were already, in their most savage present, on their date, in their place, an act of memory. (*Sauf le nom* 26)

The time signatures that denote the "here and now" of the life and writing of Assia Djebar, Hélène Cixous, and Abdelkébir Khatibi effectively draw from familial, linguistic, geographic, and cultural roots. These writers make use of their individual, idiosyncratic backgrounds to produce unprecedented literary works in French, I have maintained throughout this study. This final note, in the form of a "cadenza," touches briefly upon the many improvisational methods these wordsmiths have at their fingerprints when they draw from confessional tradition to traverse borderlines and give their own renditions in surprising, syncopated forms of testimony.

Notes

1. In an autobiographical essay, "L'animal que donc je suis," Derrida addresses this "lineage" of "confession" from Augustine to Rousseau, but throws a new factor into the equation by highlighting the presence of Descartes: "Between Saint Augustine and Rousseau, in the same, undeniable filiation, in the differentiated history of the *ego cogito ergo sum*, there is Descartes. He awaits us with his animal-machines. I assume that he won't interrupt the line of descent that, for some time now, has tied the genre of autobiography to the institution of confession" (272).

2. "Is there [. . .] an older autobiography that is free [*intacte*] of all confession, a story of the self that is untouched [*vierge*] by all confession? [. . .] An autobiography and memoirs that predate Christianity, above all, that predate the Christian institutions of confession?" ("L'animal que donc je suis" 271–72). For an insightful reading of Derrida's "Circonfession," with special attention to questions of "truth" and "contamination" in this autobiographical text, see Peggy Kamuf's "Seringues, ou les pointes aiguës du hérisson" in *Passions de la littérature*.

3. J. M. Coetzee reflects on the implications of a "secular" confession in *Doubling the Point*: "whatever authority a confession bears in a secular context derives from the status of the confessant as a hero of the labyrinth willing to confront the worst within himself" (263). In an essay titled "Deconstruction and Fiction," Derek Attridge addresses "truth" and "fiction" in literature, exploring Coetzee's treatment of "the structural interminability of confession in the secular context" (112) alongside Derrida's emphasis on the affinities between "the institution of literature" and "the notion of confession" (117).

4. Keith Walker's work reveals that confession and testimony cannot be considered synonymous, even if they are connected in certain ways. In *Countermodernism and Francophone Literary Culture*, testimony seems to prevail as a means of bringing victory to a political prisoner: "The counter-confessional testimony of the surviving political prisoner [is] a triple victory over shame, personal and collective amnesia, and the intimidation of torture and human rights abuse" (229).

5. Françoise Lionnet's lucid, detailed reading of the *Confessions* in *Autobiographical Voices* reminds us that the work's purpose is "twofold: Augustine confesses his sins to God and lets others, his brothers, know of his trials and errors so that his conversion may be an example to them" (42).

6. The most striking example of testimony may be in response to trauma, when all points of reference (including linguistic) are overthrown by the intensity of the experience. Felman's treatment of the phenomenon of testimony hints at this: "As a relation to events, testimony seems to be composed of bits and pieces of a memory that has been overwhelmed by occurrences that have not settled into understanding or remembrance, acts that cannot be constructed as knowledge nor assimilated into full cognition, events in excess of our frames of reference" (5). Sarah Kofman's work deals with the human impulse to create a story in the face of the unspeakable horrors of Auschwitz: "To speak in order to bear witness. But how? How can testimony escape the idyllic law of the story? [. . .] Robert Antelme's book *The Human Race* [. . .] underscores the need for fabulation, for the selection of events and therefore of writing, when trying to communicate unbearable truths" (36–37).

7. This is how Gayatri Spivak interprets testimony, in an essay that distinguishes it from autobiography: "Testimony is the genre of the subaltern giving witness to oppression, to a less oppressed other" ("Three Women's Texts and Circumfession" 7).

8. Felman's use of the element of surprise resonates with Derrida's evocation of surprise with respect to sincerity and truth in autobiography: "why would truth be due? And taken, surprised from the first moment, in a logic of debt and duty? Because truth would be owed to a veracity, to an unveiling of the self, to a truth of the self as sincerity?" ("L'animal" 271). Surprise (and unpredictability) is also an important element of testimony in Doris Sommer's view: "one of the most fascinating features of [Latin American *testimonios*] is their unpredictable pattern, the sense that the discourse of analysis and struggle is being created in an open-ended and syncretic process of trial, error, and surprise" (120).

Bibliography

Ahmad, Aijaz. "Jameson's Rhetoric of Otherness and the 'National Allegory.'" *The Post-Colonial Studies Reader.* Eds. Bill Ashcroft, Gareth Griffiths, and Helen Tiffin (London and New York: Routledge, 1995): 77–82.

Ahmed, Sara. *Strange Encounters: Embodied Others in Post-Coloniality.* London and New York: Routledge, 2000.

Alloula, Malek. *Le Harem colonial: Images d'un sous-érotisme.* Paris: Garance, 1981; Séguier, 2001.

American Heritage Dictionary online. http://dictionary.reference.com

Amrouche, Jean. [1939] *Chants berbères de Kabylie.* Paris: L'Harmattan, 1989.

Antelme, Robert. *L'espèce humaine.* Paris: Gallimard, 1957.

Ashcroft, Bill, Gareth Griffiths, and Helen Tiffin. *The Empire Writes Back: Theory and Practice in Post-Colonial Literatures.* London: Routledge, 1989.

———, eds. *Key Concepts in Post-Colonial Studies.* London and New York: Routledge, 1998.

———, eds. *The Post-Colonial Studies Reader.* London and New York: Routledge, 1995.

Attridge, Derek. "Deconstruction and Fiction." *Deconstructions: A User's Guide.* Ed. Nicholas Royle (New York: Palgrave, 2000): 105–118.

———. "'This Strange Institution Called Literature': An Interview with Jacques Derrida." Jacques Derrida. *Acts of Literature.* Ed. Derek Attridge (New York and London: Routledge, 1992): 33–75.

Austin, J. L. *How to Do Things with Words.* New York: Oxford University Press, 1962.

Barbé, Philippe. "Transnational and Translinguistic Relocation of the Subject in *Les Nuits de Strasbourg* by Assia Djebar." Ed. Françoise Lionnet. *L'Esprit Créateur* XVI, no. 3 (Fall 2001): 125–35.

Barthes, Roland. *La Chambre claire: Note sur la photographie.* Paris: Gallimard, 1980.
———. *Roland Barthes par Roland Barthes.* Paris: Seuil, 1975.
Ben Jelloun, Tahar. *L'Ecrivain public.* Paris: Seuil, 1983.
———. *Les Raisins de la galère.* Paris: Fayard, 1996.
———. "25ème Anniversaire de la Francophonie." *Inter treize quatorze en public du 20 mars 1995.* Radio interview aired on France Inter.
Bennington, Geoffrey, and Jacques Derrida. *Jacques Derrida.* Paris: Seuil, 1991.
Benrabah, Mohamed. *Langue et pouvoir en Algérie: Histoire d'un traumatisme linguistique.* Paris: Séguier, 1999.
Benslama, Fethi. "Identity as a Cause." *Research in African Literatures. Dissident Algeria.* Vol. 30, no. 3 (Fall 1999): 36–50.
———. *La Psychanalyse à l'épreuve de l'islam.* Paris: Aubier, 2002.
Bensmaïa, Réda. *Experimental Nations: Or, the Invention of the Maghreb.* Princeton and Oxford: Princeton University Press, 2003.
———. "La langue de l'étranger ou la Francophonie barrée." *Rue Descartes: Revue du Collège International de Philosophie* 37 (septembre 2002): 65–73.
Benveniste, Émile. *Le Vocabulaire des institutions indo-européennes.* Paris: Éditions de Minuit, 1969.
Berger, Anne-Emmanuelle, ed. *Algeria in Others' Languages.* Ithaca: Cornell University Press, 2002.
Berman, Antoine. [1985] "Translation and the Trials of the Foreign." Trans. Lawrence Venuti. *The Translation Studies Reader.* Ed. Lawrence Venuti (London and New York: Routledge, 2000): 284–97.
Bernabé, Jean, Raphaël Confiant, and Patrick Chamoiseau. *Éloge de la créolité.* Paris: Gallimard, 1989. *In Praise of Creoleness.* Trans. M. B. Taleb-Khyar. Edition bilingue. Gallimard, 1993.
Bhabha, Homi K. "DissemiNation: time, narrative, and the margins of the modern nation." *Nation and Narration.* Ed. Homi K. Bhabha (London and New York: Routledge, 1990): 291-322.
———. "Literary Engagements: The Haunting of History." Session, the 118th MLA Annual Convention. New York City. 29 December 2002.
———. *The Location of Culture.* London: Routledge, 1994.
Brunet, Guy, Pierre Darlu, and Gianna Zei, eds. *Le Patronyme: Histoire, anthropologie, société.* Paris: Éditions CNRS, 1999.
Butler, Judith. *Excitable Speech: A Politics of the Performative.* London and New York: Routledge, 1997.
Calle-Gruber, Mireille. *Du café à l'éternité: Hélène Cixous à l'œuvre.* Paris: Galilée, 2002.
———. "Le Livre d'heur(e)s d'Hélène Cixous." *Photos de racines.* (Paris: des Femmes, 1994): 163–76. "Afterword: Hélène Cixous' Book of Hours, Book of Fortune." Trans. Agnes Conacher and Catherine McGann. *The Hélène Cixous Reader.* Ed. Susan Sellers (London and New York: Routledge, 1994): 207–20.

————. "La merveille au quotidien. *Loin de Médine*: dans le passage du sacral à l'historial." *Assia Djebar ou la Résistance de l'écriture: Regards d'un écrivain d'Algérie* (Paris: Maisonneuve & Larose, 2001): 149–98.

Calle-Gruber, Mireille, and Hélène Cixous, eds. *Au Théâtre, Au cinéma, Au féminin.* Paris: L'Harmattan, 2001.

Carter, Paul. "Spatial History." *The Post-Colonial Studies Reader.* Eds. Bill Ashcroft, Gareth Griffiths, and Helen Tiffin (London and New York: Routledge, 1995): 375–77.

Caujolle, Christian. "Photographies d'informations et manipulations en tous genres." *Historiens et géographes face à la médiatisation de l'événement.* Ed. Samra Bonvoisin (Paris: Centre national de documentation pédagogique, 1999): 55–60.

Celan, Paul. *Gespräch im Gebirg.* Trans. J. E. Jackson and A. du Bouchet. *Im Strette.* Paris: Mercure de France, 1971.

Cesari, Jocelyne. *Musulmans et républicains.* Brussels: Complexe, 1998.

Chakrabarty, Dipesh. "Postcoloniality and the Artifice of History." *The Post-Colonial Studies Reader.* Eds. Bill Ashcroft, Gareth Griffiths, and Helen Tiffin (London and New York: Routledge, 1995): 383–88.

Chergui, Zebeïda, and Amazigh Kateb. *Kateb Yacine, un théâtre et trois langues.* Paris: Seuil, 2003.

Chraïbi, Driss. *Le Passé simple.* Paris: Denoël, 1954.

Cixous, Hélène. "À la source: Lévinas." *Magazine littéraire* 419 (avril 2003): 51–52.

————. "Albums et Légendes." *Photos de racines* (Paris: des Femmes, 1994): 177–213.

————. *L'Amour du loup et autres remords.* Paris: Galilée, 2003.

————. *Beethoven à jamais, ou l'existence de Dieu.* Paris: des femmes, 1993.

————. *Benjamin à Montaigne: Il ne faut pas le dire.* Paris: Galilée, 2001.

————. "The Book as One of Its Own Characters." Trans. Catherine Porter. *New Literary History* 33:3 (Summer 2002): 403–34.

————. "Coups de baguettes." *Au Théâtre, Au Cinéma, Au Féminin.* Eds. Mireille Calle-Gruber and Hélène Cixous (Paris: L'Harmattan, 2001): 41–54.

————. *Dedans.* Paris: Grasset, 1969.

————. *Entre l'écriture.* Paris: des femmes, 1986.

————. *Et soudain, des nuits d'éveils.* Paris: Le Théâtre du Soleil, September 1999.

————. "Fremdworte sind Glücksache." *La Pensée du Midi* n. 5–6 Actes Sud (October 2001): 14–22.

————. "La Fugitive." *Algérie à plus d'une langue.* Ed. Mireille Calle-Gruber. *Etudes littéraires* 33:3 Presses de l'Université Laval (Autumn 2001): 75–82.

————. "In October 1991." *On the Feminine.* Ed. Mireille Calle. *Du Féminin* (Québec: Les Éditions Le Griffon, 1993). Trans. Catherine McGann (New Jersey: Humanities Press International, 1996): 77–91.

————. "Letter to Zohra Drif." *parallax* 4:2 (1998): 189–96.

————. *Le Jour où je n'étais pas là.* Paris: Galilée, 2000.

————. *Jours de l'an.* Paris: des femmes, 1990.

————. "Le Lieu du Crime, le lieu du Pardon." *L'Indiade ou l'Inde de leurs rêves* (Paris: Théâtre du Soleil, 1987): 253–59. "The Place of Crime The Place of Forgiveness." Trans. Catherine MacGillivray. *The Hélène Cixous Reader*. Ed. Susan Sellers (London and New York: Routledge, 1994): 151–56.

————. "Letter to Zohra Drif." *parallax* 4:2 (1998): 189–96.

————. *Limonade tout était si infini*. Paris: des femmes, 1982.

————. "To Live the Orange." *The Hélène Cixous Reader*. Ed. Susan Sellers (London and New York: Routledge, 1994): 81–92.

————. *Manhattan*. Paris: Galilée, 2002.

————. "Mon Algériance." *Les Inrockuptibles* 115 (20 August–2 September 1997): 71–74. "My Algeriance, in other words: to depart, not to arrive from Algeria." *Stigmata: The Escaping Texts*. Trans. Eric Prenowitz (London and New York: Routledge, 1998): 153–72.

————. *Neutre*. Paris: Grasset, 1972.

————. *Le Nom d'Œdipe: Chant du corps interdit*. Paris: des femmes, 1978.

————. "Obstétriques cruelles." *AUTODAFE. La Revue du Parlement international des écrivains*. vol. 1 (Paris: Denoël 2000): 105–118.

————. *On ne part pas, on ne revient pas*. Paris: des femmes, 1991.

————. *OR, Les lettres de mon père*. Paris: des femmes, 1997.

————. *Osnabrück*. Paris: des femmes, 1999.

————. "Pieds nus." *Une enfance algérienne*. Ed. Leïla Sebbar (Paris: Gallimard, 1997): 55–66.

————. *Portrait de Jacques Derrida en Jeune Saint Juif*. Paris: Galilée, 2001. *Portrait of Jacques Derrida as a Young Jewish Saint*. Trans. Beverly Bie Brahic. New York: Columbia University Press, 2004.

————. "Preface." *The Hélène Cixous Reader*. Ed. and trans. Susan Sellers (London and New York: Routledge, 1994): xv–xxii.

————. *Le Prénom de Dieu*. Paris: Grasset, 1967.

————. *Prénoms de personne*. Paris: Seuil, 1974.

————. *Rêve je te dis*. Paris: Galilée, 2003.

————. *Les Rêveries de la femme sauvage: Scènes primitives*. Paris: Galilée, 2000.

————. *Révolution pour plus d'un Faust*. Paris: Seuil, 1978.

————. "Le Rire de la Méduse." *L'Arc* 61 (1975): 39–54. "The Laugh of the Medusa." Trans. Keith Cohen and Paula Cohen. *Signs* 1:4 (1976): 875–94.

————. *Rouen, la Trentième Nuit de Mai '31*. Paris: Galilée, 2001.

————. "Sorties: Out and Out: Attacks/Ways Out/Forays." *The Newly Born Woman*. Trans. Betsy Wing (Minneapolis: University of Minnesota Press): 63–132. Originally published in *Souffles* (Paris: des femmes, 1975).

————. *Souffles*. Paris: des femmes, 1975.

————. "Stigmata, or Job the Dog." *Stigmata: The Escaping Texts*. Trans. Eric Prenowitz (London and New York: Routledge, 1998): 181–94.

————. "Le Théâtre surpris par les Marionnettes." Paris: Théâtre du Soleil, 1999–2003. http://www.theatre-du-soleil.fr/tambour/txt-cisoux.shtml

———. *Three Steps on the Ladder of Writing*. (The Wellek Library Lectures at the University of California, Irvine, 1990) Trans. Sarah Cornell and Susan Sellers. New York: Columbia University Press, 1993.

———. "The Two Countries of Writing: Theater and Poetical Fiction." *The Other Perspective in Gender and Culture: Rewriting Women and the Symbolic*. Ed. Juliet Flower MacCannell (New York: Columbia University Press, 1990).

———. "Unmasked!" Trans. Eric Prenowitz. *Stigmata: Escaping Texts* (London and New York: Routledge, 1998): 131–38.

———. "La Venue à l'écriture." (1977) *Entre l'écriture* (Paris: Des femmes, 1986): 9–69.

———. *Vivre l'orange*. Paris: des femmes, 1989.

———. *Un Vrai jardin*. Paris: L'Herne, 1971, Paris: des femmes, 1986.

———. "Writing Blind: Conversation with the Donkey." Trans. Eric Prenowitz. *Stigmata: Escaping Texts* (London and New York: Routledge, 1998): 139–51.

———. *The Writing Notebooks*. Trans. Susan Sellers. New York: Continuum Publishing, 2004.

———, and Mireille Calle-Gruber. *Hélène Cixous, Photos de racines*. Paris: Des femmes, 1994. *Hélène Cixous Rootprints: Memory and Life Writing*. Trans. Eric Prenowitz. London and New York: Routledge, 1997.

———, and Catherine Clément. *La Jeune Née*. Paris: Christian Bourgois, 1975.

———, and Jacques Derrida. *Voiles*. Paris: Galilée, 1998. *Veils*. Trans. Geoffrey Bennington. Stanford: Stanford University Press, 2001.

Clerc, Jeanne-Marie. *Ecrire, Transgresser, Résister*. Paris: L'Harmattan, 1997.

Coetzee, J. M. *Doubling the Point*. Cambridge, Mass.: Harvard University Press, 1992.

Conley, Tom. "Afterword / Identity: Never More." *Identity Papers: Contested Nationhood in Twentieth Century France*. Eds. Steven Ungar and Tom Conley (Minneapolis: University of Minnesota Press, 1996): 272–82.

De Ceccatty, René. "Scènes de lecture: Table ronde." Samedi 24 mai 2003. Presentation at the colloquium "Genèses Généalogies Genres: Autour de l'œuvre d'Hélène Cixous" at the Bibliothèque nationale de France.

De Certeau, Michel, Dominique Julia, and Jacques Revel. *Une politique de la langue: La Révolution française et les patois: l'enquête de Grégoire*. Paris: Gallimard, 1975.

Deleuze, Gilles, and Félix Guattari. *L'Anti-Œdipe: Capitalisme et schizophrénie*. Paris: Éditions de minuit, 1972.

———. *Capitalisme et schizophrénie: Mille plateaux*. Paris: Éditions de minuit, 1980.

———. *Kafka: Pour une littérature mineure*. Paris: Éditions de minuit, 1975.

Derrida, Jacques. "Abraham, l'autre." *Judéités: Questions pour Jacques Derrida*. Eds. Joseph Cohen and Raphael Zagury-Orly. (Paris: Galilée, 2003): 11–42.

———. *Acts of Literature*. Ed. Derek Attridge. New York and London: Routledge, 1992.

———. "L'animal que donc je suis (à suivre)." *L'animal autobiographique: Autour de Jacques Derrida*. Ed. Marie-Louise Mallet (Paris: Galilée, 1999): 251–302.

———. "L'aphorisme à contretemps." *Psyché: Inventions de l'autre* (Paris: Galilée, 1987): 519–33.

———. *Apories*. Paris: Galilée, 1996. *Aporias*. Trans. Thomas Dutoit. Stanford: Stanford University Press, 1993 [Originally published as "Apories: Mourir-s'attendre aux limites de la vérité" in *Le Passage des frontières: Autour du travail de Jacques Derrida* (Paris: Galilée, 1993)].

———. *Chaque fois unique, la fin du monde*. Paris: Galilée, 2003.

———. "Circonfession." *Jacques Derrida*. Geoffrey Bennington and Jacques Derrida. Paris: Seuil, 1991.

———. *Cosmopolites de tous les pays, encore un effort!* Paris: Galilée, 1997.

———. *De la grammatologie*. Paris: Minuit, 1964. *Of Grammatology*. Trans. Gayatri Chakravorty Spivak. Baltimore: The Johns Hopkins University Press, 1987.

———. "Des Tours de Babel." *Difference in Translation*. Ed. Joseph E. Graham (Ithaca: Cornell University Press, 1985): 209–48.

———. *La Dissémination*. Paris: Seuil, 1972.

———. *Du droit à la philosophie du point du vue cosmopolitique*. Paris: Verdier, 1997.

———. *L'Écriture et la difference*. Paris: Seuil, 1967. *Writing and Difference*. Trans. Alan Bass. Chicago: University of Chicago Press, 1978.

———. "Fidélité à plus d'un: Mériter d'hériter où la généalogie fait défaut." *Idiomes, nationalités, déconstructions, Rencontre de Rabat avec Jacques Derrida*. Paris: Intersignes and Casablanca: Les Editions Toubkal, no. 13 (Fall 1998): 221–65.

———. "Foi et savoir." *La Religion*. Eds. Jacques Derrida and Gianni Vattimo (Paris: Seuil, 1996): 9–86. "Faith and Knowledge." Trans. Samuel Weber. *Acts of Religion*. Ed. Gil Anidjar (New York and London: Routledge, 2002): 40–101.

———. "Fourmis." Originally published in *Lectures de la difference sexuelle*. Paris: des femmes, 1994. Extract reprinted in *Photos de Racines*. Hélène Cixous and Mireille Calle-Gruber (Paris: des femmes, 1994): 123–28.

———. *Genèses, genealogies, genres et le génie: Les secrets de l'archive*. Paris: Galilée, 2003.

———. "H. C. pour la vie, c'est à dire. . . ." *Hélène Cixous croisées d'une oeuvre*. Ed. Mireille Calle-Gruber (Paris: Galilée, 2000): 13–140.

———. "La Loi du genre." *Glyph 7* (1980). "The Law of Genre." Trans. Avital Ronell. *Acts of Literature*. Ed. Derek Attridge (Routledge: New York and London, 1992): 221–52.

———. *Mal d'archive*. Paris: Galilée, 1995. *Archive Fever*. Trans. Eric Prenowitz. Chicago: University of Chicago Press, 1996.

———. "Marx & Sons." *Ghostly Demarcations: A Symposium on Jacques Derrida's Specters of Marx*. Ed. Michael Sprinker (London and New York: Verso, 1999): 213–69.

———. *Mémoires pour Paul de Man*. Paris: Galilée, 1988.

———. *Le Monolinguisme de l'autre, ou la prothèse d'origine*. Paris: Galilée, 1996. *Monolingualism of the Other or The Prosthesis of Origin*. Trans. Patrick Mensah. Stanford, California: University of Stanford Press, 1998.

———. *Otobiographies: L'enseignement de Nietzsche et la politique du nom propre*. Paris: Galilée, 1984. "Otobiographies: The Teaching of Nietzsche and the Politics of the Proper Name." Trans. Avital Ronell. *The Ear of the Other: Otobiography, Transference*. Ed. Christie McDonald. Lincoln: University of Nebraska Press, 1985.

———. *Papier machine: Le ruban de machine à écrire et autres réponses*. Paris: Galilée, 2001.

———. *Parages*. Collection "La Philosophie en effet." Paris: Galilée, 1986.

———. *Sauf le nom*. Paris: Galilée, 1993.

———. *Schibboleth, Pour Paul Celan*. Paris: Galilée, 1986.

———. *Spectres de Marx: L'État de la dette, le travail du deuil et la nouvelle Internationale*. Paris: Galilée, 1993. *Specters of Marx: The State of the Debt, the Work of Mourning, and the New International*. Trans. Peggy Kamuf. New York: Routledge, 1994.

———. *Sur Parole: Instantanés philosophiques*. Paris: Éditions de l'aube, 1999.

———. *La Voix et le phénomène*. Paris: Presses Universitaires de France, 1967.

———, and Anne Dufourmantelle. *De l'hospitalité: Anne Dufourmantelle invite Jacques Derrida à répondre*. Paris: Calmann-Lévy, 1997. *Of Hospitality: Anne Dufourmantelle invites Jacques Derrida to Respond*. Trans. Rachel Bowlby. Stanford, California: Stanford University Press, 2000.

———, and Bernard Stiegler. *Échographies de la television: entretiens filmés*. Paris: Galilée/Institut national de l'audiovisuel, 1996.

———, and Gianni Vattimo, eds. *La Religion*. Paris: Seuil, 1996.

Diocaretz, Myriam and Marta Segarra, eds. *Joyful Babel: Translating Hélène Cixous*. Amsterdam and New York: Rodopi, 2004.

Djebar, Assia. *L'Amour, la fantasia*. Paris: J-C Lattès, 1985; Albin Michel, 1995. *Fantasia: An Algerian Cavalcade*. Trans. Dorothy S. Blair. London: Quartet Books, 1985.

———. *Le Blanc de l'Algérie*. Paris: Albin Michel, 1995. *Algerian White*. Trans. Marjolijn de Jager and David Kelley. New York: Seven Stories Press, 2003.

———. *Ces voix qui m'assiègent . . . en marge de ma francophonie*. Paris: Albin Michel, 1999.

———. *La Disparition de la langue française*. Paris: Albin Michel, 2003.

———. "Droit d'auteurs." *Droit d'auteurs*. La cinquième. Interview. 30 March 1997.

———. *La Femme sans sépulture*. Paris: Albin Michel, 2002.

———. *Femmes d'Alger dans leur appartement*. Nouvelles. Paris: Des femmes, 1980. *Women of Algiers in Their Apartment*. Trans. Marjolijn de Jager. Charlottesville and London: University Press of Virginia, 1992.

———. "Leur français dans le texte." *Terres francophones*. France 3. Television Interview. 21 January 1995.

———. *Loin de Médine*. Paris: Albin Michel, 1991.

———. *La Nouba des femmes du Mont Chenoua*. Film. 1978.

———. *Ombre sultane*. Paris: J-C Lattès, 1987. *A Sister to Scheherazade*. Trans. Dorothy S. Blair. Portsmouth: Heinemann, 1993.

———. *Oran, langue morte*. Arles: Actes Sud, 1997.

———. *Les Nuits de Strasbourg*. Arles: Actes Sud, 1997.

———. "RAIS, BENTALHA. . . . Un an après." *Research in African Literatures* 30.3 (1999): 108–10.

———. *Le Roman maghrébin francophone. Entre les langues, entre les cultures: Quarante ans d'un parcours, Assia Djebar 1957–1997*. Thèse de Doctorat en Littérature et

Civilisation Françaises. Thèse présentée par Fatma-Zohra Imalhayène. Université Paul-Valéry—Montpellier III.

———. *Vaste est la prison.* Paris: Albin Michel, 1995.

———. "Voix ensevelies." *Lieux d'écriture.* ARTE. Television Interview. 9 October 1997.

———. *La Zerda et les chants de l'oubli.* Film. 1982.

Donadey, Anne. "'Elle a rallumé le vif du passé.' L'écriture-palimpseste d'Assia Djebar." *Postcolonialisme et Autobiographie: Albert Memmi, Assia Djebar, Daniel Maximin.* Eds. Alfred Hornung and Ernstpeter Ruhe. (Amsterdam and Atlanta: Rodopi, 1999): 101–15.

———. "Foreword." *An Algerian Childhood.* Ed. Leïla Sebbar (St. Paul, MN: Ruminator Books, 2001): vii–xvii.

———. "The Multilingual Strategies of Postcolonial Literature: Assia Djebar's Algerian Palimpsest." *World Literature Today* 74:1 (Winter 2000): 27–36.

———. *Recasting Postcolonialism: Women Writing Between Worlds.* Portsmouth: Heinemann, 2001.

Erickson, John. "Translating the Untranslated: Djebar's *Le Blanc de l'Algérie.*" *Research in African Literatures* 30.3 (1999): 95–107.

———. "Women's voices and women's space in Assia Djebar's *L'Amour, la fantasia.*" *Islam and the Postcolonial Narrative* (Cambridge: Cambridge University Press, 1998): 37–65.

Étienne, Bruno. "Le statut de l'islam dans l'Europe plurielle." *Revue des deux mondes: France Maghreb Paroles des deux rives* 12 (December 2000): 74–82.

Fabian, Johannes. *Time and the Other: How Anthropology Makes Its Object.* New York: Columbia University Press, 1983.

Felman, Shoshana, and Dori Laub, M.D. *Testimony: Crises of Witnessing in Literature, Psychoanalysis, and History.* New York and London: Routledge, 1992.

Fielder, Adrian. "Narrating History in the Postcolonial City: Mapping through Movement in Assia Djebar's Ombre sultane." *Assia Djebar: Studien zur Literatur und Geschichte des Maghreb.* Ed. Ernstpeter Ruhe (Würzburg: Verlag Königshausen & Neumann, 2001): 107–20.

Fisher, Claudine G. "Hélène Cixous and the Un/forgettable Child." *Women in French Studies* 10 (2002): 79–92.

Foucault, Michel. "Nietzsche, Genealogy, History." *Language, Counter-Memory, Practice.* Ed. Donald Bouchard (Ithaca, N.Y.: Cornell University Press, 1977).

Frantz, Fanon. *Peau noire, masques blancs.* Paris: Seuil, 1952. *Black Skin, White Masks.* Trans. Charles L. Markmann. London: Pluto Press, 1986.

Gafaïti, Hafid. "L'autobiographie plurielle: Assia Djebar, les femmes et l'histoire." *Postcolonialisme et Autobiographie: Albert Memmi, Assia Djebar, Daniel Maximin.* Eds. Alfred Hornung and Ernstpeter Ruhe (Amsterdam and Atlanta: Rodopi, 1999): 149–59.

Gallop, Jane. *Anecdotal Theory.* Durham, NC: Duke University Press, 2002. http://www .semcoop.com/detail/0822330385

Genette, Gérard. *Seuils*. Paris: Seuil, 1987.

Gilbert, Sandra. "Introduction: A Tarentella of Theory." Hélène Cixous and Catherine Clément. *The Newly Born Woman*. Trans. Betsy Wing (Minneapolis: University of Minnesota Press, 2001): ix–xvii.

Gilmore, Leigh. *The Limits of Autobiography: Trauma and Testimony*. Ithaca and London: Cornell University Press, 2001.

Glissant, Edouard. *Le Discours antillais*. Paris: Seuil, 1981. *Caribbean Discourse: Selected Essays*. Trans. J. Michael Dash. Charlottesville: University Press of Virginia, 1989.

Gontard, Marc. "Nom propre et interculturalité: Dans la littérature marocaine de langue française." *L'Interculturel: réflexion pluridisciplinaire* (Paris: L'Harmattan, 1995): 75–87.

Grandguillaume, Gilbert. "Préface." Mohamed Benrabah. *Langue et pouvoir en Algérie: Histoire d'un traumatisme linguistique* (Paris: Séguier, 1999): 15–19.

Gresh, Alain. "Islamophobie." *Le Monde diplomatique* (November 2001): 32.

Griffiths, Gareth. "The Myth of Authenticity." *The Post-Colonial Studies Reader*. Eds. Ashcroft, Bill, Gareth Griffiths, and Helen Tiffin (London and New York: Routledge, 1995): 237–41.

Grove Concise Dictionary of Music online. http://w3.rz-berlin.mpg.de/cmp/bartok.html

Hargreaves, Alec G., and Mark McKinney. "Introduction: The Post-Colonial Problematic in France." *Post-Colonial Cultures in France*. Eds. Alec G. Hargreaves and Mark McKinney (London and New York: Routledge, 1997): 3–25.

Hart, Kevin. "Jacques Derrida: 'The most improbable signature.'" *The Judgment of Paris: Recent French theory in a local context*. Ed. Kevin D. S. Murray. (Sydney: Allen & Unwin, 1992): 3–21.

Harzoune, Mustapha. "La Maladie de l'Islam." Book review of Abdelwahab Meddeb's *La Maladie de l'Islam* (Seuil, 2002). *hommes et migrations* 1239 (septembre-octobre 2002): 147–48.

hooks, bell. *Talking Back: Thinking Feminist, Thinking Black*. Boston, MA: South End Press, 1989.

Hornung, Alfred, and Ernstpeter Ruhe, eds. *Postcolonialisme et Autobiographie: Albert Memmi, Assia Djebar, Daniel Maximin*. Amsterdam and Atlanta: Rodopi, 1998.

———. "Discussions [with Assia Djebar]: Communication d'Anne Donadey" *Postcolonialisme et Autobiographie: Albert Memmi, Assia Djebar, Daniel Maximin* (Amsterdam and Atlanta: Editions Rodopi, 1998): 179–93.

Huggan, Graham. "Decolonizing the Map: Post-Colonialism, Post-Structuralism and the Cartographic Connection." *Ariel* 20:4 (1989): 115–31.

Huston, Nancy. *Nord perdu*. Arles: Actes Sud, 1999.

Jakobson, Roman. "On Linguistic Aspects of Translation." *On Translation*. Cambridge, MA: Harvard University Press, 1959. Reprinted in *Theories of Translation: An Anthology of Essays from Dryden to Derrida*. Eds. Rainer Schulte and John Biguenet (Chicago: University of Chicago Press, 1992): 144–51.

Kamal, Nafa. "Dynamique intertextuelle et production du sujet." *L'Intertexte à l'œuvre dans les littératures francophones*. Ed. Martine Mathieu-Job (Bordeaux: Presses Universitaires de Bordeaux, 2002): 69–110.

Kamuf, Peggy. "Seringues, ou les pointes aiguës du hérisson." *Passions de la littérature: Avec Jacques Derrida*. Ed. Michel Lisse (Paris: Galilée, 1996): 387–404.

———. *Signature Pieces: On the Institution of Authorship*. Ithaca and London: Cornell University Press, 1998.

Kateb, Yacine. *Nedjma*. Paris: Seuil, 1956.

———. *Le poète comme un boxeur: Entretiens 1958–1989*. Ed. Gilles Carpentier. Paris: Seuil, 1994.

Kéchichian, Patrick. "La francophonie, un 'exotisme de plus'?" *Le Monde des Livres*, VI, vendredi 14 mars 2003.

Kelly, Debra. *Autobiography and Independence: Selfhood and Creativity in Postcolonial African Writing in French*. Liverpool: Liverpool University Press, 2005.

Kettler Penrod, Lynn. "Hélène Cixous: Initiatory Readings, Centrifugal Readings." *On the Feminine*. Ed. Mireille Calle. Trans. Catherine McGann (Atlantic Highlands, NJ: Humanities Press International, 1996): 57–65.

Khatibi, Abdelkébir. *Aimance*. Paris: Éditions Al Manar, 2003.

———. *Amour bilingue*. Montpellier: Fata Morgana, 1983. *Love in Two Languages*. Trans. Richard Howard. Minneapolis: University of Minnesota Press, 1990.

———. *La Blessure du nom propre*. Paris: Denoël, 1974.

———. "A Colonial Labyrinth." Trans. Catherine Dana. *Post/Colonial Conditions: Exiles, Migrations, and Nomadisms*. Eds. Françoise Lionnet and Ronnie Scharfman. *Yale French Studies* 83:2 (1993): 5–11.

———. *Le Corps oriental*. Paris: Hazan, 2002.

———. *Un été à Stockholm*. Paris: Flammarion, 1990.

———. "Un étranger professionnel." *Textuel* 32 (juillet 1997): 139–41.

———. *Féerie d'un mutant*. Monaco: Le Serpent à plumes, 2005.

———. *Figures de l'étranger dans la littérature française*. Paris: Denoël, 1987.

———. "Incipits." *Du bilinguisme*. Ed. Abdelkébir Khatibi (Paris: Denoël, 1985): 171–204.

———. *La Langue de l'Autre*. New York: Éditions Les mains secrètes, 1999.

———. *Le Livre du sang*. Paris: Gallimard, 1979 and 1986.

———. *Le Lutteur de classe à la manière taoïste*. Paris: Sindbad, 1976.

———. *Maghreb pluriel*. Paris: Denoël, 1983.

———. *Le Même livre*. Paris: Éditions de l'Éclat, 1985.

———. *La Mémoire tatouée: Autobiographie d'un décolonisé*. Paris: Denoël, 1971; 10/18, 1978.

———. *Pèlerinage d'un artiste amoureux*. Paris: Éditions du Rocher, 2003.

———. "La loi du partage." *L'Intertextuel: Réflexion pluridisciplinaire* (Paris: L'Harmattan, 1995): 11–13.

———. *Vœu de silence*. Paris: Éditions Al Manar, 2000.

Kofman, Sarah. *Paroles suffoquées*. Paris: Galilée, 1987. *Smothered Words*. Trans. Madeleine Dobie. Chicago: Northwestern University Press, 1998.

Kristeva, Julia. *Micropolitique: 'Première édition' mercredi 8h25*. Paris: Éditions de l'Aube, 2001.

Kundera, Milan. *Les testaments trahis*. Paris: Gallimard, 1993. *Testaments Betrayed*. Trans. Linda Asher. New York: HarperCollins, 1996.

LaCapra, Dominick. "Trauma, Absence, Loss." *Critical Inquiry* 25:4 (Summer 1999): 696–727.

Laronde, Michel. "La littérature de l'immigration de l'institution en 1996: Réflexions à partir du paratexte de Lila dit ça" *Etudes francophones*. *Conseil international d'études francophones*, vol. XIV, no. 1 (Spring 1999): 5–21.

Lê, Linda. *Tu écriras sur le bonheur*. Paris: Presses Universitaires de France, 1999.

Lejeune, Philippe. *Le Pacte autobiographique*. Paris: Seuil, 1975.

———. "La rédaction finale de 'W ou le souvenir d'enfance.'" *Poétique: Revue de théorie et d'analyse littéraires* 133 (février 2003): 73–107.

Le Roux, Monique. "Le caravansérail du Soleil." *La Quinzaine littéraire* 854 (16 au 31 mai 2003): 21–22.

Lionnet, Françoise. *Autobiographical Voices: Race, Gender, Self-Portraiture*. Ithaca: Cornell University Press, 1989.

———. *Postcolonial Representations: Women, Literature, Identity*. Ithaca: Cornell University Press, 1995.

Littré, Émile. *Dictionnaire de la langue française*. Paris: Gallimard/Hachette, 1968.

Makherbeche, Fatima Z. "Youyous d'ici et youyous de là-bas." *hommes et migrations*, "Mélanges culturels," no. 1231 (mai-juin 2001): 45.

Mallet, Marie-Louise. *La Musique en respect*. Paris: Galilée, 2002.

———. "'. . . que le souffle avant l'hymne qui vient': quelques notes en marge de *Beethoven à jamais ou l'existence de dieu*." *Hélène Cixous croisées d'une oeuvre*. Ed. Mireille Calle-Gruber (Paris: Galilée, 2000): 301–22.

Mansour-Amrouche, Fadma Aïth. *Histoire de ma vie*. Paris: Éditions La Découverte & Syros, 2000.

McNeece, Lucy Stone. "Decolonizing the Sign: Language and Identity in Abdelkébir Khatibi's *La Mémoire tatouée*." *Yale French Studies* 83, *Post/Colonial Conditions*, eds. Françoise Lionnet and Ronnie Scharfman, (1993): 12–29.

Meddeb, Abdelwahab. *La Maladie de l'islam*. Paris: Seuil, 2002.

———. *Prétexte*. vol. 11. http://perso.club-internet.fr/pretexte/revue/entretiens/entretiens_ fr/entretiens/abdelwahab-meddeb.htm

———. *Talismano*. Paris: Éditions Christian Bourgois, 1979.

Mcrini, Rafika. *Two Major Francoophone Women Writers, Assia Djebar and Leïla Sebbar: A Thematic Study of Their Works*. New York: Peter Lang, 1999.

Miller, Nancy K. *Getting Personal: Feminist Occasions and Other Autobiographical Acts*. New York and London: Routledge, 1991.

Moi, Toril. *Sexual/Textual Politics*. London: Methuen, 1985.

Morra, Joanne, and Marquard Smith, eds. *Parallax*. "Translating 'Algeria.'" Vol. 7 (April-June 1998).

Mortimer, Mildred. "Assia Djebar's Algerian Quartet: A Study in Fragmented Autobiography." *Research in African Literatures*. Volume 28, Number 2. http://www.indiana.edu/%7Eiupress/journals/ral/ral28-2.html

———. "Entretien avec Assia Djebar, Ecrivain algérien." *Research in African Literatures* 19:2 (Summer 1988): 197–205.

Moura, Jean-Marc. *Littératures francophones et theorie postcoloniale.* Paris: Presses Universitaires de France, 1999.

Murdoch, H. Adlai. "Rewriting Writing: Identity, Exile and Renewal in Assia Djebar's *L'Amour, la fantasia.*" *Yale French Studies 83, Post/Colonial Conditions.* Eds. Françoise Lionnet and Ronnie Scharfman (1993): 71–92.

Nagy-Zekmi, Silvia. "Tradition and Transgression in the Novels of Assia Djebar and Aïcha Lemsine." *Research in African Literatures.* Vol. 33, no. 3 (Fall 2002): 1–13.

Nancy, Jean-Luc. "Borborygmes." *L'Animal autobiographique: Autour de Jacques Derrida.* Ed. Marie-Louise Mallet (Paris: Galilée, 1999): 161–79.

Niranjana, Tejaswini. *Siting Translation: History, Post-Structuralism, and the Colonial Context.* Berkeley and Los Angeles: University of California Press, 1992.

Nora, Pierre, ed. *Les Lieux de mémoire.* Paris: Gallimard, 1984, 1993.

Noudelmann, François. "Hélène Cixous: La Voix étrangère, la plus profonde, la plus antique." *Rue Descartes: Revue du Collège International de Philosophie* 37 (septembre 2002): 111–19.

O'Grady, Kathleen. "Guardian of Language: An Interview with Hélène Cixous." *Women's education des femmes* (12, 4) Winter 1996–1997: 6–10. http://bailiwick.lib.uiowa.edu/wstudies/cixous/

Ortega y Gasset, José. [1937] "The Misery and the Splendor of Translation." Trans. Elizabeth Gamble Miller. *The Translation Studies Reader.* Ed. Lawrence Venuti (London and New York: Routledge, 2000): 49–63.

Phoca, Sophia. "Hélène Cixous in Conversation." *Wasafiri* 31 (Spring 2000): 9–13.

Poncet, Emmanuel. "La névrose de classe." *Libération.* http://www.liberation.fr/quotidien/debats/020207-110005133REBO.html

Proust, Françoise. *L'Histoire à contretemps: Le temps historique chez Walter Benjamin.* Paris: Les Éditions du Cerf, 1994.

Quignard, Pascal. *La leçon de musique.* Paris: Hachette, 1987.

Rice, Alison. "The Improper Name: Ownership and Authorship in the Literary Production of Assia Djebar." *Assia Djebar: Studien zur Literatur und Geschichte des Maghreb.* Ed. Ernstpeter Ruhe (Würzburg: Verlag Königshausen & Neumann, 2001): 49–77.

Rieck, Barbara Ann. Film. *Voix ensevelies: Assia Djebar, lieux d'écriture.* ARTE. 1997.

Robin, Régine. *La Mémoire saturée.* Paris: Éditions Stock, 2003.

Rosello, Mireille. *Declining the Stereotype: Ethnicity and Representation in French Cultures.* Hanover and London: University Press of New England, 1998.

———. *Postcolonial Hospitality: The Immigrant As Guest.* Stanford, CA: Stanford University Press, 2001.

Ross, Alex. "Suspended Animation." *The New Yorker* (April 21 & 28, 2003): 189–90.

Ruhe, Ernstpeter. "Les mots, l'amour, la mort: Les mythomorphoses d'Assia Djebar." *Postcolonialism et Autobiographie.* Ed. Alfred Hornung and Ernstpeter Ruhe (Amsterdam and Atlanta, Georgia: Rodopi, 1998): 161–77.

Said, Edward W. *Covering Islam*. London: Vintage Books, 1997.
———. *Culture and Imperialism*. New York: Alfred A. Knopf, 1994.
———. *Orientalism*. New York: Vintage Books, 1979.
———. *Parallels and Paradoxes: Explorations in Music and Society*. Ed. Ara Guzelimian. London: Bloomsbury, 2003.
Samoyault, Tiphaine. "L'amour du loup." *La Quinzaine littéraire* 864 (1 au 15 novembre 2003): 12.
Sartre, Jean-Paul. *"What is Literature?" and Other Essays*. Cambridge, MA: Harvard University Press, 1988.
Savigneau, Josyane. "François Cheng, une passion française." *Le Monde des livres* (14 février 2002), <www.lemonde.fr/article/0,5987,3246-262854-00.html>.
Scharfman, Ronnie. "Regards du sujet, sujets du regard: *Vaste est la prison* d'Assia Djebar." *Assia Djebar*. Ed. Ernstpeter Ruhe (Würzburg: Königshausen & Neumann, 2001): 121–32.
Schimmel, Annemarie. "Die geheime Sprache der algerischen Frauen: Ein Gespräch mit Assia Djebar." *Literaturen: Das Journal für Bücher une Themen* (Oktober 2000): 41–44.
Sebbar, Leïla. *Je ne parle pas la langue de mon père*. Paris: Julliard, 2003.
———. "Les Jeunes filles de la colonie." *Une enfance outremer*. Ed. Leïla Sebbar (Paris: Seuil, 2001): 186–97.
———, and Jean-Michel Belorgey. *Femmes d'Afrique du Nord: Cartes postales (1885–1930)*. Paris: Bleu autour, 2002.
———, and Nancy Huston. *Lettres parisiennes: Histoires d'exil*. Paris: Bernard Barrault, 1986.
Ségalen, Victor. *Essai sur l'exotisme: Une Esthétique du divers*. Paris: Fata Morgana, 1978.
Segarra, Marta, ed. *Expressions Maghrébines. Revue de la Coordination Internationale des Chercheurs sur les Littératures Maghrébines*. "Hélène Cixous." 2:2 (Winter 2003).
Smaïl, Paul. *Vivre me tue*. Paris: Éditions Balland, 1998.
Smith, Sarah A. "Rules of the Game." *The Guardian*. May 24, 2003. http://books.guardian.co.uk/review/story/0,12084,961314,00.html
Sommer, Doris. "'Not Just a Personal Story': Women's *Testimonios* and the Plural Self." *Life/Lines: Theorizing Women's Autobiography*. Eds. Bella Brodzki and Celeste Schenck. Ithaca, NY: Cornell University Press, 1988.
Spivak, Gayatri Chakravorty. "Cixous Without Borders." *On the Feminine*. Ed. Mireille Calle (New Jersey: Humanities Press International, 1996): 38–45. Originally published as *Du Féminin*. Sainte-Foy, Canada: Les Èditions Le Griffon d'argile Inc., 1993.
———. "Three Women's Texts and Circumfession." *Postcolonialism et Autobiography: Michelle Cliff, David Dabydeen, Opal Palmer Adisa*. Eds. Alfred Hornung and Ernstpeter Ruhe (Amsterdam & Atlanta: Rodopi, 1998): 7–22.
Stevens, Christa. "Hélène Cixous, auteur en 'algériance.'" *Expressions Maghrébines*. "Qu'est-ce qu'un auteur maghrébin?" 1:1 (Summer 2002): 77–91.

Stiegler, Bernard. *Aimer, s'aimer, nous aimer: Du 11 septembre au 21 avril*. Paris: Galilée, 2003.

———. *La Technique et le temps*, vol. 3, *Le temps du cinéma*. Paris: Galilée, 2001.

Stora, Benjamin. "Women's Writing between Two Algerian Wars." *Research in African Literatures* 30.3 (1999): 78–94.

Sublet, Jacqueline. *Le Voile du nom: Essai sur le nom propre arabe*. Paris: Presses Universitaires de France, 1991.

Suleri, Sara. "Woman Skin Deep: Feminism and the Postcolonial Condition." *The Post-Colonial Studies Reader*. Eds. Bill Ashcroft, Gareth Griffiths, and Helen Tiffin (London and New York: Routledge, 1995): 273–80.

Tillion, Germaine. *L'Afrique bascule vers l'avenir: L'Algérie en 1957 et autres textes*. Paris: Les éditions de minuit, 1961.

Todorov, Tzvetan. "Bitinguisme, dialogisme et schizophrénie." *Du bilinguisme*. (Paris: Denoel, 1985).

Veinstein, Alain. "À propos de Benjamin à Montaigne: Il ne faut pas le dire," *Du Jour au lendemain*. Interview with Hélène Cixous. *France Culture*, 24 septembre 2001.

Venn, Couze. "Algeria and Occidentalism." *Parallax*. "Translating 'Algeria.'" Eds. Joanne Morra and Marquard Smith. Vol. 7 (April–June 1998): 79–88.

Vidal, Dominique. "La France des 'sans-religion.'" *Le Monde diplomatique* (septembre 2001): 22–23.

Walcott, Derek. "The Muse of History." *The Post-Colonial Studies Reader*. Eds. Bill Ashcroft, Gareth Griffiths, and Helen Tiffin (London and New York: Routledge, 1995): 370–74.

Walker, Keith. *Countermodernism and Francophone Literary Culture: The Game of Slipknot*. Durham, NC: Duke University Press, 1999.

Wideman, John Edgar. "Foreword." Zora Neale Hurston. *Every Tongue Got to Confess: Negro Folk-tales from the Gulf States* (New York: HarperCollins, 2001): xi–xx.

Wiesel, Elie. "The Holocaust as a Literary Inspiration." *Dimensions of the Holocaust*. Evanston, IL: Northwestern University Press, 1977.

Wood, Nancy. "Remembering the Jews of Algeria." *Parallax*. "Translating 'Algeria.'" Eds. Joanne Morra and Marquard Smith. Vol. 7 (April–June 1998): 169–84.

Woodhull, Winifred. *Transfigurations of the Maghreb: Feminism, Decolonization, and Literatures*. Minneapolis: University of Minnesota Press, 1993.

World Literature Today 70:4 (Autumn 1996).

Yerushalmi, Yosef Hayim. *Marranes*. Paris: Éditions de la difference, 1992.

Young, Robert J. C. "Deconstruction and the Postcolonial." *Deconstructions: A User's Guide*. Ed. Nicholas Royle (New York: Palgrave, 2000): 187–210.

Zabus, Chantal. "Encre blanche et Afrique originelle: *Derrida et la postcolonialité*." *Passions de la littérature: Avec Jacques Derrida*. (Paris: Galilée, 1996): 261–73.

———. "Relexification." *The Post-Colonial Studies Reader*. Eds. Bill Ashcroft, Gareth Griffiths, and Helen Tiffin (London and New York: Routledge, 1995): 314–18.

Index

202, 214, 299; intervals, 2;
intonation, 204, 210, 226n23; key,
202–3, 281; lamento, 154, 275; and
meaning, 206; and memory, 174n9,
209–10; minor, 27n2, 202; mode,
202, 225n18; movements, 151, 218;
note, 202–3; off beat, 22, 164; pedal
point, 209; play, 23, 26–27, 38, 66,
192, 195, 208, 210, 216, 224n13,
297; polyphony, 2, 233–34, 288;
prelude, 233; refrains, 23;
"Requiem," 215; rests, 25, 212;
rhythm, 133n32, 188, 204, 222n1,
264, 299, 306–7; scale, 251; tone,
299; transcriptions, 17, 280–81;
transposition, 17, 23, 180–81,
285n23; variation(s), 73, 101, 188,
202; voicing, 153, 178n37; vibration,
85n49, 207

Nadeau, Maurice, 13
Nagy-Zekmi, Silvia, 128n1
name, 11–13, 25, 35–85, 210, 230n46,
240, 244, 275, 178; Cixous and
Derrida, 10, 218–19, 256n19;
identity and publishing, 12; and
Islam, 78n17; and music, 55; name
changes, 51–52, 53–55; name-
dropping, 38, 229n39; naming, 25,
41, 56–57, 60–64, 67–68, 164,
224n9; naming and colonialism,
61–62, 82n35, 243, 257n22, 291;
nicknames, 60–61, 67–68;
pseudonym, 12, 52–53, 79n22,
79n25; and singularity, 40–41; and
translation, 53, 54, 278–80,
285n19; unnaming, 44–45, 64,
75n7, 83n39
Nancy, Jean-Luc, 230n46
nation. See France
Nimrod, 6, 8, 29n13
Niranjana, Tejaswini, 161–62

Nora, Pierre, 253n6
Nothomb, Amélie, 31n21

orality, 24, 125, 158, 161–62, 188,
192–99, 223–24n8, 229–30n41
Oran, 239–40, 253n4
orphan, 66–67
Ortega y Gasset, José, 227n28

palimpsest, 8, 170, 173n3, 176nn21–22,
179n40, 191, 306
parallax, 253n3
paratext, 37, 55, 70–71, 84n46
Paris, 11, 19, 33–34n39, 42, 202, 248,
264, 269, 275
Phoca, Sophia, 253n3
photographs, 148–50, 153, 167–72
postcolonial, 6, 26, 257n22, 291;
postcolonial studies, 9, 30n17, 300
Proust, Françoise, 65, 162–63, 166–67
Proust, Marcel, 314–15n43
pseudonym. See name

Reclus, Onésime, 3
recordings, 32–33n34
religion, 91–92, 94. See also Islam;
Jewishness; translation
repetition, 50, 188, 195, 210, 216, 266,
282n5
Robin, Régine, 170
Rosello, Mireille, 75n6, 176n22,
311–12n24
Ross, Alex, 213–14
Rousseau, Jean-Jacques, 31n21, 319,
322n1
Ruhe, Ernstpeter, 79n23
running, 103–4, 110

sacrifice, 47, 49–50, 77n15, 78n20,
310n13
Said, Edward, 17, 32n33, 101–3, 130n9,
136n52

~

About the Author

Alison Rice is Assistant Professor of French and Francophone Literature in the Department of Romance Languages and Literatures at the University of Notre Dame. Her teaching and research interests include autobiography, critical theory, postcolonial studies, immigrant and second-generation literature, translation theory, contemporary women's writing, music in literature, and "Francophonie" in a large sense. Her current project focuses on Eastern European authors who write in French.